CONDUCTING EDUCATIONAL RESEARCH

Bruce W. Tuckman

Rutgers University

HARCOURT BRACE JOVANOVICH, INC.

New York   Chicago   San Francisco   Atlanta

To my wife, Deanne,
my daughter, Blair Zoe,
and my son, Bret Ashley

ISBN: 0-15-512980-5

Library of Congress Catalog Card Number: 72-075077

Printed in the United States of America

PREFACE

To function effectively, the professional educator must have some knowledge of research methodology. At a minimum, each educator can be called a "consumer" of research, in that he reads and draws conclusions from research literature, or he hires someone to do research and evaluation for him. In order to evaluate and interpret research findings, the educator must understand the limitations imposed by the techniques used in data collection and analysis. He must know, among other things, that correlation does not necessarily imply causation, that generality is often limited by sample selection procedures, that changes can sometimes be accounted for by uncontrolled environmental variables, and that statistical tests suggest certain prior assumptions about the data.

The professional educator will also try many innovations whose effectiveness will need to be evaluated. Whether or not he conducts the evaluation himself, he will have to know about quasi-experimental designs, random sampling, the use of control groups, and other techniques.

In a convention symposium in 1966, Professor Marshall P. Smith coined the term *mud-pie research* to describe research undertaken not within the confines of the controllable (and usually artificial) laboratory, but rather in the real world of schools — in other words, field research or research with indistinct form and hard-to-define criteria.

As an example, Professor Smith cited research evaluating Headstart programs. Often, neither reasonable comparison groups nor instruments appropriate for use with the age and cultural group are available. In addition, the research is usually undertaken after the program has started, thus eliminating pretest data. Conducting such an evaluation, said Smith, is like making a mud-pie. To shy away from the use of research and evaluation in such situations would leave educational decisions to guesswork and intuition. It is necessary, then, to know a great deal about the research process. When a researcher is forced to compromise with some research principles, he must know the principles, the nature of the compromise, the effect of the compromise on those principles, and ways to determine the seriousness of the compromise.

This book is based on the premise that educational researchers will more often than not find that the real world must be their laboratory. Schools with fixed schedules, predetermined classes, limited space, and occasionally uncooperative personnel become the setting for research and evaluation. To train researchers to deal only with the ideal situation would leave them without many of the tools they will need in the field. Furthermore, it is the position of this writer that research should be done in the field where possible, in order to study variables that cannot be duplicated in the limited laboratory setting.

But to move into the field is to encounter "noise," or perhaps be forced to make mud-pies. Should the researcher throw up his hands in despair? The answer proposed in this book is an emphatic, NO! There are techniques to deal with the difficulties of the field. These techniques enable the researcher to incorporate many of the critical elements of research design to ensure that his findings and conclusions will have some validity. This book presents, for example, techniques called quasi-experimental designs, which are designs that provide for some control of variables that produce a threat to the internal (i.e., consistency, logic) and external (i.e., generalizability) validity of a study. These designs are offered as a tool in using real educational environments for research purposes. Not only does this tool help the researcher to move from the laboratory to the field but it helps him to retain the logical research model born of the laboratory.

Other than for the requirement of a thesis or dissertation, many educators avoid research, condemning it as scientism, cultism, or egg-headism, and viewing data collection and analysis as an activity of dubious practical value. But it is the firm philosophy of this book that research not only uncovers useful knowledge for future application but is a problem-solving tool for practicing educators. Research identifies an appropriate pattern for the collection of data relevant to a problem and then reduces that data to a manageable and interpretable form. It is a logical process that helps uncover causal relationships. Other forms of problem-solving that are quicker and cheaper often provide a misleading picture of what is happening and why, and stimulate inaccurate conclusions.

Conducting Educational Research, therefore, is based on the following premises:

1. Research is a useful tool for educators because its logical nature is essential for uncovering causal relationships and extremely useful for problem-solving.
2. Much educational research must be undertaken in the field where the problem setting exists, because to simulate it in a laboratory the critical nature of some relevant variables may be lost.

3. Field research must enlarge its focus to include the identification of relationships between the variables.
4. Field research is "muddied" by the many variables that cannot be perfectly controlled.
5. Techniques exist, and must be mastered, for controlling or partially controlling "noise" in field experiments.

For this book to be of maximal value the researcher should consider the above premises and attempt to work within them.

I would like to thank the many people who helped me with this book. My colleagues in the field, William Asher (Purdue University), Keith Edwards, (Johns Hopkins University) Mauritz Lindvall (University of Pittsburgh), and Douglas Penfield (Rutgers University) reacted to parts or all of the manuscript and provided much help. (To William Asher, in particular, I owe a major debt of thanks.) My editors, Ernst Schrader and Louise Baer, provided invaluable encouragement and assistance. My students at Rutgers in my research courses over a two-year period used parts of the book in draft form and provided encouragement and comment. For that, I owe them a debt of thanks.

My typists and editorial assistants were many — Mona De Jonghe, Sheila O'Bryan, Beverly Piano, Joanne Sheitelman, and Donna Zsoldos. Each took a personal interest in the book.

The many people who granted me permission to use their work have helped make the book a better reflection of the field. I am particularly grateful to Carl Clark and Herbert Walberg, and to Wilmot Oliver and Loraine Spenciner (my former students) who let me reprint their work in Appendix A and cite it extensively in the text. Others whose work I referenced are too numerous to mention, but I thank them all.

Many organizations and companies were gracious in letting me reprint materials they have published. I am indebted also to the literary executor of the late Sir Ronald A. Fisher, F.R.S., and to Oliver & Boyd, Edinburgh for their permission to reprint four tables (Tables I, II, III, and VII in Appendix B) from their book *Statistical Methods for Research Workers*.

Finally, I would like to thank my family, to whom this book is dedicated.

BRUCE W. TUCKMAN

CONTENTS

8 *Constructing and Using Questionnaires and Interview Schedules* *173*

1

The Role of Research

OBJECTIVES

Identify the role of internal validity. / Identify the role of external validity. / Describe the relation between internal and external validity. / Describe the characteristics of the research process. / Identify the steps in the research process. / Identify ethical considerations in research and their resolution.

1.1 WHAT IS RESEARCH?

- question
- problem
- hypotheses

Research is a systematic attempt to provide answers to questions. Such answers may be abstract and general as is often the case in *basic research*, or they may be highly concrete and specific as is often the case in *demonstration* or *applied research*. In both kinds of research, the investigator uncovers facts and then formulates a generalization based on the interpretation of those facts.

Basic research is concerned with the relationship between two or more variables. It is carried out by identifying a problem, examining selected relevant variables, constructing a hypothesis where possible, creating a research design to investigate the problem, collecting and analyzing appropriate data, and then drawing conclusions about the relationships of the variables. Basic research does not often provide immediately usable information for altering the environment. Its purpose, rather, is to develop a model, or theory, that identifies all the relevant variables in a particular environment and hypothesizes about their relationship. Then, using the findings of basic research, it is possible to develop a product—product here being used to include, for example, a given curriculum, a particular teacher-training program, a textbook, or an audio-visual aid.

A further step is to test the product, the province of applied research, often called demonstration. (In effect, applied research is a test or tryout that includes systematic evaluation.)

1.2 VALIDITY IN RESEARCH

Achieving validity in research is not an easy task, as the following examples will demonstrate.

A physicist is designing a new instructional program for college sophomore physics. He has at his disposal films, textbooks, lectures, lab experiments, and filmstrips with voice-over, and he needs to find out which of these approaches to use and in what combination. To do this he decides to teach the first unit, on force, using the lecture-textbook approach, and the second unit, on motion, using films. He can then see which has the better effect and be guided accordingly. But the physicist has created a logical trap for himself.

Suppose the unit on force were easier than the unit on motion. If this is the case, students might perform better on the end-of-unit test for force simply because the concepts covered in this unit were easier. It is possible, too, that films are a particularly good way to teach motion because of the nature of the subject matter but a poor way to teach force. If this is the case, any generalization about the advantage of films beyond the teaching of motion would be invalid. It is also possible that the particular film the physicist has chosen for teaching motion is a poor one, and its failure to instruct would not entitle him generally to condemn films for instruction in physics. Of additional concern is the fact that what the students learned about force might help them learn about motion, thereby predisposing them to do better on the second unit, regardless of pedagogical technique. Even if the two units were fairly independent in terms of subject-matter, the sophistication gained in the first unit might help in mastering the second unit. Furthermore, one of the end-of-unit tests might be easier or more representative of the learning material than the other. Finally, the outcome in the two units might occur once but have little likelihood of recurring. It might simply be an unstable outcome due to chance.

What is a researcher to do in dealing with this morass of potential pitfalls? Let us dig the hole a bit deeper with another example before trying to fill it.

A graduate student is interested in exploring the similarities and differences between teachers and disadvantaged students in matters of motivation and values. He plans to collect data from a group of 150 disadvantaged students attending a summer university program and from a group of 150 teachers attending a university summer institute. Findings are to take the form of reporting verbatim the responses to open-ended questions and attempting to detect any generalities or trends without any system for data analysis. Needless to say, the representativeness of the samples of the two groups is in serious doubt. Students and teachers who have the motivation to attend a summer program at a university are probably different in their perceptions and values than those who do not attend such programs. As for drawing conclusions based on visual inspection of some 300 or more responses, aside from the obvious difficulty and tediousness of such an approach, the likelihood that the conclusions would reflect the initial biases of the researcher is great since he may tend to see exactly what he is looking for in the data.

One final example at this point may be helpful. A faculty group is interested in assessing the effectiveness of a new teacher-education program for college seniors. They are specifically interested in the amount of identification with the teaching profession that the students in this program make. The students are asked to complete a questionnaire dealing with occupational identification during their junior year (prior to the program) and again at the end of their senior year (subsequent to the program). Unfortunately, whatever outcome is obtained is as likely to be a function of the fact that the students had matured a year as it is a function of the program. Another university also wanting to evaluate the new program was fortunate in having two campuses. Since only one campus was to have the new program, the experiment was done by comparing the identification of the students in that program with the identification of the students in the old program at the end of their senior year. Sadly, however, it is impossible to be sure that the groups were similar to begin with since the students on the two campuses were known to be different in many ways.

In the real world—as opposed to the laboratory—the educational researcher is confronted by such situations as those described. Because he often lacks the the opportunity to exercise control over what is to happen and to whom it is to happen, he is often likely to proceed as did the researchers in the examples. It is, however, the contention in this book that the research process, when properly understood, provides a basis for dealing with such situations in a more adequate and logical way.

1.3 INTERNAL AND EXTERNAL VALIDITY

To understand the shortcomings in the above research situations and how it is helpful to overcome them, consider two principles: *internal validity* and *external validity*.

A study has internal validity if the outcome of the study is a function of the program or approach being tested rather than the result of other causes not systematically dealt with in the study.

A study has external validity if the results obtained would apply in the real world to other similar programs and approaches.

The process of doing an experiment—i.e., exercising some control over the environment—contributes to internal validity while producing some limitation in external validity. As the researcher regulates and controls the circumstances of inquiry, as in an experiment, he increases the probability that what he is studying is producing the outcomes he attains (internal validity). Simultaneously, however, he decreases the probability that his conclusions will hold in the absence of the experimental manipulations (external validity). If we do not utilize procedures to provide some degree of internal validity, we may never know what has caused our observed effects to occur. Thus, external validity is of little value without some reasonable degree of internal validity giving us confidence in our conclusions before we attempt to generalize from them.*

Consider again the case of the physicist who was designing a new program for college sophomores (page 2). For several reasons his experiment lacked internal validity. To begin with, he should have applied his different teaching techniques to the same material to avoid the pitfall that some material is more easily learned than other material. In fact, he should have taught both units to one group of students using the lecture approach and both units to another group of students using films. Doing so would help offset the danger that films might be especially appropriate for a single unit since this special appropriateness would be less likely to apply to two units than to one. By using two different films and two different lectures, he would also minimize the possibility that the effect was solely a function of the merits of a specific film since both films are less likely to be more outstanding (or less outstanding) than one film. In repeating the experiment the physicist should be extremely cautious in composing his two groups; if one group contains more bright students than the other, obviously that group would have an advantage. (However, the use of two groups is the only way to insure that one teaching approach is not given the advantage of being applied last.) The physicist should also, of course, insure that his end-of-chapter tests are representative of the learning material; although, since both groups will get the same tests, their relative difficulty ceases to be as important as it was in the original plan.

*I am not denying the value of naturalistic observations made outside of a designed study. However, I am suggesting that from a logical perspective, such observations could not lead one to the same degree of confidence in one's conclusions as the controlled study. Often, naturalistic observations provide a good source of insight and a basis for generating expectations and theories which can then be tested experimentally.

The second example (pages 2–3) poses some particular problems in external validity. As was pointed out, both the student group and the teacher group are unrepresentative of the universe of teachers and of disadvantaged students. Thus, it would be difficult to generalize conclusions drawn from this investigation much beyond the specific teachers and students employed in the study. With such a limitation, the study might not be worth undertaking. The study as described also poses some problems with regard to internal validity. Converting "answers" into "data" is an important part of the research process. In effect, the researcher creates a measuring "instrument" to accomplish this conversion. This instrument like the instruments used in the physical sciences, must possess some consistency. It must generate the same readings when read by different people and when read by the same person at different points in time. If, however, the instrument reflects the researcher's own biases or hypotheses, he may overlook some relevant occurrences to the detriment of internal validity.

The final example (page 3) illustrates a common problem in achieving internal validity: the fact that human beings change over time as a function of the normal course of development and the acquisition of experience. If a study involves the passage of time, then the researcher must use a design that enables him to separate the changes resulting from normal human development from the changes resulting from the special experiences of the experimental treatment. It is tempting indeed for a researcher to take measures at Time 1 and Time 2 and conclude that any change was a function of what he had introduced during the interim period. If, however, he cannot prove that the change was a result of the experiment rather than a natural change over time, then he cannot claim to have discovered a change agent.

Evaluating Changes over Time

Researchers can be misled when examining data from two points in time with an experimental manipulation intervening to over- or underevaluate the effect of that manipulation. The data from Time 1 may itself be the result of unusual circumstances which lead it to be nonrepresentative of the prevailing conditions. Moreover, other phenomena occurring at the same time as the manipulation may account for any change that occurs. D. T. Campbell (1969) suggests that data from more than Time 1 and Time 2 be examined in order to evaluate a manipulation occurring between them. He illustrates his approach in a study of the effect of a crackdown on traffic fatalities. Figure 1.1 shows the number of traffic fatalities in 1955, before the crackdown (Time 1), and in 1956, after the crackdown (Time 2). One is impressed by the sharp reduction in fatalities and is tempted to conclude that the increase in severity of speeding penalties accounted

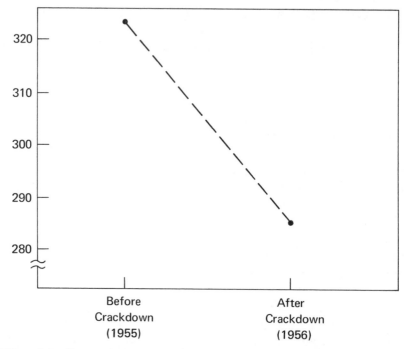

Figure 1.1 *Connecticut traffic fatalities. (After D. T. Campbell, Reforms as experiments, American Psychologist, 1969, 24, 409–429. Reprinted by permission of author and publisher.)*

for this spectacular decline (which, as it happens, turned out to be the case). Figure 1.2 shows that a simple examination of data from just two years can be somewhat misleading. In fact, it can be seen that 1955 had an unusually high amount of traffic deaths and was, therefore, not representative of the rate of fatalities on the Connecticut highways. When one encounters a single year that is so much above the average, one can expect on a chance basis that the subsequent year will be lower. Thus, an examination of data from 1951 to 1955 shows that the decline in 1956 might have been a statistical artifact—a function of the fact that 1955 was unusually high in traffic deaths. However, an examination of the data from 1956 through 1959 when compared to 1951 through 1955 shows that the trend in traffic deaths before the crackdown was an upward one while the trend after the crackdown was a downward one. Thus, the original conclusion in this instance was correct. However, one must put time changes in a proper context since certain changes will normally occur over time, having little to do with what one has imposed on the situation. One must distinguish between such changes over time and those caused by an intervention.

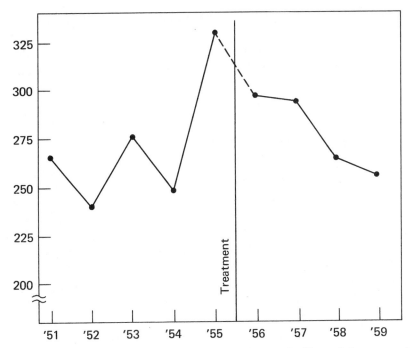

Figure 1.2 *Connecticut traffic fatalities. Same data as in Figure 1.1 presented as part of an extended time series. (After D. T. Campbell, Reforms as experiments, American Psychologist, 1969, 24, 409–429. Reprinted by permission of author and publisher.)*

Comparing Groups

A problem common to most experiments is the assignment of experimental participants to groups. Internal validity depends, in part, on the condition that the effect of a treatment* is a function of the treatment rather than a function of differences between the persons receiving the treatment and those not receiving the treatment, with these latter differences being unmeasured and uncontrolled. To be valid, an equivalent control group must be the same in composition or make-up as the group receiving the treatment. Before Teacher A can say that a teaching technique works on his students when their performance is compared to that of Teacher B's students, he must take into account the fact that his students may be more intelligent, more motivated, or more something else than B's students; it could be these other factors, alone or in combination, that account

The term treatment *is used here to label that technique or approach which is being tested or evaluated in the study.*

7

for the superior performance of A's students rather than the teaching approach per se.

In setting up a research project, it is necessary to strike a balance between the two sets of validity demands, establishing enough internal validity so that an experiment can be conclusive while remaining sufficiently within reality to be representative and generalizable.

1.4 DEALING WITH REALITY

The demands of internal validity are most easily met by confining research to a laboratory where the researcher can control or eliminate irrelevant variables and manipulate the relevant ones. However, the elimination of many variables, regardless of their centrality to the problem in question, may limit the external validity of the findings since success in the laboratory may not be any indication of success in the real world where real variables operate that have been shut out of the laboratory. Thus, many research problems require a field setting to insure external validity. The crux of the problem is to operate in the field and still achieve internal validity.

Situations in the field occur, however, where it is impossible to apply fully the rules of internal validity. Often, for example, any changes "for the better" that are to be made in a school must be made at the same time for the whole school in order to avoid raising ethical questions. To evaluate the effects of such changes, the researcher then must choose some approach other than the recommended one of applying the change to, and withholding the change from, equivalent groups. To deal with such a situation, Campbell and Stanley (1963) have developed the time-series design, which was illustrated in the traffic fatality study.

It is, however, an incontrovertible fact that research, even research done in the field (rather than the laboratory), must impose some artificialities and restrictions on the situation being studied. It is often this aspect that administrators find most objectionable. J. P. Campbell and Dunnette (1968) react to such criticism as follows:

> ...There are at least two possible replies to the perceived sterility of controlled systematic research. On the one hand, it is an unfortunate fact of scientific life that the reduction of ambiguity in behavioral data to tolerable levels demands systematic observations, measurement, and control. Often the unwanted result seems to be a dehumanization of the behavior being studied. That is, achieving unambiguous results may generate dependent variables that are somewhat removed from the original objectives of the development pro-

gram and seem, thereby, to lack relevant content. This is not an unfamiliar problem in psychological research. As always, the constructive solution is to increase the effort and ingenuity devoted to developing criteria that are *both* meaningful and amenable to controlled observation and measurement .... [J.P.Campbell and Dunnette, 1968, p. 101]

1.5 SURVEY "RESEARCH"

A particular kind of "research" that frequently appears in the education milieu is survey research. In the school survey, a procedure common in education, variables frequently are studied using a simple counting procedure with little or no attempt made to determine in a systematic fashion the relationship between them and other relevant variables. To do so would require control or comparison data, and often none are collected.

For instance, a school district is concerned with the kinds of students that enroll in high school home economics programs. A researcher goes into high school home economics classes with some form of questionnaire or interview schedule and collects data, puts this data together in frequency counts, and makes statements such as "75% of the students who go into home economics are students whose parents have required that they become active in homemaking activities in the home." Does this, then, indicate that homemaking activity at home is a necessary prerequisite and predisposing factor to entrance in home economics classes? Not necessarily, because this illustrative "experiment" has used, according to Campbell and Stanley (1963), an incorrect experimental design. Were the researcher to ask the same questions to a comparable group of high school girls who are not enrolled in home economics classes, he might discover that both groups have had the same amount of homemaking activity in the home. Therefore, while this precondition characterized the home economics students, it might, in fact, be equally true of all students and therefore could not be considered as a predisposing factor. Unfortunately, the answers the survey designer gets match the questions he asks. The inclusion of a "control" or comparison group of students who have not had the experience being evaluated helps the researcher discover whether he has asked the right questions.

Another example of research that suffers from the absence of a designed comparison is the follow-up survey of graduates of programs to determine whether the graduates have successfully attained that for which they were prepared. For example, studies show that 70 to 80 percent of vocational education graduates have been placed in occupations for which they were trained, suggesting high program success in terms of placement criterion. However, an examination of graduates of academic programs who did not go on to college (Kaufman, et al., 1967; Eninger, 1965) showed that these students often compete favorably with vocational school graduates for jobs in the same occupations. Thus, other factors beside, or in addition to, the program of study taken by students must be accounting in some degree for job placement. Obviously, then, a researcher should not draw conclusions based on an examination of the graduates of only one program. He needs to make a *comparison* between graduates of the two types of education. The term comparison should be stressed since survey research done on a single group often leads to conclusions about cause-and-effect relationships that lack validity.

Perhaps because of its simplicity, survey research abounds in education. A potentially useful technique in education as it is in public opinion polling and the social sciences, the value of the survey as a means of gathering data is not to be denied. It is recommended, however, that surveys be undertaken within a research design utilizing comparison groups. In this book, the survey as a research instrument will be dealt with in Chapter 8.

Trow (1967) makes the following observations regarding survey research in general:

> The errors and inadequacies of survey research in education appear at many points from the way problems are initially chosen and defined to the choice of the subject population, the selection of the sample, the design of the individual questions and the questionnaire as a whole, and the analysis of the resulting body of data. [Trow, 1967, p. 319.] *

Nonetheless, when properly constructed and when employed within a proper design, questionnaire and interview approaches may be used to great advantage.

1.6 CHARACTERISTICS OF THE RESEARCH PROCESS

Based on the preceding discussion, it is possible to list a set of properties that characterize the research process, at least in its ideal form.

Research Is Systematic

Since research is a structured process (that is, there are rules for carrying it out), it follows that it is systematic. The rules include procedural specifications

See also Sieber (1968).

10

for identifying and defining variables, for designing studies in which these variables will be examined and their effect on other variables determined, and for relating the data thus collected to the originally stated problem and hypothesis. (There are other processes for arriving at conclusions, such as deduction, that are equally systematic, but processes such as "guestimation" and intuition lack the systematic quality that characterizes research.)

Research Is Logical

Research follows a system that employs logic at many points. By logical examination of the procedures employed in an experiment, and, in the context of internal validity, the researcher is able to check the validity of the conclusions drawn. Applying logic, he may also check generalizations in the context of external validity. The logic of valid research makes it a valuable tool for decision-making, certainly far superior to intuiting or using "off-the-top-of-the-head" observations for data.

Research Is Empirical

Research has a reality-referent. Much deduction may precede its application, but data is the end result of research procedures. It is the collection of data that identifies research as an empirical process. To determine the extent to which his empirical findings can be generalized beyond the immediate situation in which the research took place, the researcher must evaluate the reality-referent of a particular undertaking in terms of its external validity. Other processes involved in understanding the world or making decisions within it may equal research in their logic but fail to match its empirical quality.

Research Is Reductive

When a researcher applies analytic procedures to the data he has collected, he reduces the confusion of individual events and objects to more understandable categories of concepts. In doing this he sacrifices some of the specificity and uniqueness associated with the individual objects or events, but gains in terms of the power to identify general relationships, a process which requires some degree of conceptualization. This process of reduction is part of the attempt to translate from reality to an abstract or conceptual state in order to understand the relationships between events and attempt to predict how these relationships might operate in other contexts. Reductionism, thus, enables research to play an explanatory role rather than simply a descriptive one.

Research Is Replicable and Transmittable

Because it is recorded, generalized, and replicated, research is considerably less transitory in nature than are the products of other problem-solving processes. Thus, individuals other than the researcher himself may use the results of a study, and one researcher may build upon the research results of another. Moreover, the process and procedures are themselves transmittable, enabling others to replicate them and to assess their validity. This transmittable property of research is critical both to its role in extending knowledge and its role in decision-making.

1.7 STEPS IN THE RESEARCH PROCESS

The purpose of this book is to provide the potential researcher with those skills necessary to carry out the research process. Following is a listing and brief description of the steps in the research process, each of which will be discussed in detail in subsequent chapters.

Identifying a Problem

For a student, identifying a problem is the most difficult step in the research process. He must discover and define not only a problem area but also a specific problem within that area that he chooses to study. In Chapter 2, sample models are presented for helping to define and identify problem areas and problems in education.

Constructing a Hypothesis

Once a problem has been identified, the researcher often employs the logical processes of deduction and induction to formulate an expectation of the outcome of the study. That is, he conjectures or hypothesizes about the relationship between the concepts identified in the problem.

12

Identifying and Labeling Variables

After formulating a hypothesis, the researcher must identify and label the variables both in the hypothesis and elsewhere in the study. In Chapter 3 the following five types of variables are outlined: independent, dependent, moderator, control, and intervening.

Constructing Operational Definitions

Since research is composed of a series of operations, it is necessary to convert variables from an abstract or conceptual form to an operational form. Operationalizing variables means stating them in an observable and measurable form, making them available for manipulation, control, and examination. After establishing the need for operational definitions, Chapter 4 presents methods for identification of variables and discusses the criteria used for construction of operational definitions.

Manipulating and Controlling Variables

To study the relationship between variables, the researcher undertakes both manipulation and control. The concepts of internal and external validity, which will be discussed in detail in Chapter 5, are basic to this undertaking.

Constructing a Research Design

A research design is a specification of operations for the testing of a hypothesis under a given set of conditions. In Chapter 6 specific types of true and quasi-experimental designs are described and diagrammed in the context of internal and external validity.

Identifying and Constructing Devices for Observation and Measurement

Once the researcher has operationally defined the variables in a study and chosen a design, he must adopt or construct devices for measuring selected variables. In Chapter 7, standardized tests are enumerated, and techniques are presented for the development of achievement and attitude measures. Basic measurement concepts are also covered.

Constructing Questionnaires and Interview Schedules

Since many studies in education and in allied fields rely on questionnaires and interviews as their main source of data, Chapter 8 provides a description of techniques for constructing and using these measurement devices.

Carrying Out Statistical Analyses

A researcher uses measuring devices to collect data in order to test hypotheses. Once data have been collected, they must be reduced by statistical analysis so that conclusions or generalizations can be drawn from them (i.e., so that hypotheses can be tested). In Chapter 9, worksheets for six basic statistical tests are provided, along with a model for selecting a suitable test for a given situation.

Using the Computer for Data Analysis

The computer is a useful tool for data analysis. Its efficient use requires that data be suitable rostered, that appropriate programs be identified, that programs be modified for their desired use, and that final printouts be interpreted. The basic skills and information necessary for computer use in data analysis are presented in Chapter 10.

Writing a Research Report

Chapter 11 deals in detail with report writing, providing instruction and examples. The construction of each section of a research proposal and the construction of a final research report are covered with recommendations offered as to structure and format.* Information about the construction of tables and graphs is also presented.

*Before continuing with this book, the reader might find it useful to read parts of Chapter 11, particularly the procedures for writing the introduction and method sections of a research proposal.

Conducting Evaluation Studies

While evaluation does not represent a discrete step in the research process, today's educational researcher must have a clear conceptualization and grasp of it. The two types of evaluation, formative and summative, are described in Chapter 12 with an emphasis on the latter (since this type of evaluation is part of the demonstration process).

1.8 SOME ETHICAL CONSIDERATIONS

4 factors

The matter of ethics is an important one for educational researchers. Because their subject of study is the learning and behavior of human beings, often children, the nature of such research may embarrass, hurt, frighten, impose on, or otherwise negatively affect the lives of the people who are making the research possible by their participation. To deal with this problem, organizations such as the American Psychological Association have developed a code of ethics for research with human subjects. Also, agencies such as the United States Office of Education have established screening procedures for evaluating on ethical grounds a grant recipient's test and questionnaire materials.

Of course it is possible to ask, "Why do research at all if even one person might be compromised?" However, the educational researcher must begin by asserting, and accepting the assertion, that research has substantially contributed to the body of scientific knowledge and all the human and technological advances that have been made based on this knowledge. Thus, research has the potential to help men improve their lives and themselves and, therefore, must remain an integral part of human endeavor. Accepting the assertion that research has value in contributing to knowledge and, ultimately, to human betterment, it is still necessary to ask: "What ethical considerations *must* the researcher take into account in designing experiments in order not to invade human rights?" These considerations and how to deal with them are outlined below.

The Right to Remain Anonymous

All participants in human research have the right to remain anonymous, that is, the right to insist that their individual identities not be a salient feature of the research. To insure anonymity, two approaches are often used. First, researchers are usually interested in group data rather than individual data; thus scores obtained from individuals in a study are pooled or grouped together and reported as averages. Since his individual scores cannot be identified, such a reporting process provides each participant with anonymity. Second, whereever possible subjects are identified by number rather than by name.

Before starting the testing, it is wise to explain to the subjects that they have not been singled out as individuals for study, but rather, they have been randomly selected in an attempt to study the population of which they are representatives. Thus, they need not fear that the researcher would have any reason to compromise their right to anonymity.

The Right to Privacy

The right to privacy, as distinguished from the right to anonymity, refers to the right of a participant in a study to keep from the public certain information about himself. For example, many people would regard test items in psychological inventories that ask about religious convictions or personal feelings about parents as an invasion of privacy. To safeguard the privacy of his subjects, the researcher should (1) take care to avoid asking unnecessary questions, (2) avoid recording individual item responses if possible, and (3) obtain direct consent for participation from adults and consent from parent and teacher for children.

The Right to Confidentiality

Similar to the concern over privacy is the concern over confidentiality: Who will have access to the data? In school studies, students and teachers both are concerned with others having access to research data and using them to make judgments of character or performance. Certainly participants have every right to insist that data collected from them be treated with confidentiality. To guarantee this, the researcher should (1) roster all data by number rather than by name, (2) destroy the original test protocols as soon as the study is completed, and (3) when possible provide participants with stamped, self-addressed envelopes to return questionnaires directly to him (rather than turning them in to a teacher or principal).

The Right to Expect Experimenter Responsibility

Finally, every participant in a study has the right to expect that the researcher be sensitive to human dignity and well-meaning in his intentions.

Researchers should reassure potential participants, particularly assuring them that they will not be "hurt" by their participation. Although some studies, by their very nature, require that their true purpose be camouflaged (or, at least, not divulged) before their completion, participants have the right to insist that the researcher explain the study to them after it is completed, particularly to overcome any negative effects that might result from participation.

RECOMMENDED READINGS

Bergmann, G. *Philosophy of science.* Madison: University of Wisconsin Press, 1957.
Brodbeck, May. Logic and scientific method in research on teaching. In N. L. Gage (Ed.) *Handbook of research on teaching.* Chicago: Rand McNally, 1963, pp. 44–93.
Feigl, H. and Brodbeck, May (Eds.) *Readings in the philosophy of science.* New York: Appleton-Century-Crofts, 1953.
Northrup, F. *The logic of the sciences and the humanities.* New York: Macmillan, 1947.
Townsend, J. C. *Introduction to experimental method.* New York: McGraw-Hill, 1953.

COMPETENCY TEST EXERCISES

1. Consider the following experiment:

    There were two first grades in a particular school. One first grade was taught readiness and then sight reading while the second was given a pre-primer and then primer using the phonics method. The second group earned higher scores at the end of the year on the Davis Reading Test.

    Below are five statements applicable to this experiment. Some represent threats to internal validity; some represent threats to external validity; some do not represent threats at all. Write *i* next to threats to internal validity, *e* next to threats to external validity, and nothing next to all others.

    a. no attempt to establish group equivalence
    b. reading gain due to maturation
    c. groups not representative of all first graders
    d. teachers of the two classes have different style
    e. combinations of treatments are contrived

2. Which of the following statements best describes internal validity?
    a. insuring that an experiment is reasonably representative of reality.
    b. insuring that the results really occurred
    c. insuring that the experimenter followed the rules
    d. insuring that the results were really a function of the experimental treatment.

3. Which of the *above* statements best describes external validity?

4. Which of the following statements best describes the relationship between internal and external validity?
    a. If there is no internal validity to an experiment there can be no external validity.
    b. If there is no external validity to an experiment there can be no internal validity.
    c. Internal validity and external validity are essentially unrelated.

5. I have just read about an experiment. I cannot apply the results because the conditions of the experiment are so different from conditions in which I operated. Thus, for my purposes the experiment lacks_____ (internal, external) validity.

6. I have just read about an experiment. I cannot apply the results because I cannot believe that the results are a function of the treatment. The conclusions do not seem warranted based on the design of the experiment. The experiment lacks_____ (internal, external) validity.

7. Describe (in one sentence) each of the following characteristics of the research process:

a. systematic
b. logical
c. empirical
d. reductive
e. transmittable

8. Some of the following statements represent steps in the research process. Write a number next to those statements indicating their place in the sequence of the research process.
   a. constructing operational definitions
   b. carrying out data analysis
   c. teaching students how to teach
   d. identifying a problem
   e. writing a final report
   f. constructing devices for measurement
   g. resolving discipline problems
   h. identifying and labeling variables
   i. constructing an experimental design
   j. adjusting individual initiative
   k. constructing an hypothesis.

9. Which of the following represent individual ethical rights in an experiment?
   a. the right to privacy
   b. the right to unlimited exposure
   c. the right to expect experimenter responsibility
   d. the right to confidentiality
   e. the right to total participation
   f. the right to remain anonymous
   g. the right to free expectation

10. Describe (in one sentence) each of the individual ethical rights checked above.

2

Selecting a Problem and Constructing Hypotheses

OBJECTIVES

Select a research problem characterized by both practicality and interest. / Identify specific and general hypotheses and observations, and describe their difference. / Construct alternative hypotheses from a problem statement. / Determine the appropriateness of a hypothesis using deduction and induction. / Identify concepts, given operational statements, that can be used for generating hypotheses. / Construct a null hypothesis from a hypothesis given in positive form.

2.1 CHARACTERISTICS OF A PROBLEM

Although selecting a research problem is one of the most difficult steps for a student in the research process, it is unfortunately one for which the least guidance can be given. Problem selection is not subject to the same degree of technical rules or requirements as are research design, measurement, or statistics; fortunately, however, some guidelines can be offered.

A problem statement must have the following characteristics which we will examine in detail.

1. It should ask about a relationship between two or more variables.
2. It should be stated clearly and unambiguously, usually in question form.
3. It should be possible to collect data to answer the question(s) asked.
4. It should not represent a moral or ethical position.

Relationship between Variables

The type of problem that will be dealt with in this book examines the relationship between two or more variables. In this kind of problem the researcher manipulates a minimum of one variable to determine its effect on other variables, as opposed to a purely descriptive study in which the researcher observes, counts, or in some way measures the frequency of appearance of a particular variable in a particular setting. For instance, in a descriptive study the problem might be: How many students in School X have I.Q.'s in excess of 120? Since no attempt need be made to deal with a relationship between variables, this problem requires only a "bookkeeping" procedure. If, however, the problem were worded: Are boys more likely than girls to have I.Q.'s in excess of 120?, then it would involve the relationship between variables.

For purposes of this book, a problem statement will require the inclusion of at least two variables and their relation. The examples given in the next subsection are illustrative of this point.

The Problem Is Stated in Question Form

As can be seen from the following examples, the problem is best stated in the form of a question.

- What is the relation between I.Q. and achievement?
- Do students learn more from a directive teacher or a nondirective teacher?
- Is there a relationship between racial background and dropout rate?
- Do more students continue in training programs offering stipends or in programs not offering stipends?
- Can students who have had pretraining be taught a learning task more quickly than those who have not had pretraining?
- Does the repetitious use of prompting in a learning program impair the effectiveness of programmed materials?
- Do students who are described unfavorably by their teacher tend to describe themselves more unfavorably than those students described favorably?
- What is the relationship between rote learning ability and socioeconomic status?
- Does the ability to discriminate among parts of speech increase with chronological age and education level?

Empirical Testability

⌐A problem should be testable by empirical methods—that is, through the collection of data.⌐ Moreover, for a student's purposes, it should lend itself to study by a single researcher, on a limited budget, within a year. The nature of the variables included in the problem is a good clue to its testability. An example of the kind of problem that is wise to avoid is: Does an extended experience in communal living improve a person's outlook on life? In addition to the magnitude and probable duration of studying such a problem, the variables themselves would be difficult to manipulate or measure.

Avoidance of Moral or Ethical Judgments

Questions about ideals or values are often more difficult to study than questions about attitudes or performance. Examples of problems that would be difficult to test are: Should men disguise their feelings? Should children be seen and not heard? Problems such as: Are all philosophies equally inspiring? Should students avoid cheating under all circumstances? represent moral and ethical issues and should be avoided as such. After completing Chapter 4 on operational definitions, you may feel you can bring some ethical questions into the range of solvable problems, but in general they are best avoided.

2.2 NARROWING THE RANGE OF PROBLEMS

Since an infinite number of problems exists "out there," it is wise for the researcher to narrow the range of problems in terms of his interests and skills. To accomplish this, ⌐some scheme for classifying problems is useful. Two such schemes are offered in Figures 2.1 and 2.2. (They are only basic illustrations; you should feel free to use any other scheme that more clearly fits your frame of reference.)⌐

To use the first scheme, simply look at the categories and ask yourself: In which category am I most interested and most competent? Suppose that your answer is Teacher Education. You would then divide this category into subcategories; for instance, teacher recruitment and selection, teacher competencies, teaching style, teacher-education programs (these being further subdivided into preservice and inservice), and program evaluation. Having listed the subcategories, you might then ask yourself: What is it about inservice education that particular-

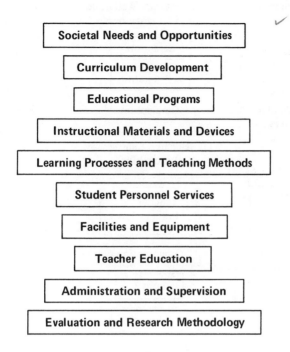

Figure 2.1 *A one-dimensional model for problem consideration.*

ly interests me? If your interest is in changing the behavior of inservice teachers, you could do a study on the relative effects of feedback from students and supervisors in changing teacher behavior. (See Appendix A, Sample Study I.)

To use the second scheme, you would attempt to discover an area of interest in column 1 and link it to an interest in column 2 and column 3. However, it is not necessary to begin with column 1 nor to use all three columns. You may begin in any column and use only two. Thus, if your major interest is career development (possibly a subcategory of meeting individual needs shown in column 3), you might link it to services (column 2) and then further refine services to a particular interest you might have, group guidance. Thus, you might ask: Is group guidance as effective as individual guidance in facilitating an individual's career development (i.e., does it increase his ability to make an appropriate career choice for himself)? Bringing in the first column (prospective students) you might ask: Is group guidance more effective in facilitating career development among students with clearly defined goals compared to students without clearly defined goals?

Models such as these or others may prove useful in helping you to narrow the range of problems for consideration.

Available Inputs	Instructional Activities and Organization	Anticipated Outcomes

Available Inputs

- Prospective Students
- Prospective Teachers
- Attitudes
- Job Markets
- Institutional Relations

Instructional Activities and Organization

- Selection
- Program
- Curriculum
- Teacher–Learner Relationships
- Teacher Preparation
- Organization
- Policy
- Services

Anticipated Outcomes

- Meeting Societal Needs
- Meeting Individual Needs
- Attitude Change
- Social Change
- Competency Acquisition

Figure 2.2 *A three-dimensional model for problem consideration.*

2.3 FORMULATING HYPOTHESES

What is a hypothesis?

The next step after the selection of the problem is to state a hypothesis (or hypotheses). A hypothesis, a suggested answer to the problem, has the following characteristics:

1. It should conjecture upon a relationship between two or more variables.
2. It should be stated clearly and unambiguously in the form of a declarative sentence.
3. It should be testable; that is, it should be possible to restate it in an operational form which can then be evaluated based on data. (This is dealt with in Chapter 4.)

Thus, hypotheses that might have been derived from the problem statements listed on page 21 are:

- I.Q. and achievement are positively related.
- Directive teachers are more effective than nondirective teachers.
- The dropout rate is higher for black students than for white students.

- Programs offering stipends are more successful at retaining students.

- Speed of learning a task is directly proportional to the amount of pretraining.

- The repetitive use of prompting in a learning process impairs the effectiveness of programmed materials.

- As the description of a student by his teacher becomes increasingly unfavorable, his description of himself becomes increasingly unfavorable.

- Error rate in a rote learning task and socioeconomic status are inversely related; that is, middle class youngsters make fewer errors in a rote learning task than lower class youngsters.

- The ability to discriminate among parts of speech increases with chronological age and educational level.

Observations versus Specific and General Hypotheses

Hypotheses are often confused with observations. These terms, however, refer to quite different things. An observation refers to *what is*—that is, to what is seen. Thus, a researcher may go into a school and after looking around observe that most of the students are black.

From that observation, he may then *infer* that the school is located in a poor neighborhood. Though the researcher does not *know* that the neighborhood is poor (i.e., he has no data on income level), he *expects* that the majority of people living there are poor. What he has done is make a *specific hypothesis** setting forth an anticipated relationship between two variables, race and income level.

To test this specific hypothesis, the researcher could walk around the neighborhood, observe the homes, and inquire of the residents as to their income levels. After making the observations needed to provide support for the specific hypothesis (i.e., that the neighborhood the school is in is poor) the researcher might make a *general hypothesis*: areas containing a high concentration of black persons are characterized by a high incidence of low income. The second hypothesis represents a generalization and must be tested by making observations, as was the specific hypothesis. Since it would be impossible—or impractical—to observe all neighborhoods, the researcher will take a sample of neighborhoods and reach conclusions on a probability basis, that is, the likelihood of the hypothesis being true. (Specific hypotheses require fewer observations for testing than general hypotheses. For testing purposes a general hypothesis is reformulated to a more specific one.)

A hypothesis, then, could be defined as an expectation about events based on

In Chapter 4, the term prediction *will be introduced to mean a specific hypothesis.*

generalizations of the assumed relationship between variables. Hypotheses are abstract and are concerned with theories and concepts, while the observations used to test hypotheses are specific and are based on facts.

Where Do Hypotheses Come from?

Given a problem statement, for example, Are A and B related? there are three possible hypotheses. These are

a. Yes, as A increases so does B.
b. Yes, as A increases B decreases.
c. No, A and B are unrelated.

Of course as more variables are simultaneously considered, the number of possible hypotheses increases greatly. Also, the above possibilities have been limited to simple linear relationships, so that there are conceivably more possibilities, such as, as A increases B initially increases and then levels off.

After deciding that the relationship between variables A and B is the problem to be studied, the researcher has two logical processes to draw upon in developing a hypothesis. These processes are called *deduction* and *induction*.

Deduction is a process which goes from the general to the specific. For example, it can be generally stated that the extent to which a person believes feedback and is therefore likely to change as a result of it depends on the motives he perceives the feedback-giver to have and the degree to which he feels the feedback-giver has accurate information to convey. Feedback received from a person who is perceived as having accurate information and having the best interests of the recipient in mind is more likely to provoke change than feedback received from a person perceived as lacking these characteristics. It can also be generally stated that change from feedback will depend on the power of the giver over the recipient, being greater as this power increases.

Considering the first general statement, the researcher would deduce that teachers would be more receptive to feedback from students than from supervisors (the hypothesis offered in Sample Study I, Appendix A). Considering the second general statement, the researcher would deduce that teachers would be more receptive to feedback from supervisors than from students. Thus, the specific hypothesis deduced depends on the more general or theoretical position started from. When general expectations about events based on presumed relationships between variables are used to arrive at more specific expectations (or anticipated observations), that process is called deduction.

In the inductive process the researcher starts with specific observations and combines them to produce a more general statement of relationship, namely a hypothesis. Many researchers begin by searching the literature for relevant specific findings in order to induce a hypothesis, and others often run a series of exploratory studies before attempting to induce a hypothetical* statement about the relationship between the variables in question. The findings that obese people eat as much immediately after a meal as they do some hours after a meal, that they eat much less unappealing food than appealing food, that they eat more when they think it is dinner time even though little time had elapsed since their previous meal led Schachter (1968) to induce that for obese persons hunger is controlled externally rather than internally as it is for persons of normal weight.

Induction begins with data and observations (empirical events) and proceeds toward hypotheses and theories, while deduction begins with theories and general hypotheses and proceeds toward specific hypotheses (or anticipated observations).

Constructing Alternative Hypotheses

From any problem statement, it is generally possible to derive more than one hypothesis. As an example, consider Sample Study I, Appendix A. One of the problems identified was: What is the relationship between a teacher's amount of teaching experience and his likelihood to change when given feedback? Three simple possible hypotheses can be generated from this statement:

 a. Teaching experience and receptivity to feedback are positively related— the more experienced the teacher, the more likely he is to change when given feedback.
 b. Teaching experience and receptivity to feedback are negatively (or inversely) related—the less experienced the teacher, the more likely he is to change when given feedback.
 c. Teaching experience and receptivity to feedback are unrelated—less experienced teachers are neither more nor less likely to change when given feedback than are more experienced teachers.

Both induction and deduction are needed to choose among these possibilities. Many theories, both psychological and educational, deal with the stabilization (and rigidifying) of behavior patterns as a function of their use. Thorndike's (1931) Law of Frequency states that the likelihood of recurrence of a behavior increases with frequency. Since the frequency of occurrence of normal classroom behaviors will be increasingly greater with experience, the logical deduction is

*The terms hypothetical, conceptual, and theoretical are used interchangeably to refer to inferred or anticipated events or relationships.

that hypothesis (b), which cites an inverse relationship between experience and receptivity to feedback, is the most "appropriate" expectation of the three. Moreover, there tends to be a strong positive relation between years of teaching experience and age (more experienced teachers are older). Research findings are also cited in Sample Study I that establish an inverse relationship between age and tendency to change. Therefore, reasoning inductively, hypothesis (b) again is the most appropriate.

Consider Sample Study II in Appendix A from which a second example will be drawn. In this study the problem is to determine the effect of massive, positive, verbal rewards on the reading achievement of children. At first glance these three hypotheses might be offered:

  a. Rewards will increase reading achievement.
  b. Rewards will decrease reading achievement.
  c. Rewards will have no effect on reading achievement.

Ample evidence has already been obtained in the laboratory to support hypothesis (a) (rewards enhance performance). However, upon closer examination, the primary purpose of this study is to determine whether the enhancing effect of rewards can be incorporated into a real classroom setting to facilitate children's learning to read. Based on the assumption that the "laws" of learning should apply in a classroom, if perhaps more subtly than in a laboratory, and on the laboratory findings that support the assumed relationship between rewards and performance, the logical conclusion would be that rewards would have a demonstrable enhancing effect on classroom performance. This conclusion is based on the first assumption arrived at deductively and the second arrived at inductively.

Consider one further example of choosing among possible hypotheses. A researcher interested in the possible relationship between birth order and achievement motivation asks: Are first-born children more likely to pursue higher education than later-born children? There are three possible hypotheses:

  a. First-borns are more likely to pursue higher education than later-born children.
  b. First-borns are less likely to pursue higher education than later-borns.
  c. First-borns and later-borns are equally likely to pursue higher education.

There are data available to the researcher to indicate that in specific instances first-borns were more concerned with parental approval. Therefore, he knows from prior studies that under the conditions of those studies first-born children sought parental approval more than later-borns. Moreover, he has observed specific occasions when educational accomplishment was a source of parental approval. On those occasions, parents were likely both to approve and to reward the educational attainments of their children. Based on the specific observations that

(1) first-borns seek parental approval, and (2) such approval may be gained from education pursuits, he is able to *induce* the more general expectation that first-borns are more education-oriented than later-borns—hypothesis (a). From this general hypothesis, arrived at inductively, it may be deduced that in this year's graduating class at Harvard, more first-borns will be found than later-borns.

Researchers formulate hypotheses using induction and deduction, thus giving due consideration to both potentially relevant theory and prior research findings. Since one of the goals of research is to produce the *pieces* for generalizable bodies of theory which will provide *answers* to practical problems, the researcher, where possible, should try to work out of or toward a general theoretical base. Hypothesis construction and testing enable researchers to generalize their findings beyond the specific conditions in which they were obtained.

⌈The decision to pursue a particular study is usually based on considerations of the potential importance of definitive findings and their likelihood of being obtained. Since a hypothesis is a formulation of anticipated findings, students are advised to develop a hypothesis as a means of demonstrating the basis for their study to themselves and their readers.⌋ Moreover, the tasks of introducing a study and discussing the findings are facilitated by the existence of a hypothesis —integrating relevant research and logic.

2.4 HYPOTHESES BASED ON CONCEPTUALIZING

⌈The researcher deals with reality on two levels, the *operational* level and the *conceptual* level. On the operational level he must define events in observable terms in order to operate with the reality necessary to do research. On the conceptual level he must define events in terms of underlying communality (usually causal) with other events.⌋ Defining at a conceptual level, the researcher can abstract from single specific instances to general ones and thus begin to understand how phenomena operate and variables interrelate. ⌈The formulation of a hypothesis very frequently requires going from the operational or concrete level to the conceptual or abstract level.⌋ It is this movement to the conceptual level that enables the results of research to be generalized beyond the specific conditions of a particular study and thus to be of wider applicability.

⌈Research requires the ability to move from the operational to the conceptual level and vice versa.⌋ This ability is required not only in constructing experiments but in applying their findings as well.

Consider the following hypothetical study. A State Department of Education has decided to run three inservice workshops for staff development to be open to all the schools in the state. The purpose of the workshops is to help teachers and administrators work together in establishing priorities and programs for helping disadvantaged students in their districts.

Let us label these workshops A, B, and C. At first glance it would appear that the research problem is to compare the relative success of each workshop in developing communication and problem-solving skills among its participants, success to be judged in terms of program planning outcomes. However, such a comparison might not indicate those features characteristic of the most successful workshop that differentiated it from the others and thus may have contributed to its greater success. In other words, rather than merely seeking to conclude that one workshop was more successful than the others, it would be more useful to have some basis for determining how the workshops were different in order to discover what it was about one that led to greater effectiveness.

Two dimensions or concepts were identified to classify these workshops. The first was the concept of structure, that is, predesignated specification of what was to happen, when, and for what purpose.

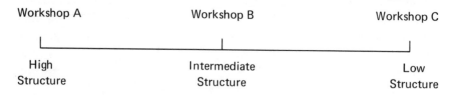

Workshop A   Workshop B   Workshop C

High   Intermediate   Low
Structure   Structure   Structure

The second concept dealt with the task orientation of the workshop, that is, what kinds of problems were to be dealt with. The distinction was made between cognitive problems (those dealing with thinking and problem-solving) and affective problems (those dealing with feelings and attitudes).

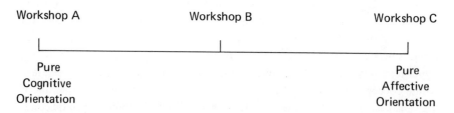

Workshop A   Workshop B   Workshop C

Pure   Pure
Cognitive   Affective
Orientation   Orientation

Workshop A was very traditional, utilizing a very highly developed agenda and focusing on generating solutions to pre-ordained, real-world problems. Institute C was almost entirely human relations oriented and utilized no set agenda. Emotional and attitude problems were dealt with as they emerged. Finally, Institute B was in the middle; both "in-the-head" and "in-the-heart" problems were dealt with, and a somewhat specific agenda was employed.

It was hypothesized that Workshop B would be the most effective because it provided structure without eliminating the possibility for changes in the agenda and because it dealt with both cognitive and affective concerns. Knowing that moderate levels of structure and a mixed orientation are most conducive to success, developers of very different kinds of institutes and other training programs may be able to apply the results to their situations. They could generalize beyond the specifics of each workshop to those underlying dimensions on which the workshops differed. Generalizability depends on conceptualization.

Consider a second example in which programmed instruction is being compared to traditional instruction. The terms "programmed instruction" and "traditional instruction" are operational terms. In order to gain greater generalizability, these operational terms should be examined for underlying conceptual similarities and differences. This process of making conceptual contrasts between operational programs is called *conceptualizing* or *dimensionalizing*. Dimensions useful for contrasting programmed and traditional instruction might be degree of feedback, rate of positive reinforcement, uniqueness of presentation format, control of pacing, size of instructional units, and degree of incorporation of student performance feedback in instructional design. These six dimensions or concepts could be used for classifying any instructional model as a basis for understanding its relation to other models. Such classification at this abstract level would help one not only to hypothesize whether instructional model A will be more effective than model B on certain specific criteria, but to begin to understand why model A is better and thus to be able to build "model A-ness" into other instructional procedures.

Moving from the operational to the conceptual level and vice versa is a critical ingredient of the research-to-demonstration process.

2.5 TESTING A HYPOTHESIS

The purpose of testing a hypothesis is to determine the probability that it is supported by fact. However, because a hypothesis is a general expectation about the relationship between variables, there is an extremely large number of instances under which it can be tested, and it would be impractical to attempt to gain support in all of these instances.

A hypothesis which says, for instance, that nondirective teachers are more effective than directive teachers would have to be tested for many groups of teachers, in many subjects and many settings, and with many criteria before it could be accepted. If, however, on the basis of limited testing the hypothesis fails to yield confirming results, then it would be fair to reject it.

Since it is extremely difficult to obtain unequivocal support for a hypothesis, the researcher instead attempts to test and disprove its negation. The negative or "no differences" version of a hypothesis is called a *null hypothesis*. A null hypothesis suggests that minor differences can occur due to chance variation and thus are not real differences (this concept will be dealt with further in the chapter on statistics).

Consider the possible three hypotheses concerning a comparison of the effectiveness of directive and nondirective teachers:

a. Nondirective teachers are more effective than directive teachers.
b. Directive teachers are more effective than nondirective teachers.
c. Nondirective and directive teachers are equally effective.

Hypothesis (c) is the null or no-differences hypothesis. (In fact, in each of the three sets of hypotheses stated on pages 27 and 28, hypothesis (c) was the null hypothesis.) While the researcher has developed a rationale for alternative (a), nondirective teachers are more effective than directive teachers, he will *implicitly* turn it into the null hypothesis, nondirective and directive teachers are equally effective, for purposes of testing it statistically. He can reject the null hypothesis if he feels that differences found are large enough to be real. That is, he can say that the statement, nondirective and directive teachers are equally effective, is unlikely to be true since one group has been shown clearly to be more effective than the other. He is not justified in saying, however, that he has *proven* that nondirective teachers are more effective. He must be satisfied with his rejection of the null hypothesis indicating that the effectiveness of the two groups of teachers is, in the greatest likelihood, not equal. It is unwise to conclude that a hypothesis is absolutely true or false since different kinds of errors may lead to the acceptance of hypotheses that are false or to the rejection of hypotheses that are true.

It is not necessary to state a hypothesis in null form; it is easier to discuss and understand when it is stated in positive or directional form. However, for purposes of statistical testing and interpretation the researcher always uses the null hypothesis.

Thus far in the discussion of hypotheses, words and phrases such as "effective" and "receptivity to change" have been employed. As you may have recognized, words and phrases such as these do not lend themselves to experimental testing. A hypothesis, therefore, even a null hypothesis, is not directly testable in the form in which it is generally stated. Its very generality, a distinguishing characteristic, limits its direct testability. To become testable, it must be transformed into a more specific or operationalized statement. A hypothesis is operationalized (made testable) by providing operational definitions for the terms (variables) of the hypothesis. This conversion is the subject of Chapter 4. But before variables can be defined, we must specify what our variables are—this being the subject of the next chapter.

RECOMMENDED READINGS

Adelson, J. The teacher as a model. In N. Sanford (Ed.) The *American College*, New York: Wiley, 1962, pp. 396–417.

Bachrach, A. *Psychological research*. New York: Random House, 1962.

Gage, N. L. Paradigms for research on teaching. In N. L. Gage (Ed.) *Handbook of research on teaching*. Chicago: Rand-McNally, 1963, pp. 94–141.

Hyman, R. T. (Ed.) *Teaching: vantage points for study*. Philadelphia: Lippincott, 1968.

Sellitz, Claire, Jahoda, Marie, Deutsch, M., and Cook, S. W. *Research methods in social relations* (revised). New York: Holt, Rinehart, & Winston, 1964.

Van Dalen, D. B. *Understanding educational research*. New York: McGraw-Hill, 1966. (Especially Chapter 8 and Appendices.)

Willower, D. J. Some illustrated comments on hypothesis construction and research. *Journal of Educational Research*, 1962, *56*, 210–213.

COMPETENCY TEST EXERCISES

1. Indicate which of the following three statements is a specific hypothesis, which is a general hypothesis, and which is an observation.
   a. Johnny has never been tested but it is expected that he has a high I.Q.
   b. Boys of Johnny's age have higher I.Q.'s than girls of the same age.
   c. Johnny was just given an I.Q. test and obtained a high score.

2. Indicate which of the following three statements is a specific hypothesis, which is a general hypothesis, and which is an observation.
   a. The phonics approach to reading is better than any other currently in existence.
   b. The Johnson Phonics Reading Program worked better in the Cleveland schools than any others tried.
   c. The Johnson Phonics Reading Program should work better in the Martin Luther King School than any presently in use.

3. In the above two items, indicate briefly the difference between the two types of hypothesis and observations.

4. Problem: To find out whether blind children or partially-sighted children will be better liked by their sighted peers. Construct three hypotheses from this problem. (Note that this is the subject of Sample Study III in Appendix A.)

5. Problem: To find out whether students who use this textbook will learn more about research methods than students who use the Brand X textbook. Construct three hypotheses from this problem.

6. Given two hypotheses: (a) team teaching is more effective than individual teaching, and (b) team teaching is no more effective than individual teaching. Which of these hypotheses would you judge to be more appropriate given the following:
   i. All students cannot be expected to like all teachers.
   ii. Research has shown that male models and female models are both important in socialization.
   Why did you choose the one you did?

7. Which of the statements (i or ii) in exercise 6 — is deductive? Which is inductive?

8. Some students are going to receive instruction on the environment in a classroom. Other students will receive this instruction out-of-doors. We are interested in identifying concepts that will distinguish between these two learning locations. Below are a list of concepts. Check those that might be useful in distinguishing between these locations.

   environmental relevance   _____

   unrestrictedness   _____

appropriateness   _____

learning level   _____

motivation   _____

9. Take those concepts above that you checked and indicate how they might be used (or applied) to differentiate between in-classroom and out-of-doors learning environments.

10. Rewrite the following hypotheses in null form:
    a. Youngsters who read below grade level will find school less pleasant than those who read at or above grade level.
    b. Intelligence and ordinal position of birth are positively related, i.e., first-borns are more intelligent than later-borns.
    c. A combination of reading readiness training and programmed reading instruction will be more effective in teaching reading than normal classroom instruction in sight reading.

11. State three potential research problems. Critique each in terms of (a) its interest to you, and (b) its practicality as a researchable problem.

12. Take each of the research problems you stated in exercise 11 and show how each fits into (a) the one-dimensional model shown in Figure 2.1 on page 23, (b) the three-dimensional model shown in Figure 2.2 on page 24.

3

Identifying and Labeling Variables

OBJECTIVES

Identify variables and label them as one of five types: independent, dependent, moderator, control, and intervening. / Describe the characteristics of each type of variable. / State several factors to be considered in labeling variables as one of the five types.

3.1 A HYPOTHESIS AND ITS VARIABLES

Among students of the same age and intelligence, skill performance is directly related to the number of practice trials particularly in boys but less directly among girls. This would seem to indicate that practice increases learning. In such a hypothesis the variables which must be considered are:

Independent variable: number of practice trials
Dependent variable: skill performance
Moderator variable: sex
Control variables: age, intelligence
Intervening variable: learning

3.2 THE INDEPENDENT VARIABLE

The independent variable, which is a stimulus variable or input, operates either within a person or within his environment to affect his behavior. It is *that factor* which is measured, manipulated, or selected by the experimenter to determine its relationship to an observed phenomenon. If an experimenter studying the relationship between two variables, X and Y, asks himself, "What will happen to Y if I make X greater or smaller?" he is thinking of variable X as his independent variable. It is the variable that he will manipulate or change to cause a change in some other variable. He considers it independent because he is interested only in how it affects another variable, not in what affects it. He regards it as an antecedent condition, a condition required preceding a particular consequence.

3.3 THE DEPENDENT VARIABLE

The dependent variable is a response variable or output. It is an observed aspect of the behavior of an organism that has been stimulated. The dependent variable is *that factor which is observed and measured to determine the effect of the independent variable*, i.e., that factor that appears, disappears, or varies as the experimenter introduces, removes, or varies the independent variable. In the study of the relationship between the two variables X and Y when the experimenter asks, "What will happen to Y if I make X greater or smaller?" he is thinking of Y as the dependent variable. It is the variable that will change as a result of variations in the independent variable. It is considered dependent because its value depends upon the value of the independent variable. It represents the consequence of a change in the person or situation studied.

3.4 THE RELATIONSHIP BETWEEN INDEPENDENT AND DEPENDENT VARIABLES

Most experiments involve many variables, not just a single independent and a single dependent variable. The additional variables may be independent and dependent variables or they may be moderator or control variables. But in this section for the purpose of explanation we will deal solely with the relationship between a single independent and a single dependent variable.

In many experiments, the independent variable is *discrete* (i.e., categorical) and takes the form of the presence versus the absence of a particular treatment or approach being studied or a comparison between different approaches. In other experiments, the independent variable may be *continuous*, and the experimenter's observations of it may be stated in numerical terms indicating its degree. When two continuous variables are compared, as in correlation studies, deciding which variable to call independent and which dependent is sometimes rather arbitrary. In fact, in such cases the variables are often not labeled as independent or dependent since there is no real distinction.

Independent variables may be called *factors* and their variations may be called *levels*. In a study of the effect of music instruction on ability to concentrate, experimental treatment (music instruction) versus no experimental treatment (no music instruction) represents a single independent variable or factor with two levels. The amount of music instruction is the factor. The first level is some degree of music instruction; the second level is no degree of music instruction. A study of the effectiveness of (a) programmed instruction versus, (b) instruction by lecture alone versus, (c) instruction combining lecture and discussion has a single independent variable or factor (type of instruction) with three levels. *Be careful not to confuse an independent variable with two levels for two independent variables or an independent variable with three levels for three independent variables, and so on.*

Townsend (1953) uses diagrams to illustrate the relationship between a discrete independent variable and a dependent variable. An application of his approach is shown in Figure 3.1 on page 39.

Some Examples of Independent and Dependent Variables

A number of hypotheses drawn from studies undertaken in a research methods course are listed below; the independent and dependent variables have been identified for each one.

- **Hypothesis 1.** Under intangible reinforcement conditions, middle-class children will learn significantly better than lower-class children.

    Independent variable: middle-class versus lower-class

    Dependent variable: ease or speed of learning

- **Hypothesis 2.** Girls who plan to pursue careers in science are more aggressive, less conforming, more independent, and have a greater need for achievement than girls who do not plan such careers.

    Independent variable: girls who plan to pursue careers in science versus those who do not

    Dependent variable: aggressiveness, conformity, independence, need for achievement*

It is difficult if not impossible to determine whether the career chosen has caused the personality characteristics, the personality has caused the career chosen, or both have been caused by a third factor. Thus, the labeling of independent and dependent variables is arbitrary. In such cases, there is no real need to label the variables, other than for discussion purposes, and then labeling may be based on presumed causality.

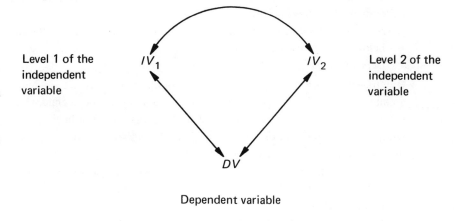

Level 1 of the independent variable — IV_1 ... IV_2 — Level 2 of the independent variable

DV

Dependent variable

HYPOTHESIS: As IV_1 is changed to IV_2, DV will increase (decrease).

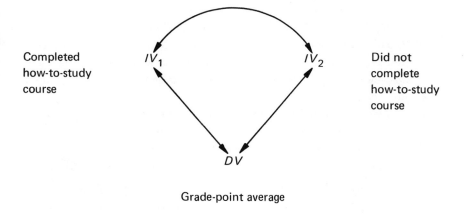

Completed how-to-study course — IV_1 ... IV_2 — Did not complete how-to-study course

DV

Grade-point average

HYPOTHESIS: Students who have completed a how-to-study course will make significantly higher grade-point averages than students who have never taken such a course.

Figure 3.1 *Diagrams of the relation between independent and dependent variables. Adapted from Townsend, J. C.,* Introduction to Experimental Method, *McGraw-Hill, 1953.*

- **Hypothesis 3.** In the elementary school age group, above average height children are more often chosen as leaders by their classmates than are children below average height.

    Independent variable: children above average height versus children below average height

    Dependent variable: selections as leader by classmates

- **Hypothesis 4.** In a middle class, suburban, public school district in which a child is expected to meet the standards of a set curriculum, a child who is under five years of age upon entrance to kindergarten is less likely to be ready for first grade in one year than a child who is five years of age or more at the time of entrance to kindergarten.

    Independent variable: children under five years of age upon entrance to kindergarten versus children five years of age or more upon entrance to kindergarten

    Dependent variable: readiness for first grade

- **Hypothesis 5.** Culturally advantaged first graders are more mature in perceptual-motor development than their lower-class disadvantaged counterparts.

    Independent variable: culturally advantaged first graders versus lower-class disadvantaged first graders

    Dependent variable: level of perceptual-motor development attained

- **Hypothesis 6.** Individuals who graduate with a Doctor of Education (Ed. D.) degree in educational administration attain better paying jobs than those who received a Specialist in Education (Ed. S.) in educational administration.

    Independent variable: degree attained: Ed. D. in educational administration versus Ed. S. in educational administration

    Dependent variable: pay level of jobs attained

    Consider also the following two examples drawn from journal sources.

- **Hypothesis 7.** Perceptions of the characteristics of the "good" or effective teacher are in part determined by the perceiver's attitudes toward education.

    Independent variable: perceiver's attitudes toward education

    Dependent variable: perceptions of the characteristics of the "good" or effective teacher.

- **Hypothesis 8.** Test-wiseness affects test performance.

    Independent variable: test-wiseness: much test-taking experience versus little test-taking experience

    Dependent variable: test performance

3.5 THE MODERATOR VARIABLE

The term moderator variable describes a special type of independent variable, a secondary independent variable selected for study to determine if it affects the relationship between the primary independent variable and the dependent variables. The moderator variable is defined as *that factor which is measured, manipulated, or selected by the experimenter to discover whether it modifies the relationship of the independent variable to an observed phenomenon.* The word moderator simply acknowledges the reason that this secondary independent variable has been singled out for study. If the experimenter is interested in studying the effect of independent variable X on dependent variable Y but suspects that the nature of the relationship between X and Y is altered by the level of a third factor Z, then Z can be in the analysis as a moderator variable.

Consider two illustrations. First, suppose the researcher wants to compare the effectiveness of the phonic approach to teaching reading to the effectiveness of the sight approach. Suppose further he suspects that, while one method may be more effective for average readers, the other may be more effective for slow readers. When all readers are tested together, the results of the two methods may appear to be the same; but when fast and slow readers are separated, the two methods may have different results in each subgroup. If so, reading level would be seen to moderate the relationship between reading approach (the independent variable) and effectiveness (the dependent variable). This moderating relationship (usually established via analysis of variance or regression analysis) is shown graphically in Figure 3.2. (These data are fictional.)

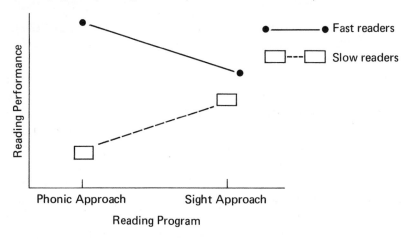

Figure 3.2 *Relationship between reading program (independent variable) and reading performance (dependent variable) as moderated by reading level.*

A second illustration (borne out by real data) is a study of the relationship between the conditions under which a test is taken (the independent variable) and test performance (the dependent variable). Assume that the experimenter varies test conditions between ego orientation ("write your name on the paper, we're measuring you") and task orientation ("don't write your name on the paper, we're measuring the test"). The test-taker's test anxiety level, a "personality" measure, is analyzed as a moderator variable. The results showed that high test anxious persons functioned better under task orientation and low test anxious persons functioned better under ego orientation. This interaction between the independent variable, the moderator variable, and the dependent variable, is shown graphically in Figure 3.3.

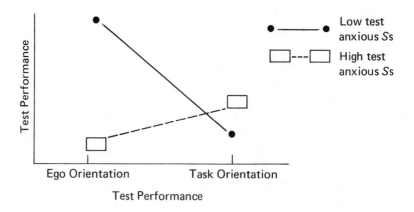

Figure 3.3 *Relationship between test conditions (independent variable) and test performance (dependent variable) as moderated by test anxiety level.*

Because the situations in educational research investigations are usually quite complex, the inclusion of at least one moderator variable in a study is highly recommended. Often the nature of the relationship between X and Y remains poorly understood because of the researcher's failure to single out and measure vital moderator variables—Z, W, and so on.

Some Examples of Moderator Variables

Listed below are a number of hypotheses drawn from various sources including students' research reports; the moderator variable (along with the independent and dependent variable) has been identified for each one.

- **Hypothesis 1.** Situational pressures of morality cause nondogmatic school superintendents to innovate while situational pressures of expediency cause dogmatic school superintendents to innovate.

    Independent variable: type of situational pressure—morality versus expediency

    Moderator variable: level of dogmatism of the school superintendent

    Dependent variable: degree to which superintendent innovates

- **Hypothesis 2.** Male experimenters get more effective performances from both male and female subjects than female experimenters, but they are singularly most effective with male subjects.

    Independent variable: the sex of the experimenter

    Moderator variable: the sex of the subject

    Dependent variable: effectiveness of performance of subjects

- **Hypothesis 3.** First-born male college students with a Machiavellian orientation get higher grades than their non-Machiavellian counterparts of equal intelligence, while no such differences are found among later-borns.

    Moderator variable: It is optional whether first-born versus later-born or Machiavellian versus non-Machiavellian is considered the moderator variable, while the other would be considered the independent variable.

    Dependent variable: grades

- **Hypothesis 4.** Grade point average and intelligence are more highly correlated for boys than for girls.

    Independent variable: either grade point average or intelligence may be considered the independent variable; the other, the dependent variable

    Moderator variable: sex (boys versus girls)

3.6 CONTROL VARIABLES

All of the variables in a situation (situational variables) or in a person (dispositional variables) cannot be studied at the same time; some must be neutralized to guarantee that they will not have a differential or moderating effect on the relationship between the independent variable and the dependent variable. These variables whose effects must be neutralized or controlled are called control variables. They are defined as *those factors which are controlled by the experimenter to cancel out or neutralize any effect they might otherwise have on the observed phenomenon*. While the effects of control variables are neutralized, the effects of moderator variables are studied. (As you will see in Chapter 5, the effects of control variables can be neutralized by elimination, equating across groups, or randomization.)

Certain variables appear repeatedly as control variables, although they occasionally serve as moderator variables. Sex, intelligence, and socioeconomic status are three subject variables that are commonly controlled; noise, task order, and task content are common control variables in the situation. In constructing an experiment, the researcher must always decide which variables will be studied and which will be controlled. Some of the bases for deciding this matter are discussed in section 3.9.

Some Examples of Control Variables

Control variables are not necessarily specified in the hypothesis. It is often necessary to read the methods section of a study to discover which variables have been treated as control variables. The examples below, however, specifically list at least one control variable in the hypothesis.

- **Hypothesis 1.** First-born college students with a Machiavellian orientation get higher grades than their non-Machiavellian counterparts of equal intelligence, while no such differences are found among later-borns.
  Control variable: intelligence

- **Hypothesis 2.** Among boys there is a correlation between physical size and social maturity, while for girls in the same age group there is no correlation between these two variables.
  Control variable: age

- **Hypothesis 3.** Task performance by high need achievers will exceed that of low need achievers in tasks with a 50% subjective probability of success.
  Control variable: subjective probability of task success

- **Hypothesis 4.** Under intangible reinforcement conditions, middle-class children will learn significantly better than lower-class children.
  Control variable: reinforcement conditions

In each of the above illustrations, there are undoubtedly other variables, such as the subjects' relevant prior experiences or the noise level during treatment, which are not specified in the hypothesis but which must be controlled. Because they are controlled by routine design procedures, universal variables such as these are often not systematically labeled.

3.7 INTERVENING VARIABLES

All of the variables described thus far—independent, dependent, moderator, and control—are concrete. Each independent, moderator, and control variable can be manipulated by the experimenter, and each variation can be observed by him as it affects the dependent variable. What the experimenter is trying to find out by manipulating these concrete variables is often not concrete, however, but hypothetical: the relationship between a hypothetical underlying or intervening variable and a dependent variable. An intervening variable is *that factor which theoretically affects the observed phenomenon but cannot be seen, measured, or manipulated; its effect must be inferred from the effects of the independent and moderator variables on the observed phenomenon.*

In writing about their experiments, researchers do not always identify their intervening variables, and are even less likely to label them as such. It would be helpful if they did.

Consider the role of the intervening variable in the following hypotheses.

- **Hypothesis 1.** As task interest increases, measured task performance increases.
   Independent variable: task interest
   Intervening variable: learning
   Dependent variable: task performance

- **Hypothesis 2.** Children who are blocked from reaching their goals exhibit more aggressive acts than children not so blocked.
   Independent variable: being or not being blocked from goal
   Intervening variable: frustration
   Dependent variable: number of aggressive acts

- **Hypothesis 3.** Teachers given more positive feedback experiences will have more positive attitudes toward children than teachers given fewer positive feedback experiences.
   Independent variable: number of positive feedback experiences for teacher
   Intervening variable: teacher's self-esteem
   Dependent variable: positiveness of teacher's attitudes toward students

The researcher must operationalize his variables in order to study them and conceptualize his variables in order to generalize from them. Researchers often use the labels independent, dependent, moderator, and control to describe operational statements of their variables. The intervening variable, however, always refers to a conceptual variable—that which is being affected by the independent, moderator, and control variables, and, in turn, affects the dependent variable.

A researcher, for example, is going to contrast presenting a lesson on closed-circuit TV versus presenting it via live lecture. His independent variable is mode of presentation; his dependent variable is some measure of learning. He asks himself, "What is it about the two modes of presentation that should lead one to be more effective than the other?" He is asking himself what the intervening variable is. The likely answer (likely but not certain since intervening variables are neither visible nor directly measureable) is *attention*. Closed-circuit TV will not present more or less information but it may stimulate more attention. Thus, the increased attention could consequently lead to better learning.

Why bother to identify intervening variables? The reason is for purposes of generalizing. In the above example, it may be possible to develop taped classes that lead to more than increased attention, or other, nontelevised techniques for stimulating attention. If attention is the intervening variable, then the researcher must examine attention as a factor affecting learning and use his data as a means of generalizing to other situations and other modes of presentation. Overlooking the conceptual or intervening variable would be like overlooking the flow of electrons in a live wire or the ions in a chemical reaction. Researchers must concern themselves with *why* as well as what and how.

Consider the following statements:

1. Students taught by discovery (a_1) will perform better on a new but related task (c) than students taught by rote (a_2).
2. Students taught by discovery (a_1) will develop a search strategy (b_1)—an approach to finding solutions—that will enable them to perform better on a new but related task (c) while students taught by rote will learn solutions but not strategies (b_2), thus limiting their ability to solve transfer problems (c).

The symbols a_1 and a_2 refer to the two levels of the independent variable while c refers to the dependent variable. The intervening variable (presence or absence of a search strategy) is identified as b_1, b_2 in the second statement.

The intervening variables can often be discovered by examining a hypothesis and asking the question: What is it about the independent variable that will cause the predicted outcome?

3.8 THE COMBINED VARIABLES

The relationship between the five types of variables described in this chapter is illustrated in Figure 3.4. Note that independent, moderator, and control variables are inputs or causes, the first two being those that are studied while the third, control variables, are neutralized or "eliminated." At the other end, dependent variables represent effects, while intervening variables are conceptualizations which intervene between operationally-stated causes and operationally-stated effects.

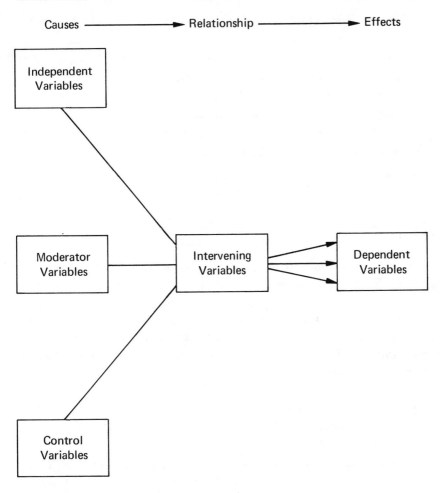

Figure 3.4 *The combined variables.*

Example 1

Consider a study of teacher style and its effect on satisfaction among different types of students. Suppose the hypothesis states that directive teachers would yield more course satisfaction among students whose personality style is measured as "concrete," while nondirective teachers would yield more course satisfaction among students measured as "abstract."

- The *independent variable* is teacher style with two levels being compared.

- The *moderator variable* is student personality style with two levels being included, concrete and abstract.

- The *control variables*, while not mentioned in the hypothesis, would be likely to include subject matter taught, class size, students' age, students' sex, and others.

- The *intervening variable* would probably deal with classroom structuring and formality as provided by the different types of teachers and as desired by the different types of students.

- The *dependent variable* would be students' satisfaction with the course.

Example 2

Consider Sample Study I, Appendix A, wherein teachers are given feedback as to their in-class behavior from (a) students, (b) supervisors, (c) both students and supervisors, and (d) neither. Students' judgments are again obtained after 12 weeks to determine if teachers given the different sources of feedback have shown differential change of behavior in the direction advocated by the feedback. Differential outcomes are also considered in terms of years of teaching experience of each teacher.

- The *independent variable* is source of feedback. Note that it represents a single independent variable or factor with four levels, each corresponding to a condition (a, b, c, and d).

- The *moderator variable* is years of teaching experience. This is also a single factor and in this particular study has three levels (1-3 years of teaching experience, 4-10 years of teaching experience, or 11 or more years of teaching experience).

- *Control variables* are students' grade level (10th, 11th, or 13th grade), students' curricular major (vocational only), teachers' subject (vocational only), and class size (approximately 15 students).

- The *intervening variable* would be identified as the responsiveness of the teacher to the different feedback sources based on the perceived motivation and perceived level of information of each.

- The *dependent variable* is change in teachers' behavior (as perceived by students).   The purpose of the study is to see how different feedback sources affect a change in teachers' behavior.

Example 3

Consider Sample Study II, Appendix A, in which students considered as potential drop-outs were divided into groups, some of which received "massive" rewards in the form of praise for remedial reading while the remainder did not receive rewards. Results were measured in terms of performance on a standardized reading test.

- The *independent variable* or cause, containing two levels, would be receipt of massive rewards versus receipt of no rewards.

- There was no *moderator variable* in this study.

- The *control variables* were students' age, students' overall performance, students' pre-experimental intelligence test scores,* assignment of students to conditions, control period (allowing for any novelty effect to wear off), the use of the reward recording system by both experimental and control groups to control for *Hawthorne effect†*, and the assignment of teachers to conditions.

*Rather than treating intelligence as a moderator variable by manipulating groups in terms of it, it was treated as a control variable by cancelling out its effects via a statistical procedure called analysis of covariance.

†This effect was discovered and labeled by Mayo, Roethlisberger, and Dickson during performance studies at the Hawthorne Works of the General Electric Company in Chicago, Illinois during the late 1920's (see Brown, 1954). While attempting to determine the effect of changes in the physical characteristics of the work environment as well as incentive rates and rest periods, it was discovered that production increased regardless of the conditions imposed. It was then concluded that the workers were reacting to their role in the experiment and the importance placed on them by management. The Hawthorne effect, thus, refers to performance increments prompted by mere inclusion in an experiment.

- The *intervening variables* would be motivation and self-expectation, since rewards are considered a source of motivation and a basis for constructing self-expectations.

- The *dependent variable* would be reading test scores.

Example 4

Consider a study reported by Feshback (1969) in a recent issue of the *Journal of Educational Psychology*. Feshback hypothesized that:

> ... student teachers (would) prefer children whose behaviors reflected control, caution, and conformity as compared to children whose behaviors reflected independence, challenge, and flexibility and that since some of these behaviors are sex typed, interactions are expected between the sex of the child and the personality triad being assessed; for example, while it is hypothesized that assertiveness and independence will receive less favored ratings when displayed by boys or girls, it should be even less acceptable in girls since these traits are less compatible with the female role. [Feshback, 1969, p. 167]

- The *independent variable* is the personality triad of the child, controlled, cautious, and conformist children versus independent, challenging, and flexible children.

- The *moderator variable* is sex of the child, boy versus girl.

- Some of the *control variables* are sex of the teacher (all female), experience of the teacher (all student teachers), and age of the teachers.

- The *intervening variable* is the values that teachers place on particular personality characteristics of the child.

- *The dependent variable* is the preference expressed by the teachers for different students.

3.9 SOME CONSIDERATIONS FOR VARIABLE CHOICE

After selecting the independent and dependent variables, the researcher must decide which variables to include as moderator variables and which to exclude or hold constant as control variables. He must decide how to treat the total pool of other variables (other than the independent) that might affect the dependent variable. In making these decisions (which variables are "in" and which are "out") he should take into account three kinds of considerations. These are described below.

1. *Theoretical Considerations.* In treating a variable as a moderator variable, the researcher learns how it interacts with the independent variable to produce differential effects on the dependent variable. In terms of the theoretical base from which he is working and in terms of what he is trying to find out in a particular experiment, certain variables may highly qualify as moderator variables. In choosing a moderator variable the researcher should ask:

- Is the variable related to the theory with which I'm working?

- How helpful would it be to know if an interaction exists? That is, would my theoretical interpretations and applications be different?

- How likely is there to be an interaction?

2. *Design Considerations.* Beyond the questions cited above are questions which relate to the experimental design which has been chosen and its adequacy for controlling for sources of bias. The researcher should ask the following question:

- Have my decisions about moderator and control variables met the requirements of experimental design in terms of dealing with sources of invalidity?

3. *Practical Considerations.* A researcher can only study so many variables at one time. There are limits to his human and financial resources and the deadlines he can meet. By their nature some variables are harder to study than to neutralize, while others are as easily studied as neutralized. While researchers are bound by design considerations, there is usually enough freedom of choice so that practical concerns can come in to play. In dealing with practical considerations, the researcher must ask questions like the following:

- How difficult is it to make a variable a moderator as opposed to a control variable?

- What kinds of resources are available and what kinds are required to create moderator variables?

- How much control do I have over the experimental situation?

This last concern is a highly significant one. In educational experiments researchers often have less control over the situation than design and theoretical considerations might necessitate. Thus, they must take practical considerations into account when selecting variables.

RECOMMENDED READINGS

MacCorquodale, K. and Meehl, P. E. Hypothetical constructs and intervening variables. *Psychological Review*, 1948, *55*, 95–107.

Townsend, J. C. *Introduction to experimental method*. New York: McGraw-Hill, 1953.

COMPETENCY TEST EXERCISES

1. Define each of the following:
   a. independent variable
   b. dependent variable
   c. moderator variable
   d. control variable
   e. intervening variable

2. Connect the terms in column A with those in column B.

	A		B
a.	independent variable	1.	avoided
b.	dependent variable	2.	inferred
c.	moderator variable	3.	cause
d.	control variable	4.	modifier
e.	intervening variable	5.	effect

3. Consider Sample Study III in Appendix A (Differences between blind and partially-sighted children in rejection by sighted peers in integrated classrooms, grades 2–8). In this study, identify the
   a. independent variable
   b. moderator variable
   c. control variable
   d. intervening variable
   e. dependent variable

4. Suggest three moderator variables that might have been included in the above study (but were not).

5. For each of the moderator variables you have suggested in exercise 4,
   a. state three theoretical considerations that might lead to the inclusion or exclusion of this variable as a moderator;
   b. state three practical considerations that might lead to the inclusion or exclusion of this variable as a moderator.

6. Hypothesis: With I.Q. held constant, boys with perceptual-motor training will perform better on eye-hand coordination tasks than boys without this training while such differences will not appear among girls.
   a. independent variable: _____
   b. moderator variable: _____
   c. control variable: _____
   d. intervening variable: _____
   e. dependent variable: _____

7. Hypothesis: Inexperienced male teachers are more likely to change their attitudes toward teaching after having a microteaching experience than without having such an experience while experienced male teachers are equally likely to maintain their attitudes either with or without microteaching.

   a. independent variable: _____

   b. moderator variable: _____

   c. control variable: _____

   d. intervening variable: _____

   e. dependent variable: _____

4

Constructing Operational Definitions of Variables

OBJECTIVES

Identify reasons and situations for constructing operational definitions of variables. / Distinguish between operational definitions and other types of definitions. / State minimal observable criteria to include in an operational definition. / Construct three different types of operational definitions. / Distinguish between operational definitions in terms of their "uniqueness." / Construct predictions from hypotheses.

4.1 WHY HAVE OPERATIONAL DEFINITIONS?

"You say I was speeding?"

"Yes, you were going over 15 miles per hour. The speed limit is 15 miles per hour in a school zone; according to the speedometer in my patrol car you were going 20."

"The children are all in school and no child was along the street. How could my speed have been unsafe?"

"The law is the law. Here is your ticket."

The purpose of this conversation is to show how an everyday situation involves operational definitions of terms. The officer is correct that the law defines "speeding in a school zone" as: *A car which is going at more than 15 miles per hour in a school zone which is marked by appropriate signs.* The law guides the officer. All he has to do is observe the cars moving within a marked school zone and measure their speed; if the speed exceeds 15 miles per hour, the car is speeding and the driver is given a ticket.

In contrast, the driver tried to use a different operational definition of speeding in a school zone: *In a marked school zone, a car is speeding only if the speed exceeds 15 miles per hour when children are near or on the street.* According to the driver, a car is speeding if (1) the speed of the car exceeds 15 miles per hour in a school zone, and (2) children are near or on the street. The driver believes that the speed of the car is important only when children are present.

Another operational definition, but one which is impractical, is to define speeding in a school zone on the basis of what has happened, that is, after the fact: *If a car going at any speed in a school zone hits a child and hurts him, then the car was speeding.* Thus, if a child hit by a car is injured, the car was speeding but if the child gets up and walks away uninjured, the car was not speeding, even though it ran into a child. For obvious reasons, this operational definition of speeding in a school zone is not useful.

Consider an illustration nearer to the subject at hand. Suppose you were the school principal and a teacher came to you and asked you to remove a youngster from her class because he was too aggressive. And suppose you responded by indicating that you liked aggressive learners, that you felt "aggressiveness" (i.e., active challenging of the relevance of instructional experiences) was a useful quality to bring to the learning situation. Suppose now that you asked the teacher what she meant by "aggressive" and she replied "filled with hate and potentially violent."

From these illustrations it is possible to conclude:

1. Situations exist which require operational definitions.
2. An operational definition identifies the observable criteria of that which is being defined.
3. A concept or object may have more than one operational definition.
4. An operational definition may be unique for the situation in which it is to be used.

Such situations illustrate communication problems; the same word or phrase can have different meanings for different persons. Research is a communication process, though it is not always thought of as such. The researcher employs certain techniques to find out something about the world and then attempts to communicate these findings to others, and this communication requires a preciseness of language far more exacting than that demanded of the novelist, poet, or everyday conversationalist. The novelist and poet are often purposely trying to evoke a *range* of reactions to the words and images they use, while participants in everyday conversations often share a common language background. The researcher, however, must convey his meanings in sufficient preciseness so that any reader from any background understands *exactly* what he is saying and in sufficient detail to make replication possible.

4.2 AN OPERATIONAL DEFINITION IS BASED ON OBSERVABLE CRITERIA

There are a variety of ways to define something. Often definitions are simply synonymous; while at other times they may be conceptual, providing a hypothetical description of what or why something is. *An operational definition is a definition based on the observable characteristics of that which is being defined.* The word "observable" is the significant word in describing an operational definition. If it is possible for a researcher to make some relatively stable observations of an object or phenomenon, then these observations can be made by others, thus enabling them to identify that which has been so defined. What is important is the nature of these observations upon which operational definitions are based, how they are made, and of what they are made.

Conceptual definitions, on the other hand, identify something in terms of conceptual or hypothetical criteria rather than observable ones. Defining the ego as the sense of self or effective teaching as teaching which promotes learning would be two examples. In the conceptual definition, a concept is defined with reference to another concept rather than with reference to observable reality characteristics as is the case in an operational definition. Conceptual definitions play an important role in the processes of logic associated with hypothesis formulation. However, they are of little use in creating a bridge between the domain of the hypothetical or general and that of the real and specific. This latter role is played by operational definitions. Ultimately, for purposes of investigation, concepts must be defined operationally.

Another form of definition is definition by synonym. Being irate is defined as being mad or angry. Being aggressive is defined as being forceful, pushy, or demanding. Being intelligent is defined as being smart. Such definitions do provide some information but they cannot be relied on to link one's concepts to the observable world. Finally, there are dictionary definitions, which include many kinds of definitions, in an attempt to clarify every word in a way that would be of some use to everyone, Again, while dictionary definitions are useful and informative, they are no substitute for formal operational definitions which clearly spell out the observable criteria uniquely associated with some object or state.

4.3 ALTERNATIVE WAYS OF GENERATING OPERATIONAL DEFINITIONS

There are three approaches to constructing operational definitions, which, theoretically, make it possible to construct three operational definitions for any object or phenomenon. These have been arbitrarily labeled type A, type B, and type C.

Type A Operational Definitions

A type A *operational definition can be constructed in terms of the operations that must be performed to cause the phenomenon or state being defined to occur.* Very often in an experiment a researcher causes the phenomenon being studied to occur through the use of a certain procedure. It is the description of this procedure that forms a type A operational definition. (This type of operational definition is often more appropriate for defining a phenomenon or state rather than an object or thing.)

Here are some examples of type A definitions. Frustration may be operationally defined as that state which results when an individual is blocked from reaching a highly desired goal which he is close to attaining. A child may be shown a piece of candy that is held beyond his reach, thus utilizing an operation which fulfills the type A operational definition of frustration. A drive may be operationally defined as that state which results when a person is deprived of a needed substance or activity. Hunger may be operationally defined as the result of being deprived of food for 24 hours. Using this definition, observers would all agree on whether a person was hungry by determining when he had eaten last. Table salt can be operationally defined as the result of the chemical combination of sodium and chlorine. A culturally-disadvantaged youngster might be operationally defined as one who has been raised in a community with a particular population density by a parent or parents receiving an income of less than $3,000 a year, and who is attending a school in that community. Thus, cultural disadvantagement is operationally defined via a type A operational definition by stating those features which cause its existence. Finally, aggression might be defined with a type A operational definition as the behavior of a person who has been repeatedly blocked from reaching a highly desired goal. Note that another type of operational definition for aggression may be more appropriate (page 60).

In each case, a type A operational definition is a statement of what manipulations or preconditions the experimenter creates or looks for to indicate that a certain phenomenon or state exists. He defines that phenomenon operationally by stating the preceding operations or events which have reliably led to its occurrence. While the label of the state or phenomenon may often be somewhat arbitrary, the preconditions are quite concrete and observable and thus constitute an adequate definition for scientific purposes. While more than one operational definition can often be constructed for something, each must be sufficiently operational to meet the criterion of uniqueness (which will be subsequently dealt with).

A few additional examples of type A operational definitions follow:

- Fear—state produced by exposing a person to an object which he has indicated is highest in his hierarchy of objects to be avoided.
- Conflict—state produced by placing two or more persons in a situation where each has the same goal, but only one can attain it.
- Positive self-expectation of success—telling a person that the results of an intelligence test he has taken indicate that he is likely to be academically successful.

Because type A operational definitions tell what manipulation to use to induce a particular state, they are useful for defining independent variables as prescriptions to be carried out by the experimenter. The same variable may, of course, be operationally defined by more than one type of definition but when that variable is the independent variable—one to be manipulated—a type A operational definition is often the most useful.

Type B Operational Definitions

A type B operational definition can be constructed in terms of how the particular object or thing being defined operates, that is, what it does or what constitutes its dynamic properties. An intelligent person can be operationally defined as a person who gets high grades in school or a person who demonstrates a capability for solving symbolic logic problems. Operationally defined, table salt can be a water soluble substance that conducts electricity, and a hungry person can be a person who will depress a lever at the rate of 10 times a minute to get food. A directive teacher might be operationally defined as one who gives instructions, personalizes criticism or blame, and establishes formal relationships with students.

Note that type B operational definitions seem particularly appropriate in an educational context for describing a type of person (a person of a certain quality or a person in a particular state). Since the dynamic properties of people are represented as behavior, a type B definition describes a particular type of person in terms of concrete and observable *behaviors* associated with the type or state of the person. Thus, while aggression was operationally defined with a type A definition as behavior by a person blocked from attaining a goal, it can also be defined with a type B definition as acting out, fighting, or speaking loudly and abusively. The type B definition suggested here may be more unique than its type A counterpart.

A few additional examples of type B operational definitions follow.

- Subject matter preference—given a room containing materials from different subject matters in equal numbers, the characteristic of reliably selecting to examine or use materials from one subject matter more frequently than from the others.

- Motor activity—excursions by the subject from his assigned position.

- Sensitivity—tendency of teacher to smile at, touch, or exchange pleasantries with students during class.

- Motivation—persistent attendance of students in school. Or alternatively: Motivated person—person who manifests persistent school attendance.

Though they may be used to define other variables, type B definitions are particularly useful for defining the dependent variable when it is to be operationally based on behavior.

Type C Operational Definitions

A type C operational definition can be constructed in terms of what the object or phenomenon being defined looks like, that is, what constitutes its static properties. An intelligent student can be defined, for instance, as a person who has a good memory, a large vocabulary, good reasoning ability, good arithmetic skills, etc. Table salt can be operationally defined as a substance having cubical crystals. Type C operational definitions utilize observable structural properties of the object.

In educational research, many operational definitions are based on the characteristics that persons or states possess, many of which ultimately lend themselves to measurement through the use of tests or scales. For example, course satisfaction may be defined as liking a course, indicated by perceiving it as an interesting and effective learning experience. This operational definition may then lead to the development of a questionnaire constructed to measure course satisfaction. Teaching effectiveness can be operationally defined (type B) as judgments of a teacher's behavior in terms of the teacher's willingness to report her own feelings, to encourage students to report their feelings, and to praise them for constructive criticism of her teaching; or if it is defined by the outcomes that are produced, such as student learning and student satisfaction, a type C definition exists.

A few additional examples of type C operational definitions follow.

- Introversion—tendency or characteristic of person to prefer to engage in solitary rather than group activity (to view oneself as a "loner").

- Attitudes toward school—receptiveness and acceptability of school activities, school rules, school requirements, and school work.

- Arithmetic achievement—competency attainment in arithmetic including mastery of basic skills (addition, subtraction, multiplication, and division), fractions, decimals, and whole numbers.

- Team teaching—utilization of two or more teachers to develop lesson plans and teach in one or more subject matter areas for a fixed group of students.

Note that type C operational definitions describe the qualities, traits, or characteristics of people or things. Thus, they may be used for defining any type of variable. When used for defining a person's characteristics, they specify the static or internal qualities rather than his behavior as does the type B definition. Type C operational definitions often lend themselves to *measurement* by tests although the ability to be tested is not a requisite part of the definition. However, operational definitions are statements of observable properties—traits, appearances, behaviors—and statements of such properties are a prerequisite to their measurement.

Many researchers refer to scores on tests or rating scales as operational definitions (type C). Such instruments do not themselves constitute operational definitions but they must embody operational definitions. Thus, mathematics achievement might be measured by a mathematics achievement test and be defined as the manifestation of representative skills in algebra such as solving equations with one unknown, adding and subtracting imaginary numbers, and so on. While the test itself measures these skills, it is the demonstration of these *specified* skills that is referred to as the operational definition. Once having settled on such an operational definition, the researcher would set out to uncover or develop a test or measurement procedure suitable for the measurement of the state or phenomenon as operationally defined.

The typology of operational definitions is offered as an aid in constructing them, in recognizing them, and in understanding why a single state or object may be operationally defined in more than one way. While the classification of an operational definition into the typology may be somewhat arbitrary, the construction of the operational definition is not. The researcher uses the operational definition best suited to bringing his concepts and variables to a sufficiently concrete state for study and examination. Indeed, the notion of typing an operational definition is often an after-the-fact consideration. What is of principal importance is the manner in which the object or state will be examined in an experiment.

4.4 THE CRITERION OF UNIQUENESS

It is possible to define operationally an aggressive child as one who gets into a fight. It is also possible to define operationally an aggressive child as one who gets into fights habitually. Still another possibility is one who gets into fights habitually, even when unprovoked. Each of these operational definitions identifies a more unique set of observable criteria associated with aggressiveness than the one preceding it. *The more unique an operational definition, the more useful it is* because it conveys more information, makes it possible to exclude other objects or states from consideration that the definition is not intended to cover, and increases the possibility that the sense of the variable as used can be replicated. However, carrying uniqueness to an extreme restricts the generalizability of a concept by restricting its external validity. It is necessary to strike a "happy medium" between the demands of internal validity for greater uniqueness and the demands of external validity for lesser uniqueness.

If a researcher were to define school learning as presence in a classroom he would not be wrong. However, many students present in a classroom are not learning, so that the definition would not be very unique. If the definition was enlarged to include the appearance of enjoyment, the uniqueness would be increased but would not exclude students who are happy but not learning. Thus, the operational definition would still be of limited usefulness. It is necessary to specify in the definition some observable characteristic of the learner, such as his achievement, change in behavior, or gain in skills that distinguishes the learner from the non-learner. Thus, school learning might be defined as increase in ability to solve specific types of problems after having been present in a classroom.

When formulating any operational definition, consider how distinctly the observable criteria chosen for use in the definition identify that which is being defined as unique from everything else.

4.5 EXAMPLES FROM THE SAMPLE STUDIES

The first example of the process of operationally defining will be drawn from Sample Study I, Appendix A. The first hypothesis of this study states that "teachers receiving feedback would change more than teachers not receiving feedback." Prior to the statement of the hypothesis, an operational definition of *change* was provided although not necessarily identified as such. The procedure for determining this change is quoted below.

> Students were asked to rate their teacher twice, with a 12-week interval separating these ratings . . . . Behavior change by teachers was inferred from a difference between post-interval and pre-interval ratings.

Since the pre- and post-interval measuring instrument asked students to rate the teachers' likeability, relevance, etc., change was operationally defined as teachers becoming more likeable, more interesting, more relevant, etc., over time as perceived by students. This type B operational definition was not based directly on teacher behavior but on student perception of teacher behavior.

Feedback to the teacher was operationally defined as information about the teacher in terms of likeability, relevance, etc., as seen by students and/or supervisors and reported both graphically and verbally to the teacher (a type A definition). Specifically, for student feedback.

> Students completed the SOQ, and their ratings on the 10 scales were averaged. The teacher was presented with a graph showing the average student judgment for each item. In addition, a summation of the students' responses on the open-ended questions was provided. Teachers were told that the feedback was from their students.

In the second hypothesis of this study, "feedback source" appears as a variable. Its operational definition appears in the "Problem" section where the three sources—students, supervisors, and a combination of students and supervisors—are delineated.

For additional examples of operational definitions, consider Sample Study II, Appendix A. The authors hypothesized that learning among potential dropouts can be enhanced through the use of massive rewards. Operational definitions were required for "learning," "potential dropouts," and "massive rewards." Learning was operationally defined as improvement in reading skills as evidenced by scores on the "Science Research Associates Reading Test, Intermediate Form" given on a pre and post basis. This is a type C definition. Potential dropouts were defined as students who "were from one to four years behind typical levels of children in the same age and grade" (another type *C* definition).

Massive rewards were described as follows:

> After six sessions the reward rates per child and per teacher appeared to stabilize and the five teachers . . . of the experimental groups were . . . asked to double or triple the number of rewards while the four teachers of the control groups were asked to "keep up the good work." After these requests were made, large increments appeared in the number of tally marks on cards for the experimental group while the numbers for the control group remained at approximately the same levels.

This is a methodological description from which the following concise operational definition of massive rewards may be offered: frequently-given praise by teachers which students recorded by making a mark on a tally sheet. Since it describes what must be done to create a reward, this last definition would be type *A*.

4.6 OPERATIONAL DEFINITIONS AND THE RESEARCH PROCESS

Within the process of testing a hypothesis, the researcher must move on multiple occasions from the hypothetical to the concrete and vice versa. In order to get the maximum value from his data, he must be able to make generalizations that apply to situations other than the experiment itself. Thus, the researcher often begins at the conceptual or hypothetical level in developing hypotheses which pose possible linkages between concepts. A research study, however, operates in reality so that it is necessary to transform the conceptual statements of the variables as they appear in the hypotheses to operational statements. For example, after constructing an hypothesis such as "Students prefer nondirective teachers to directive teachers," the researcher must ask himself: What do I mean by prefer? What do I mean by nondirective and directive teachers? The answers to these questions take the form of operational definitions. *Prefer* may be operationally defined as relative liking of a specific teacher by a student in comparison to other teachers. (This is a type *C* definition.) Preference may be ultimately measured by asking the student to rank order all his teachers according to liking. Using a type *B* operational definition, a *directive* teacher may be defined as a teacher who exhibits the following behaviors:

Structure

    formal planning and structuring of the course

    minimizing informal work and group work

    structuring group activity when it is used

    rigidly structuring individual and classroom activity

    requiring factual knowledge from students based on absolute sources

Interpersonal

    using absolute and justifiable punishment

    minimizing the opportunity to make and learn from mistakes

    maintaining a formal classroom atmosphere

    maintaining a formal relationship with students

    taking absolute responsibility for grades

In designing the study or experiment, operational definitions of all relevant variables must be transformed into a specific methodology and a specific set of measuring devices or techniques. In fact, the methods section of a research report is really a detailed set of measurement specifications based on operational definitions. However, the process of formulating operational definitions must be completed before the details of measurement are decided upon. Thus, operational definitions of the concepts dealt with in the hypotheses should appear in the introductory section of a report. (The organization of a report will be dealt with in detail in Chapter 11.

Following an experiment, the operational findings are then related back to those concepts included in the original hypotheses of the study and generalizations are made. Thus, the processes of conceptualizing and operationalizing have been combined and recombined in the total research process.

Testability

The testability of any hypothesis depends on whether suitable operational definitions can be constructed for its variables. If a researcher hypothesizes that junior-college deans will be more effective administrators when they are trained in programs designed for junior-college administrators rather than in programs designed for administrators in universities or secondary schools, then he is faced with the task of constructing a useful operational definition for effectiveness of a junior-college administrator. One possibility is to use the perceptions of effectiveness by other administrators, but this approach leaves much room for error.

It would be more useful to think in terms of a type *B* definition, that is, how does an effective administrator behave which differentiates him from an ineffective administrator. After compiling a list of such behaviors and tightening it to reduce overlap the researcher could define an effective administrator as one who can make decisions quickly, can delegate responsibility, is well-liked by his superiors and subordinates, and is reacted to with confidence and trust by teachers and students.

The administrator's role can be operationalized as including individual task functions (or decision-making), group task functions (or delegating responsibility), and sociability functions (or relations with teachers). Thus, an adequate operational definition of the effective administrator paves the way for testing hypotheses which include the concept of an effective administrator.

Predictions

Defining the variables in a hypothesis in order to make it testable results in the construction of a prediction. *A predicition is a statement of expectations, in which the conceptual statements of the variables in the hypothesis have been replaced by operational definitions.* Thus, a prediction is a testable derivative of a hypothesis. In fact, to use a terminology developed earlier, a prediction is a *specific hypothesis.* Since variables can be given different operational definitions, alternative predictions (or alternative specific hypotheses) can be derived from any one (general) hypothesis.

Consider the following examples:

- **Hypothesis.** Attitudes toward school and aggressive behavior in school are inversely related.

  Prediction: Students who see the school as a place they enjoy and in which they like to be will be less frequently cited for fighting or talking back to a teacher than those who see the school as a place they neither enjoy nor like.

- **Hypothesis.** Programs offering stipends are more successful at retaining students.

  Prediction: The dropout rate among adults enrolled in training and retraining programs will be smaller in those programs where students are paid a stipend to attend.

- **Hypothesis.** Performance in paired-associate tasks and socioeconomic status are inversely related.

     Prediction: Students whose parents earn more than $5,000 a year will require fewer trials to perfectly learn a paired-associate list than students whose parents earn less than $5,000 a year.

- **Hypothesis.** Authoritarian school superintendents will be less inclined to respond to rational pressures and more inclined to respond to expedience pressures in deciding on curricular innovations than nonauthoritarian school superintendents.

     Prediction: School superintendents who react to the world in terms of superordinate-subordinate roles and power and toughness will less frequently acknowledge the opinion of subject-matter experts as a source of influence in judging curricular innovations and more frequently acknowledge their superiors than those who do not react to the world in these terms.

4.7 THE RESEARCH SPECTRUM

The researcher has now developed operational definitions of his variables and restated his hypotheses in the operational form called predictions. He is now ready to conduct a study to test these predictions and thus his hypotheses. His next step will be to decide how to control and/or manipulate his variables through a research design.

In order to place those steps and procedures already described in perspective, relative to those to be dealt with in the remainder of this book, and to outline the sequence of activities in research which form the basis for this book, the schematic of the research spectrum is presented in Figure 4.1.

Note that research begins with a problem and the utilization of both theories and findings in arriving at hypotheses. (This point was covered in Chapter 2.) These hypotheses contain variables which must be labeled and then operationally defined, as described in this chapter, to construct predictions. These steps might be considered the *logical* stages of research. These stages are followed by the *methodological* stages, which culminate in the development of a research design, the development of measures, and finally in the findings themselves. These processes, namely designing a study or experiment, developing measures, and collecting and analyzing data, are the subjects of the six chapters to follow, two on design, two on measurement, and two on analysis.

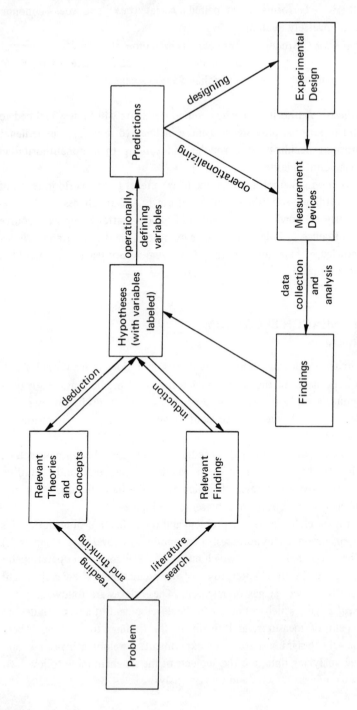

Figure 4.1 *The research spectrum.*

RECOMMENDED READINGS

Boring, E. P. et al. Symposium on operationism. *Psychological Review*, 1945, *52*, 241–294.

Bridgman, P. W. *The logic of modern physics*. New York: Macmillan, 1927.

Kerlinger, F. N. *Foundations of behavioral research*. New York: Holt, Rinehart & Winston, 1965.

COMPETENCY TEST EXERCISES

1. Which of the following are reasons for using operational definitions?
   a. replication
   b. validity
   c. communication
   d. precision

2. Which of the following definitions is operational?
   a. partially-sighted child—one having 20/70 or less vision in the better eye with correction but who is a print reader
   b. partially-sighted child—one who is not blind but does not see too well
   c. partially-sighted child—one who would like to see better

3. As stated, which of the following are observable criteria of a teacher?
   a. he is confident
   b. he stands in front of a classroom
   c. he identifies himself as a teacher
   d. he is liked by students

4. Below are three definitions. Identify the three types—A, B, and C.
   a. blind child—child reared in total darkness from birth
   b. blind child—child who cannot identify any letter on Snellen eye chart
   c. blind child—child who can read only by Braille

5. Below are three more definitions. Again, label the three types—A, B, and C.
   a. interest—state evidenced by a person's own admission to that effect
   b. interest—state provoked by showing someone something that he has said would appeal to him
   c. interest—state evidenced by increase of activity and attention to a new stimulus

6. Construct a type A operational definition of (a) achievement motivation, (b) cohesiveness (i.e., group solidarity).

7. Construct a type B operational definition of (a) achievement motivation, (b) cohesiveness.

8. Construct a type C operational definition of (a) achievement motivation, (b) cohesiveness.

9. Which of the following two operational definitions is the more unique?
   a. freedom—state of being able to do whatever you want
   b. freedom—state of being able to do whatever you want short of interfering with the right of another person to do whatever he wants

10. Write a third operational definition of freedom which is more unique than the two above.

11. Hypothesis: Socioeconomic status and academic ability are positively related. Rewrite this hypothesis as a prediction.

12. Hypothesis: The more unstructured a classroom climate, the more creative the students will be. Rewrite this hypothesis as a prediction.

5

Identifying Techniques
for the Manipulation
and Control of Variables

OBJECTIVES

Identify the reasons for the use of a control group. / Identify and describe the sources of internal and external invalidity which a control group is an attempt to overcome. / Describe the procedures for controlling against the various sources of invalidity. / Identify within a given piece of research, procedures used for controlling against the various sources of invalidity and describe their adequacy. / Describe procedures for determining whether a manipulation has been successful.

5.1 THE CONTROL GROUP

The essence of experimental research is *control*. It is impossible to make a valid assessment of the effect of a particular condition or treatment unless other conditions or factors that also influence the obtained effect have been eliminated (or limited).

To deal with the problem of eliminating the other factors, researchers use a control group*. *A control group is a group of subjects[†] whose selection and experiences are identical in every way possible to the treatment or experimental*

Often referred to as a comparison *group.*
[†]Subjects *is the term used to designate participants in an experiment.*

group except that they do not receive the treatment (i.e., the independent variable is absent). (See Figure 5.1.)

Let us consider an example offered by Townsend (1953) which illustrates why a control group is necessary.

> Suppose an investigator believes that he has found a drug or chemical which if administered to feeble-minded subjects will raise their intelligence quotients. In order to test the effectiveness of his drug, he would make it the independent variable in an experiment, and the intelligence quotient of his group of subjects the dependent variable. If he were simply to administer the drug to, let us say, one hundred subjects and then again measure their I.Q.'s, how might he interpret his data if he found a significant increase in the I.Q.'s?
>
> The investigator could not say that the increase in I.Q. was caused by the drug he administered. Why not? Because he would not know whether the I.Q.'s of the subjects would have raised even if he had not given them the drug. It is possible that the subjects were more highly motivated on the second administration of the test than they were on the first administration. Further, the entire group might have received a better diet, been exposed to a more favorable environment, and been given closer and perhaps better medical attention because they were under observation, or perhaps there were certain transfer effects or carry-over from the first to the second administration of the tests. Any one of these conditions, and many more, might have been responsible for the apparent increase in I.Q. [Townsend, 1953, p. 62.]

Experimental Group		**Control Group**	
Environmental Stimuli	Subjects' Responses	Environmental Stimuli	Subjects' Responses
S_x ---------------------------	R_x	S_0 ---------------------------	R_0
S_1 ---------------------------	R_1	S_1 ---------------------------	R_1
S_2 ---------------------------	R_2	S_2 ---------------------------	R_2
S_3 ---------------------------	R_3	S_3 ---------------------------	R_3
S_4 ---------------------------	R_4	S_4 ---------------------------	R_4

S_x: independent variable (level 1); s_0: independent variable (level 2)*
S_1, S_2, S_3, S_4: control variables (number is arbitrary)
R_x, R_0: dependent variable (levels)
*May be either absence of treatment or comparison treatment

Figure 5.1 *Experimental and control groups in an experiment.*

To deal with the problem posed by Townsend, the experimenter would utilize a control group made up of feeble-minded persons who would also receive a "drug" at the same time as the first group, although the control group would be given a *placebo* such as a salt tablet. The subject would not know whether he was receiving the real drug or the placebo; he would be operating in the *blind*. Because the person administering the drug can subtly reveal whether he is giving the "real thing" or not, he too will not be informed what each pill is; he too will be operating in the blind (this is commonly referred to as the *double-blind* technique).

In creating a control group for the purpose of cancelling or neutralizing the effects of extraneous variables, all conditions other than the independent and moderator variables must be kept constant for both experimental and control groups. (The moderator variable is controlled by treating it as an independent variable and systematically examining its effects.) It is helpful to identify and classify variables which, when not adequately controlled, would make it impossible to reach valid conclusions about the outcome of an experiment. Campbell and Stanley (1963) have organized these variables into two broad categories: those that pose threats to internal validity and those that pose threats to external validity. Within each category are a number of subcategories, each of which will be discussed in turn.

5.2 FACTORS AFFECTING INTERNAL VALIDITY

For an experiment to have internal validity the researcher must establish experimental controls that will enable him to conclude that differences occur as a result of his experimental treatment. In an experiment lacking internal validity, the researcher does not know whether his experimental treatment or uncontrolled factors produced the difference between groups. Campbell and Stanley (1963) identified eight classes of extraneous variables which can be a source of internal invalidity, if not controlled.

History

In research, the term "history" refers to events occurring in the environment at the same time that the experimental variable is being tested. If a specific curriculum is being tested on a group of students, and this group of students is simultaneously experiencing a high state of stress by virtue of an external event, then the measured outcomes of the experimental test may not reflect upon the experimental curriculum, but rather on the external historical event. Limitations on internal validity by virtue of history are dealt with by using a control group which can be expected to have the same external or historical experiences during the course of the experiment as those of the experimental group. If both groups experience the same history, then this factor becomes less important.

In addition, experimental participants and their controls must experience a comparable "history" *within* the experiment in all regards other than for those experiences which are being tested. Specifically, materials, conditions, and procedures used within the experiment must be identical for experimental and control subjects other than those specific to one of the variables being manipulated (i.e., independent or moderator variable).

Maturation

Maturation refers to the processes of change that take place within those persons who are participating in the experiment. Experiments that extend for long periods of time can be expected to be confounded by uncontrolled processes occurring simultaneously, such as developmental changes within the subjects. Since people (and typically students) are known to change as a result of the course of normal development, it could well be this change rather than any experimental treatment which produces the final outcome. The use of a control group composed of comparable persons who can be expected to have the same (or similar) maturational and developmental experiences will enable the experimenter to make conclusions about the experimental treatment independent of the confounding maturation effect.

Testing

Testing refers to the effects of taking a pretest on the subsequent posttest performance of individuals. Many experiments include the use of a pretest to determine the initial state of the subject with regard to some particular variable. The effect of taking this pretest may increase the likelihood that the individual will do better on the subsequent posttest, particularly when it is identical to the pretest. The posttest, then, may not be measuring simply the effect of the experimental treatment. Indeed, the posttest may be reflecting the pretest experience more than the treatment experience itself (or, in the case of the control group, the absence of treatment experience). A pretest can cause differences between experimental and control groups to disappear by providing the control group with an experience more relevant to the posttest than the experimental treatment.[*]

A recent book entitled *Unobstrusive Measures* (Webb et al., 1966), advocates more frequent use of those kinds of measurement techniques that do not require acceptance or awareness by the experimental subject, thus minimizing the possibility that testing will jeopardize internal validity. (If subjects do not directly provide data by voluntarily responding to a test, they are not afforded a test exposure with the opportunity to benefit from this exposure.)

In more traditional experimental designs, the problem of testing can be avoided simply by avoiding the use of a pretest entirely (since they are often unnecessary). In the next chapter, designs will be presented that avoid the use of pretests. Apart from the possible bias described above, pretests are expensive and time-consuming.

Instrumentation

Instrumentation refers to changes that occur in the measurement or observation procedures during an experiment. Such procedures typically include tests, mechanical measuring instruments, and observers or scorers. While it is not likely that mechanical measuring instruments will undergo a change during the course of an experiment, it is not *unlikely* that observers and scorers may change their manner of data collecting and recording as the experiment proceeds. Because interviewers tend to become more proficient (or perhaps more bored) as an experiment proceeds, they may inadvertently provide different cues to the interviewee, take different amounts and kinds of notes, or even score or code protocols differently.

Another threat to validity is the possibility that the observers, scorers, or interviewers will become aware of the purpose of the experiment and, consciously or unconsciously, attempt to increase the likelihood that the desired hypotheses will be supported. Both the measuring instruments of an experiment and the data collectors should remain "*constant across time* as well as *constant across groups* (or conditions).

The recent work of Welch and Walberg (1970) tends to minimize this pretest sensitization effect on internal validity. It may be that this source of bias has been overstressed.

Selection

In an experiment attempting to compare the effects of different experiences or treatments on different groups of individuals, the group experiencing one treatment might be brighter, more receptive, older, and so on, than the group receiving either no treatment or some other treatment. With regard to the first group, the effects of the treatment may occur not because it is better but because the group receiving the treatment is different. The personal reactions and behaviors of individuals comprising a group can influence the results. In other words, "people factors" can introduce a bias.

The use of random assignment, a procedure in which any person in the subject pool has an equal probability of being assigned to either the experimental or control group, minimizes the problems of selection. Since there is no reason to expect experimental or control subjects assigned randomly to differ in general characteristics, it is unlikely that any treatment effects in the study can be attributed to the special characteristics of a particular group. When selection is to be a variable under manipulation, then subjects are separated systematically into different groups based on some individual difference measure, thus providing for control.

Obviously if a researcher fails to control selection bias, then the outcome of his study may be a function of initial differences between groups rather than of the treatment being evaluated. Detailed procedures for minimizing selection bias are described in Section 5.4.

Statistical Regression

When groups are chosen on the basis of extreme scores on a particular variable, problems of statistical regression occur. Say, for instance, that a group of students are given an I.Q. test and only the highest third and the lowest third are selected for the experiment, with the middle third being eliminated. There would be a tendency on any posttest measurement for the scores of the higher scorers to decrease toward the mean while the scores of the lower scorers would increase toward the mean. Thus there would be differences between the groups on the posttest *even if no treatment were given*. The reason is that chance factors are more likely to contribute to extreme scores than to average scores, and such chance factors are unlikely to reappear during a second testing (or in testing on a different measure). The problem is avoided by avoiding the selection of extreme scorers to the exclusion of average scorers.

Experimental Mortality

In any study it is desirable to obtain posttest data from *all* of the subjects who were originally included in the study because subjects who withdraw from an experimental study may be different from those who remain. To the extent that such differences exist and are relevant to the dependent variable, posttest bias (or internal invalidity based on mortality) will be present. This bias also occurs when a study contains more than one condition and subjects are lost differentially from the different conditions.

As an example, graduates of two different programs are being followed up and compared. However, some members of each group are unavailable by virtue of, for example, having joined the armed forces. Moreover, one of the two groups has lost more members than the other. The original samples may now be biased by the selective loss of some persons. Since the groups have not lost equally, the losses may not be random but rather may reflect some bias in the group or program. If the purpose of the follow-up were to assess attitudes toward authority (to pursue the armed forces example), it is entirely possible that those graduates in the armed services differ systematically from other graduates on this variable. The failure to obtain data from these persons, then, would bias the outcome in terms of assessing the attitudes produced by the educational program in question. If data from a representative sample of the graduates were included, the conclusions might be quite different. To avoid problems created by experimental mortality it is often necessary to choose reasonably large groups, take steps to insure their representativeness, and attempt to follow up a portion of those who leave the study or were intitally unavailable.

Stability

Bias due to stability (see D. T. Campbell, 1969) refers to the tendency for a finding or result to be unreliable, i.e., to occur once but not thereafter. This whimsy in data can be examined through the use of statistical tests (see Chapter 9). Such tests provide information on the probability that a finding was not a chance event.

Interactive Combinations of Factors

It is possible, of course, for the factors that affect validity to occur in combination. For example, a source of invalidity might be a selection-maturation interaction. If experimental and control groups were not equated on age, there would be, in addition to problems of selection, certain problems of maturation since children at some ages mature or change at a greater rate than children at other ages. Moreover, the nature of the changes taking place at one age might be more systematically related to the experimental treatment than the changes taking place at another age. Thus, two sources of invalidity can combine to restrict the validity of the experiment.

5.3 FACTORS AFFECTING EXTERNAL VALIDITY

Campbell and Stanley (1963) use the term "external validity" to refer to the generalizability or representativeness of the findings of a study. A researcher, in doing an experiment, hopes that the results can be applied during later time periods to groups of people in other geographical locations. In order for findings to have any generality and, therefore, to be more broadly useful, it is necessary that consideration be given to external validity* in the experimental design. To this question of generalizability at least four factors must be taken into account.

Reactive Effects of Testing

If pretesting has been used which sensitizes the experimental subject to the particular treatment, then the effect of the treatment may be partially the result of the sensitization of the pretest. In another set of conditions wherein the pretest is not used, the treatment would not have the same effects. If, for example, a study of attitude change were to begin with a pretesting of attitudes, the participants could become sensitized to the attitudes in question and, therefore, pay more attention to the communication and show more attitude change as a result. Should the same communication be used in a different group without pretest, the effect of the treatment will most likely be different, especially if the treatment requires the pretest as a necessary precondition.

Also, subjects often try to "help" the experimenter by providing the result they think he is anticipating. One reason they may react differently to the

---

*External validity here refers to the generalizability of a set of findings based on the design of the study. Recall that generalizability can also be contributed to through the formulation of conceptual hypotheses and intervening variables as described in Chapters 2 and 3.

treatment after a pretest is that they think they then know from the pretest what the experimenter's aim is.*

Interaction Effects of Selection Bias

If the samples drawn for a study are not representative of the larger population, then it will be difficult to generalize findings from the samples to the population. An experiment run with students in one part of the country, for instance, might not be valid for students in another part of the country; or a study run with urban dwellers might not apply to rural dwellers if there is something unique about the urban population that contributes to the effects of the experiment. Thus, it is desirable for purposes of external generality to use samples that are representative of the broadest population possible. The techniques for accomplishing this are described in Section 8.5.

Reactive Effects of Experimental Arrangements

The arrangements of the experiment or the experience of participating in it may create sufficient artificiality to limit the possibility that the results will be generalizable to a nonexperimental test of the treatment. The following anecdote illustrates how subjects behave differently in experimental settings.

Two experimenters, after fastening a subject to the side of a swimming pool into which water was being placed in order to study the effects of stress from near-drowning, forgot that they were carrying out this experiment and returned to the pool just in time to turn off the water before the subject was drowned. The experimenters, quite frightened by this experience and somewhat in a state of shock, pulled the subject from the pool and loosened him from the bonds. Upon being asked by the experimenters, "Weren't you frightened?" the subject calmly replied, "Oh no, it was only an experiment."

Often a curriculum will work on an experimental basis because of what has been called the *Hawthorne effect*. This effect led participants, pleased by having been singled out to participate in an experimental project, to react more strongly to their pleasure than to the treatment. However, such projects when tried on a nonexperimental basis often yield very different results.

Again, the work of Welch and Walberg (1970) tends to indicate that pretesting may be a lesser source of invalidity than heretofore assumed. It is worth re-emphasizing, however, that the pretest is costly and time-consuming and may, in certain situations be avoided (see Chapter 6).

Multiple Treatment Interference

When experimental participants are subjected to a number of treatments simultaneously, some of which may be experimental and others not, the treatments often interact in ways that cause the representativeness of the effects of any one of them to be reduced. For example, if students serve as subjects, they will be experiencing a variety of other treatments as part of their normal school activity in addition to the experimental treatment. The treatments in combination may produce effects that will not be reproduced under circumstances where only the experimental treatment is being applied.

5.4 CONTROLLING FOR SELECTION: EQUATING EXPERIMENTAL AND CONTROL GROUPS

By selecting a control group made up of persons who as nearly as possible have the same idiosyncracies as the experimental group subjects the researcher will minimize selection invalidity—that is, that the outcome of an experiment is as much, or more, a function of uncontrolled individual differences as of the treatment.

Because selection problems are a common source of consternation for researchers, a number of approaches have been developed to deal with them.

Randomization

Randomization (also called random assignment) is a procedure for controlling selection variables without first having to identify them. Its purpose is to avoid introducing a systematic basis of selection by reducing to chance the probability that more of one type of person than another is in the experimental or control group.

A researcher randomizes by beginning with a subject pool and randomly assigning members of this pool to the experimental and control groups. Operationally, this may be accomplished by drawing names out of a hat or assigning numbers to subjects (Ss) and using a table of random numbers (see Appendix B) to assign subjects to groups. With 50 Ss for example, a researcher might alphabetize the list and number each person from 1 to 50. Then he would go down the random numbers list looking only at the first two digits in a column. If the first number began with a 22, subject 22 would be assigned to the experimental group. If the second number began with 09, the subject 9 would be assigned to the experimental group. He would continue in this manner until half of the *Ss* were assigned to the experimental group. The remainder would then be assigned to the control group. Equal group sizes are desirable.

In a study in which pretest data on the dependent variable are to be collected, randomized assignment of subjects to conditions should be undertaken independently of pretest scores.* That is, subjects should be assigned to conditions on the random basis described above rather than on the basis of pretest scores. Pretest scores may be subsequently examined but no group reassignment should occur as a result.

To insure random assignment[†] the researcher either must assign subjects to conditions or determine that such assignment while undertaken independently of him was done without bias. Even when the assigner may contend that assignments were not undertaken on any systematic basis, it is often unwise for the experimenter to consider his groups to have been randomly composed: the researcher himself must find some objective basis for concluding that assignment to conditions was without bias.

The use of intact classes (that is classes to which students have been assigned by their school prior to an experiment) poses a particular problem. While it is often tempting to consider these as randomly assigned groups, it is usually a better course of action to consider them as nonrandom groups and proceed with specific designs for use with intact groups (described in Chapter 6). It is sometimes possible for a researcher to demonstrate that assignment to such intact groups has been done on essentially a random basis. When in doubt, however, it is better to assume nonrandomness.

Matched-Pair Technique

To use the matched-pair technique the researcher must first decide which control variables applicable to individual differences are his most prominent sources of problems (i.e., his most likely sources of internal invalidity due to selection) in the experiment he is designing. Among these often are sex, age,

---

*Pretest scores would be used in the analysis of such data by using them as a covariate in an analysis of covariance, by examining change scores (posttest minus pretest), or by comparing group pretest scores after-the-fact as a check on the distribution of selection factors across groups. Moreover, subjects may be paired on pretest scores, and then one member of each pair, chosen randomly, would be assigned to the experimental group, the other to the control group. This is described under matched pairs.

[†]The discussion here concerns the procedure for assigning Ss to conditions to minimize internal invalidity due to selection bias. Random selection of a sample from a population, a procedure for increasing external validity, is described in Chapter 8.

socioeconomic status, race, I.Q., achievement, various personality measures, and pretest scores on the dependent variable. It is necessary then for the researcher to identify within the subject pool the pairs of persons who are most equivalent on the specific variable(s) he wants to control. Thus, an 11 year old male of low I.Q. (as defined operationally) would be paired with another 11 year old male of low I.Q. All subjects in the pool eventually would be paired. Instead of having 50 individual subjects, there would be 25 pairs of subjects matched on the chosen selection measures. Then, one member of each pair, chosen from among the two members on a *random* basis, would be assigned to the experimental group and one to the control group. Each of the remaining pairs would be split similarly. The resultant two groups would be considered reasonably equal on the measures in question, thus providing control over selection variables*

Such matching can also be done on a pretest measure of the dependent variable. If the dependent variable were, for instance, mathematics achievement, pairs could be matched on initial level of mathematics achievement, and then randomly assigned to groups, thereby controlling for intitial level on the dependent variable. This procedure is an alternative to the randomization procedure described on pages 81–82 where no matching or sorting is done on any measure. Of the two, randomization by itself is preferred.

Matched-Group Technique

A similar but less extensive matching procedure is the assignment of individuals to groups in such a way that the means of the groups on the critical selection variables are the same. Thus, two groups might be composed such that the mean age in each case were 11.5 or between 11 and 12. Equivalent pairs might not exist across groups but the groups on the average would be equivalent. Groups can also be matched on the average on a pretest measure of the dependent variable in order to guarantee average equivalence of the groups at the start of the experiment. Often, statistical comparisons are required to insure that the groups have been adequately matched. Note, however, that this technique may lead to regression effects (see page 77) and should be avoided in favor of randomization and matched-pairing in other than uncommon circumstances.

It is not uncommon for subjects to be assigned randomly to groups and then a check made on the distribution of control variables by comparing the groups to assess their equivalence on these variables. This is an after-the-fact check, though, rather than matching, per se.

It is important that extreme scorers not be eliminated in this procedure nor certain combinations of scores favored for inclusion. To do this would produce statistical regression effects.

Using Subjects as Their Own Controls*

If all subjects serve as both the experimental and the control group, then selection variables can usually be considered to be adequately controlled; however, there are many situations where this technique cannot be used because the experimental experience will have an effect on a person's performance in the control acitivity or vice versa. In learning and teaching studies, for instance, after having completed the experimental treatment, the subject will no longer be naive and his performance on the control task will reflect his experience on the experimental task. In other words, this technique while controlling adequately for selection bias often creates insurmountable problems of *maturation* or *history*; control and experimental subjects may be the same persons but their relevant history, hence their present level of maturation, is different in completing the second task because of having experienced the first.

In instances where subjects can be used as their own controls, it is important to control for order effects by counterbalancing. Half of the subjects, chosen at random, should receive the experimental treatment first while the remainder first serve as control. (See pages 86-87.)

Limiting the Population

The population is the "group" you set out to study. The sample is made up of those persons from that group who are chosen to participate in the study. By narrowly restricting the population (for instance, to college sophomores in universities with graduate psychology departments), it is possible to control a number of possibly confounding selection variables. In fact, in most experiments some boundaries on the population in question are adopted. However, when these boundaries become too restrictive, the "price paid" for the increase in internal validity via selection is very high in terms of reduction of external validity. Severely limiting the population may limit the conclusions to a restricted group rather than enabling them to be more universal.†

This procedure is labelled repeated measurement *or* correlated measures *for statistical purposes.*

†When a researcher describes his variables in conceptual terms, i.e., as intervening variables, he often extends their generality beyond the specific sample studied. By doing this, he gains external validity—that is, he may broaden his delineation of the population of which his sample is representative. Psychologists have, for example, conducted many studies on samples of college sophomores but because of their conceptualizations may often apply their findings to the population of all people.

The Moderator Variable as a Selection Device

If a particular individual difference measure seems extremely likely to be a potential influence on the hypothesis being tested, it can be both controlled (as a source of confounding or bias) and studied (as it interacts with the independent variable) by manipulating it within an experiment as a moderator variable. To control a variable in a study by making it a moderator variable, a factorial statistical design is used (this will be described in Chapter 6). Such a design is an important means of dealing with selection variables because it enables the researcher to examine interactions, that is, effects on the dependent variable that are the result of the independent and moderator variables acting in combination.*

5.5 CONTROLLING FOR HISTORY: EQUATING EXPERIMENTAL AND CONTROL CONDITIONS

Outside of the independent variable, the control group insofar as possible should have the same experiences or history as the experimental group. It is difficult to insure that the experiences of the two groups will be comparable outside of the experimental setting; realistically the maximum amount of control that can be exercised is simply to *have* a control group which is drawn from the same population as the experimental group. However, within the experiment itself, there are many potentially confounding variables (i.e., sources of internal invalidity due to history) which must be adequately controlled. A number of techniques are available.

Method of Removal

Where possible, extraneous influences should be entirely removed from the experiences in both the experimental and control conditions. Extraneous noises, interruptions, and changes in environmental conditions should be scrupulously avoided. For example, rather than encountering possible confounding from subjects asking questions while taking either the pretest or posttest, the possibility of interruptions by questions and answers is removed by disallowing questions.

---

*There is a statistical procedure for eliminating the potential effect of a particular selection factor. This procedure is called analysis of covariance and is described in most statistics textbooks. It differs from the above technique in that it treats the potentially confounding variable as a control variable (i.e., a variable to be neutralized) rather than as a moderator variable (i.e., a variable to be assessed).

The double-blind technique described earlier (page 74) is another way of avoiding the possibility of an administrator's influencing a subject's responses.

Method of Constancy

Experiences, other than those resulting from the manipulation of the independent variable, should be *constant* across the experimental and control groups. If instructions need be given, these should be written in advance and then read to both groups to guarantee their constancy across conditions. Tasks, experiences, or procedures not unique to the treatment should be identical for experimental and control groups. Experimental settings should also be the same in both cases. In experiments where the presence of an experience is to be contrasted with its absence do not leave uncontrolled the factors of time, involvement in the experiment, and exposure to materials. To maintain constancy on these factors, the control group, rather than having no experience, should be given an irrelevant experience, which takes as long as the treatment, provides the same amount of exposure, and thus the same amount of involvement.

What is difficult is not how to provide constancy but on *what* to provide constancy. If the experimenter fails to provide constancy on a potential confounding variable, his design will lack internal validity and, hence, his conclusions will not be justified. Variables such as time spent in the experiment, attention from the experimenter, and amount of material exposed to are occasionally overlooked as control variables.

Although experimental studies are often thought of as comparing the presence of a treatment to its absence (the control), in fact control subjects should be having some type of experience while their experimental counterparts are experiencing the treatment. (See Figure 5.1, page 73; note S_0.) Rather than ignoring the activities of control subjects during this period, it is recommended that the researcher provide an alternative, "irrelevant" experience or use some other means to insure constancy. A design appropriate for controlling for the Hawthorne effect, which may result if experimental Ss are treated and control Ss ignored, is discussed in the next chapter (Section 6.7).

Method of Counterbalancing

In experiments where subjects perform more than one task or take more than one test, it is often necessary to control for the effects of order, that is, for apparent progressive shifts in a subject's response as he continues to serve in the experiment. These shifts may be a function of practice or of fatigue (so-called constant errors). This is particularly relevant in those instances where subjects serve as their own controls—that is, when the same subjects are used in both experimental and control groups (see page 84) but is equally applicable where there are multiple treatments or multiple dependent measures.

Where there are two tasks (A and B) and subjects must perform each once, counterbalancing is achieved by randomly dividing the group in half and giving each half the tasks in the opposite order.

Group I   Group II

A   B   B   A

When there are two tests to be taken, the same approach can be used.

In instances where each of two experiences is to occur more than twice for each subject, a counterbalanced order A B B A enables the constant errors to be equalized across experiences. Where subjects are to react to pictures of dogs and cats, the order can be DOG CAT CAT DOG.

If a single constant task order is used (A B), the effect of this order as a potential source of history bias must be independently assessed. Since such assessment is difficult and burdensome, constant task orders should be avoided. Counterbalancing of task order has the advantage of enabling the researcher to assess task order effects within the experiment and thereby determine if such effects occur and how they affect the treatment. Randomizing task order (i.e., giving the tasks in a randomly chosen order) has the advantage of enabling the researcher to neutralize task order effects. If task order effects are of interest, then counterbalancing should be employed, making task order a moderator variable. Most often, however, these effects are not of specific interest. They are then most easily controlled by randomizing the order of the tasks or tests across subjects. In this way, order effects are neutralized rather than systematized. Moreover, subsequent statistical analyses are simpler, sample sizes need not be as large, and no assumptions about order need be made by the researcher.

Method of Multiple Counterbalancing*

The counterbalancing technique described above applies to instances where each subject is to experience two tasks two or more times. When the number of

*Townsend (1953) refers to this procedure as the method of systematic randomization.

tasks or experiences to be equated and ordered across subjects exceeds two, the technique of multiple counterbalancing can be employed. This technique is merely a complex or multiple form of counterbalancing which is achieved when many things are counterbalanced simultaneously. It is easiest to describe by example.

Consider the experiment by Lewin, Lippitt, and White (1939) in which subjects serving as their own controls experienced three social climates each: autocratic, democratic, and laissez-faire; furthermore, the subjects experienced three leaders who "created" those climates by playing appropriate roles. Thus, in such an experiment the following factors had to be controlled:

1. the number of times each climate was experienced
2. the number of times each leader was experienced
3. the number of times each leader played each role
4. the order in which the three climates were experienced
5. the order in which the three leaders were experienced

You will notice by examing Figure 5.2 below that six groups were used, with three experiences per group, to provide the controls. Each group experienced each social climate once and each leader once, while each leader played each role twice. There were six possible orders of the three climates and each group experienced a different one of these orders. Likewise, there were six possible orders of the three leaders and each group experienced a different one of these orders.

	Group 1	Group 2	Group 3
Time 1	Autocratic climate	Autocratic climate	Democratic climate
	Leader 1	Leader 3	Leader 2
Time 2	Democratic climate	Laissez-faire climate	Autocratic climate
	Leader 2	Leader 2	Leader 1
Time 3	Laissez-faire climate	Democratic climate	Laissez-faire climate
	Leader 3	Leader 1	Leader 3

	Group 4	Group 5	Group 6
Time 1	Democratic climate	Laissez-faire climate	Laissez-faire climate
	Leader 3	Leader 2	Leader 1
Time 2	Laissez-faire climate	Autocratic climate	Democratic climate
	Leader 1	Leader 3	Leader 3
Time 3	Autocratic climate	Democratic climate	Autocratic climate
	Leader 2	Leader 1	Leader 2

Figure 5.2 *Multiple counterbalancing of social climates and leaders in the Lewin, Lippitt, and White (1939) experiment.*

There are some combinations of experiences that could not be systematically controlled in this experiment because it would have required either too many groups or too many experiences per group. For instance, the unique combination of leader and climate would ideally require that each group experience each leader playing the role appropriate to each climate. Added to this was the problem of the order in which each leader would lead each group with what climate. Ideally each group should have experienced each leader playing each role in a different order. But for practical reasons Lewin et al. could not include all possible leader-climate and leader-climate-order combinations in their research design. Instead, they used randomization of the various combinations that could not be dealt with through counterbalancing as a safeguard against systematic bias.

5.6 CONTROLLING FOR INSTRUMENTATION

Instrumentation bias is based on the extent to which vicissitudes in subjects, raters, environment, and so on, affect the readings obtained on the measuring instruments employed. Ways in which the potential bias from such vicissitudes can be minimized or controlled will be described in detail in Chapter 7 (Observation and Measurement) and in Chapter 8 (Interviews and Questionnaires). Some of the major points covered in these chapters will be itemized here to provide an overview in the context of internal validity.

Instrumentation bias can be often dealt with in the following ways

1. Establish the reliability or consistency of test scores over items and over time, thus showing that the test tends to measure something consistently (see Section 7.1).
2. Use the same measure for both pre- and posttest or use alternate forms of the same measure (see Section 7.1).
3. Establish the validity of a test measure, thus showing that what you intended to measure has been measured (see Section 7.2).
4. Establish a relative scoring system for a test (i.e., norms) so that scores may be adapted to a common scale (see Section 7.3).
5. Use more than one judge or observer, keep the same judges or observers throughout the course of a study, and compare their judgments to establish an index of inter-judge agreement (see Section 7.8).

Other techniques for controlling instrumentation bias also exist but the above five are the most commonly encountered. The purpose of the subspeciality called "psychometrics" is essentially to deal with instrumentation bias in behavioral measurement.

5.7 AN ANALYSIS OF CONTROL IN THREE STUDIES

Sample Study I (Appendix A)

Sample Study I utilized both a control group (no feedback) and three comparison groups (feedback from students, supervisors, and from both). Aside from these differences in feedback, for each of the four groups the environment and procedures were as alike as could be possible. Let us consider Sample Study I in terms of the categories of internal validity.

The *history* of the subjects (*Ss*, in this case, teachers) can be expected to be the same in each of the conditions. All the participants were teaching vocational subjects; thus their experiences can be considered comparable on a group basis. The use of *comparison groups* and a *control group* minimized the likelihood that individual histories of *Ss* outside of, but simultaneous to, the experiment differentially affected the performance of *Ss* in the experiment.

Within a 12-week period, the amount of *maturation* expected among 30 and 40 year old persons is minimal and, therefore, should not differ from condition to condition.

Since the data for the dependent variable were not collected from the subjects of the experiment (the teachers), invalidity due to *testing* is not possible. Had teacher behavior been measured by self-report (which it was not), testing might have been a problem.

Instrumentation was maintained as a constant across the four conditions by using students as judges on all pretest and posttest measurement and using the same instrument in each instance. Had the measuring instruments or judges differed from condition to condition (as they did not), this would have caused a problem. It is interesting to note that the judges did not manifest constancy over time even though they were the same students. Ratings in the spring were lower than ratings the previous winter. However, since this effect occurred across all conditions, it did not pose a validity threat.

Selection was dealt with through the use of a moderator variable and random assignment. Because it was expected that the effects of feedback would differ as a function of a teacher's level of experience, years of teaching experience was dealt with as a moderator variable. Three levels were identified on this variable. One-fourth of the teachers in each experience level were randomly selected for each feedback (or no feedback) condition. Thus, random assignment of subjects to the experimental conditions controlled for selection on all characteristics other than years of teaching experience, which was treated as a moderator variable (i.e., systematically manipulated).

Statistical regression effects were unlikely in Sample Study I because groups were not chosen on the basis of extreme scores. The full range of teachers on the measure of years of experience was employed. .

Few teachers dropped out of the study. Those that did were spread across the four experimental conditions, thus eliminating *experimental mortality* as a source of concern. When *Ss* are randomly assigned to conditions, losses can be expected to be randomized across conditions.

To insure external validity, *strict* generalizations would have to be limited to the population studied, the specific situation, and procedures; although at the conceptual level, the finding that teachers were most influenced by student feedback can be expected to apply to teachers regardless of the subject matter taught or school setting. However, its application requires students of sufficient maturity to complete the feedback questionnaire employed.

Sample Study II (Appendix A)

Within Sample Study II, two sources of internal invalidity posed a major threat: selection and history. Selection was dealt with in the following manner:

> Fortunately, for our experiment, the administrators and teachers cooperated insofar as to enable random assignment of pupils to class as well as classes to experimental and control conditions.

In all school studies, the use of intact classes to which students have been assigned as part of the school's normal procedures poses a threat to internal validity. Since it is often difficult, if not impossible, to conduct both experimental and control conditions in the same classroom, the researcher may end up by *randomly* assigning intact classrooms to conditions. While the use of more than one intact class per condition and the random assignment of intact classes to conditions controls for selection bias to a far greater extent than the assignment of intact classes to conditions on some nonrandom basis, the assignment of whole classes is not comparable to the random assignment of individual students to conditions by the researcher as a control for selection bias. It is possible that intact classes have built-in selection biases. For example, among two classes, one might contain considerably more bright youngsters than the other. Whichever of two conditions the brighter total class was randomly assigned to would then have an advantage over the condition receiving the second, less bright class. The researcher would not be loading his treatment in his favor because random assignment of intact classes means that he has no control over which class gets which experience, but, nevertheless, the condition receiving the brighter class would gain an advantage. The use of more than one class per condition, coupled with random assignment of classes to conditions in Sample Study II, helped to limit potential selection bias. In addition, the random assignment of students to classes in this study provided the maximum in control for selection bias.

In studies such as Sample Study II where academic performance is the criterion or dependent variable, controlling for selection bias becomes critical, since intelligence, a common selection factor, is known to affect this criterion. When not adequately controlled for, intelligence differences may have a greater effect on outcomes than the treatment. The randomizing procedures employed in this study were entirely adequate to control for intelligence differences as a potential source of selection bias. Moreover, the researchers attempted to control for I.Q. beyond randomizing by collecting I.Q. data and introducing it as a covariate in an analysis of covariance procedure.

It was the intention of the authors of Sample Study II to manipulate rewards but to control for all other experiences within the experiment. Two threats to internal validity based on *history* are called the "gadget effect" and the "Hawthorne effect" by the authors. (For more information about controlling for the latter effect, see Section 6.7.) To eliminate these effects, both control and experimental *Ss* received reward tally cards and tallied their rewards daily. Thus, both were afforded the appearance of being in an experiment and had access to the manipulanda of the experiment (the tally cards).

The absence of a pretest eliminates testing effects; the use of standardized tests minimizes validity threats based on instrumentation. No mortality data are presented but we can assume that either no *Ss* were lost or that losses were random across conditions, since *Ss* were assigned at random.

Of course generalizability in this study must be restricted to the population studied, namely inner-city students who are behind in their school performance levels.

The Lockmiller-DiNello Study

Consider the study by Lockmiller and DiNello (1970), entitled: "Words in color versus a basal reader program with retarded readers in grade 2," from the *Journal of Educational Research*. The problem and method sections have been reproduced below (the problem section was included for background purposes).

LOCKMILLER–DINELLO*

THE PROBLEM

At present, research regarding the effectiveness of *Words in Color* with elementary school children is quite limited. Research comparing the progress of retarded readers using *Words in Color* with that of retarded readers using a basal approach has not been reported. It therefore seemed appropriate to conduct such a study.

Specifically, the purpose of this study was to seek answers to the following questions:

1. On the basis of two methods of teaching phonics, the *Words in Color* approach versus the phonics program contained in one particular basal reader, are the differences in the post-test scores of two treatment groups of second-grade retarded readers on the McKee Inventory of Phonetic Skills statistically significant?

2. On the basis of two methods of teaching reading, the *Words in Color* approach versus one particular basal reader approach, are the differences in the posttest scores of two treatment groups of second-grade retarded readers on the California Reading Test statistically significant?

SUBJECTS AND PROCEDURE

Subjects of this study were forty-eight second-grade retarded readers enrolled for remedial reading instruction in the Education Center of Clovis, New Mexico. Of the forty-eight subjects, twenty-four were boys and twenty-four were girls. Twelve boys were randomly selected for assignment to the experimental group and the twelve boys remaining were assigned to the control group. In a like manner, the girls were assigned to experimental and control groups.

The ethnic makeup of the experimental groups included three Negro, sixteen Mexican-American, and five white children.

Seventeen of the children had been retained in first grade and three of the seventeen retainees were repeating second grade also. After the subjects had been assigned to experimental and control groups, it was found that eleven of the retainees were in the experimental group and six in the control group. There were three

From P. Lockmiller and M. C. DiNello, Words in color versus a basal reader program with retarded readers in grade 2, Journal of Educational Research, 1970, 63, 330-334. Reprinted by permission of authors and publisher.

retainees in the boys experimental group, three in the boys control group, six in the girls experimental group, and five in the girls control group.

Information concerning ages and I.Q.'s of the four groups is shown below.

	Age Range (years and months)	Mean Age	I.Q. Range	Mean I.Q.
Boys				
Experimental	6-9 to 9-0	7-9	67–95	82.08
Control	6-10 to 8-0	7-6	70–91	81.08
Girls				
Experimental	6-8 to 10-8	7-5	63–98	83.67
Control	6-9 to 9-0	7-4	61–94	79.50

F-tests revealed the differences between ages and mean I.Q.'s among the four groups to be not significant.

All subjects were tested for I.Q. with the Lorge-Thorndike Intelligence Test, Primary Battery, Level Two, Form A, on October 20, 1966; and for color blindness with the New Practical Test Cards for Colour-Blindness on February 28, 1967. To secure pretest measures in reading and phonics, the California Reading Test, Lower Primary, Form W and the McKee Inventory of Phonetic Skills, Test One were administered on September 6, 1966, and February 27, 1967, respectively.

The September administration of the California Reading Test was a part of the regular school testing program; and the results, used to assign students to the Education Center for remedial reading instruction, were made available for use in this study.

McKee's Inventory of Phonetic Skills, Test One, selected for use in this study, was designed to test for knowledge of the phonic elements introduced in the McKee reading series through the first-grade reader, *Up and Away*, which was to be used with the control group. Experience with the McKee phonics test and knowledge of the slow rate of growth in phonics and reading already shown by the subjects of the study led the investigators to believe that the test would provide sufficient test ceiling for use in this study without biasing the results in favor of the control group.

At the end of the study, posttest measures in reading and phonics were obtained through the administration of the California Reading Test, Lower Primary, Form X on May 15, 1967, and the readministration of the McKee Inventory of Phonetic Skills, Test One, on May 16, 1967.

The reading program employed with the boys and the girls experimental groups was Gattegno's *Words in Color* and that of the boys and girls control groups was Houghton Mifflin's *Up and Away*, the first grade reader in the McKee reading series.

The same level reader was employed with all subjects in the control group because all had made satisfactory progress through the primer level and were ready to begin reading at the first grade level. Some were able to read at the first grade level, and a few could manage to read in the beginning second grade reader, but in either case only with difficulty because of general deficiencies in word attack skills and a relatively low reading vocabulary.

The experiment was conducted between February 27 and May 17, 1967. Equal amounts of instruction were provided for all groups by the same teacher. The same teacher was used as a means to attempt to hold the experimenter variable constant.

Treatment of data was by means of a Model 1620 IBM Computer. Analysis of variance was employed to test the significance of the difference of the mean pretest scores of the experimental and control groups. Posttest measures were similarly treated. Throughout the study the test of significance was the *F*-test at the .05 level.

The chief internal validity concern in this study was *selection*. Selection variables included sex, age, I.Q., color vision, ethnic background, grade retention, grade level, retardation, initial reading level, and so on. To control these, variables *Ss* were assigned to experimental and control groups on a random basis. However, a post-assignment check was made on age and I.Q. levels of experimental and control groups to assure their equivalence. Rather than using a matching procedure to control for selection bias, Lockmiller and DiNello employed randomization. However, a further check on this control was undertaken for selected control variables by comparing group means on these variables after the assignment process had been completed. This is considered to be a highly effective control procedure for selection bias.

Since all *Ss* were retardates, the retardate-nonretardate variable was controlled by the exclusion of nonretardates. Of course this limits external validity and restricts conclusions to retardates.

Matching was employed to control for sex with equal numbers of boys and girls participating in the study and equal numbers being assigned to each condition. Assignment of girls and boys to conditions was done randomly with the restriction that equal numbers of each sex would be included in each condition.

Neither ethnic makeup nor retention (number of times left back) was controlled as such although data on each were reported. (Color vision was probably used as a screening measure for the experimental condition in which colored materials were used.)

Pretest scores of the experimental and control *Ss* on the two reading measures were statistically compared to assess their equivalence. First, *Ss* were *randomly* assigned to experimental and control groups. Then, reading scores were compared across groups. This technique is called randomization with a check for post-assignment equivalence of groups on selected control variables (see page 83). This approach provides for control of selection bias through randomization plus the subsequent examination of specific control variables thought to be a particular source of confounding. Had the groups turned out not to be equivalent on pretest readings, a statistical technique such as analysis of covariance would be used to control for this nonequivalence.

History factors controlled for were the reading level of the experimental and control materials (these being at the same level), the amount of instruction provided each group (these being equal), and the teacher effects (the same teacher being used for experimental and control conditions). The use of the same teacher for both conditions eliminates invalidity based on teacher differences but creates another source of invalidity—that based on the interaction of teacher effect and treatment effect. Suppose the teacher is better with the experimental materials than with the control materials, thus creating a threat to internal validity in favor of the experimental condition. The preferred approach would be to have multiple experimental and multiple control classrooms, each one headed by a different teacher who is assigned randomly to a classroom. This would minimize the possibility that teachers would differentially contribute to outcomes (that is, would help the experimental group more than the control or vice versa). However, with as few as two classes—one experimental and one control, using a different teacher for each—the strong possibility of differential teacher effects would be left open. Thus, given a small number of groups, it is probably better to use the same teacher or teachers in both conditions in order to eliminate the differential teacher effect. (Note, however, that the single teacher approach sets limits on external validity since positive outcomes may not be attributable to the treatment alone, but to the combination of the treatment and a specific teacher.)

The use of pre- and posttests creates the possibility of a *testing* effect, which can be further minimized in the case of one of the tests by using alternative forms. Standardized test use limits invalidity due to *instrumentation*. The short duration of the experiment and the use of comparison groups limits invalidity due to *maturation*.* No *mortality* data are presented and *regression* effects are minimal

---

Compounding of these biases is further minimized through the use of randomizing procedures for assigning Ss to conditions.

since the samples were homogenous. Further they are equal across conditions since random assignment of Ss to conditions was used.

Note that in a study comparing educational programs such as this one, the heavy control emphasis concerns selection and history factors. These are typically the greatest threats to internal validity and require the greatest efforts at control. The more specific control variables employed, the greater the likelihood that these factors will be adequately controlled.

In terms of external validity, a major limiting factor in this study is the use of retardates. Generalizations to the nonretardate population can be made only with caution. A further limit is based on the fact that only one teacher was used in all conditions. While the use of one teacher enhances internal validity, it limits external validity since identical findings may not be obtained with other teachers. The specific characteristics of the teacher employed may be part of the outcome, and thus limit generalizability.

5.8 APPRAISING THE SUCCESS OF THE MANIPULATION

In some experiments the manipulation of the independent variable is quite straightforward—you introduce a particular experience to your experimental group and withhold it from your control group. If the independent variable is operationally defined by a type *B* or type *C* definition (pages 59–62) then you simply have to find an appropriate measuring device to detect the presence and absence of the observable criteria associated with the levels of this variable. However, if you are going to create your independent variable (a type *A* operational definition, pages 58–59), then it is usually necessary to check during the experiment to determine if the state you have created has the same dynamic and static properties as the state you were trying to create.

Let us say you are interested in studying the effect of fear on behavior. You tell your experimental group a story intended to produce fear in them. At this point it is wise to check if your manipulation (the story) has produced the desired effect (fear). To accomplish this, you might possibly give both your experimental and control groups an emotional symptomatology questionnaire or measure their palmar skin electrical conductivity to see if the groups differed in the desired direction.

Consider another illustration from the research of Lewin, Lippitt, and White (1939) cited in Section 5.5. As you recall, the purpose of this experiment was to compare the effects of autocratic, democratic, and laissez-faire social climates on the performance and social behavior of children. To control for leader personality differences, it was decided that each leader would generate each of the three climates. Thus, each climate required a type *A* operational definition and each leader had to be trained to use behaviors called for in the definition. Here are the definitions of the three climates as they appeared in Lippitt and White (1958).*

> *Plan for authoritarian leadership role.* Practically all policies as regards club activities and procedures should be determined by the leader. The techniques and activity steps should be communicated by the authority, one unit at a time, so that future steps are in the dark to a large degree. The adult should take considerable responsibility for assigning the activity tasks and companions of each group member. The dominator should keep his standards of praise and criticism to himself in evaluating individual and group activities. He should also remain fairly aloof from active group participation except in demonstrating.

> *Plan for the democratic leadership role.* Wherever possible, policies should be a matter of group decision and discussion with active encouragement and assistance by the adult leader. The leader should attempt to see that activity perspective emerges during the discussion period with the general steps to the group goal becoming clarified. Wherever technical advice is needed, the leader should try to suggest two or more alternative procedures from which choice can be made by the group members. Everyone should be free to work with whomever he chooses, and the divisions of responsibility should be left up to the group. The leader should attempt to communicate in an objective, fact-minded way the bases for his praise and criticism of individual and group activities. He should try to be a regular group member in spirit but not do much of the work (so that comparisons of group productivity can be made between the groups).

> *Plan for laissez-faire leadership role.* In this situation, the adult should play a rather passive role in social participation and leave complete freedom for group or individual decisions in relation to activity and group procedure. The leader should make clear the various materials which are available and be sure it is understood that

The Lippitt and White (1958) study is a rewritten version of the original Lewin, Lippitt, and White (1939) study. From R. Lippitt and R. K. White, An experimental study of leadership and group life, in E. E. Maccoby, T. M. Newcomb, and E. L. Hartley (Eds.), Readings in Social Psychology, 3rd ed. Copyright 1947, 1952, © 1958 by Holt, Rinehart and Winston, Inc. Reprinted by permission of Holt, Rinehart and Winston, Inc.

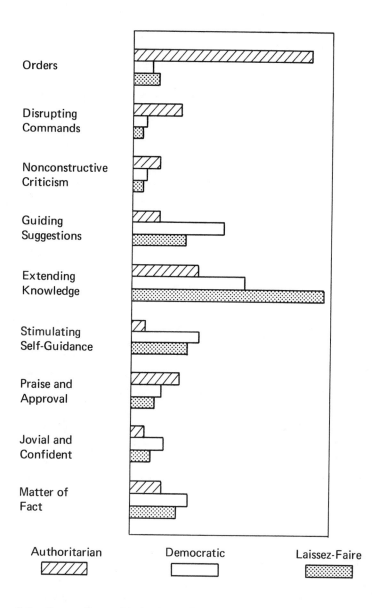

Figure 5.3 *Comparison of behaviors of average authoritarian, democratic, and laissez-faire leaders. (From R. Lippitt and R. K. White, An experimental study of leadership and group life, in E. E. Maccoby, T. M. Newcomb, and E. L. Hartley (Eds.),* Readings in Social Psychology, *3rd ed. Copyright 1947, 1952, © 1958 by Holt, Rinehart and Winston, Inc. Reprinted by permission of Holt, Rinehart and Winston, Inc.)*

he will supply information and help when asked. He should do a minimum of taking the initiative in making suggestions. He should make no attempt to evaluate negatively or positively the behavior or production of the individual or the group as a group, although he should be friendly rather than "stand-offish" at all times.

(You will note that these are type *A* operational definitions because they specify what a person should do to *create* a particular climate.)

It was necessary for the researchers in this study to assure themselves that each leader in fact played the role for each climate as it was specified. If the three leaders behaved differently when they were all supposed to be autocratic (authoritarian), it would be unlikely that the expected effects of the autocratic climate would be obtained.

To determine if the manipulation was successful, trained observers watched each leader playing each role and coded every leadership act into one of nine categories. A breakdown of each category according to the role the leader was playing appears in Figure 5.3.

As you can see, the autocratic leader (here called "authoritarian") primarily gave orders, the democratic leader gave suggestions, and the laissez-faire leader gave information (he extended the boys' knowledge). This conforms closely to the operational definitions of the climates. Thus, it may be concluded that the experimental conditions "took," and when the authors talk about the three climates, they are justified in labeling them as they do.

In most studies, the independent variable may be measured or "canned" (i.e., prepared in advance as a package). However, in those instances when the experimenter must make a state or condition occur as the independent variable, it is useful to check and see (as Lippitt and White did) that the manipulation produced the desired state or condition.

RECOMMENDED READINGS

Campbell, D. T. and Stanley, J. C. Experimental and quasi-experimental designs for research on teaching. In N. L. Gage (Ed.) *Handbook for research on teaching.* Chicago: Rand-McNally, 1963, pp. 171–246. (Also available as a monograph from Rand-McNally.)

Townsend, J. C. *Introduction to experimental method.* New York: McGraw-Hill, 1953.

COMPETENCY TEST EXERCISES

1. A coach has given some boys training in swimming. Which of the reasons given below would *not* be valid in establishing the need for a control group to evaluate the effects of the training?
   a. The boys might have had superior potentials for becoming good swimmers.
   b. The coach may not have sufficient free time to continue the training program.
   c. The experience in the water may have contributed more than the training per se.
   d. Normal physical development may have accounted for any improvement.

2. Youngsters initially showing much aggressive behavior toward teachers and classmates have reduced this aggressiveness considerably after a special counseling program. Which of the reasons given below would *not* be valid in establishing the need for a control group to evaluate the effects of the counseling?
   a. Judgments of aggressive behavior following the program were biased by the judges' desire to see the program as succeeding.
   b. The oldest of the problem children never completed the program.
   c. People running the program were well-trained counselors.
   d. Special attention given to these students really accounted for their change in behavior.

3. Six of the above eight choices [1(a), 1(b), 1(c), 1(d), 2(a), 2(b), 2(c), 2(d)] represent sources of internal invalidity. Label each completion according to the source of internal invalidity, leaving blank the two chosen as answers for exercises 1 and 2.

   1(a)   2(a)

   1(b)   2(b)

   1(c)   2(c)

   1(d)   2(d)

4. Match up each source of external invalidity with its proper label.
   a. reactive effect of testing   1. people behave differently in experiments
   b. interaction effects of selection bias   2. pretest sensitizing to treatment

c. reactive effects of experimental arrangements	3. combined effect of two or more treatments
d. multiple treatment interference	4. posttest sensitizing to treatment
	5. treatment interferes with outcome
	6. nonrepresentativeness of sample

5. In one sentence per item, describe each of the techniques listed below for controlling against sources of invalidity.
   a. randomized assignment
   b. matched pairs
   c. matched groups
   d. *Ss* as their own controls

6. In one sentence per item, describe each of the techniques listed below for controlling against sources of invalidity.
   a. removal
   b. constancy
   c. counterbalancing
   d. multiple counterbalancing

7. Consider Sample Study III (Differences between blind and partially-sighted children . . .) in Appendix A. What was done by the experimenter to avoid or overcome selection bias?

8. You are interested in determining the effect of programmed mathematics material on the level of mathematics achievement. What steps would you undertake to control for history, maturation, testing, instrumentation, selection, regression, and mortality biases?

9. In the above example (exercise 8), what steps would you undertake to control for the various sources of external invalidity?

10. You are interested in finding out whether a film about careers increases the tendency of students to make career decisions. What steps would you undertake to control for history, maturation, and selection biases?

11. You have designed an experiment to compare directive and nondirective counselors. You are using the same counselors in both conditions but have trained them to counsel differently for each. How would you check to see if your counselors were behaving directively and nondirectively in the appropriate conditions as directed?

12. You are interested in studying the effects of anger on problem-solving. You attempt to make *Ss* angry by finding fault with their behavior and yelling at them. What can you do subsequent to this anger manipulation to determine whether the desired result has occurred?

6

Constructing
Research Designs*

OBJECTIVES

Distinguish between pre-experimental designs, true experimental designs, and quasi-experimental designs based on their adequacy for handling the different threats to validity. / Construct true experimental designs including factorial designs given predictions. / Identify circumstances which call for or necessitate the use of quasi-experimental designs. / Identify the threats to validity not completely controlled by each of the quasi-experimental designs. / Construct quasi-experimental designs given predictions and specific circumstances in the situation which preclude the use of true designs. / Describe the circumstances which call for or necessitate the use of the criterion group or co-relational designs and, given such situations, construct these designs. / Construct designs for the control of reactive effects, that is, the Hawthorne and expectancy effects, given predictions and situations in which such effects may operate.

6.1 A SHORTHAND FOR DISPLAYING DESIGNS

The system of symbols described below will be used in the research designs.

An X will be used to designate a *treatment* (the presence of a treatment) and a blank space to designate a *control* (the absence of a treatment). When treatments are compared, they will be labeled X_1, X_2, and so on.

*This chapter is based in large measure on D. T. Campbell and J. C. Stanley, *Experimental and quasi-experimental designs for research on teaching*, in N. L. Gage, Ed., Handbook of Research on Teaching, *Chicago, Rand-McNally, 1963, Chapter 5.*

An O will be used to designate an *observation* or measurement and each O will carry an arbitrary subscript for ease of identification and referral (O_1, O_2, and so on).*

The letter R will indicate that factors, (for example, selection) have been controlled by using *randomization* or some other technique described in Chapter 5. Finally, a dashed line will show that *intact groups* have been used, indicating incomplete control of selection bias.

6.2 PRE-EXPERIMENTAL DESIGNS (NONDESIGNS)

There are three common designs (used unfortunately all too often) which do not qualify as legitimate experimental designs because they do not control adequately against the sources of internal invalidity. These nondesigns are described below. They are referred to as *pre-experimental* designs because they are the component pieces or elements of experimental designs. However, there is value in knowing what you should not do as well as what you should do. Because they are inadequate as they stand, they are also called nondesigns.

One-Shot Case Study

The one-shot case study can be diagrammed as follows:

$$X \quad O$$

In this "study" some treatment (X) is tried on a single group; an observation (O) is then made on the members of that group to assess the effects of the treatment. The lack of a control group (a group that does not receive X) and the lack of information about the persons who experience X violate most of the principles of internal validity in a design. On the basis of a one-shot case study there is no justification for concluding that X *caused O*.

Consider an example. Suppose that a school institutes a free lunch program (X). After the program has been in operation for six months, teachers are interviewed and they report (O) that instances of disruptive classroom activity are minimal. The school principal then concludes that the school lunch program is reducing student tension and aggression. However, the principal does not know (1) whether specific experiences or occurrences (history) other than the lunch program have contributed to the observed behavior change, (2) whether there

---

These subscripts are used solely for differentiation; they have no systematic meaning in terms of sequence.

really was a change relative to past behavior, and, if there was, whether it is stable, or (3) whether students participating in the lunch program were likely to change anyway as a function of selection or maturation.

One-Group Pretest-Posttest Design

The one-group pretest-posttest design can be diagrammed as shown below:

$$O_1 \quad X \quad O_2$$

This study differs from the one-shot case study by using a pretest, which provides some information about the sample. However, this design (or nondesign) fails to control for history, maturation, testing, or statistical regression and thus cannot be considered legitimate. While it provides some information about selection because the pretest describes the initial state of the selected Ss on the dependent variable, it falls far short of handling the other sources of internal invalidity.

Intact-Group Comparison

The intact-group comparison* can be diagrammed as shown below:

$$\frac{X \quad O_1}{O_2}$$

A second group or control group which does not receive the treatment (X) as a source of comparison for the treatment-receiving group is utilized in this approach. Because a control (non-treatment) group is employed, validity factors such as history (and, to a lesser extent, maturation) are controlled for by the control (non-treatment) group. That is, if some other coincidental event affected the outcome, it would as likely affect O_2 as O_1, thus controlling for history.

However, the control group subjects and experimental group subjects are neither selected nor assigned to groups on a random basis (or on any other of the bases required for the control of selection bias). The dashed line between the groups indicates they are intact groups. Moreover, by failing to pretest the subjects, it is impossible to ascertain whether the control and experimental group subjects are essentially equivalent. Thus, this approach is unacceptable because it fails to control not only for selection invalidity but also for invalidity based on experimental mortality. That is, there is no way of telling whether one group was already higher on O (or some other related measure) before the treatment which may have caused it to outperform the other on the posttest.

Campbell and Stanley (1963) refer to this design as the static-group comparison. The term used here is more consistent with the terminology used in this book.

While it is unlikely that differences between O_2 and O_1 are based on different histories and rates of maturation during the experiment, it should not be assumed that these differences are not based on differences which the subjects bring with them to the experiment. Thus, the intact-group comparison is considered to be a pre-experimental design—that is, a design that in itself does not control satisfactorily all sources of invalidity to be acceptable or legitimate. By virtue of their shortcomings, this and the other nondesigns do not eliminate alternative explanations of the findings.

6.3 TRUE EXPERIMENTAL DESIGNS

There are some designs that can be called *true* experimental designs because they provide completely adequate controls for all sources of internal invalidity. They represent no compromise between experimental design requirements and the nature and reality of the situation in which a study is being undertaken. Two of these true designs will be described in turn.*

Posttest-Only Control Group Design

The posttest-only control group design is the potentially most useful true design. It can be diagrammed as shown below

$$R \quad X \quad O_1$$
$$R \quad \quad O_2$$

This design utilizes two groups, one of which experiences the treatment while the other does not, thus controlling for history and maturation. Furthermore, group assignment is made on a random basis which controls for selection and mortality. In addition, no pretest is given to either group in order to control for simple testing effects and the interactions between testing and treatment. This design is quite ideal, then, in that it controls all threats to validity or sources of bias.

The posttest-only control group design is both simple and efficient. Selection variables can often be adequately controlled for by randomization, thus minimizing the need for pretest data. Where random assignment of Ss to conditions is

*A third, the Solomon Four-Group Design, is not covered in this book because of its limited usefulness. The reader is referred to Campbell and Stanley (1963).

possible, this design is recommended. Not only does it control for all sources of invalidity, but it also does not require the experimenter to identify in advance particular sources of selection bias. All potentially biasing selection variables are controlled by randomizing.

The appropriate analysis for dealing with data from the posttest-only control group design would be a comparison between the mean for O_1 and the mean for O_2.

Sample Study II, Appendix A, illustrates the posttest-only control group design. Two conditions were employed with Ss randomly assigned to each (R). No pretest on the dependent variable was used. One group experienced massive reward (X) while the other group did not. Both groups then completed a reading test (O_1, O_2). Posttest reading scores were compared to assess the effect of the treatment, with I.Q. scores serving as a statistical control variable.* The potentially sensitizing effects of a pretest were avoided.

Another example of the useful posttest-only control group design comes from a study by Childers and Haas (1970). This study sought to compare the writing efficiency of a group of college freshmen exposed to a special program of extensive preguidance, periodic checking, and detailed correction and comment on the development of a paper to the writing efficiency of a group of freshmen given no special help or feedback in the development of the same paper. Students from two sections of freshman English at the University of Wisconsin were used as subjects. The authors undertook a detailed examination of the registration procedure to satisfy themselves (and their readers) that the assignment of students to sections occurred on an essentially random basis. Having obtained this assurance, they utilized the posttest-only control group design with one section receiving the treatment. The use of a control group and the unbiased assignment of Ss to conditions provide a suitable control for all sources of internal validity. The posttest-only control group design is recommended where such requirements can be met.

Pretest-Posttest Control Group Design

The pretest-posttest control group design can be diagrammed as shown below.

$$R \quad O_1 \quad X \quad O_2$$
$$R \quad O_3 \qquad O_4$$

Through the use of analysis of covariance it is possible to control the effects of a variable statistically.

As can be seen from the diagram, two groups are employed in this design; one group, the experimental group, receives a treatment (X) while the second group, the control group, does not. (The assignment of subjects to both groups is accomplished on a random basis.)* Both groups are given a pretest and a posttest —the use of a pretest being the only difference between this design and the previous one.

By the utilization of a control group, which has all the same experiences as the experimental group other than the experience of the treatment itself, this design controls for history, maturation, and regression. By randomizing subjects across experimental and control conditions, both selection and mortality are controlled. This design, therefore, controls many threats to validity or sources of bias.

However, the use of a pretest does introduce additional slight design difficulties than those encountered in the posttest-only control group design. There is no control for a *testing effect* (i.e., gain on the posttest due to experience on the pretest) which may reduce internal validity; nor is there any control for the possible sensitization to the treatment that a subject might gain by having the pretest experience, thus affecting external validity. In other words, a testing by treatment interaction is not controlled for in this design. Moreover, this design lacks control for the artificiality of an experiment, a set which may well be established through the use of a pretest.

In summary, then, what may be said about this design is that it controls for all the simple sources of invalidity, but by virtue of its use of a pretest does not control for the testing sources of invalidity (both simple and interactive) that may often plague a study. When the researcher feels a strong need to collect pretest data on the dependent variable and has little fear that the pretest will provide a simple posttest gain or a differential sensitivity to the treatment, he may use this design. However, when the researcher has a reason to suspect that the pretest may provide such factors, it is recommended that he use the posttest-only control group design. Indeed, under most circumstances the posttest-only control group design should be used since random assignment of Ss to conditions is generally considered adequate for control of selection bias—avoidance of a pretest also saves time and money. Obviously, however, when the experimenter is interested in assessing degree of change, the availability of pretest data is necessary.

In analyzing the data from the pretest-posttest control group design, the researcher can compare gain scores for the two groups. That is, he can compare the mean of $O_2 - O_1$ with the mean of $O_4 - O_3$ in order to determine whether the

Matching may be used prior to randomizing if desired.

treatment had a differential effect on the groups. It is also possible to compare the groups on the pretest (O_1 mean versus the mean for O_3). If the groups are equivalent, the posttest means (O_2 versus O_4) can be compared to evaluate the treatment.

The use of this design is aptly illustrated in the study by Lockmiller and DiNello (1970), two sections of which appear on pages 93–95. In this study a reading test and a phonics skills test were administered to experimental and control groups on a pretest basis. (Assignment of Ss to experimental and control conditions was accomplished on a random basis.) Experimental Ss then experienced a *Words in Color* reading program while control Ss experienced a traditional basal reader program. Following the treatment, all Ss were retested on an alternate form of the reading test and the same form of the phonics skills test.

Data analyses were undertaken for pretest and posttest administrations *separately* on each of the two measures (and for boys and girls separately). That is, rather than comparing gain scores (posttest minus pretest) for experimental and control Ss, pretest scores for each group were compared to assess pre-experiment equivalence of groups (even though Ss had been assigned randomly to groups), and posttest scores for each group were then compared to determine the effects of the treatment. This procedure is commonly used and is an acceptable alternative to the comparison of gain scores.*

6.4 FACTORIAL DESIGNS

Factorial designs are modifications of the true experimental designs described above with the further complication that additional independent variables (usually moderator variables) are included in addition to the treatment variable. An illustration of the modification of the posttest-only control group design with one treatment variable into a factorial design with one treatment variable and one moderator variable (the moderator variable is indicated by the letter Y with two levels, Y_1 and Y_2) is diagrammed as follows

$$
\begin{array}{cccc}
R & X & Y_1 & O_1 \\
R &   & Y_1 & O_2 \\
R & X & Y_2 & O_3 \\
R &   & Y_2 & O_4
\end{array}
$$

*Often posttest scores are analyzed by means of a statistical procedure called analysis of covariance, using the pretest scores as a statistical covariate to control for initial group differences.

It is shown that two groups receive the treatment and two groups do not. One group receiving the treatment and one group not receiving the treatment are simultaneously categorized as Y_1 while the remaining two groups, one receiving and one not receiving the treatment, are categorized Y_2. Thus, if Y_1 represented a high intelligence subgroup and Y_2 a lower intelligence subgroup, only half of the high intelligence subgroup would be receiving the treatment, with only half of the lower intelligence subgroup receiving the treatment. Moreover, the half to be given or not given the treatment is determined on a random basis.

It is equally possible to create a factorial design by modifying the pretest-posttest control group design. This is illustrated below, again for a two-factor situation.

$$
\begin{array}{cccccc}
R & O_1 & X & Y_1 & O_2 \\
R & O_3 & & Y_1 & O_4 \\
R & O_5 & X & Y_2 & O_6 \\
R & O_7 & & Y_2 & O_8
\end{array}
$$

The above design was utilized in Sample Study I, Appendix A. A pretest was utilized since the dependent variable was a measure of change thus requiring a baseline against which change could be measured. In Sample Study I, teachers were separated into three Y groups (Y representing years of teaching experience). Teachers from each Y group were then randomly assigned to one of four treatment groups (X). Pretest and posttest data were collected in each condition. The design for Sample Study I appears in Figure 6.1.

In dealing with an independent variable and a moderator variable, it is important to recognize that when the moderator variable is an individual difference measure (as was true in Sample Study I), subjects cannot be randomly assigned to the different levels of the moderator variable. The moderator variable in Sample Study I identifies teachers with different amounts of teaching experience to be assigned to the appropriate level of that variable or factor. However, teachers within each level on the moderator variable are then randomly assigned to each condition or level on the independent variable to insure that all other selection characteristics (other than amount of teaching experience) are randomized across conditions within each level of teaching experience.

All that can be said of the true experimental designs can be said of factorial designs with the addition that the factorial design makes it possible to deal systematically with more than one independent variable. That is, within the factorial designs, more than one variable can be manipulated and thus studied.

Treatments (X)

R	O_1	X_1	Y_1	O_2	X_1	student feedback
R	O_3	X_2	Y_1	O_4	X_2	supervisor feedback
R	O_5	X_3	Y_1	O_6	X_3	student plus supervisor feedback
R	O_7	X_0	Y_1	O_8	X_0	no feedback (control)

- - - - - - - - - - - -

R	O_9	X_1	Y_2	O_{10}
R	O_{11}	X_2	Y_2	O_{12}
R	O_{13}	X_3	Y_2	O_{14}
R	O_{15}	X_0	Y_2	O_{16}

- - - - - - - - - - - - Moderator (Y)

R	O_{17}	X_1	Y_3	O_{18}	Y_1	1–3 years of teaching experience
R	O_{19}	X_2	Y_3	O_{20}	Y_2	4–10 years of teaching experience
R	O_{21}	X_3	Y_3	O_{22}	Y_3	11 or more years of teaching
R	O_{23}	X_0	Y_3	O_{24}		experience

Figure 6.1 *Factorial design (4 × 3) for Sample Study I.*

Within the factorial design, it is possible to assess the effect of each independent variable separately as well as their conjoint or simultaneous effect.* Thus, the researcher can see how one of the variables might moderate the other. The diagram below illustrates the relationship between the various observations (of the dependent variable) in the factorial design and the two independent variables being studied. (One of these latter variables is typically called a moderator variable.) By comparing the observations under X_1 (i.e., O_{X1}) to the observations

$$
\begin{array}{c c c}
 & X_1 & X_0 \\
Y_1 & \boxed{\begin{array}{cc} O_1 & O_2 \end{array}} & O_{Y1} \\
Y_2 & \begin{array}{cc} O_3 & O_4 \end{array} & O_{Y2} \\
 & O_{X1} & O_{XO}
\end{array}
$$

Statistically, the procedure used is an analysis of variance. The above illustration would require a two-way analysis of variance (see Chapter 9).

under X_0 (i.e., O_{X0}), it is possible to contrast the effects of the treatment with the control. By comparing the observations in the Y_1 row (i.e., O_{Y1}) to the observations of the Y_2 row (i.e., O_{Y2}), it is possible to contrast the effects of level 1 of the Y variable to the effects of level 2 of the Y variable. Furthermore, by contrasting the individual cell effects, O_1 versus O_3 and O_2 versus O_4, it is possible to identify the simultaneous effects of X and Y variables that might exist.*

Suppose, for example, that X_1 was an intensive program to improve memory, while X_0 was a control condition including reading but no memory training. The moderator variable (Y) might then be immediate memory span, with Y_1 being persons high on this measure and Y_2 persons low on this measure. The findings might be something like those illustrated in Figure 6.2

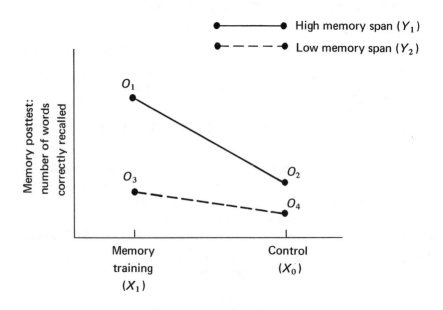

Figure 6.2 *Results of memory experiment.*

The data suggest that the training is having an overall salutory effect (both O_1 and O_3 are higher than O_2 and O_4), and that high memory span persons do better than low memory span ones (O_1 is higher than O_3, O_2 is higher than O_4). In addition, the Y variable seems to moderate the X variable. That is, the effects of the training are more pronounced for persons of high memory span than for

*This simultaneous effect is called an interaction. It is described in the discussion of analysis of variance in Chapter 9. (See, particularly, Figure 9.3.)

those of low memory span. Thus, the two independent variables seem to have a conjoint effect as well as separate effects. (Of course, these conclusions would have to be substantiated by an analysis of variance.) The factorial design is useful because it allows the researcher to identify the simultaneous as well as separate effects of independent variables. That is, it allows for the inclusion of one or more moderator variables.

6.5 QUASI-EXPERIMENTAL DESIGNS

Quasi-experimental designs are partly—but not fully—true experimental designs; they control some but not all of the sources of internal invalidity. Although they are not as adequate as the true experimental designs (since the sources of bias are not amply controlled), they are substantially better than the pre-experimental designs, with regard to control of the threats to validity.

Quasi-experimental designs exist for situations in which complete experimental control is difficult or impossible. The real educational world, i.e., that world confronting the educational researcher, is fraught with real limitations upon the researcher's ability to select or assign subjects and manipulate conditions. It is possible that school systems may not accept new programs for testing on an experimental basis, may not allow intact classes to be disrupted or divided to provide for random or equivalent samples, may not allow for a "treatment" to be given to some and withheld from others, while insisting—if it seems good— that it be given to all, and—if it seems bad—that it be given to none, and may not provide an opportunity for pretesting in advance of the implementation of some program or change.

In the past, researchers often would throw up their hands in despair and retreat to the laboratory or advance upon the real "noise" (the uncontrolled and uncontrollable variables) of the educational milieu with the pre-experimental designs as their inadequate tools. Now the quasi-experimental designs, because they carry experimental control to its reasonable limit within the realities of a particular situation (while acknowledging those factors not dealt with as completely as would have been possible using the true experimental designs) present a workable solution.

Campbell and Stanley (1963) suggest many quasi-experimental designs.* The ones most generally applicable will be dealt with here.

While knowledge of these designs has been with us for some time, their popularity and more widespread use in educational research is a recent development.

Time-Series Design

As has been discussed earlier, there are times when a comparison or control group cannot be included in an experiment. When a change is to occur in an entire school system, for example, it may be impossible to find a second school system which (1) is in most ways comparable to the first, (2) has not also incorporated the change, and (3) is willing to cooperate. Change often occurs without providing a control group for the comfort of the researcher. Faced with this predicament, he might consider the one-shot case study or the one group pretest-posttest design. However, a third solution which provides better control is the time-series design diagrammed below:

$$O_1 O_2 O_3 O_4 \quad X \quad O_5 O_6 O_7 O_8$$

The time-series design differs from the one group pretest-posttest design in that a series of pretest and posttests are given, rather than a single test of each. Administered over a period of time, these series provide for the control of maturation (particularly) and in some degree for history—two important sources of internal invalidity totally uncontrolled by the one group pretest-posttest design. The time series also offers the advantage of controlling for testing effects, since repeated exposure to a single pretest is likely to lead to adaptation or desensitization while any testing effects that do occur may not be expected to persevere through the series of posttests.

It is impossible to rule out history as a source of invalidity when using this design, but its effect usually can be minimized. In general, any effects of extraneous events should occur across all of the observations and could then be inferred from an examination of O_1 to O_8. The possible (but improbable) simultaneous occurrence of an extraneous event to the application of the treatment X, neither preceding it nor following it, but only being coincident with it, would invalidate conclusions drawn from this design for reasons of historical bias. (See Figure 6.3.)

Although the time-series design does not control for history as well as a true experimental design, it does help the researcher to interpret the extent to which history is a source of confounding and thus is more adequate than alternative single-group designs. In addition, the time-series design controls threats to validity (except, perhaps, instrumentation).

One practical limitation in the use of this design is the unavailability of data to serve as the multiple pretest observations (O_1-O_4). A researcher is often dependent on the school system to collect this data as a regular part of its assessment program. If such data represent achievement, they are usually available as a regular

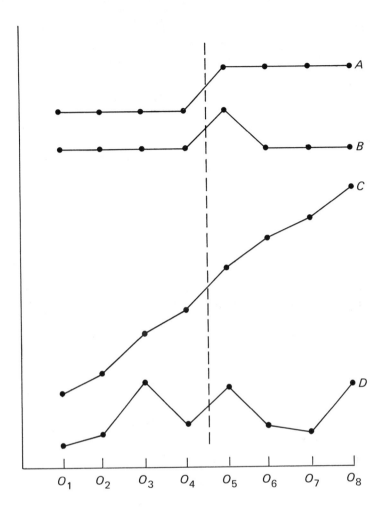

Figure 6.3 *Some possible outcomes using the time-series design with measurements O_1–O_8 and a treatment (X) between O_4 and O_5. (While the O_4–O_5 gain is the same in each instance, the inference of an effect is most justified in A and B and unjustified in C and D.)*

part of school records (such as regular achievement test scores). However, if such data represent attitudes, the researcher would have to plan well in advance of the treatment to begin to collect these data. Webb et al. (1966) suggest the *morale ballot*, a new measurement device for inclusion in the school's regular assessment battery. If attitude data were made available on a regular basis, the time-series design would increase in practicality. Eliminating advance planning and testing would also reduce the likelihood that testing would function as a source of external invalidity by sensitizing participants to the treatment.

The use of the time series is illustrated in Chapter 1 in the example concerning traffic fatalities in Connecticut.*

Equivalent Time-Samples Design

Like the time-series design, the equivalent time-samples design is used when only a single group is available for study and the group's pattern of experience with the treatment is highly predetermined—that is, the researcher must expose the group to the treatment on some systematic basis. This design is diagrammed below:

$$X_1 \quad O_1 \quad X_0 \quad O_2 \quad X_1 \quad O_3 \quad X_0 \quad O_4$$

It, too, is a form of time-series design but, rather than introducing the treatment (X_1) only a single time, it is introduced and reintroduced, with some other experience (X_0) being available in the absence of the treatment.

The equivalent time-samples design satisfies the requirements of internal validity, including controlling for historical bias. In this regard, it is superior to the time-series design. The likelihood that a compelling extraneous event will occur simultaneously with each presentation of the treatment (X_1) is highly unlikely. Thus, a comparison of the average of O_1 and O_3 with the average of O_2 and O_4 will yield a result which is not likely to be invalidated by historical bias. Moreover, as shown below, the analysis can be set up to determine order effects as well:

	First Administration	Second Administration
X_1	O_1	O_3
X_0	O_2	O_4

Consider the following example of the use of this design. An art teacher wishes to determine the effect of a museum field trip on the attitudes and knowledge of his students in art. He takes his class to the local art museum in lieu of the regularly scheduled art class for the week (X_1). Following the trip, he admin-

*Simple statistical comparisons of O_4 and O_5 are to be avoided in analyzing the results of a time-series experiment. Comparisons among all pairs of adjacent points or measures of the slope and intercept characteristics of the series are recommended.

isters a test of art knowledge and a measure of attitudes (O_1). The following week he holds his regular art appreciation class (X_0) and subsequently measures knowledge and attitudes toward art (O_2). In the third week he returns with his class to the local museum and concentrates on another portion of the collection (X_1). Knowledge and attitudes are again measured (O_3). The last week involves normal class activity (X_0) and measurement (O_4).

The analysis of the data in this study is set up as shown above. A comparison of O_1 and O_3 with O_2 and O_4 allows the teacher to compare the two experiences. The interaction between the four measurements allows him to check on differential changes over time. Simple time effects can be determined by comparing O_1 and O_2 to O_3 and O_4. Selection factors are controlled by using the same Ss in both conditions (using Ss as their own controls).* History bias is unlikely to affect just the museum trips and not the regular classes, particularly since the treatment is experienced on two separate occasions. Other sources of invalidity do not pose any major threat to this design.

One weakness in the equivalent time-samples design is in the area of external validity. If the effect of the treatment is different when continuous than when dispersed, it will be impossible to generalize beyond the experiment. That is, if the effect of X_1 when it is administered over time $(X_1 \longrightarrow)$ is different from its effect when introduced and reintroduced (as it is in the equivalent time-samples designs, $X_1 X_0 X_1 X_0$, then it would be difficult to make valid conclusions about the continuous effect of X_1 from a study using the equivalent time-samples design. Moreover, some treatments lead to adaptation as a function of repeated presentation, again lessening the external validity of this design.

Thus, the equivalent time-samples design is an improvement on the time-series design in controlling for history, but it introduces certain problems of external validity which, if relevant, weaken its applicability. Like all of the quasi-experimental designs, this one has strengths and weaknesses and must be used in situations which maximize its strengths.

Nonequivalent Control Group Design

Often in educational research, the researcher is not in a position to assign subjects randomly to treatments. While the principal of a school may be willing to make two math classes available for testing, he is not likely to permit a researcher to break them up and reconstitute them; rather, he intends them to be kept as intact groups. Moreover, there is reason to believe that these classes may

*This procedure for controlling selection threats to validity was described in Chapter 5.

have been originally composed on some systematic basis (thus creating a bias for researcher purposes). In working with such intact nonequivalent groups, the nonequivalent control group design, shown below, is recommended.

$$O_1 \quad X \quad O_2$$
$$- \; - \; - \; - \; - \; -$$
$$O_3 \qquad O_4$$

This design is identical to the pretest-posttest control group design in all respects *except for the random assignment of subjects to conditions.* If the assignment to conditions is not made by the experimenter, he cannot assume randomness unless he can demonstrate satisfactorily that assignment by the school's scheduling staff was done on a random basis. Should there be any doubt, or any bias suspected, then this design rather than a true design should be used. The procedures for this design are the same as for a true design except that intact groups rather than randomly assigned ones are used, creating a control problem in terms of selection bias. This problem mandates the use of a pretest to demonstrate initial equivalence of the intact groups on the dependent variable.

The use of intact nonequivalent classes rather than randomized or matched groups (shown by the use of a dashed line between groups and the absence of the R designation) creates potential difficulty in controlling for selection and experimental mortality bias. To overcome the potential selection bias that the use of this design might create, the researcher can compare the intact groups on pretest scores (O_1 versus O_3) and on scores on any control variables appropriate to selection and potentially relevant to the treatment such as I.Q., sex, age, and so on. Note that the use of the pretest is quite essential here as compared to a true experimental design.

In the recommended posttest-only control group design, no pretest is used. In the pretest-posttest control group design, a pretest is used but only as a baseline to evaluate changes that occur or as a further safeguard, beyond random assignment, to control for selection bias. In the nonequivalent control group design, a pretest *must* be employed to provide any control for selection bias. Only through a pretest can initial group equivalence be demonstrated (in the absence of randomized assignment).

Failure to have randomly assigned groups necessitates some basis for initially comparing groups; the pretest provides this basis. Thus, faced with two intact classes for comparing the process approach to teaching science with the traditional textbook approach, the researcher at the outset of the experiment would compare groups on science achievement, primarily, but also possibly on age and sex to be sure that the groups were equivalent. If they prove to be equivalent, the researcher can continue with less concern about selection (or mortality) bias operating as a threat to internal validity. If the groups are not equivalent on relevant measures, then alternative designs must be sought. However, what is more often true is first, that the bias which possibly might occur in group assignment in a study is on irrelevant variables and second, that pretest means on the dependent and control variables of the study are equivalent, thus making this design a good choice.

The nonequivalent control group design, therefore, is not as good as the pretest-posttest control group design but it is greatly superior to the one-group pretest-posttest design. There is one situation in which caution must be exercised in the use of the nonequivalent control group design: where the experimental group is self-selected, that is, they are volunteers. Comparing a group of volunteers to a group of nonvolunteers does not control for selection because volunteers are different from nonvolunteers—at least in terms of the volunteering behavior and all that underlies it. Where the researcher has maximum control over group assignment, he should recruit twice as many volunteers as the treatment can accommodate and randomly divide them into two groups—an experimental group which receives the treatment and a control group from which it is withheld. Effects of the treatment versus its absence on some dependent variable would then be evaluated using one of the two true experimental designs. When the volunteers cannot be split into the two groups, the separate-sample pretest-posttest design should be used (see next page). The nonequivalent control group design, on the other hand, is usually inappropriate where one intact group is composed of volunteers, the other not. While it is intended for the situation where there is reason to suspect some bias in the assignment of persons to intact groups, its use requires that this bias not be relevant to the dependent variable (as evidenced by group pretest equivalence). The bias imposed by comparing volunteers to nonvolunteers is typically relevant to almost any dependent variable.

A study conducted by a group of three students in a research methods course illustrates the use of the nonequivalent control group design. The purpose of their study was to assess the effects of a program intended to improve handwriting among third graders. The school they were able to gain access to consisted of two third-grade classes, but there was no evidence that the classes had been composed without bias. The principal of the school was not willing to allow the researchers to alter the composition of the classes and it was not possible to undertake both treatment and control conditions in the same classroom (i.e., the treatment was a class activity). Consequently, the nonequivalent control group design was employed. The decision of which of the two classes was to receive the treatment was made on a random basis (a coin was flipped). A handwriting test, measuring the dependent variable, was administered on a pre- and posttreatment basis. Moreover, the equivalence of the two intact classes on a number of control variables was ascertained, namely: sex, chronological age, standardized vocabulary test score, standardized reading comprehension test score, involvement in instrumental music lessons, and presence of physical disorders. Thus the researchers satisfactorily established that the possible selection bias existing between the groups was not strongly relevant to the comparisons to be made in the study. The effect of the treatment was assessed by comparing the gain scores (that is, posttest minus pretest) of the two groups on the dependent variable.*

In summary, the nonequivalent control group design, in terms of its ability to control for selection bias, is midway between the unacceptable intact-group comparison (a pre-experimental design) and the pretest-posttest control group design (a true experimental design). It is weaker than the latter for failure to include randomized assignment of Ss to groups but stronger than the former by virtue of the inclusion of a pretest providing initial data on the equivalence of the intact groups on dependent and control variables. Where intact groups (i.e., groups whose membership were not determined by the researcher) are employed for experimental and control purposes, the researcher can partially control for selection bias by demonstrating that the groups are initially equivalent on relevant variables.

Separate-Sample Pretest-Posttest Design

Consider a research situation in which it would be impossible to provide the treatment to all the subjects at the same time—for instance, a training program which is to be made available to 1000 students but can accommodate only 100 persons *at one time*. Thus, the program would have to run continuously, filling its ranks anew each time it started over again. (Many training and remedial treatment programs, in fact, do operate in this manner.) Because all of the students are being included in the program at some point in time, they cannot be assigned to training and nontraining conditions; thus it would be impossible to use a true design. Since each person would receive the treatment only once and would be unavailable for advance testing, the equivalent time-samples and time-series designs could not be used.

Analysis of covariance is also often used in these cases.

To deal with a situation that at first glance seems uncontrollable, it is possible to take an inadequate design, the one-group pretest-posttest design, and repeat it twice as shown below:

$$O_1 \quad X \quad O_2$$

$$- \; - \; - \; - \; - \; - \; - \; -$$

$$O_3 \quad X \quad O_4$$

By repeating the one-group pretest-posttest design ($O_1 \; X \; O_2$) twice, it is possible to overcome one of the major shortcomings of this pre-experimental design: its failure to control for history. In the one-group pretest-posttest design it is possible to conclude that some other event occurring simultaneously to X caused O_2. Using the separate-sample pretest-posttest design, if $O_2 > O_1$ and $O_4 > O_3$, it is unlikely that some other event would have occurred simultaneously to X on *both administrations*, thus lending validity to the conclusion that X caused O. While the other-event "theory" (i.e., history bias) is still a possibility, it is rather unlikely.

In particular this separate-sample pretest-posttest design is vulnerable to three sources of internal invalidity. The first of these is invalidity due to a simple *testing* effect brought on by the use of a pretest. Since a pretest is essential to this design in controlling for selection bias, the researcher must avoid the use of highly sensitizing pretest measures.

A second source of invalidity is *maturation*. The major control comparison in this design is O_3 versus O_2. However, the second group is usually at an earlier maturational point at its inception than the first group is at its completion. If a group of students begins a one-year training program at an average age of 18, then O_2 occurs at an average age of 19 for the group while O_3 occurs at an average age of 18. Comparing 19 year olds to 18 year olds creates the possibility that maturation will serve as a threat to validity. This threat may be compensated for by converting one of the groups in the separate-sample design to a kind of time-series design as follows:

$$O_1 \quad X \quad O_2$$

$$- \; - \; - \; - \; - \; - \; - \; -$$

$$O_5 \qquad O_3 \quad X \quad O_4$$

Note that O_5 has been added, making this version of the separate-sample design also a version of the nonequivalent control group design. However, it is often impossible to make such a change since one of the conditions necessitating the use of the separate-sample design is being able to test subjects only immediately before and after the treatment.

The threat posed by maturation to a separate-sample pretest-posttest type of design is further illustrated in a doctoral study (mentioned on page 3) of the effects of student teaching on students' perceptions of the teaching profession. To control for the history bias encountered when this kind of study is done without a control group, the doctoral candidate used this separate-sample design:

$$O_1 \qquad O_2 \qquad \text{(Juniors)}$$
$$-\ -\ -\ -\ -\ -\ -\ -\ -$$
$$O_3 \qquad O_4 \quad X \quad O_5 \qquad \text{(Seniors)}$$

The subjects of the study experience student teaching in the spring of the senior year. It would be difficult to evaluate the effects of student teaching on students' perceptions of the profession without the availability of a comparable control group. Students not in the teacher education program would make a poor control group since their perceptions of teaching as a profession are likely to be different from those in the program, and the use of a longitudinal study perhaps involving the time-series design would require more time than most doctoral candidates can be expected to have. The researcher solved the problem by utilizing juniors in the teacher education program to serve as a "control," creating a variant of either the separate-sample or nonequivalent control group designs. While the use of juniors as a control group controlled for threats to internal validity without creating insurmountable bias based on selection, maturation posed a major threat. Seniors are older and have had more educational experiences than juniors and can be expected to differ, therefore, on perceptions of their chosen profession simply as a function of maturation. To check this, O_3 was added. If $O_4 - O_3$ exceeded $O_2 - O_1$, then the latter difference could be considered to be a function of maturation rather than of the treatment of student teaching.

The third source of invalidity to which the separate-sample pretest-posttest design is susceptible is based on the *interaction of selection and maturation*. Little can be done to offset this possibility.

"Patched-Up" Design

The separate-sample pretest-posttest design was essentially built on a pre-experimental design ($O\ X\ O$) being used twice. The patched-up design shown here is based on two different pre-experimental designs, neither of which by itself is adequate, but which, in combination, can create an adequate design.* It is especially useful in situations like those previously described where a particular training program runs continuously with new persons (students graduating and entering) and where the researcher has no opportunity to withhold treatment from anyone. Moreover, the patched-up design shown here allows the study to begin in the middle of a training program rather than at its inception.

Recall that the one-group pretest-posttest design ($O \ X \ O$) provided some control over selection effects but totally failed to control for history, maturation, and regression. Recall also that the intact-group comparison $\left(\dfrac{X \_ \ O_1}{O_2} \right)$ controlled for maturation and history but totally failed to control for selection. The patched-up design shown below combines these two pre-experimental designs to merge their strengths and overcome their shortcomings.

$$\text{Class A} \quad X \quad O_1$$
$$\text{-- -- -- -- -- --}$$
$$\text{Class B} \qquad \quad O_2 \quad X \quad O_3$$

The comparison O_2 versus O_1 is the intact-group comparison and cannot be explained away by maturation or history. O_3 versus O_2 is the one-group pretest-posttest comparison and cannot be explained away by selection. If the O_2 versus O_1 and O_3 versus O_2 comparisons are reasonably equal, then neither history, maturation, nor selection can be considered to account for the outcome.

This design illustrates the creative aspect of generating quasi-experimental designs, particularly from the building blocks of the pre-experimental designs, to deal with situations where total experimental control (a prerequisite for true experimental designs) is not possible. In using this patched-up design, everybody gets the treatment; this cannot be controlled by the experimenter. However, he can control when and to whom the treatment is given at a particular point in time. Thus, the groups get the treatment sequentially and are compared: the pretest score of the second group to its own posttest score, and to the posttest score of the first group.

6.6 EX POST FACTO DESIGNS

The term *ex post facto* is used here to refer to an experiment in which the researcher examines the effects of a naturalistically-occurring treatment after

The two variants of the separate-sample pretest-posttest design illustrated in the preceding section can also be considered "patched-up" designs.

that treatment has occurred rather than creating the treatment himself. The experimenter attempts to relate this after-the-fact treatment to an outcome or dependent measure. While the naturalistic or ex post facto experiment may not always be diagrammed differently from other designs that have been described, it is different in that the treatment is included by selection rather than manipulation. For this reason, it is not always possible to assume a simple causative relation between independent and dependent variables. If the relationship fails to be obtained, then it is likely that no causative relationship holds. But if the predicted relationship *is* obtained, this does not necessarily mean that the variables studied are causally related. (This point will be dealt with in more detail later.) Two types of ex post facto designs—the co-relational design and the criterion-group design—will be discussed below.

Co-Relational Study

A co-relational study* involves the collection of two or more sets of data from a group of subjects with the attempt to determine the subsequent relationship between those sets of data. This type of approach might be diagrammed as follows:

$$O_1 \quad O_2$$

Consider the following example. Borkowski (1970) attempted to show a relationship between the quality of a music teacher's undergraduate training and his subsequent teaching effectiveness. Measures of the quality of a music teacher's undergraduate training (O_1) included grades in specific courses, overall grade average, self-ratings, etc. Measures of teaching effectiveness (O_2) included indices of pupil performance, pupil knowledge, judgments by experts, etc. Correlations between all measures were obtained to determine the relationship. Note that the researcher could not assign teachers to training programs, nor control training through the use of a control group. At most, this study could show that a relationship existed, after-the-fact, between quality of teacher preparation and teaching effectiveness.

Occasionally, an experimenter will suggest, following a co-relational study,

---

*This designation has been chosen to suggest that the purpose of the design is simply to show that a relationship exists between variables. While correlations are the statistics typically employed in analyzing such data, they are by no means exclusive in this regard.

that the variable that O_1 is measuring has caused O_2. However, a strong relationship between O_1 and O_2 suggests one of three possible interpretations:

1. the variable that O_1 is measuring has caused O_2 (as the experimenter has suggested);
2. the variable that O_2 is measuring has caused O_1;
3. some third, unmeasured, variable has caused both O_1 and O_2.

Since the experimenter has not caused any variable to operate by his own manipulation or assignment but has merely sampled the existence of characteristics, he cannot tell which of the above three interpretations accounts for the relationship. A weak relationship or no relationship suggests that he reject all three interpretations but a strong relationship does not help him choose among the possibilities.

Co-relational studies serve a useful purpose in determining the relationship among measures and *suggesting* possible bases for causality. While correlation does not necessarily imply causation, causation necessarily implies correlation. As a next step, the researcher can design a study employing a treatment which he himself controls.

Co-relational studies, then, are not adequate themselves for establishing causal relationships among variables but may be a useful first step in this direction.

Criterion-Group Design

When a researcher is working in an ongoing educational environment, particularly when he is interested in generating some hypotheses about what causes a particular state or condition, it is often helpful to begin by contrasting the characteristics of a state with the characteristics of its opposite state using the criterion-group approach.

Suppose, for example, that a researcher were interested in studying the factors that contribute to teaching effectiveness. Before he could conduct a true experiment intended to produce effective teachers by design, he would first need some ideas about what factors make a difference between effective and ineffective teaching. In the criterion-group approach, he would begin by identifying the two criterion groups: effective teachers and ineffective teachers. This might be done by employing students' judgments or supervisors' judgments. The next step would be to contrast the classroom behavior of these two groups of teachers in order to identify possible outcomes of teacher effectiveness. The researcher could also examine the background and skills of these two teacher groups to discover what might "cause" only some teachers to be effective.

Contrast this example with the one offered to illustrate the co-relational study. In the latter example, Borkowski (1970) attempted to determine whether teacher training contributed to teacher effectiveness. Rather than comparing effective versus ineffective teachers (i.e., using the criterion-group approach), he examined teachers along a range or continuum of effectiveness in terms of the quality of their undergraduate preparation. The criterion-group study and co-relational study are simply alternative ways of identifying an existing relationship between two variables.

However, it would be incorrect to conclude from either study that the *causes* of teaching effectiveness are thus identified since identification was accomplished on an after-the-fact basis. To establish a causal relationship, it would be necessary to create a training program and compare the effectiveness of teachers who have gone through the program with teachers trained in some other manner. Another possibility would be to examine the relationship between every conceivable cause of teaching effectiveness and subsequent effectiveness to gain confidence in drawing any conclusions about causation.

The criterion-group design can be diagrammed as follows:

$$C \quad O_1 \qquad\qquad O_1 \quad C \quad O_2 \qquad\qquad C \quad O_1{}^*$$
$$\text{or} \quad -\ -\ -\ -\ - \quad \text{or} \quad -\ -\ -$$
$$O_2 \qquad\qquad O_3 \qquad O_4 \qquad\qquad O_2$$

Rather than using X, which stands for a manipulated experience or treatment, the letter C, standing for selection of an experience according to a criterion, has been employed. Such an approach is used in instances where the assignment of subjects with criterion experiences is done randomly from among a larger group of Ss all qualifying on the criterion variable or where intact groups of criterion and non-criterion Ss are used. Similarly, the criterion-group approach can be used in a factorial design, as shown below:

$$\begin{array}{ccc} C_1 & Y_1 & O_1 \\ \hline C_2 & Y_1 & O_2 \\ \hline C_1 & Y_2 & O_3 \\ \hline C_2 & Y_2 & O_4 \end{array}$$

*Note the similarity between this design and the co-relation design ($O_1\ O_2$). This design is similar to a nondesign. However, it is not used primarily to establish cause and effect relationships.

This approach is illustrated in a study by Tuckman (1968) contrasting directive and nondirective teaching styles. Rather than attempting to train teachers to behave in directive and nondirective ways, an instrument was developed to determine the manner in which the teacher taught naturally. This instrument was then used to identify a group of directive teachers (C_1) and a group of nondirective teachers (C_2). The performance and attitudes of students in the classes of the directive teachers (O_1, O_3) were subsequently compared with the performance and attitudes of students having nondirective teachers (O_2, O_4). (Teachers were further subdivided into vocational Y_1 and nonvocational Y_2.) Rather than a manipulation, a naturalistic difference was exploited by selecting teachers on the criterion measure and comparing the reactions of their students. Contrast this to the Lippitt and White (1958) experiment, described in the previous chapter, in which teaching (or leadership) styles were created by instruction, making the use of a true experimental design possible.

The criterion-group approach is thus used in two contexts. In the *first* context, an attempt is made to determine what characteristics are associated with the criterion group and have presumably preceded and thereby caused the criterion behavior—that is, how have those people who possess the criterion been previously trained, or what experiences have they had, or what kinds of personalities do they have, and so on. While it is difficult to establish causality, it is possible to identify *potential* causes which often can then be tested more directly by manipulation. Consider the following illustration. Suppose a researcher wanted to determine the origins of creativity. To this end he might administer a battery of tests designed to measure creativity to a group of students. On the basis of those test scores he would then identify a criterion group of students who score high on these tests and their counterparts, students who score low. He might then administer a questionnaire to the parents of both groups to identify particular experiences that the criterion group have had that their counterparts have lacked. Because the experiences have not been manipulated by the experimenter with *Ss* being randomly assigned to conditions he could not conclude that these experiences have caused creativity. He might, however, have generated some testable hypotheses from this criterion-group approach (some of which might be testable using a criterion-group approach; the others would probably require a quasi- or true experimental design).

In the *second* context, illustrated by the directive versus nondirective teacher study, the criterion-group approach might better have been called a *naturalistic study*. In this context, a criterion group (directive teachers) and its counterpart (nondirective teachers) are also identified but the purpose of the study, then, is to assess the differential effects of the criterion group and its counterpart on an entirely different group (their students).* In this context, the criterion-group approach is a way to bring to bear a differential treatment. It too has limitations in the identification of causality. Since nothing is created by the experimenter, he cannot be sure whether the criterion group (i.e., teachers) characteristic caused the behavior of the student group or whether the reverse was true. While the former is often more likely than the latter, it is not unquestionable.

6.7 DESIGNS TO CONTROL FOR EXTERNAL INVALIDITY BASED ON REACTIVE EFFECTS[†]

Whenever an innovation or experimental intervention of any sort is tested in a real environment such as an educational system, the likelihood arises that an effect will accrue based not on the specifics of the intervention but rather on the simple fact that the experiment is being conducted. This has been referred to as the *reactive effect of experimental arrangements*—a common threat to external validity (see page 80). The Hawthorne effect, based on industrial studies completed in the late 1920's in the General Electric Hawthorne works in Chicago, is a prevalent reactive effect. The Hawthorne studies showed that workers' productivity increased during their participation in an experiment regardless of what other experimental changes were introduced. Apparently workers changed because of the fact that they were being observed and considered themselves to be important by virtue of their participation in an experiment. (See page 49.)

Many studies in which an experimental treatment in a school system is compared to a no-treatment or no-intervention condition may result in differences based not on the specifics of the intervention, but on the fact that some intervention took place. That is, the benefits may not accrue from what the intervention consists of but from the fact that there was simply some form of intervention. The effects may not be *true* but *reactive*—i.e., a function of the experiment—and thus externally invalid.

Similar problems in experiments can result from the expectancy that certain key figures in an experiment, such as teachers, may have about the effects that are likely to occur—another reactive effect. Such expectancies operate, for instance, in drug research. If the drug administrator were to know what drug was

*In essence, the first use of this design is to identify the antecedents of the criterion characteristic while the second is to identify its consequences. A third use is to identify concomitants of the criterion (Are more creative youngsters more intelligent than less creative ones?).

[†]This section is based on material reported by Rosenthal (1966) and Rosenthal and Jacobson (1968). While some of the findings of the latter study have been challenged, the methodology dealt with here has not been.

being administered he would have certain expectancies regarding its potential effect. For this reason, it is considered best for the drug administrator to operate in-the-blind, that is, to be unaware of the kind of drug in order that his expectancies not affect the outcome of the experiment.

Designs to Control for Hawthorne Effect

Rather than designing an experiment to test an experimental intervention by including the typical two groups (the experimental group and the control group) there is value in introducing a *second* control group which specifically provides for the control of the Hawthorne effect. What is the difference between a no-treatment control and a *Hawthorne control*? A no-treatment control, typically employed in intervention studies, involves no contact at all between the experimenter and the subjects except for the collection of pretest (where necessary) and posttest data. The Hawthorne control, on the other hand, represents a systematic intervention and interaction on the part of the experimenter with the subjects; the purpose is to introduce a new procedure that is not anticipated to have specific effects related to the effects of the treatment or intervention being evaluated. That is, in the Hawthorne control experiment an *irrelevant, unrelated* intervention is deliberately introduced in order to create the Hawthorne effect which is often associated with intervention. Thus, the experimental condition and the Hawthorne control condition are comparable in that both can be expected to produce a Hawthorne or facilitating effect since both include an intervention. However, the Hawthorne control condition is, in fact, a control condition since the intervention employed is intended to be totally unrelated and irrelevant to those measures serving as the dependent variables.

If, for example, the experimental intervention were a technique for teaching first graders to read and the dependent variable was a measure of reading achievement, then the Hawthorne intervention might take the form of playing games with the children during the same period of time that the experimental group was experiencing the reading training. The no-treatment control condition, on the other hand, would involve no contact whatever between experimenter and subjects.*

Some studies utilize only the Hawthorne control group for comparison purposes and omit the regular, no-contact control group. In studies where the likelihood of a Hawthorne effect is great, there may be little value in running a control group that does not control for Hawthorne effect. Sample Study II, Appendix A, is illustrative of the comparison between an experimental group and a Hawthorne control group.

The Hawthorne control contributes considerably to the external validity of an experiment. Because an experiment involves some artificiality and often confronts subjects with experiences and people that they are not normally confronted with (or are normally confronted with but in a different context), it is likely that an experiment will create some Hawthorne effect (a typical reactive effect) to improve its outcome above-and-beyond the specific effects of the intervention. The Hawthorne control enables the experimenter to separate the "true" effects based on the intervention as a specific experience from those reactive effects resulting from the subjects' participation in an experiment and their interaction with the experimental staff. Such assessment of Hawthorne effect is impossible with only a no-treatment control.

Designs Providing for Expectancy Controls

An additional threat to external validity is that the agent of change may, by virtue of his expectation regarding the outcome of an experiment, affect that very outcome which he is interested in observing. In that case the outcome is not a function of the intervention alone, but in part a function of the intervention *and* of the expectation of the agent of change—and thus a reactive effect. In many educational experiments, the agent of change is the teacher. If the teacher has certain expectations associated with a particular educational treatment, then as a result of these expectations, the likelihood exists that the teacher can unconsciously and unintentionally effect the outcome of the experiment in the anticipated direction.

In order to control for the invalidating effects of expectancy, the researcher could employ a design in which four rather than two conditions are included. Instead of the dual design including treatment and no-treatment conditions, he would employ two treatment and two no-treatment conditions. In one of the experimental treatment conditions, the teacher would believe that the experimental innovation would be successful. The outcome then would be a combination of the treatment plus the teacher's expectation for success. In the alternative treatment condition, the teacher would be led to believe that the treatment was only a control condition; thus the combination of treatment and no expectation of success would exist. Similarly, in one control condition the teacher would be led to believe that the condition was only a control condition which, in fact, would be the truth. In the other control condition, however, the teacher would be led to believe that the control was actually an experimental intervention and therefore should result in success or benefit to the experimental participants. This design appears in Figure 6.4.

$$R \quad X \quad E_p \quad O_1$$
$$R \quad X \quad E_n \quad O_2$$
$$R \quad H \quad E_p \quad O_3$$
$$R \quad H \quad E_n \quad O_4$$

X Experimental (relevant) treatment
H Hawthorne control (irrelevant experience)
E_p Positive teacher expectation created
E_n Neutral teacher expectation created

Figure 6.4 *Experimental design with controls for reactive effects: Hawthorne and expectancy effects.*

Since the pure no-treatment control involves no interaction between experimenter and subject, it would be very difficult—probably impossible—to make teachers believe that they were participating in the experiment. (Teachers would certainly be hard pressed to believe that some benefit was to accrue to subjects when in fact *no* intervention at all was taking place.) However, as you recall in the Hawthorne control, an irrelevant interaction between subjects and experimenter takes place in order to establish a Hawthorne effect without establishing a treatment effect. It would be more likely in this condition that teachers could be led to believe that this was in fact an experimental treatment (which of course it was not) in order to create positive teacher expectation in the absence of the experimental treatment.

Thus, the four conditions displayed in Figure 6.4 are (1) an experimental procedure with positive teacher expectation, (2) the experimental procedure with a neutral teacher expectation, (3) a Hawthorne control with positive teacher expectation, and (4) a Hawthorne control with a neutral or no teacher expectation. These four conditions would make it possible to control for or systematically assess the effects of both the Hawthorne phenomenon and teacher expectancy. By using the statistical technique of analysis of variance (described in Chapter 9), it is possible to determine independently the effect of the experimental procedure versus the control and the effect of teacher positive expectation versus neutral or no expectation. It would also be possible to determine the interaction between the expectation phenomenon and the experimental procedure.

This design is particularly recommended for situations in which teachers are used as agents of change in an experimental procedure because of the likelihood that such procedures will be affected by teacher expectancy. In order to establish external validity and to be able to generalize from an experiment it is necessary that the effects of the treatment be separated from both kinds of reactive effects —teacher expectancy and Hawthorne effect. The design described above makes it possible to do just this. In addition, with this design it would be possible to anticipate in nonexperimental situations what effects can be expected from the treatment in the absence of both Hawthorne effect and positive teacher expectation, neither of which can necessarily be counted upon to apply to a nonexperimental setting.

RECOMMENDED READINGS

Campbell, D. T. and Stanley, J. C. Experimental and quasi-experimental designs for research on teaching. In N. L. Gage (Ed.) *Handbook for research on teaching.* Chicago: Rand-McNally, 1963, pp. 171–296. (Also available in a monograph from Rand-McNally.)

Kirk, R. E. *Experimental design: Procedures for the behavioral sciences.* Belmont, Calif.: Brooks/Cole, 1969.

COMPETENCY TEST EXERCISES

1. Match up the following:
   a. intact-group comparison
   b. pretest-posttest control group design
   c. posttest-only control group design
   d. one-shot case study
   e. equivalent time-samples design
   f. separate-sample pretest-posttest

   1. true design with no testing effect
   2. one-group design repeated twice
   3. does not control for history or selection
   4. true design with possible testing effect
   5. does not control for selection
   6. improved control for history but weak on external validity

2. Match up the following:
   a. nonequivalent control group design
   b. posttest-only control group design
   c. time-series design
   d. one-group pretest-posttest design
   e. factorial design
   f. patched-up design

   1. true design for dealing with multiple independent variables
   2. imperfect control of selection but better than nondesign
   3. true design with no pretest bias
   4. imperfect control of history but better than nondesign
   5. combination of two nondesigns
   6. inadequate control of history

3. In terms of controlling for history bias, rank order the three following designs in terms of their adequacy.
   1. most adequate
   2. next most adequate
   3. least adequate

   a. time-series design
   b. one-group pretest-posttest design
   c. pretest-posttest control group design

4. In terms of controlling for selection bias, rank order the four following designs in terms of their adequacy.
   1. most adequate
   2. next most adequate
   3. next least adequate
   4. least adequate

   a. patched-up design
   b. intact-group comparison
   c. posttest-only control group design
   d. nonequivalent control group design

5. Prediction: Student teachers who are randomly assigned to urban schools for experience are more likely to choose urban schools for their first teaching assignment than student teachers who are randomly assigned to non-urban schools.

   Construct an experimental design to test this prediction.

6. Prediction: Students given programmed math instruction will gain more in math achievement than students not given this instruction but this effect will be more pronounced among high math aptitude students than among low.

Construct an experimental design to test this prediction.

7. Which of the following circumstances necessitate the use of a quasi-experimental design? (More than one may be right.)
   a. experimenter cannot assign Ss to conditions
   b. experimenter must employ a pretest
   c. experimenter must collect the data himself
   d. the program to be evaluated has already begun

8. Which of the following circumstances necessitate the use of a quasi-experimental design? (More than one may be right.)
   a. there is more than one independent variable
   b. no control group is available
   c. the pretest is sensitizing
   d. everybody must receive the treatment

9. A patched-up design has been created where this years' first graders serve as the control group for a treatment being tried on this years' second graders. Which validity threat is not controlled?
   a. selection
   b. history
   c. maturation
   d. mortality

10. Prediction: Student teachers who choose urban schools for experience are more likely to choose urban schools for their first teaching assignment than student teachers who choose non-urban schools.
   a. Why must a quasi-experimental design be employed to test this prediction?
   b. Construct one.

11. A school decides to implement a dental hygiene program for all its students. It predicts that cavities will be reduced as a result of this program.
   a. Why must a quasi-experimental design be employed to test this prediction?
   b. Construct one.

12. Sample Study III, Appendix A, utilizes a criterion-group design.
   a. Why is this design employed rather than an experimental design?
   b. Diagram this design as used in Sample Study III.

13. Prediction: Children from broken homes will create a greater discipline problem in school (as evidenced by demerits) than children from intact homes.
   a. Why must a criterion-group design be employed to test this prediction?
   b. Construct one.

14. Prediction: An after-school dance program will improve the physical skills and social skills of first-graders.
    a. Why does the testing of this prediction call for a Hawthorne control?
    b. Construct a design for testing it.

15. A researcher has just designed a special program to increase verbal I.Q. It is a series of classroom lessons. He wants to try it out in some schools.
    a. Why would a Hawthorne control be a good idea?
    b. Why would teacher expectancy controls be a good idea?
    c. Construct a design to test this program.

7

Identifying and Describing Procedures for Observation and Measurement

OBJECTIVES

Identify and describe the different approaches to the estimation of test reliability. / Identify and describe the different approaches to the estimation of test validity. / Distinguish between four types of measurement scales: nominal, ordinal, interval, and ratio. / Identify and describe different techniques for describing test performances including percentiles, standard scores, and norms. / Describe procedures for test identification using the *Mental Measurements Yearbook*. / Identify different categories of standardized tests and specific tests in each category. / Describe procedures for constructing a paper-and-pencil performance test and for performing an item analysis on the items. / Describe procedures for constructing and using an attitude scale of the Likert or Semantic Differential type. / Describe procedures for constructing and using observation recording devices such as a rating scale or coding scheme.

7.1 TEST RELIABILITY

Test reliability means that a test is *consistent*. A ruler made of rubber would not be a reliable ruler since it could stretch or contract to give varying measures. Similarly, another example of unreliability would be an I.Q. test on which Johnny scored 135 on Monday and 100 on the following Friday, with no significant event or experience occurring to account for the discrepancy in scores. A test that is not reliable is not a good test regardless of its other characteristics.

Among the factors which contribute to the unreliability of a test are (1) familiarity with the particular test form (such as a multiple choice question), (2) fatigue, (3) emotional strain, (4) physical conditions of the room in which the test is given, (5) health of the test taker, (6) fluctuations of human memory, (7) amount of practice or experience by the test taker of the specific skill being measured, and (8) specific knowledge that has been gained outside of the experience being evaluated by the test. A test which is overly sensitive to these unpredictable (and often uncontrollable) sources of error is not a reliable test. Test unreliability creates *instrumentation bias,* a source of internal invalidity in an experiment.

Before drawing any conclusions from an experiment, the reliability of the test instruments used in that experiment should be assessed. Standardized tests available commercially have been checked for reliability; data relative to this point can be found in the test manual. When using homemade instruments, the researcher should assess their reliability either before or during the experiment. Four approaches for determining reliability are discussed briefly below. (For more detail, study the sources recommended at the end of this chapter.)

Test-Retest Reliability

One way to measure reliability is to give the same people the same test on more than one occasion and then compare each person's performance on both testings. In this procedure, known as *test-retest reliability*, the scores obtained by each person on the first administration of the test are related to his score on the second administration to provide a reliability coefficient.* This coefficient can vary from *0* (no relationship) to *1.00* (perfect relationship), but coefficients near zero are rare. Since the coefficient is an indication of the extent to which the test is measuring stable and enduring characteristics of the test-taker rather than variable and temporary ones, reasonably high coefficients are, of course, desirable.

Test-retest has the advantage of requiring only one form of a test but the disadvantage of being influenced by practice and memory. It can also be influenced by whatever events occur between testing sessions.

Since the determination of test-retest reliability requires two test administrations while the other three reliability procedures (described below) require only one, it is a more difficult procedure to follow. However, it is the only one of the four that provides information about a test's consistency over time. This particular quality of a test is often important enough in an experiment to justify its determination, particularly when both pre- and posttesting will be done.

*This relationship is usually computed by means of a correlation, described in Chapter 9.

Alternate-Forms Reliability

Alternate-forms reliability is determined by administering alternate forms of a test to the same people and computing the relation between each person's score on the two forms. This approach requires two forms of a test which parallel one another in the content and mental operations required—that is, the two tests must have items on one form matched to items on the other form with corresponding items measuring the same quality.

This approach can be used to assess the reliability of either of the two forms by comparison with the other or to determine the extent to which the two forms are parallel. This latter determination is particularly important if one form is to be used as a pretest and the other as a posttest.

Split-Half Reliability

The two approaches to reliability described above involve the determination of test consistency over time and over forms, but it is also possible to determine the internal consistency of a test relatively quickly: split a test into two halves, usually the odd-numbered items and the even-numbered items, and then relate the scores obtained by each person on one half with those obtained by each person on the other. This procedure which yields an estimate called the *split-half reliability* enables a researcher to determine whether the halves of a test are measuring the same quality or characteristic. He then enters the relation obtained (r_1) into the Spearman-Brown formula (shown below) to calculate the whole test reliability (r_2).

$$r_2 = \frac{nr}{1 - (n-1)r_1}$$

r_2 = corrected reliability
r_1 = uncorrected reliability
n = number of parts
(e.g., for halves, $n = 2$)

Since the actual test scores to be used as data in an experiment are based on the total test score rather than either half test score, the split-half reliability can be corrected by the above formula to reflect the increase in reliability gained by combining the halves.

Kuder-Richardson Reliability

When test items are scored either *a* or *b* (e.g., right or wrong) on an untimed test assumed to measure one characteristic or quality, the extent to which the test items are all measuring this same characteristic or quality can be determined by examining individual item scores rather than part or total scores (as in the split-half method), and then applying a *Kuder-Richardson formula*. This formula (known as *K-R* formula 20) is shown below and is equivalent to the average of *all possible* split-half reliability coefficients.

$$ r_{K\text{-}R} = \left(\frac{K}{K-1} \right) \left(\frac{\sigma^2 - \Sigma\, p_i\, q_i}{\sigma^2} \right) $$

$r_{K\text{-}R}$ = Kuder-Richardson reliability coefficient

K = number of items in the test

σ^2 = test variance (a measure of variability)

p_i = proportion of students responding correctly to item i

q_i = proportion of students responding incorrectly to item i

7.2 TEST VALIDITY

The validity of a test represents the extent to which a test measures what it purports to measure. In simple words, does the test really measure the characteristic that it is being used to measure? For example, a test of mathematical aptitude must in fact be a *true* indication of a student's mathematical aptitude. When you use a ruler to measure an object, you do not end up with a valid indication of how much that object weighs.

Following is a discussion of four types of validity. Within the manual of a test, these various forms of validity will be reported so that the potential test user can assess whether it measures what the title says it measures.

Predictive Validity

Validity can be established by relating a test to some actual behavior of which the test is supposed to be predictive. For example, a test intended to be predictive of a student's "staying power" in college could be validated by administering the test to students at the start of freshman year and seeing what percentage of the high scorers survive four years of college and what percentage of the low scorers drop out. If a test can be used to predict an outcome in terms of some performance or behavior criterion, then the *predictive validity* of that test can be obtained by relating test performance to subsequent performance on the related criterion.

Concurrent Validity

For some tests, particularly those that measure characteristics or qualities, it is difficult to establish predictive validity since it is not easy to identify specific performance outcomes that are related to that characteristic or quality. What is usually done in this case is to relate performance on the test with performance on another, well-reputed test (if such exists). This procedure is termed *concurrent validity*. Intelligence tests, for example, are often validated concurrently by comparing performance on a newer, more experimental one with performance on an older, more established one.

Another procedure for establishing the concurrent validity of a test is to compare qualities or performance as assessed by that test to the qualities or performance as assessed by another procedure, such as human judges. For example, results of a test intending to measure the extent to which persons are neurotic could be compared to judgments of the same sort made by a panel of clinical psychologists not aware of the test results (i.e., working in-the-blind). Agreement between test and judges would be an indication of the test's concurrent validity.

Construct Validity

A test builder might reason that a student with a high level of self-esteem would be more inclined to speak out when unjustly criticized by an authority figure; i.e., that such behavior can be *explained* by the construct (or concept) self-esteem.* Such a proposed relationship between a construct and a derivative behavior might provide a basis by which the *construct validity* of a test of self-esteem could be determined. Thus, the construct validity of a test of self-esteem might be established by demonstrating its relation to a proposed derivative

To relate the term "construct" to one previously used, it can be said that some independent variable causes self-esteem—an intervening variable or construct—which in turn leads to the speaking-out behavior.

behavior (such as speaking out in one's defense) where the construct measured by the test attempts to explain the behavior.

Construct validity, therefore, is established by relating a presumed measure of a construct or hypothetical quantity with some behavior or manifestation that it is hypothesized to underlie (or conversely, relating a behavior to a test of some construct that is an attempt to explain it).

As another example, a test maker might expect that more sensitive teachers would express more positive feeling toward their students than less sensitive teachers. By comparing the number of times positive feelings toward students were expressed during a class period by teachers scoring high on a test of the construct-sensitivity with teachers scoring lower, he could assess the construct validity of the test of sensitivity.

Content Validity

A test is an attempt to determine how an individual will function in a set of actual situations. Rather than placing the individual in each actual situation, a test is used as a shortcut to determine his behavior or performance in the set of situations. Thus, constructing the test requires a selection or sampling of situations from the total set. On the basis of the individual's performance on these sample situations, the researcher should be able to generalize regarding the full set of situations. A test in which the sample of situations or performances measured is *representative* of the set from which the sample was drawn (and about which generalizations are to be made) is considered to have *content validity*.

For example, suppose a researcher constructed a performance test of secretarial skills to be used by companies for screening applicants for jobs. The content validity of this test could be established by comparing the skill areas covered in the test, and the number of test items devoted to each, to the skill requirements of the job and the relative importance (e.g., time spent) of each. If the former (the sample) is representative of the latter (the set), then the test has content validity. Similarly, a final exam for Algebra I should be representative of the topics covered in the course and relative time devoted to each topic.*

Within the manual of a test, these various forms of validity will be reported (if available) so that the potential test user can assess whether the test measures what its title says it measures.

A further example of establishing content validity appears in Chapter 12.

7.3 TYPES OF MEASUREMENT SCALES

A *measurement scale* is a set of rules for quantifying or assigning numerical scores to a particular variable. Measurement scales (hereafter simply called scales) can be either *nominal, ordinal, interval,* or *ratio*. Each will be discussed in turn.

Nominal Scales

The term nominal means to name. Hence, a nominal scale basically does not measure but rather names. In other words, observations are simply classified into categories with no necessary relation existing between the categories. Suppose a researcher were interested in the number of happy and unhappy students in a class. If an interviewer were to talk to each child and classify him as happy or unhappy, then this classification system would represent a nominal scale. No mathematical relationship between happy and unhappy is implied; they simply are two different categories.* Thus, the happiness variable is being measured nominally.

When the independent variable of a study is made up of two levels—a treatment and a no-treatment control (or of two different treatments)—the independent variable would be considered nominal since two discrete conditions are being compared. As another example, splitting I.Q. scorers into high and low would make I.Q. into a two-category nominal variable. While high and low denote an order and could therefore be considered ordinal (see below), they can also be treated simply as category names and thus be dealt with as nominal data. (For statistical purposes, two-category orders are usually best treated as nominal data, as will be seen in Chapter 9.)

Ordinal Scales

The term ordinal means to order. In other words, an ordinal scale is a rank ordering of things, with a categorization in terms of *more than* or *less than* (When the number of things is two, the distinction between nominal and ordinal measurements is arbitrary. As previously mentioned, such cases of two will be considered nominal since this is usually preferable for statistical purposes.)

These categories may be scored 0 and 1, thus implying a mathematical relationship in its simplest form, i.e., presence versus absence.

Suppose the observer in the previous example interviewed each child in the class and then rank-ordered him in terms of happiness. Now he could specify how happy a child was in terms of his ranking. Since he had specified the order of things, the observer would have generated an ordinal scale.

While ordinal measurement may be a bit more difficult than nominal, it is also more informative since it gives more precise data.

Interval Scales

Interval scales not only tell the order of things; they also tell the interval or distance between judgments. For instance, on a classroom test one student gets a score of 95 while another gets a score of 85. Not only has the first performed better than the second, but this performance was 10 points better. If a third student has scored 75, then the second student would have outperformed him by as much as he was outperformed by the first student. Thus, on an interval scale, a distance of so many points may be considered a relative constant at any point on the scale where it occurs.

Rating scales and tests are considered to be interval scales. One unit on a rating scale or test is assumed to be equal in size to any other unit. Moreover, in the case of tests, raw scores can be converted to standard scores (as described in the next section) to insure interval scale properties. As you will see, most behavioral measurement is considered to be interval in nature.

Ratio Scales

Ratio scales are encountered in the physical sciences but not the behavioral sciences. Because this scale includes a true *zero value,* that is, a point on the scale that represents complete absence of the characteristic involved, ratios are comparable at different points on the scale. Thus, nine ohms is three times the resistance of three ohms while six ohms stands in the same ratio to two ohms. Because an I.Q. scale, on the other hand, is an interval scale, a person with an I.Q. of 120 is more comparable to one with an I.Q. of 100 (they are 20 scale points apart) than is a 144 I.Q. person to one with a 120 I.Q. (they are 24 scale points apart), even though the ratios between the two sets of scores are equal. This happens because the I.Q. scale, as an interval scale, has no true zero point; intervals of equal size are equal regardless of where on the scale they occur. Were the I.Q. scale a ratio scale (which it is not), these scores would be comparably related because each pair is of the ratio 6:5.

However, because of their absence in the behavioral sciences, this book will not be concerned with ratio scales but will be limited to the other three scales.

Scale Conversion

If a researcher were interested in measuring the extent of happiness among a group of children, he might:

1. count categories: happy versus unhappy,
2. rank order in terms of happiness, or
3. rate each child on a happiness scale.

If he were to make the choice to rate each child on a happiness scale (3) and thus collect interval data, he could always convert this interval data to rank-orderings (ordinal data) or, alternatively, divide the children into the most happy half and the least happy half (nominal data). In educational research, it is standard procedure to convert from a higher to a lower order of measurement whereas conversion from a lower to a higher order of measurement is not ordinarily done.

To select the appropriate statistical tests, it is important to be able to identify the scale with which you are dealing—be it nominal, ordinal, or interval. A more detailed description of the process of converting data from one scale of measurement to another will be provided in Section 9.4.

7.4 DESCRIBING TEST PERFORMANCES

It is difficult to interpret an individual's test score, or to place it in its proper perspective without some basis for comparison or standard. There are techniques available for comparing a test score to others within a single group of test takers and to others within a larger group of those who have previously taken the test. In order to deal in depth with such approaches it would be necessary to go beyond the scope of this book. However, brief mention will be made of some of these statistics or labels for describing and comparing test scores.

Percentiles

A test score can be expressed as a percentile (an ordinal measure) by describing its relative standing among a group of scores. A percentile is a number which represents the percent of scores that a particular raw score exceeds. It is computed by counting the number of scores which the score in question exceeds and then dividing this number by the total number of scores and multiplying by 100. Consider the following 20 test scores:

95	85	75	70
93	81	75	69
91	81	74	65
90	78	72	64
89	77	71	60

The score of 89 is higher than 15 of the 20 scores. Dividing 15 by 20 and multiplying by 100 yields 75. Thus, the score of 89 is at the 75th percentile.

Now, suppose the same test as that on which the above scores were obtained were given to another class of 20 yielding the following scores:

98	93	88	80
97	92	86	80
95	91	85	79
94	91	83	77
94	89	81	75

The same score of 89 in this group exceeds only 10 of the 20 scores, and thus is at the 50th percentile. This illustration shows that it is difficult (and misleading) to interpret a test score on an absolute basis. It is helpful to interpret scores relative to other scores.

Standard Scores

Standard scores are scores expressed as deviations or variations from the mean* or average score for a group in terms of *standard deviation* units.* A standard deviation unit is a unit of magnitude equal to the measure of spread of a group of scores around the average score for that group. Its use allows a researcher to adjust scores from absolute to relative to reflect the relationship between all the scores in a group. Moreover, standard scores are interval scores since the standard deviation unit is a constant interval throughout the scale. An *absolute* raw score is converted to a *relative* standard score by (1) subtracting

*See Chapter 9 for a more complete description of these terms and their determination.

the group mean on the test from it, (2) dividing the result by the standard deviation, and (3) adding a constant (usually of 50) to avoid minus signs and multiplying by 10 to avoid decimals. (This procedure is described by Thorndike and Hagen, 1961.)

By converting raw test scores into standard scores, it is possible to compare scores within a group and between groups and to add the scores from two or more tests to obtain a single score. Figure 7.1 illustrates the relation between standard scores and the normal distribution curve.* In Figure 7.1, raw scores falling at the mean of the distribution are assigned the score of 50, scores falling one standard deviation above the mean are assigned the score of 50 plus 10 or 60, and so on. Each standard deviation is set to span 10 points on the standard scale. This system gives scores a meaning in terms of their relation to one another by being fitted to the distribution described by the total group of scores.

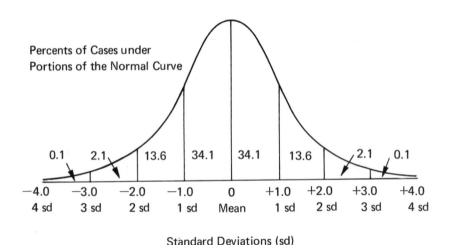

Figure 7.1 *Relationship between the normal curve and standard scores.*

See Chapter 9 for a more complete description of this term and its determination.

The purpose of norms is to describe a test score in terms of its location relative to a large body of scores which have already been collected. Rather than relating a group of 10 scores only to one another, it is possible to relate them to a larger group of scores to the extent that other persons have previously taken the same test.

Figure 7.2 shows some norms for four of the scales of the Edwards Personal Preference Schedule (EPPS) as they appear in the test manual. The norms in this figure are expressed in percentiles and are applicable only to men. Separate norms are supplied for women. The norms shown are based on data collected from 760 male college students which represent, in this case, the *normative population*. If you were to administer the EPPS to a college age male and he were to obtain a score of 20 on the achievement (*ach*) scale, you could, by virtue of the norms, relate this single score to the 760 scores of the normative population and assign it a percentile rank of 86. This indicates that a score of 20 exceeds 86 percent of the scores contained in the normative sample of 760. Note that on the *ach* scale, scores of 14 and 15 are farther apart on a relative basis (40th and 50th percentile, respectively) than scores of 21 and 24 (91st and 99th percentile, respectively). Thus, norms are invaluable in assessing the "meaning" of a score by comparing it to other scores.

Norm tables are found in the test manuals of standardized tests. The term *standardized test* indicates a test for which norms are available, as well as information on reliability and validity. In the EPPS manual norms are expressed as standard scores, in addition to being expressed as percentile scores. Either may be used. When dealing with a sample from a population on which no norms are available, the researcher must test a sufficiently large number of persons to generate his own norms. Without norms, you cannot tell how high or low a particular score is. This is a relative question.

7.5 STANDARDIZED TESTS

The most complete guide to standardized tests is the *Mental Measurements Yearbook* compiled by Oscar Krisen Buros and generally found on library reference shelves. This volume is a compendium of more than 1,000 commercially available mental and educational tests and has appeared a number of times over the past thirty years; new, updated versions are published regularly.

Percentile Scores on Subscales

raw score	ach	def	exh	ord	aut
28					
27					
26					
25					
24	99				99
23	98				98
22	95		99		96
21	91		98		94
20	86		97	99	91
19	83	99	93	97	86
18	74	98	89	96	82
17	66	96	81	95	76
16	58	93	72	92	68
15	50	88	62	88	61
14	40	81	49	84	52
13	30	73	37	78	43
12	22	63	28	71	34
11	16	52	21	63	28
10	10	43	15	54	22
9	7	34	9	46	15
8	4	23	6	36	11
7	2	16	3	27	6
6	1	10	1	19	3
5		6		14	2
4		3		9	1
3		1		6	
2				3	
1				1	
0					

ach, need for achievement
def, need for deference
exh, need for exhibition
ord, need for order
aut, need for autonomy

MEN
N = 760

Figure 7.2 *Percentiles for college students on the Edwards Personal Preference Schedule (EPPS). (Reproduced by permission. Copyright 1954, 1959 by The Psychological Corporation, New York, N. Y. All rights reserved.)*

A sample entry from the *Yearbook* along with its explanation appears below (Buros, 1965, p. 182).

$$\boxed{182}$$

*STUDY OF VALUES: A SCALE FOR MEASURING THE DOMI-NANT INTERESTS IN PERSONALITY, THIRD EDITION. Grades 13 and over; 1931-60; 6 scores: theoretical, economic, aesthetic, social, political, religious; 1 form ('60, 12 pages identical with test copyrighted in 1951); revised manual ('60, 19 pages); $4 per 35 tests; 60¢ per specimen set; postage extra; (20 minutes); Gordon W. Allport, Phillip E. Vernon, and Gardner Lindzey; Houghton Mifflin Co.

The words in bold type represent the name of the test, and the edition. The asterisk means this test has been revised or supplemented since the last *Yearbook*. The grade range of the test (13 and over) is listed next, followed by the inclusive copyright or publication dates (1931-60). The scoring categories of the test are then listed followed by forms, edition dates, and pages; then costs in bulk and costs for a specimen test are itemized. Finally, a time estimate for completing the test is given as are the names of the test authors and the publisher.* In addition, reviews of the tests by distinguished psychometricians are often included.

Achievement Batteries

Achievement batteries are sets of tests to measure the amount of *knowledge* that an individual has *acquired* in a number of discrete subject matter areas at one or more discrete grade levels. The use of such standardized batteries makes possible comparisons of learning among students in different parts of the country. Because such batteries serve an important evaluative function, many elementary and secondary schools (as well as colleges) use achievement batteries as a built-in part of their programs.

The *Yearbook* describes such batteries as:

1. American College Testing Program Examination (ACT)
2. California Achievement Tests
3. Graduate Record Examinations: The Area Tests

---

*Specimen test kits are available for most tests and can be ordered from the publishers whose addresses are listed in the back of the Yearbook.

4. Iowa Tests of Educational Development
5. Metropolitan Achievement Tests
6. National Educational Development Tests
7. SRA Achievement Tests
8. Sequential Tests of Educational Progress (STEP)
9. Stanford Achievement Tests

as well as others. Lengthy reviews of each are also included.

Aptitude Batteries

Another section of the *Yearbook* deals with multi-aptitude batteries, which are intended to measure an individual's *potential for learning* rather than what he has already learned. While achievement tests measure acquired knowledge in specific areas (such as, mathematics, science, reading), aptitude tests measure potential for acquiring knowledge in broad underlying areas (for example, verbal, quantitative). Among those multi-aptitude batteries described are the following:

1. Differential Aptitude Test (DAT)
2. Flanagan Aptitude Classification Tests (FACT)
3. General Aptitude Test Battery (GATB)
4. SRA Primary Mental Abilities (PMA)

Intelligence Tests

Intelligence as a concept is not highly dissimilar from that of aptitude, each being a function of learning potential. General intelligence is typically taken to mean "abstract intelligence—the ability to see relations in, make generalizations from, and relate and organize ideas represented in symbolic form" (Thorndike and Hagen, 1961, p. 222). The *Yearbook* divides intelligence tests into *group, individual,* and *specific*. Among the group tests, i.e., those that can be administered to more than one person at the same time, are listed:

1. American Council on Education Psychological Examination for College Freshmen (ACE)
2. Army General Classification Test (AGCT)
3. California Test of Mental Maturity (CTMM)

4. College Entrance Examination Board Scholastic Aptitude Test (SAT)
5. Cooperative School and College Ability Tests (SCAT)
6. Culture Fair Intelligence Test (IPAT)
7. Graduate Record Examinations Aptitude Test
8. Henmon-Nelson Tests of Mental Ability
9. Kuhlmann-Anderson Intelligence Tests
10. Lorge-Thorndike Intelligence Tests
11. Miller Analogies Test
12. Otis Group Intelligence Scale
13. Otis Quick-Scoring Mental Ability Tests
14. Progressive Matrices
15. SRA Tests of Educational Ability (and of General Ability)
16. Wonderlic Personnel Test

Among the individually-administered intelligence tests are:

1. Merrill Palmer Scale of Mental Tests
2. Peabody Picture Vocabulary Test (PPVT)
3. Quick Test
4. Stanford-Binet Intelligence Scale
5. Wechsler Adult Intelligence Scale (WAIS)
6. Wechsler-Bellevue Intelligence Scale
7. Wechsler Intelligence Scale for Children (WISC)

So-called specific intelligence tests measure specific traits thought to relate to intelligence (such as creativity). Such tests are:

1. Kit of Reference Tests for Cognitive Factors
2. Marianne Frostig Developmental Test of Visual Perception
3. Match Problems
4. Subsumed Ability Test

Tests of Specific Subject-Matter Achievement and Aptitude

Another category of tests are those that measure achievement and aptitudes in discrete and specified subject matter areas. The *Yearbook* includes lists of tests in

1. Business Education
2. English
3. Fine Arts
4. Foreign Languages
5. Mathematics
6. Reading*
7. Science
8. Social Studies

and many other areas listed under the heading of "Miscellaneous."

Character and Personality Tests

Character and personality tests measure an individual's characteristic ways of relating to his environment and the people in it, as well as his personal and interpersonal needs and his way of dealing with them. These tests have been subdivided into *nonprojective* and *projective*. Nonprojective tests are the typical paper-and-pencil variety and require that the individual respond to written statements by choosing a response, while projective tests use either words or pictures to elicit a free or unstructured response (e.g., look at an ink-blot and tell what you see; look at a picture and make up a story about it). Among the more well-known nonprojective character and personality tests listed are the following:

1. California Psychological Inventory (CPI)
2. California Test of Personality
3. Edwards Personal Preference Schedule (EPPS)
4. Embedded Figures Test
5. Gordon Personality Inventory (and Profile)
6. Guilford-Zimmerman Temperament Survey
7. Maudsley Personality Inventory
8. Minnesota Multiphasic Personality Inventory (MMPI)
9. Myers-Briggs Type Indicator
10. Sixteen Personality Factor Questionnaire (16PF)
11. Study of Values (Allport-Vernon-Lindzey)
12. Welsh Figure Preference Test

*The SRA Reading Test was employed as a measure of the dependent variable in Sample Study II, Appendix A.

Among the more well-known projective character and personality tests listed are the following:

1. Bender-Gestalt Test
2. Holtzman Inkblot Technique
3. Kent-Rosanoff Free Association Test
4. Machover Figure Drawing Test
5. Rorschach
6. Rosenzweig Picture Frustration Study
7. Thematic Apperception Test (TAT)

Sensory-Motor Tests

Also included in the *Yearbook* is a section on sensory-motor tests with listings of tests of hearing, vision, and motor coordination. These tests are intended to measure an individual's sensory capacities and motor abilities. Some examples are the Granson-Stadler Audiometers and the Test for Color Blindness.

Tests of Vocations (including Vocational Interests)

The concluding section of the *Yearbook* concerns vocations. This section includes listings of tests of vocationally relevant skills and knowledge and tests intended to determine a person's interests as an aid to making a vocational choice. (Such interest tests typically present sets of three activities and the respondent must indicate his preference.) Listings in this section include:

1. clerical tests
2. manual dexterity tests
3. mechanical ability tests
4. selection and rating forms
5. miscellaneous tests
6. tests of specific vocations (e.g., accounting, law, nursing, etc.)
7. interest inventories, including the Kuder Preference Record and the Strong Vocational Interest Blank

7.6 CONSTRUCTING A PAPER-AND-PENCIL PERFORMANCE TEST

In order to construct a performance test, obviously, you must first identify those performances that you would like to measure. Begin by constructing a list of instructional objectives for the course, program, treatment, or subject area (if such a list does not already exist) and then outlining all those performance capabilities that students should possess if successfully taught. On the basis of this content outline, you then write performance items and develop scoring keys. The use of the content outline should establish content validity in that test items based on the outline assess or sample the mastery of that content which they are intended to test. To build in content validity it is first necessary to develop a content outline.*

More items should be generated in each specific content area than will ultimately be used. In these items the specific examples used in teaching the content should be modified to make possible the measurement of transferability of skills rather than rote learning. For example, if Shakespeare's *Macbeth* had been used in teaching iambic pentameter as a meter of writing, *Hamlet* might be used in testing students' knowledge of this meter.

The items generated should then be administered to a pilot group. Total scores on such measures as number of items passed should be obtained for each student in the pilot group. Performance on each item should then be compared to total scores using the following procedure, called *item analysis*.

1. Subdivide students based on total score into
   a. high third scorers
   b. middle third scorers
   c. low third scorers.
2. Identify the number of high third and low third scorers who pass each item (see Figure 7.3 for an illustration).

Discriminability refers to the extent to which a test item is responded to correctly by those students possessing more of the quality being measured and incorrectly by those students possessing less of this quality. Such items serve the purpose for which they were written—separating more knowledgeable students from less knowledgeable ones. Only six of the ten items in Figure 7.3 have satisfactory discriminating power in that two-thirds (.67) or more of those who get them right are in the high third group (i.e., the index of discriminability for these items is above .67). These are items 1, 3, 4, 6, 7, and 8.

*Another illustration of this procedure appears in Chapter 12 on evaluation.

Item	Number of High 1/3 Who Pass	Number of Low 1/3 Who Pass	Index of Difficulty	Index of Discriminability
1	10	0	.50	1.00
2	10	9	.05	.53
3	3	0	.85	1.00
4	9	2	.45	.82
5	5	5	.50	.50
6	10	3	.35	.77
7	7	1	.60	.87
8	9	3	.40	.75
9	2	4	.70	.33
10	8	9	.15	.47

$$\text{Index of Difficulty} = \frac{\text{number who fail an item}}{\text{total number in both groups}}$$

$$\text{For Item 1: } \frac{20 - (10 + 0)}{10 + 10} = \frac{10}{20} = .50$$

$$\text{Index of Discriminability} = \frac{\text{number of high 1/3 who pass an item}}{\text{total number in both groups who pass the item}}$$

$$\text{For Item 1: } \frac{10}{10 + 0} = \frac{10}{10} = 1.00$$

Figure 7.3 *Sample item analysis on the data from among a group of thirty.*

Difficulty refers to the extent to which a test item can be responded to correctly by any student. It differs from discriminability in that it does not include any differentiation between students. Of the 10 items, two are too easy (items 2 and 10) since fewer than 1/3 (.33) got them wrong (i.e., the index of difficulty for these items is below .33). Moreover, two items are too difficult (items 3 and 9) since more than 2/3 (.67) got them wrong (i.e., the index of difficulty for these items is above .67. Taking both considerations into account, items 1, 4, 6, 7, and 8 would survive this pilot test since they have both satisfactory discriminability (above .67) and reasonable difficulty (between .33 and .67). Of course, you have a certain degree of flexibility in setting the cutoffs for discriminability and difficulty; in choosing to exercise this flexibility, you should understand what these values mean and what you are doing to your test as you change them.

Notice that on those items in which a great number of lower scorers pass, the index of discriminability dips below .50 (items 9, 10). Of course, these items must be discarded.* Sometimes it does not hurt to retain an extremely easy item like item 2. Since it is uniformly easy, it may have motivational value, and because of its uniform ease for both low and high scorers, it will not affect the relative position of scores.

In building a performance test, therefore, it is essential to:

1. outline content areas to be covered to insure content validity;
2. try the test out to obtain data for an item analysis in terms of item difficulty and discriminability.

It is also useful to administer any other comparable or related test to your pilot group to see whether your test relates to another test. If your test shows a relationship to another performance test[†], you can then demonstrate concurrent validity. If it relates to an aptitude test (as an example), then this may contribute to construct validity. Finally, if classroom performance records are available, additional validity tests can be made. For a performance test, however, the establishment of content validity (a non-statistical concept) and the use of item analysis are usually sufficient for test construction.

Attempts to establish forms of validity other than content validity are usually unnecessary for tests of performance, although it is useful to establish their reliability. While an item analysis contributes to the establishment of internal reliability, the Kuder-Richardson formula can also be used for this purpose (see Section 7.1).

7.7 CONSTRUCTING A SCALE

Scales are devices constructed or employed by researchers to quantify the responses of a subject on a particular variable (see Section 7.3). Scales may be used to obtain interval data concerning Ss' attitudes, judgments, or

---

*Even though these items may be measuring some things of value, it is presumably outside the scope of the content outline and therefore outside the scope of what the test is intended to measure. However, in such cases you might consider altering the content outline or developing another test to measure those other concepts.

†The relationship is usually tested by means of a correlation, a measure of the extent to which two sets of scores are related. Correlation techniques are described in Chapter 9.

perceptions about almost any subject or object. The most comn
scales are

a. Likert Scale
b. Semantic Differential
c. Thurstone Scale

Only types (a) and (b) will be discussed here. The reader is referred to *Techniques of Attitude Scale Construction* by Allan Edwards (1957) for information on type (c) and for additional details on types (a) and (b). (The use of scales or scaled responses in questionnaires and interviews is discussed in the next chapter.)

Likert Scale

A Likert scale is a five-point scale in which the interval between each point on the scale is assumed to be equal.* It is actually called an equal-appearing interval scale. This scale is used to register the extent of agreement or disagreement with a particular statement of an attitude, belief, or judgment. An example appears below.

Red China should be admitted to the United Nations.

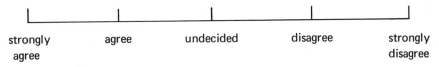

| strongly | agree | undecided | disagree | strongly |
| agree | | | | disagree |

The respondent indicates his opinion or attitude by making a mark on the scale above the word(s) he chooses.

On the sample Likert-type attitude scale in Figure 7.4, the respondent is instructed to circle the letter(s) indicating his opinion. This scale was built by first identifying the attitude areas (or subtopics) included within the topic of vocational education in the comprehensive high school. The subtopics turned out to include areas such as:

1. opportunities for the vocational student
2. quality of such programs

Since analyses of data from Likert scales are usually based on summated scores over a number of items, the equal-interval assumption is workable. In Thurstone scaling procedures, on the other hand, items are scaled by Ss and chosen to satisfy the equal-interval requirement. This procedure is considerably more complex than the Likert scale approach.

Vocational Education in the Comprehensive High School

This scale has been prepared so that you can indicate how you feel about vocational education in the comprehensive high school. Please *circle* the letter(s) on the left indicating how you feel about each statement. (*SA* strongly agree, *A* agree, *U* undecided, *D* disagree, *SD* strongly disagree.)

SA A U D SD   1.   Vocational education should be included in the comprehensive high school.

SA A U D SD   2.   Vocational students in the comprehensive high school have the opportunity to participate in a variety of activities.

SA A U D SD   3.   Vocational students will not feel like they really "fit in" in a comprehensive high school

SA A U D SD   4.   Students enrolled in a vocational course in a comprehensive high school are well prepared to enroll in college.

SA A U D SD   5.   Vocational courses do not prevent high school dropouts in a comprehensive high school

SA A U D SD   6.   Vocational education in the comprehensive high school enables each student to feel worthwhile.

SA A U D SD   7.   Richer and more varied experiences are available to the vocational student in the comprehensive high school.

SA A U D SD   8.   Students who receive their vocational training in the comprehensive high school tend to be inadequately trained.

SA A U D SD   9.   Vocational education in a comprehensive high school jeopardizes the school's accreditation.

SA A U D SD   10.   Vocational education in the comprehensive high school provides students an opportunity to learn to accept and respect all students.

SA A U D SD   11.   Vocational programs in the comprehensive high school do not tend to be quality programs.

SA A U D SD   12.   Vocational experiences in a comprehensive high school are limited.

SA A U D SD   13.   High school should be a general education which includes vocational education.

SA A U D SD   14.   Social climate in a comprehensive high school prevents many students, who might benefit, from enrolling in vocational education.

SA A U D SD   15.   Vocational education students in the comprehensive high school do not have an opportunity to develop leadership qualities.

SA A U D SD   16.   Facilities available in a comprehensive high school restrict the vocational education offerings.

SA A U D SD   17.   Each high school graduate should be exposed to courses in vocational education.

SA A U D SD   18.   Vocational education expenses are lower in comprehensive high school because teacher time can be better utilized than it can in separate vocational schools.

SA A U D SD   19.   Vocational education is more economical when both academic and vocational education are provided in one institution.

SA A U D SD   20.   The insurance rates of a comprehensive high school are higher when vocational facilities are included.

Figure 7.4 *Sample Likert scale.*

3. making the vocational student feel like a first-class citizen
4. economic considerations

Then items were written for each area or subtopic; some items were written in a positive (pro) direction and some in a negative (con) direction. A positive item was scored by the following key:

$$SA = 5, A = 4, U = 3, D = 2, SD = 1$$

A negative item was scored by the following key:

$$SA = 1, A = 2, U = 3, D = 4, SD = 5$$

The reason for reversing the scoring of negative items was to provide a total score that reflected positiveness toward the object in question. A person favoring vocational education in the comprehensive high school would agree with positive items and disagree with negative ones, while a person opposing such programs would do the opposite, disagree with positive items and agree with negative ones.

The total pool of items was then administered to a pilot group of Ss. The responses given by the Ss to each individual item were correlated (a statistical procedure described in Chapter 9) with the total scores obtained by the Ss on the whole test. This item analysis procedure provides an indication of the degree of agreement or overlap between each individual item and the total test, that is, the extent to which each item measures what the total test measures. The purpose of this procedure is to identify those items that best agree with the test and will thus yield the greatest degree of internal consistency. Using this procedure it was possible to identify the 20 best items, i.e., those items showing the greatest amount of agreement with the total score. (The choice of the number 20 was based on the fact that 20 items showed high agreement with the total score and would make up a scale that could be completed in a reasonably short time.) Furthermore, item selection was made in order to include roughly an equal number of positive and negative items covering a range of topics. Thus, a scale was built and ready to use.

Semantic Differential

The semantic differential is an attitude measuring technique developed by Osgood, Suci, and Tannenbaum (1957). A sample of the semantic differential containing nine bipolar adjective scales is shown in Figure 7.5. This technique

RED CHINA

	(7)	(6)	(5)	(4)	(3)	(2)	(1)*	
strong	___ :	X :	___ :	___ :	___ :	___ :	___ :	weak
bad	___ :	X :	___ :	___ :	___ :	___ :	___ :	good
fast	___ :	___ :	X :	___ :	___ :	___ :	___ :	slow
passive	___ :	___ :	___ :	___ :	___ :	X :	___ :	active
pleasant	___ :	___ :	___ :	___ :	___ :	X :	___ :	unpleasant
small	___ :	___ :	___ :	___ :	___ :	X :	___ :	large
heavy	X :	___ :	___ :	___ :	___ :	___ :	___ :	light
dull	___ :	___ :	___ :	X :	___ :	___ :	___ :	sharp
clean	___ :	___ :	___ :	X :	___ :	___ :	___ :	dirty

These scoring numbers do not appear on the actual copy of the scale.

Figure 7.5 *Sample semantic differential.*

enables a researcher to measure judgments of the evaluation, potency, and activity of a concept in a fairly circumspect way. The respondent is instructed to judge the word (or concept) at the top of the page (in the example, "RED CHINA") on each of the bipolar adjective scales by placing an X in one of the seven spaces on each scale. In Figure 7.5, according to the pattern of X's given by the respondent in the sample, he sees Red China as moderately bad, extremely unpleasant, and slightly dirty. The three scales of bad—good, pleasant—unpleasant, and clean—dirty have been shown to measure the same factor, namely, the *evaluative* dimension.

Notice also that the respondent rates Red China as moderately strong, extremely large, and extremely heavy. These three scales—strong—weak, small—large, and heavy—light—have been shown to measure the same factor, namely, the *potency* dimension.

Finally, the respondent rates Red China as slightly fast, extremely active, and slightly sharp. The scales for passive—active, fast—slow, and dull—sharp measure the same factor, namely, the *activity* dimension.

If a researcher were interested in measuring attitudes toward some concept only on the evaluative factor (rather than all three factors), he could look in the Osgood et al. (1953) book, *The Measurement of Meaning,* and get a list of evaluative adjective pairs and choose that number desired for the task at hand.

Although most of the adjectives might not seem related to the concept to be judged, this apparent lack of meaningfulness of the adjectives often puts the respondent off his guard, and leads to more honest responses. Critics of this approach claim that the adjectives are irrelevant to the concepts to be judged, but it is this apparent irrelevance that is the strength of this approach since it often limits the tendency to produce socially acceptable responses.

Judgments on the semantic differential are quantified on a one-to-seven scale (see the numbers under the strong-weak scale in Figure 7.5) with seven representing the most positive judgment. On the actual copy of the scale, these numbers do not appear.

7.8 CONSTRUCTING AN OBSERVATION RECORDING DEVICE

There are basically two devices for recording observations: the rating scale (or the checklist) which represents a summary of occurrences, and the coding system which represents an occurrence-by-occurrence account.

Rating Scales

A rating scale is a device which can be used by an observer to summarize his judgment of the activity or behavior that he has observed. Such a scale may have three, five, seven, nine, one hundred, or an infinite number of points on a line with descriptive statements on either end, and perhaps in the middle as well. (Scales of three, five, and seven points are the most common.) Following a selected period of time, an observer (who is often pretrained) records his impression, thereby providing a quantitative estimate of what has transpired. Some examples are shown in Figure 7.6.

An example of an entire rating scale taken from Tuckman (1968) is given in Figure 7.7 (pages 163-164). The observers, in this case classes of high school students, worked independently and described their teachers by filling out the 17 scale items. This scale was designed to assess a teacher's teaching style on the directive-nondirective dimension based on the operational definition given on page 65.

When human beings are used as measuring instruments, by having them complete rating scales, their perception is subject to many influences. One of these influences is called the *halo effect,* which means that observers have a tendency when they like a person to rate him positively on all scales, thus causing the scales

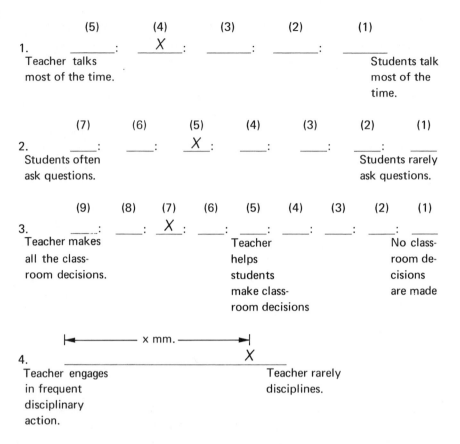

1.

(5)	(4)	(3)	(2)	(1)
_____:	_X_ :	_____:	_____:	_____

Teacher talks most of the time.   Students talk most of the time.

2.

(7)	(6)	(5)	(4)	(3)	(2)	(1)
___:	___:	_X_ :	___:	___:	___:	___

Students often ask questions.   Students rarely ask questions.

3.

(9)	(8)	(7)	(6)	(5)	(4)	(3)	(2)	(1)
___:	___:	_X_ :	___:	___:	___:	___:	___:	___

Teacher makes all the class-room decisions.   Teacher helps students make class-room decisions   No class-room decisions are made

4.

|← ——— x mm. ———→|

X

Teacher engages in frequent disciplinary action.   Teacher rarely disciplines.

5. Using any whole number from 0 to 100, indicate the amount of time the teacher talked (100 = all the time; 0 = none of the time). _30_

Figure 7.6 *Sample rating scales.*

to measure simply the general positiveness of the observer's perception. When an extremely strong relationship is found between a series of somewhat unrelated scales, the researcher should be suspicious that the ratings are subject to the halo effect.

Because a rating scale uses human recorders whose perceptions, as noted before, are subject to influences, the scale then is subject to a number of inconsistencies or errors. Because these errors constitute threats to internal validity via instrumentation, it is necessary to determine the consistency or "accuracy" of your rating procedure. This is usually accomplished by employing two (or more) raters and having each complete the scale and then correlating the two ratings to

STUDENT PERCEPTION OF TEACHER STYLE (SPOTS)

1. Your teacher is mainly interested in

1	2	3	4	5	6	7	8	9
How many facts you know			If he gets an idea across to you			Whether you can "think for yourself"		

2. The teacher

1	2	3	4	5	6	7	8	9
Makes you do what he wants you to most of the time			Makes you do what he wants you to sometimes			Lets you make your own decisions most of the time		

3. The teacher

1	2	3	4	5	6	7	8	9
Doesn't like to talk about any subject that isn't part of your course			Talks about your course subject a lot but encourages the discussion of other matters			Likes to talk about different subjects and is interested in your personal opinions		

4. The students in our class

1	2	3	4	5	6	7	8	9
Only speak when the teacher asks them a question			Feel free to ask the teacher questions			Feel free to speak up in class at almost any time		

5. When the teacher or another student says something you don't agree with

1	2	3	4	5	6	7	8	9
You try not to start an argument and feel that it's not your job to tell him he's wrong			You tell why you disagree when the teacher asks you to			You feel free to discuss and argue your point of view whether the teacher asks you or not		

6. The teacher

1	2	3	4	5	6	7	8	9
Usually bases his opinions on what the book says or what the principal says			Usually gives you another point of view in addition to what the book says			Tells you that books, teachers, principals and customs are not always right		

7. If you were to call your teacher by his first name,

1	2	3	4	5	6	7	8	9
He wouldn't like it and would tell you not to do it			He would tell you that it's all right to call him by his first name outside of school but that he would prefer you to call him by his last name while he is teaching			He wouldn't mind at all		

8. The teacher

1	2	3	4	5	6	7	8	9
Never tells jokes while he's teaching and does not like it when the students joke around			Sometimes tells a joke or a humorous story to get a point across			Always tells funny stories and encourages the students to tell about funny things that happened to them		

Figure 7.7 *A complete rating scale instrument (Tuckman, 1968, p. 82-84).* *

Also reprinted in Tuckman, 1970, p. 398-400.

9. The teacher spends a lot of time

1 2 3	4 5 6	7 8 9
Telling you about tests, grades, and about how the course is planned	Giving you an idea about tests, grades, and the course but not too much time giving you the details	Asking you to make your own decisions about tests, grades, the course plan or group projects

10. When we are working on a group project or in a committee, the teacher

1 2 3	4 5 6	7 8 9
Tells us exactly what to do	Suggest ways that the project might be handled	Lets the group members decide how the project should be handled

11. The teacher usually

1 2 3	4 5 6	7 8 9
Makes all the students do the same thing in class (working, studying)	Makes some students work on projects and some students study, depending on how far behind they are	Lets the students do what they like as long as they complete the number of projects or chapters assigned by the end of the week

12. When you get angry at the teacher,

1 2 3	4 5 6	7 8 9
You usually hold it in because the teacher would punish any show of anger	You feel that you can tell the teacher why you're angry	You feel that you could show your anger without the teacher becoming angry

13. The teacher

1 2 3	4 5 6	7 8 9
Acts like a teacher all of the time	Acts like a teacher most of the time but sometimes seems more like a friend	Acts like a friend more than he acts like a teacher

14. The first thing the teacher does when he comes into the room

1 2 3	4 5 6	7 8 9
Is to tell you to be quiet so that he can take attendance	Is to take attendance and ask you why some students are absent (if they are sick, etc.)	Is to let you start your projects or studying and then takes attendance while you're working

15. In this class, homework

1 2 3	4 5 6	7 8 9
Is assigned every day and must be handed in the next day	Is divided between work which is due every day and a few long-term projects each term	Usually consists of long-term projects

16. In our class pupils work together in a group or on a committee

1 2 3	4 5 6	7 8 9
Never	Sometimes	A great deal

17. When there is work which has to be done with another student we are

1 2 3	4 5 6	7 8 9
Usually told with whom to work	Can sometimes choose our own partner	Can usually decide with whom we want to work

Figure 7.7 (*continued*)

obtain a coefficient of *inter-rater reliability*. (See Chapter 9 for a description of correlation procedures.) If this correlation is sufficiently high (arbitrarily, it should be about .70 or better), you can usually conclude that individual differences in rater perception are within tolerable limits, thus reducing potential internal invalidity based on instrumentation.

It is further recommended that the average or *mean* of the two sets of rater judgments be used as data if you intend to use these data in your actual study.* By doing this, you produce data that are more reliable than the ratings from either judge alone. When using mean ratings across judges, it is permissable to modify your reliability coefficient using the Spearman-Brown correction formula, shown on page 138 (since the mean is more reliable than either judgment alone). In many studies, two or more raters are purposely employed in order to produce more reliable data for analysis. Moreover, a comparison of the judgments made by the raters makes possible the determination of the inter-rater reliability, a measure of the accuracy of the ratings.

While the rating scale is an efficient and ubiquitous recording technique, it is highly subject to human error. Consequently, the humans who use the scale must be checked for error and this error *must* be reported, thus helping both the researcher and the reader assess instrumentation as a threat to the validity of a study.

A variation of the rating scale is an observer checklist, which is simply a series of statements (such as might appear on a rating scale) in which an observer indicates in retrospect which of two statements is a more accurate description of the behavior he has observed. It is like a series of two-point rating scales where a check means "occurred" and no check means "did not occur." In a checklist, the observer is limited to describing what has or has not transpired rather than indicating the degree of presence or absence of the behaviors in question (as would be the case with a rating scale).

Coding Systems

A coding system is a means for recording the occurrence of specific preselected behaviors as they happen—a set of categories into which ongoing behavior is classified.† Like rating procedures, coding techniques represent an attempt to quantify behavior. If you are interested in determining the effect of class size on the number of question-asking behaviors in a class, you would code

Sometimes, reliability data are collected separately from the study itself. At other times, data to be employed in a study are also used to establish reliability.

†*Coding may be done after-the-fact from tape recordings or video tapes.*

question-asking behavior during a designated block of time in large and small classes in order to establish a *measure* of this behavior as a dependent variable. Rating and coding schemes convert behavior into measures. While rating scales are completed in retrospect, and represent the memory of what happened overall, coding scales are completed as the coder observes (or hears) the behavior. A coding system is a technique for recording the frequency of the occurrence of specific (usually individual) acts that have been predesignated, while rating scales are used to summarize the occurrence of types of behavior in a more global fashion.

There are two kinds of coding systems. The first kind uses a set of behavioral categories and each time one of these preselected codeable behaviors occurs, it is coded in the appropriate category. The decision of when to code is a function of the occurrence of behaviors which have been predesignated for coding. For example, if a coding system included "suggestions" as a codeable act, the coder would have to code every time a suggestion was made.

An example of such a *sign coding* system for coding group problem-solving activities appears in Figure 7.8. The scheme shown, developed by Bales (1950), lists 12 behaviors. Whenever one of these 12 behaviors occurs, an observer records the occurrence of that behavior by category (1-12). In addition to coding the occurrence of the behaviors listed in Figure 7.8, the observer is also instructed to keep a record of the person who performs the behavior and the person toward whom the coded behavior is directed. Observers need a good deal of practice to be able to record occurrences of such frequency and rapidity.

The second kind of coding system also employs a set of behavioral categories. However, in this system, coding is done not only of preselected or signed acts but of every act that occurs during a preselected time interval. Thus, the behavior taking place every three seconds might be recorded; or every ten seconds an observation might be made and the behavior taking place recorded. An example of such *time-coding* is the scheme of Flanders (1965), called Interaction Process Analysis, shown in Figure 7.9 (page 168). You will notice that the same act may be coded many times if it persists through a number of coding time periods. Thus, time-coding yields percent-of-time data for each category while sign coding yields number of occurrences data for each category.

Compared with rating as a means of quantifying observations, coding has both its advantages and disadvantages. On the negative side of the ledger, it is difficult to train coders and hard to establish inter-coder reliability; it is difficult and time consuming to carry out coding activities (often this is done from tape recordings—which produces other difficulties); when you are finished coding, it may be hard to say what you have besides a set of category tallies. However, on the positive side, data yielded from coding approaches more closely what the physical scientist calls "hard data." Coding techniques have the potential for

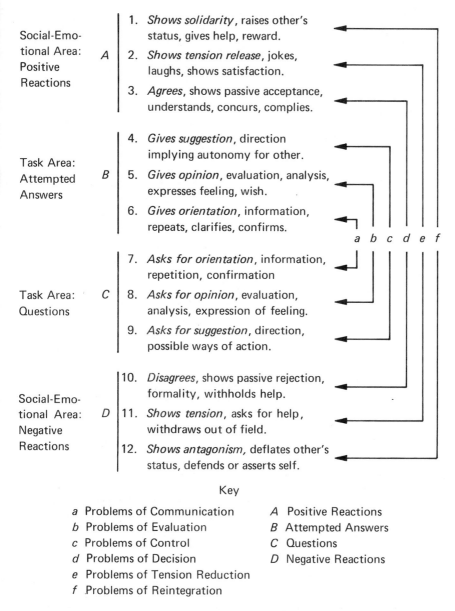

Social-Emotional Area: Positive Reactions	A	1. *Shows solidarity*, raises other's status, gives help, reward.
		2. *Shows tension release*, jokes, laughs, shows satisfaction.
		3. *Agrees*, shows passive acceptance, understands, concurs, complies.

Task Area: Attempted Answers	B	4. *Gives suggestion*, direction implying autonomy for other.
		5. *Gives opinion*, evaluation, analysis, expresses feeling, wish.
		6. *Gives orientation*, information, repeats, clarifies, confirms.

a b c d e f

Task Area: Questions	C	7. *Asks for orientation*, information, repetition, confirmation
		8. *Asks for opinion*, evaluation, analysis, expression of feeling.
		9. *Asks for suggestion*, direction, possible ways of action.

Social-Emotional Area: Negative Reactions	D	10. *Disagrees*, shows passive rejection, formality, withholds help.
		11. *Shows tension*, asks for help, withdraws out of field.
		12. *Shows antagonism*, deflates other's status, defends or asserts self.

Key

a Problems of Communication A Positive Reactions
b Problems of Evaluation   B Attempted Answers
c Problems of Control   C Questions
d Problems of Decision   D Negative Reactions
e Problems of Tension Reduction
f Problems of Reintegration

Figure 7.8 *Categories for classifying interpersonal behavior.* (From R. F. Bales, Interaction Process Analysis: A Method for the Study of Small Groups, *Addison-Wesley, 1950, p. 9.* *

For recent and associated research see R. F. Bales, Personality and Interpersonal Behavior, *Holt, Rinehart, and Winston, 1970.*

TEACHER **TALK**	INDIRECT INFLUENCE	1. **Accepts feeling:** accepts and clarifies feeling tone of the students in a non-threatening manner. Feelings may be positive or negative. Predicting and recalling feelings are included. 2. **Praises or encourages:** praises or encourages student action or behavior. Jokes that release tension, not at the expense of another individual, nodding head or saying "uhhuh?" or "go on" are included. 3. **Accepts or uses ideas of student:** clarifying, building, or developing ideas or suggestions by a student. As teacher brings more of his own ideas into play, shift to category five. 4. **Asks questions:** asking a question about content or procedure with the intent that a student answer.
	DIRECT INFLUENCE	5. **Lectures:** giving facts or opinions about content or procedure; expressing his own idea; asking rhetorical questions. 6. **Gives directions:** directions, commands, or orders with which a student is expected to comply. 7. **Criticizes or justifies authority:** statements intended to change student behavior from non-acceptable pattern; bawling someone out; stating why the teacher is doing what he is doing, extreme self-reference.
STUDENT **TALK**		8. **Student talk-response:** talk by students in response to teacher. Teacher initiates the contact or solicits student statement. 9. **Student talk-initiation:** talk by students, which they initiate. If "calling on" student is only to indicate who may talk next, observer must decide whether student wanted to talk. If he did, use this category.
		10. **Silence or confusion:** pauses, short periods of silence, and periods of confusion in which communication cannot be understood by the observer.

Figure 7.9 *Summary of categories for interaction analysis.* (*Flanders, 1965, p. 20*).

generating a somewhat more objective picture of what has happened than do rating scale techniques.

Considering both sides of the issue, it is advisable to avoid coding in favor of rating unless a well-developed coding system is available, such as the Flanders scheme, and you possess the resources required to hire and train coders and have them listen to lengthy tape recordings.

This chapter has considered the measurement process in a variety of forms (for example, tests, scales) as well as some of the properties of measuring instruments (such as, reliability, validity). The next chapter will deal with the concrete problem of constructing questionnaires and interview schedules.

RECOMMENDED READINGS

APA, AERA, and NCME. *Standards for educational and psychological tests and manuals.* Washington, D.C.: American Psychological Association, 1966.

Buros, O. K. *Tests in print: comprehensive bibliography of tests for use in education, psychology, and industry.* Highland Park, New Jersey: The Gryphon Press, 1961.

Buros, O. K. *The sixth mental measurement yearbook.* Highland Park, N.J.: The Gryphon Press, 1965.

Dick, W. and Hagerty, Nancy. *Topics in measurement.* New York: McGraw-Hill, 1971.

Educational Testing Service. *Tests and measurement kit.* Princeton, N.J.: Educational Testing Service, 1965.

Edwards, Alan. *Techniques of attitude scale construction.* New York: Appleton–Century–Crofts, 1957.

Medley, D. M. and Mitzel, H. E. Measuring classroom behavior by systematic observation. In N. L. Gage (Ed.) *Handbook of research on teaching.* Chicago: Rand McNally, 1963, pp. 247–328.

Osgood, C. E., Suci, G. S., and Tannenbaum, P. H. *The measurement of meaning.* Urbana, Ill.: University of Illinois Press, 1957.

Payne, David. *The specification and measurement of learning outcomes.* Waltham, Mass.: Blaisdell Publishing Co., 1968.

Remmers, H. H. Rating methods in research on teaching. In N. L. Gage (Ed.) *Handbook of research on teaching.* Chicago: Rand McNally, 1963, pp. 329-378.

Sellitz, Claire, et al. *Research methods in social relations.* New York: Holt, Rinehart and Winston, 1964.

Thorndike, Robert L. and Hagen, Elizabeth. *Measurement and evaluation in psychology and education* (2nd ed.). New York, Wiley, 1961.

Webb, Eugene J., et al. *Unobtrusive measures: nonreactive research in the social sciences.* Chicago: Rand McNally, 1966.

COMPETENCY TEST EXERCISES

1. Match up the items on the left with those on the right.
   2 a. test-retest reliability
           1. odd versus even items across test takers
   4 b. alternate forms reliability
           2. scores at time A versus scores at time B
      c. split-half reliability
           3. direct comparison of item scores by formula
      d. Kuder-Richardson reliability
           4. scores on form A versus scores on form B

2. Describe procedures for determining test-retest reliability as compared to split-half reliability.

3. Match up the items on the left with those on the right.
      a. predictive validity
           1. test adequately samples from total range of relevant behaviors
      b. concurrent validity
           2. test of concept relates to hypothetically-related behavior
   2 c. construct validity
           3. test relates to behavior it is presumed to predict
      d. content validity
           4. test relates to another test of same thing

4. Describe procedures for determining the concurrent validity of an I.Q. test as contrasted to its construct validity.

5. Match up the items on the left with those on the right.
   3 a. nominal scale
           1. more apples, less apples
   1 b. ordinal scale
           2. two apples, three apples
   2 c. interval scale
           3. apples and oranges

6. An interval scale and an ordinal scale can be converted to a nominal scale and an interval scale can be converted to a nominal scale but a nominal scale is not ordinarily converted to an ordinal scale. TRUE or FALSE.

7. Match up the items on the left with those on the right.
   2 a. percentile score
           1. deviation score from the mean
   1 b. standard score
           2. number of scores one exceeds
   3 c. norms
           3. set of relative scores

8. Look at Figure 7.2, page 148. A student obtained a raw score of 13 on the autonomy scale of the EPPS.
   a. What would this students's percentile score be?

b. If 1,000 students took the test, how many students would be expected to get a lower score on this scale?

c. If this score were calculated to fall exactly 1 sd below the mean, what would the standard score be? (For part (c), use Figure 7.1, page 146.)

9. Go to the library and find the *Sixth Mental Measurements Yearbook*. Answer the following questions about the "Pictorial Test of Intelligence":

a. test number   f. age range
b. page number   g. number of scores
c. author   h. number of forms
d. publisher   i. cost for examiner's kit
e. time to complete full test   j. date of publication

10. The *Sixth Mental Measurements Yearbook* lists tests of sex knowledge. Which of the tests that they list would you use if you were doing a study of sex knowledge and why?

11. Using the *Sixth Mental Measurements Yearbook* match up the items on the left with those on the right.

a. group intelligence test   1. Structured Doll Play Test
b. nonprojective character test   2. Pupil Record of Educational Progress
c. vocational interest test   3. English Usage: Every Pupil Test
d. achievement battery   4. The Quick Test
e. projective personality test   5. Qualifications Record
f. individual intelligence test   6. Jensen Alternation Board
     7. Secondary Verbal Tests
     8. Test of Basic Assumptions

12. Which of the following is a projective character test?

a. FIRO-B
b. Human Relations Inventory
c. It Scale for Children
d. Children's Apperception Test
e. Welsh Figure Preference Test

13. Consider the following test scores of six people on a four-item test ($\checkmark$ = right, X = wrong).

	1	2	3	4	5	6
Item 1	$\checkmark$	X	X	$\checkmark$	X	X
Item 2	$\checkmark$	$\checkmark$	$\checkmark$	$\checkmark$	X	$\checkmark$
Item 3	X	X	$\checkmark$	$\checkmark$	$\checkmark$	X
Item 4	$\checkmark$	X	X	$\checkmark$	X	$\checkmark$

Calculate the indices of difficulty and discriminability of each item. Which item would you eliminate?

14. In constructing a paper-and-pencil performance test, the following steps are undertaken. List them in the proper order in which they are done.
    a. performing an item analysis
    b. eliminating poor items
    c. developing a content outline
    d. collecting pilot data
    e. establishing content validity
    f. writing test items

15. To test the items on a Likert-type attitude scale, the items are administered to a pilot group and then correlations are run between _____
_____ .

16. The semantic differential measures three dimensions. These are _____
_____ , _____ , and _____ .

17. Observer rating scales must be tested for accuracy. This is accomplished by having two or more raters use the scales to rate the same activity and then
_____ .

18. A coding system that counts preselected codeable behaviors each time they occur is called a _____ coding system while one that records the behavior that takes place during preselected time periods is called a _____ coding system.

19. Two raters rated a set of behaviors and obtained an inter-rater reliability of .88. This can be converted to a corrected reliability of _____ if the average of their judgments is used.

8

Constructing
and Using Questionnaires
and Interview Schedules

OBJECTIVES

Identify the various purposes for which questionnaires and interviews are used; identify shortcomings in the use of each. / Identify different question formats and response modes and describe their relative characteristics. / Describe the bases for choosing between a questionnaire and an interview and for choosing a response mode for a specific set of conditions and purposes. / Construct a series of items (for example, a questionnaire or interview) designed to get answers to specific questions. / Describe sampling procedures for use in questionnaire and interview studies. / Describe procedures for administering a questionnaire including the preparation of a cover letter. / Describe procedures for conducting an interview. / Describe procedures for coding and scoring interview and questionnaire data.

8.1 WHAT DO QUESTIONNAIRES AND INTERVIEWS MEASURE?

Questionnaires and interviews are used by researchers to convert into data the information directly given by a person (subject). By providing access to what is "inside a person's head", these approaches make it possible to measure what a person knows (knowledge or information), what a person likes and dislikes (values and preferences), and what a person thinks (attitudes and beliefs). Questionnaires and interviews can also be used to discover what experiences have taken place (biography) and what is occurring at the present. This information can be transformed into numbers or quantitative data by using the attitude scaling or rating scale techniques, described in the previous chapter or by counting the number of respondents who give a particular response, thus generating frequency data.

Questionnaires and interviews are a way of getting data about a person by *asking* him rather than by watching him behave or by sampling a bit of his behavior. However, the self-report approach incorporated in questionnaires and interviews does present certain problems because (a) the respondent must cooperate when completing a questionnaire or interview, (b) he must tell what is— rather than what he thinks ought to be or what he thinks the researcher would like to hear, and (c) he must know what he feels and thinks in order to report it. Thus, these techniques measure not what a person believes but what he says he believes, not what he likes but what he says he likes.

In preparing questionnaires and interviews, the researcher should be very cautious. He must constantly apply the criteria

(1) To what extent might a question influence the respondent to show himself in a good light?

(2) To what extent might a question influence a respondent to be unduly helpful by attempting to anticipate what the researcher wants to hear or find out?

(3) To what extent might a question be asking for information about a respondent that he is not certain, and perhaps not likely, to know about himself.

The validity of questionnaire and interview items will be limited by all three kinds of considerations. However, certain information cannot be obtained any way other than by asking the person, and, even when an alternative is available, the "asking" route may be the most efficient (and often is). Thus, the advantages and disadvantages of a questionnaire or interview as a source of data must be considered in each specific case before a decision can be made.

8.2 HOW MAY THE QUESTIONS BE ASKED?

In this kind of research there are certain forms of question and certain response modes that are commonly used. This section will deal with *question formats*, and the following section with response modes.

Direct versus Indirect Questions

The difference between direct and indirect questions lies in how obvious the question is in soliciting a specific piece of information. If, for instance, a researcher asks a person whether or not he likes his job, that would be a direct question. In the indirect approach he could ask a person what he *thinks* of his job or selected aspects of it and then attempt to build inferences from patterns of responses. By making the purpose of questions less obvious, the indirect approach is more likely to engender frank and open responses, though it may take a greater number of indirect questions to collect information relevant to a single point. (There are, however, specific administrative procedures that may be used to engender frank responses to direct questions. These will be described later.)

Specific versus Non-Specific Questions

One form of question deals very specifically with an object, person, or idea toward which an attitude, belief, or concept is being solicited, for example, an attitude toward a specific painting. Its alternate form probes a more general area, such as a style of painting—abstract. An interviewer can ask a factory worker how he likes operating a lathe or he can ask him how he likes operating machinery or working with his hands. He can ask a student how much he likes a particular teacher versus how satisfied he is with a particular class (which happens to be taught by the teacher in question). Specific questions, like direct ones, may cause a respondent to become cautious or guarded and give less-than-honest answers. Non-specific questions may lead circuituously to the desired information but with less alarm by the respondent.

Fact versus Opinion

Another option the interviewer has is between questions requesting that the respondent provide facts and those requesting opinions. A factual question would ask the respondent for the type of car he owns or for his marital status. The opinion question would ask him if he prefers Fords or Chevrolets or reasons why (or why not) he thinks marriage contributes to a meaningful relationship between a man and a woman. Because the respondent may have a faulty memory or a conscious desire to create a particular impression, factual questions do not always elicit factual answers. Nor do opinion questions necessarily elicit honest opinions because with them distortions based on *social desirability* may occur, i.e., respondents may reply to show themselves in the most socially acceptable light. In both forms, questions must be structured, and questionnaires and interviews administered, to minimize these sources of bias.

Questions versus Statements

On many topics the interviewer can either ask the respondent a direct question or he can provide him with a statement and ask him whether he agrees or disagrees (or whether he thinks it is true or false). In this manner statements can be used as an alternative to questions as a way of obtaining information. In fact, in attitude measurement it is more common to see statements rather than questions used as a stimuli. Consider the following:

- Do you think that the school day
  should be lengthened?   YES   NO

    versus

  The school day should be shortened   AGREE   DISAGREE

There is no basis for distinguishing between these two formats in terms of their potential for eliciting an honest response. Usually the researcher chooses between them on the basis of the response mode which will be discussed in the next section.

Predetermined versus Response-Keyed Questions

Some questionnaires require the respondent to complete every item. Others are designed so that subsequent questions may or may not be answered, depending upon the response to a keyed question. For example, a key item may ask the respondent if he is a college graduate. If he responds "no", he would then be instructed to skip the next question. The decision of whether or not he should answer the question would be keyed to the response he gave on whether or not he graduated from college.

Consider another example of response keying. An interviewer asks a school superintendent if he likes a nationally-known curriculum. Two possible questions are keyed to his response. If he says he likes the curriculum, he will be asked why he likes it; if he says he dislikes the curriculum, he will be asked why he dislikes it. The two questions are obviously similar, though not identical, but note that in neither does the interviewer merely ask the respondent "why"?

8.3 HOW MAY THE QUESTIONS BE ANSWERED?

Not only are there a variety of ways that questions may be asked but there are a multiplicity of forms or modes that responses can take. A number of different *response modes* will be described below.

Unstructured Response

The unstructured response, perhaps more commonly called the open-ended question (although it is the response that is open-ended and not the question), allows the subject to give his own response in whatever form he chooses. Open-ended and non-open-ended questions may be identical. What differentiates the unstructured (open-ended) from the structured is the type of response that the respondent is allowed to make. For instance, if a respondent were asked if he thinks schools should be ungraded and he said yes, he would then be asked why he thinks so. His unstructured response might take several minutes and include a series of arguments, facts, ramblings, etc. A structured response would offer the respondent, say, five reasons and ask him to choose one.

Some examples of the use of the unstructured response mode are listed below. (Also see items II and IV in Figure 8.1 (page 180) as illustrative of the unstructured response mode.)

- Why do you think you didn't try harder in high school? _____
  _____
  _____
  _____

- What led you to go to college? _____
  _____
  _____
  _____

- Describe the feelings you are having as you think of your father.
  _____
  _____
  _____

Thus, the unstructured response mode is a response form over which the researcher attempts to exert little control other than by virtue of the questions he asks and the amount of space (or time) he provides. Once a question is asked, the response may be stated in the way the respondent chooses. Allowing the respondent such control over his response ensures that the respondent will give his own answers rather than agreeing with one of yours. However, this procedure does raise problems in quantification, which will be discussed in detail in Section 8.8 on coding and scoring procedures.

In contrast, an advantage of the structured response format is ease of scoring and quantification of the data. A number of ways to use this format are discussed.

Fill-In Response

The fill-in response mode can be considered the transitional mode between unstructured and structured forms. Though it requires that the individual generate rather than choose a response, it typically limits the range of possible responses by limiting the answer to a word or a phrase. Consider the following examples.

- What is your father's occupation?_____

- In what school did you do your
  undergraduate work?_____

- Looking at the above picture, what one word would you use to best describe the way that it makes you feel?_____

Note that the difference between the unstructured response mode and the structured, fill-in mode is one of degree. In the fill-in mode, respondents are restricted to a single word or phrase and are usually asked to report factual information (although the third example elicits something other than facts). The very wording of the question restricts the number of possible responses the respondent can make, and the number of words he can use.

Tabular Response

A tabular response mode is like a fill-in although somewhat more structured because the respondent must fit his responses into a table. Here is an example.

Next Previous Job Title	Specify Type of Work Performed	Name of Employer	Annual Salary	Dates	
				From	To

Typically the tabular response requires numbers, words, or phrases (often factual information of a personal nature), but it may also be used for respondents to reflect their degree of endorsement or agreement along some scale as shown in Item I, Figure 8.1. (This latter use of the tabular mode will be described in more detail in the following section on scaled response.)

The table is a convenient way of organizing a complex response, that is, a response that includes a variety of information rather than a single piece of information. However, it is otherwise not a distinct response mode. The responses to be made within the tabular organization will either be of the *fill-in* type (as in the above example) or of the *scaled* type (as in Item I, Figure 8.1).

Scaled Response

A commonly used structured response mode is that of a scale (i.e., a series of gradations) on which the respondent is asked to express endorsement or rejection of an attitude statement or to describe some aspect of himself. Item I in Figure 8.1 (which utilizes the tabular form of organization) is illustrative of the scaled response mode. Note that the respondent is asked to consider each concern which is a potential obstacle to job advancement and to indicate the effect of that concern on his acceptance of a new job using the following scale.

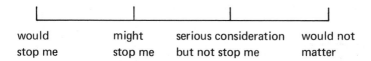

This is a four-point scale of *degree* of influence, from total influence at the left to no influence at the right.

Consider also items III and V in Figure 8.1. Identical in wording but referring to different goals, they ask the respondent to assess his likelihood of reaching a goal, using the following five-point scale.

By choosing one of the above five categories, the respondent indicates the *degree* to which he sees goal attainment as likely.

Halpin (1966) in his *Organizational Climate Descriptive Questionnaire* (OCDQ) uses a scale to indicate *frequency* (Figure 8.2). The respondent, usually

I. Suppose you were offered an opportunity to make a substantial advance in a job or occupation. Place a check opposite each item in the following list to show how important it would be in stopping you from making that advance.

	Would stop me	Might stop me from making change	Would be a serious consideration but wouldn't stop me	Wouldn't matter at all
Endanger your health				
Leave your family for some time				
Move around the country a lot				
Leave your community				
Leave your friends				
Give up leisure time				
Keep quiet about political views				
Learn a new routine				
Work harder than you are now				
Take on more responsibility				

II. Looking at your present situation, what do you expect to be doing five years from now?

_____

III. What are your chances of reaching this goal?

____ excellent ____good ____ fair ____poor ____very poor

IV. What would you *like* to be doing five years from now?

_____

V. What are your chances of reaching this goal?

____ excellent ____good ____fair ____poor ____very poor

Figure 8.1 *A sample questionnaire.*

a teacher, is given a descriptive statement about the behavior of teachers and principals and is asked to indicate the frequency with which this behavior occurs, using, the following four point scale.

| rarely | sometime | often | very frequently |
| occurs (RO) | occurs (SO) | occurs (OO) | occurs (VFO) |

The OCDQ is used primarily to assess whether the climate of a school is open or closed.

All scaled responses measure degree of either frequency or agreement (although a variety of response words may be used) and are based on the assumption that a response on a scale is a quantitative measure of judgment or feeling. (Refer to Section 7.7, on constructing a scale.) Unlike an unstructured response which has to be coded to be useful as data, a structured, scaled response is collected in the form of usable and analyzable data. Moreover, in some research situations, scaled responses can be considered to be *interval* scales.[*] For example, the difference in frequency between *RO* and *SO* in the Organizational Climate Descriptive Questionnaire would be considered equivalent to the difference between *SO* and *OO* and between *OO* and *VFO*. Provided other requirements are met, such interval data can be analyzed using powerful parametric statistical tests. (These statistical procedures will be described in Chapter 9 on statistics.)

Ranking Response

If a researcher gives a respondent a series of statements and asks him to rank-order them in terms of a particular criterion, he will obtain results in terms of ordinal position (i.e., it is *ordinal* measurement). Consider the following example:

- Rank the following activities in terms of their *usefulness* in your learning how to write behavioral objectives. (Use numbers 1 through 5 with 1 indicating the activity most useful and 5 indicating the least useful. If any activity was of no use at all, indicate this by a 0.)

  ＿＿＿ Initial presentation by consultants

  ＿＿＿ Initial small group activity

*See Section 7.3 for a discussion of the types of measurement scales.

Instructions:

Following are some statements about the school setting. Please indicate the extent to which each statement characterizes your school by circling the appropriate response at the right of each statement.

RO—rarely occurs, SO—sometimes occurs, OO—often occurs, VFO—very frequently occurs

1. Teachers' closest friends are other faculty members at this school.	RO	SO	OO	VFO
2. The mannerisms of teachers at this school are annoying.	RO	SO	OO	VFO
3. Teachers spend time after school with students who have individual problems.	RO	SO	OO	VFO
4. Instructions for the operation of teaching aids are available.	RO	SO	OO	VFO
5. Teachers invite other faculty members to visit them at home.	RO	SO	OO	VFO
6. There is a minority group of teachers who always oppose the majority.	RO	SO	OO	VFO
7. Extra books are available for classroom use.	RO	SO	OO	VFO
8. Sufficient time is given to prepare administrative reports.	RO	SO	OO	VFO
9. Teachers know the family background of other faculty members.	RO	SO	OO	VFO
10. Teachers exert group pressure on non-conforming faculty members.	RO	SO	OO	VFO
11. In facutly meetings, there is the feeling of "let's get things done".	RO	SO	OO	VFO
12. Administrative paper work is burdensome at this school.	RO	SO	OO	VFO
13. Teachers talk about their personal life to other faculty members.	RO	SO	OO	VFO
14. Teachers seek special favors from the principal.	RO	SO	OO	VFO
15. School supplies are readily available for use in classwork.	RO	SO	OO	VFO
16. Student progress reports require too much work.	RO	SO	OO	VFO

Figure 8.2 *The Organizational Climate Descriptive Questionnaire (OCDQ). From A. W. Halpin,* Theory and Research in Administration, *New York, Macmillan, 1966, pp. 148-150.* * *(Reprinted by permission of the author and publisher.)*

*The OCDQ is published by the Macmillan Company. It cannot be reproduced in any form without permission from the publishers.

17. Teachers have fun socializing together during school time.	RO	SO	OO	VFO
18. Teachers interrupt other faculty members who are talking in staff meetings.	RO	SO	OO	VFO
19. Most of the teachers here accept the faults of their colleagues.	RO	SO	OO	VFO
20. Teachers have too many committee requirements.	RO	SO	OO	VFO
21. There is considerable laughter when teachers gather informally.	RO	SO	OO	VFO
22. Teachers ask nonsensical questions in faculty meetings.	RO	SO	OO	VFO
23. Custodial service is available when needed.	RO	SO	OO	VFO
24. Routine duties interfere with the job of teaching.	RO	SO	OO	VFO
25. Teachers prepare administrative reports by themselves.	RO	SO	OO	VFO
26. Teachers ramble when they talk in faculty meetings.	RO	SO	OO	VFO
27. Teachers at this school show much school spirit.	RO	SO	OO	VFO
28. The principal goes out of his way to help teachers.	RO	SO	OO	VFO
29. The principal helps teachers solve personal problems.	RO	SO	OO	VFO
30. Teachers at this school stay by themselves.	RO	SO	OO	VFO
31. The teachers accomplish their work with great vim, vigor, and pleasure.	RO	SO	OO	VFO
32. The principal sets an example by working hard himself.	RO	SO	OO	VFO
33. The principal does personal favors for teachers.	RO	SO	OO	VFO
34. Teachers eat lunch by themselves in their own classrooms.	RO	SO	OO	VFO
35. The morale of the teachers is high.	RO	SO	OO	VFO
36. The principal uses constructive criticism.	RO	SO	OO	VFO
37. The principal stays after school to help teachers finish their work.	RO	SO	OO	VFO
38. Teachers socialize together in small select groups.	RO	SO	OO	VFO
39. The principal makes all class-scheduling decisions.	RO	SO	OO	VFO
40. Teachers are contacted by the principal each day.	RO	SO	OO	VFO

Figure 8.2 (continued)

41. The principal is well prepared when he speaks at school functions.	RO	SO	OO	VFO
42. The principal helps staff members settle minor differences.	RO	SO	OO	VFO
43. The principal schedules the work for the teachers.	RO	SO	OO	VFO
44. Teachers leave the grounds during the school day.	RO	SO	OO	VFO
45. Teachers help select which courses will be taught.	RO	SO	OO	VFO
46. The principal corrects teachers' mistakes.	RO	SO	OO	VFO
47. The principal talks a great deal.	RO	SO	OO	VFO
48. The principal explains his reasons for criticism to teachers.	RO	SO	OO	VFO
49. The principal tries to get better salaries for teachers.	RO	SO	OO	VFO
50. Extra duty for teachers is posted conspicuously.	RO	SO	OO	VFO
51. The rules set by the principal are never questioned.	RO	SO	OO	VFO
52. The principal looks out for the personal welfare of teachers.	RO	SO	OO	VFO
53. School secretarial service is available for teachers' use.	RO	SO	OO	VFO
54. The principal runs the faculty meeting like a business conference.	RO	SO	OO	VFO
55. The principal is in the building before teachers arrive.	RO	SO	OO	VFO
56. Teachers work together preparing administrative reports.	RO	SO	OO	VFO
57. Faculty meetings are organized according to a tight agenda.	RO	SO	OO	VFO
58. Faculty meetings are mainly principal-report meetings.	RO	SO	OO	VFO
59. The principal tells teachers of new ideas he has run across.	RO	SO	OO	VFO
60. Teachers talk about leaving the school system.	RO	SO	OO	VFO
61. The principal checks the subject-matter ability of teachers.	RO	SO	OO	VFO
62. The principal is easy to understand.	RO	SO	OO	VFO
63. Teachers are informed of the results of a supervisor's visit.	RO	SO	OO	VFO
64. The principal insures that teachers work to their full capacity.	RO	SO	OO	VFO

Figure 8.2 (continued)

_____ Weekly faculty sessions

_____ Mailed instructions and examples of behavioral objectives

_____ Individual sessions with consultant

Ranking has the value of forcing respondents to choose between alternatives. If a respondent were asked to rate (that is, scale) or accept–reject each of the above activities, he could credit them all equally, but ranking forces him to be critical in his estimation of the value of each activity.

Typically, ranked data is analyzed by summing the rank of each response across subjects, thus obtaining an overall or group rank order of alternatives. Such an overall ranking generated by one group (for example, teachers) can be compared to that generated by a second group (for example, administrators) using non-parametric statistical techniques. (See Chapter 9.)

Checklist Response

In a checklist item the respondent replies by selecting one of the possible choices offered to him. This form of response, however, does not represent a scale because the answers do not represent points on a continuum; rather they are *nominal* categories. Two examples are given below.

- The kind of job that I would most prefer would be:
  Check one:

  _____ (1) A job where I am almost always certain of my ability to perform well.

  _____ (2) A job where I am usually pressed to the limit of my abilities.

- I get most of my professional and intellectual stimulation from:
  Check *one* of the following blanks:

  _____ A. Teachers in the system

  _____ B. Principal

  _____ C. Superintendent

  _____ D. Other professional personnel in the system

  _____ E. Other professional personnel elsewhere

  _____ F. Periodicals, books, and other publications

Nominal judgments as required by a checklist are often easier to make than scalar judgments and take less time for the respondent, but they yield less information for the researcher. Nominal data are usually analyzed by means of the chi-square statistical analysis (which will be described in the next chapter).

Categorical Response

The categorical response mode, similar to the checklist but simpler, offers the respondent only two response possibilities for each item. (Admittedly, the checklist item also offers only two responses: check or no check, each on a series of choices. However, the checklist is more complex since the choices cannot be considered independently, as in the categorical mode, and, after a check is made, no further option exists on the remaining choices in the list.)

Yes-no is often used in the categorical response mode:

- Are you a veteran?   Yes _____ No _____

True-false may be used with attitude items:

- Guidance counseling does not begin early enough. True _____ False _____

It is possible to render true-false data into *interval* form by using the number of true (or number of responses indicating favorableness) as the respondent's score. The total or cumulative number of true responses made by an individual S on a questionnaire then becomes an indication of the degree or frequency of agreement by that S—an interval measure. Counting the number of Ss who indicate agreement on a single item provides a nominal measure.

8.4 CONSTRUCTING A QUESTIONNAIRE OR INTERVIEW SCHEDULE

How do you go about constructing a questionnaire or interview schedule? What questions do you ask and in what format? What response modes do you employ? To answer, begin by asking, "What am I trying to find out?"

Specifying the Variables to Be Measured

The questions to be asked on a questionnaire or in an interview reflect what it is you are trying to find out, that is, your hypotheses or research questions. To find out what to measure you need only write down the names of all the variables you are dealing with in your study. A study which is attempting to relate source of occupational training (i.e., high school, junior college, or on-the-job) to degree of geographic mobility would have to measure where the individual was trained for the job and places where the individual has lived. A study concerned with a comparison between eighth graders and twelfth graders in terms of how favorably they perceive the high-school climate would have to ask respondents to indicate their grade level (8th or 12th) and have them react to statements about the high-school climate in such a way as to indicate whether they saw it as favorable or not. A study concerned with the relative incomes of terminal academic and vocational high school graudates five years after graduation would have to ask respondents to indicate whether they were academic or vocational high-school graduates and how much money they were presently earning. Thus, the first step in constructing questionnaire or interview questions is to *specify your variables by name.* Your variables are what you are trying to measure. They tell you where to begin.

Choosing the Question Format

The first decision you must make about question format is whether to use a written questionnaire or an oral interview. Because it is more convenient and economical, the questionnaire is more commonly used, although it does limit the kinds of questions that can be asked and the kinds of answers that are obtained. Personally sensitive and revealing information is difficult to obtain from a questionnaire and it is also difficult to get answers to indirect, nonspecific questions that represent probes. Also, on questionnaires you must decide all of your questions in advance, and other than through some limited response-keyed questions, you must ask all respondents the same questions. The best possibilities for response-keyed questions are with interviews.

Table 8.1 summarizes the relative merits of interviews and questionnaires. Ordinarily, a researcher undertakes the additional cost and unreliability of interviewing only when the nature of the area he is studying is sensitive and/or when he wants to personalize the questioning. (Interview unreliability is based on the fact that the researcher is dependent on the interviewer to elicit, record, and often code the response.) In general, when the researcher chooses to use the unstructured response mode, interviewing tends to be the better choice because people find it easier to talk than write and consequently more information is generated.

The choice of question format is, of course, based on whether you are attempting to measure facts, attitudes, preferences, and so on. Use direct, specific, clearly-worded questions and keep response-keying to a minimum in constructing a questionnaire. In constructing an interview schedule you may sacrifice specificity for depth and use indirect, subtle probes to work into an area of questioning. Response-keyed questions—questions that the answers to which determine which subsequent questions, if any, must be answered—are also recommended as a labor-saving shortcut.

Table 8.1 *Summary of relative merits of interviewing versus questionnaires.*

Consideration		*Interview*	*Questionnaire*
(1)	Personnel needed to collect data	Requires interviewers	Requires a clerk
(2)	Major expense	Payment to interviewers	Postage and printing
(3)	Opportunities for response-keying (personalization)	Extensive	Limited
(4)	Opportunities for asking	Extensive	Limited
(5)	Opportunity to probe (follow leads)	Possible	Difficult
(6)	Relative magnitude of data reduction	Great (because of coding)	Mainly limited to to rostering
(7)	Typically, the number of respondents who can be reached	Limited	Extensive
(8)	Rate of return	Good	Poor
(9)	Sources of error	Interviewer, instrument, coding, sample	Limited to instrument and sample
(10)	Overall reliability	Quite limited	Fair
(11)	Emphasis on writing skill	Limited	Extensive

Choosing the Response Mode

There are no specific rules for response mode selection. In some cases the kind of information you are seeking will determine the most suitable response mode, but often you must choose between equally acceptable forms. You can, for instance, provide a respondent with a blank space and ask him to fill in his age or, alternatively, you can give him a series of age groupings (e.g., 20–30, 30–40, etc.) and ask him to check the one into which his age fits.

The decision of which response mode to employ should be based on the manner in which the data will be treated, although, unfortunately, researchers do not always decide this before the data are collected. It is recommended that data analysis decisions be made in conjunction with the selection of response modes so that the researcher (1) can be assured that data will serve his intended purposes, and (2) can begin to construct data rosters and to prepare for the analyses (see Chapter 10). To return to the previous example, if age data will ultimately be grouped into ranges to provide nominal data for a chi-square statistical analysis, the researcher would want to design his questionnaire item for collecting these data in grouped form.

Scaled responses most readily lend themselves to parametric statistical analysis since they often can be considered to be interval data. Ranking procedures may provide less information since they generate ordinal data. Fill-ins and checklists usually provide nominal data, which, unless otherwise coded, lend themselves to chi-square analysis. Thus, the ultimate criterion in choosing a response mode is the nature of your variables and your intentions for statistically testing your hypotheses.* If the statistical tests to be used to analyze the data are not determined in advance, the best rule-of-thumb is to use the scaled response mode since the interval data so collected can always be transformed into ordinal or nominal data (see Chapter 9).

Certain other practical considerations must also be taken into account when choosing a response mode. Scaled responses may take longer than the true-false type for the respondent to complete (and longer for the researcher to score). If your questionnaire is already lengthy, the true-false response mode may be preferable insofar as it will reduce the burden placed upon the respondent. Fill-ins have the advantage of not biasing the respondent's judgment as much as the other types but they have the disadvantage of being more difficult to score or code. Response-keyed questions provide the respondent with greater response flexibility but, like the fill-ins, may be more difficult to score and do not provide parallel data for all respondents. Some of these considerations are summarized in Table 8.2

Thus, selection between response modes requires a consideration of the following:

1. *Type of data desired* (for analysis purposes). If you seek interval data, as required for some types of statistical analysis, scaled and checklist

Conversely, should the response mode be chosen first, it should be the criterion for choosing the statistical tests.

Table 8.2 *Considerations in selecting a response mode.*

Response Mode	Type of Data	Chief Advantages	Chief Disadvantages
Fill-in	Nominal	Less biasing; greater response flexibility	More difficult to score
Scaled	Interval	Easy to score	Time consuming; can be biasing
Ranking	Ordinal	Easy to score; forces discrimination	Difficult to complete
Checklist or categorical	Nominal (may be interval when totalled)	Easy to score; easy to respond	Provides less data and fewer options

Note: The tabular mode is just a way of organizing fill-in or scaled responses and thus has been omitted from the table as a distinct category.

responses are best. (The checklist item must be coded to yield interval data and responses must be pooled across items. An individual checklist-type item yields nominal data.) Ranking provides ordinal data and fill-ins and some checklists provide nominal data.

2. *Response flexibility.* Fill-ins allow the respondent the greatest degree of choice; yes-no and true-false items the least.

3. *Time to complete.* Ranking procedures generally take the most time to complete although scaled items may be equally tedious.

4. *Potential response bias.* Scaled responses and checklist responses offer the greatest potential for bias. Respondents may be biased not only by social desirability considerations but by a variety of other factors, such as a tendency to overuse the "true" or "yes" answer and the selection of one point on the scale using it as the response to every item. Others are inclined to avoid the extremes of a rating scale, thus shrinking the scale. These troublesome tendencies on the part of respondents are strongest on long questionnaires, which provoke fatigue and annoyance. Ranking and fill-in modes are less susceptible to such difficulties. In particular, ranking forces the respondent to discriminate between response alternatives.

5. *Ease of scoring.* Fill-in responses must usually be coded and therefore are considerably more difficult to score. The other types of responses discussed are approximately equally easy to score.

Preparing Interview Items

As pointed out earlier, the first step in preparing items for an interview schedule is to specify the variables that you are trying to measure; then construct questions that focus on these variables. If, for example, one of your variables is
openness of climate, an obvious question to ask classroom teachers would be:
How open is the climate here? Less direct but perhaps more concrete would be
questions such as: Do you feel free to take your problems to the principal? Do
you feel free to adopt new classroom practices and materials? Note that the questions are based on the operational definition of the variable openness, which in
this case has been operationally defined as freedom to change, freedom to

1. Would you say overall that your experience in the State Home was a favorable
   or an unfavorable one?
2. What made it favorable (or unfavorable)?
   a. Would you comment on the school program?
   b. On the cottage officers?
   c. On the doctors?
   d. On the other boys?
3. Choose the one of the above that provokes the most negative feeling. What
   would you have us do to overcome the problems you have identified with?
   (e.g. the doctors)　　　　　　　　　　
4. What do you plan to do now that you are leaving?
   a. (If not mentioned specifically)　What kind of job will you look for (ask
      only if the boy is 16 or older and indicates he will not return to school)?
   b. (If he mentions a job) What made you choose that job?
   c. (If he mentions a job) Do you have any skill in that area?
5. Have you had any experiences here that will help you when you leave? (Try
   to elicit specific answers.)
6. What were some of the worst experiences you have had? Describe them.
   (Try to elicit specific answers.)
   Can you think of any more? (Repeat until no more can be thought of.)
7. What were some of the best experiences you have had? Describe them. (Try
   to elicit specific answers.)
   Can you think of any more? (Repeat until no more can be thought of.)
8. Do you have any more comments or feelings about your experiences in the
   State Home?

Figure 8.3 *A sample interview schedule.*

approach superiors, and so on. In writing questions, make sure they incorporate the properties set forth in the operational definitions of your variables. (Recall that these properties may be either dynamic or static, depending on whether a type B or type C operational definition was employed; see Chapter 4.)

It is quite acceptable to employ more than one question format and more than one response mode in an interview schedule or questionnaire. A sample interview schedule appears in Figure 8.3. It seeks to measure the favorableness of the incarceration experience of boys in a state home, the factors and experiences contributing positively and negatively to the favorableness, and future plans. It is a reasonably unstructured interview schedule. Some of the questions are response-keyed. Most of them are nonspecific while all responses are open-ended.

Preparing Questionnaire Items

The procedures for preparing questionnaire items parallel those for preparing interview schedule items. Again, the relationship between the items and the variables as operationally defined is of critical importance. Thus, you must constantly ask about your items: Is this what I want to be measuring? Three sample questionnaires appear in Figures 8.4, 8.5, and 8.6.

The questionnaire in Figure 8.4 (Buzzell, 1970) is only two parts of a lengthy questionnaire which seeks to measure in depth a man's employment history and job training. Section IV of the questionnaire deals with the source of technical training. After determining if the respondent was trained in a high school, post-high school institution, or on the job, the questions seek to determine the nature of this training.

Note that questions 17–20 determine where the training occurred, with the remaining questions response-keyed to questions 17, 18, and 19. Once the respondent has indicated where he was trained, he need only fill out those items (21, 22–24, or 25–28) dealing with his source of training. Section V of the same questionnaire deals with his occupational history. Here the researcher is primarily interested in the number of different jobs held by an individual (this section incidentally continues, providing more space for individuals having held more than three jobs). However, the researcher is also interested in finding out if the jobs were different, and to what degree, so he employs a scaled response in addition to the tabular, fill-in approach.

The sample questionnaire in Figure 8.5 (page 195) uses the scaled response and is an attempt to measure attitudes toward business education training

Section IV   **SOURCE OF TECHNICAL TRAINING**

17. Did you receive your technical training for the technology in which you are now employed in high school? ☐ No ☐ Yes (If Yes, skip to Question 21)

18. If No, did you receive your technical training for the technology in which you are now employed in a post-high school? (i.e., Technical Institute, 2-Year College, 4-Year College, Armed Forces Training School, etc.) ☐ No ☐ Yes (If Yes, skip to Question 22)

19. If No, did you receive your technical training for the technology in which you are now employed on-the-job? (i.e. Apprentice Training, MDTA, In-Plant Training, etc.) ☐ No ☐ Yes (If Yes, skip to Question 25)

20. If No, please explain how you received your technical training _____

_____

HIGH SCHOOL TECHNICAL TRAINING

21. If you answered Yes to Question 17, how would you describe the high school in which you received your technical training?
   A. Vocational High School   ☐
   B. Regular High School   ☐
   C. Other (Please specify) _____

POST-HIGH SCHOOL TECHNICAL TRAINING (Including Armed Forces Training)

22. If you answered Yes to Question 18, how would you describe the post-high school in which you received your technical training?
   A. Vocation-Technical School   ☐
   B. Technical Institute   ☐
   C. Two-Year College   ☐
   D. Science Program in a Four-Year College or University   ☐
   E. Engineering Program in a Four-Year College or University ☐
   F. Armed Forces Training School ☐
   G. Other (Please specify) _____

23. If you attended more than one type of post-high school, identify the type you feel made the most significant contribution to your technical skill training by circling the letter preceding it.

24. What were the actual number of months spent in obtaining the training you have identified above as most significant? (Do not count summer vacation time.) months _____

ON-THE-JOB TECHNICAL TRAINING

25. If you answered Yes to Question 19, how would you describe the type of on-the-job training.
   A. Formal employer training program (including regular classtime scheduled away from the "bench").   ☐
   B. Informal training at the bench   ☐
   C. Apprentice Training   ☐
   D. Manpower Development Training Program (MDTA)   ☐
   E. Other (Please specify) _____

26. If you received more than one type of on-the-job training, identify the type you feel made the most significant contribution to your technical skill training by circling the letter preceding it.

27. What were the actual number of months spent in obtaining the training you have identified above as most significant? months _____

Figure 8.4 *Sample Questionnaire I. (From C. H. Buzzell, Incidents of geographic and occupational mobility among certified electronic technicians in the middle-Atlantic States, New Brunswick, N.J., Rutgers University, unpublished doctoral dissertation, 1970, pp. 164–166. (Reprinted by permission of the author.)*

28. How many hours per day were spent in this traning program? hours _____

Directions: The following questions are designed to assess the degree to which
           your employment, as a technician has changed.

29. How many different full-time jobs have you had as a technician since you
    completed your technical training?

30. How many different full-time jobs have you had since you completed your
    technical training which would not be classified as technical jobs?

31. Please complete one section for every job (technical and non-technical) you
    have held since you completed your training as a technician. Start with
    your present job. If additional space is required please supply on insert page.

Present Job Title	Specific Type of Technical Work Performed	Name of Employer	Annual Salary	Date From	To
					Present

A. Are the skills and knowledge required of this job different from those
   required of your previous job?

   ☐ No   ☐ Somewhat   ☐ Considerably   ☐ Completely
   0   2   4   6

B. Are the products and/or services associated with this job different from
   those of your previous job?

   ☐ No   ☐ Somewhat   ☐ Considerably   ☐ Completely
   0   1   2   3

32.

Next Previous Job Title	Specific Type of Work Performed	Name of Employer	Annual Salary	Date From	To

A. Were the skills and knowledge required of this job different from those
   required of the job you held before this one?

   ☐ No   ☐ Somewhat   ☐ Considerably   ☐ Completely
   0   2   4   6

B. Were the products and/or services associated with the job different from
   those of the job you held before this one?

   ☐ No   ☐ Somewhat   ☐ Considerably   ☐ Completely
   0   1   2   3

33.

Next Previous Job Title	Specific Type of Work Performed	Name of Employer	Annual Salary	Date From	To

A. Were the skills and knowledge required of this job different from those
   required of the job you held before this one?

   ☐ No   ☐ Somewhat   ☐ Considerably   ☐ Completely
   0   2   4   6

B. Were the products and/or services associated with this job different
   from those of the job you held before this one?

   ☐ No   ☐ Somewhat   ☐ Considerably   ☐ Completely
   0   1   2   3

Figure 8.4 (continued)

Directions: Please circle the number that best describes your viewpoint.

	I certainly do	I think so	At times I do	I don't think so	I certainly do not
16. Do you feel your high school business education program is effectively preparing you to obtain your first office position?	5	4	3	2	1
17. Do you feel you could find work as an office employee without being graduated from a high-school business education program?	5	4	3	2	1
18. Do you expect to have difficulty obtaining an office position?	5	4	3	2	1
19. Do you feel minority group and white job applicants have the same chances of being hired for office employment?	5	4	3	2	1
20. Do you expect to take an aptitude or a typewriting test before you are hired for an office position?	5	4	3	2	1
21. Do you feel you will be accepted quickly by your fellow employees?	5	4	3	2	1
22. Do you feel it important that you get along with fellow employees?	5	4	3	2	1
23. Do you feel a need for a great amount of on-the-job training before you become a productive office employee?	5	4	3	2	1
24. Do you feel pressure will be placed on you to meet work deadlines?	5	4	3	2	1
25. Do you expect your office promotions to be based on reports written by your boss?	5	4	3	2	1
26. Do you feel promotion from your beginning office position will require education beyond high school?	5	4	3	2	1
27. Do you feel it desirable that you obtain training beyond high school to be promoted from your beginning office position?	5	4	3	2	1
28. Do you plan to further your education beyond high school?	5	4	3	2	1
29. If you decided to enroll in a night school course, would you expect your office employer to pay a part of the cost of this course?	5	4	3	2	1
30. Do you feel your office employer should make a profit on your work? (Should you be worth mòre to your employer than what you are paid?)	5	4	3	2	1

Figure 8.5 *Sample Questionnaire II. (From E. Brower, The office employment expectations of white and non-white business education students, Philadelphia, Temple University, unpublished doctoral dissertation, 1970, pp. 195-196. Reprinted by permission of the author.)*

received in a high-school program (Brower, 1970). Note that for each item a five-point scale is available for responding and that the question format is utilized. Note further that some of the items have been *reversed* (e.g., 18, 23). That is, the questions have been written in two directions so that agreement on some items indicates positivity while others have been written so that disagreement indicates positivity. Agreement with an item such as number 16, for example, reflects a positive attitude toward the business education program while disagreement with item 18 also reflects a positive attitude. This technique is a protection against the form of response bias in which an individual simply circles the same response number for each item. Under this system, he will not delude you into thinking he is extremely positive or extremely negative, but he will come out neutral since half of the items are written in each direction. Another feature of this questionnaire is the inclusion of items not specifically related to its objective. Item 19, for instance, deals with an attitude area that is unrelated to the one being measured. It is a *filler* item and serves to make the true purpose of the instrument less visible. Filler items are particularly useful in test situations where the potentially obvious purpose of the test and social desirability considerations may be biasing factors.

A third sample questionnaire is shown in Figure 8.6.

Developed by Bryan (1963), this student-opinion questionnaire (SOQ) was the measuring instrument employed in Sample Study I in Appendix A to determine teacher behavior as perceived by students. Items 1–10 are scaled items, each utilizing a five-point scale as the response mode. Note the format includes both a statement and a question (the statement appearing first in block letters and the corresponding question following in parentheses). No attempt has been made to counteract for response bias by reversing the direction of some of the items; each item has been written so that agreement indicates positivity. Obviously, these items are susceptible to biased response based on considerations other than respondent's judgment. The questionnaire also includes four open-ended items, numbers 11–14, although responses to them were not included in the analyses in Sample Study I but were part of the feedback process. (These open-ended items were exempted from analysis in Sample Study I because of their difficulty to code, that is, to convert to numerical scores on a variable.)

Pilot Testing and Evaluating a Questionnaire

It is usually highly desirable to run a pilot test on a questionnaire and to revise it based on the results of the test. A pilot test, which uses a group of respondents

STUDENT-OPINION QUESTIONNAIRE (SOQ), Form 6

Please answer the following questions honestly and frankly. Do not give your name. To encourage you to be frank, your regular teacher should be absent from the classroom while these questions are being answered. Neither your teacher nor anyone else at your school will ever see your answers.

The person who is temporarily in charge of your class during this period will collect all reports and seal them in an envelope addressed to _____ University. Your teacher will receive from the university a summary of the answers by the students in your class. The university will mail this summary to no one except your teacher unless requested to do so by your teacher.

After completing this report, sit quietly or study until all students have completed their reports. There should be no talking.

Underline your answer to each question on this page. Write your answers to questions 11 to 14 on the other side of this page.

WHAT IS YOUR OPINION CONCERNING:

1. THE KNOWLEDGE THIS TEACHER HAS OF THE SUBJECT TAUGHT? (Has he a thorough knowledge and understanding of his teaching field?)
   Below Average   Average   Good   Very Good   The Very Best

2. THE ABILITY OF THIS TEACHER TO EXPLAIN CLEARLY? (Are assignments and explanations clear and definite?)
   Below Average   Average   Good   Very good   The Very Best

3. THIS TEACHER'S FAIRNESS IN DEALING WITH STUDENTS? (Is he fair and impartial in treatment of all students?)
   Below Average   Average   Good   Very Good   The Very Best

4. THE ABILITY OF THIS TEACHER TO MAINTAIN GOOD DISCIPLINE? (Does he keep good control of the class without being harsh? Is he firm but fair?)
   Below Average   Average   Good   Very Good   The Very Best

5. THE SYMPATHETIC UNDERSTANDING SHOWN BY THIS TEACHER? (Is he patient, friendly, considerate, and helpful?)
   Below Average   Average   Good   Very Good   The Very Best

6. HOW MUCH ARE YOU LEARNING IN THIS CLASS? (Are you learning well and much? Are you really working?)
   Below Average   Average   Good   Very Good   The Very Best

Figure 8.6 *Sample Questionnaire III. (From R. C. Bryan, Reactions to teachers by students, parents, and administrators, Kalamazoo, Mich. Western Michigan University (U.S. Office of Education Cooperative Research Project No. 668), 1963, p. 53. Reprinted by permission of the author.)*

7. THE ABILITY THIS TEACHER HAS TO MAKE CLASSES INTEREST-ING? (Does he show enthusiasm and a sense of humor? Does he vary teaching procedures?)

   Below Average   Average   Good   Very Good   The Very Best

8. THE ABILITY OF THIS TEACHER TO GET THINGS DONE IN AN EFFICIENT AND BUSINESS-LIKE MANNER? (Are plans well made? Is little time wasted?)

   Below Average   Average   Good   Very Good   The Very Best

9. THE SKILL THIS TEACHER HAS TO GET STUDENTS TO THINK FOR THEMSELVES? (Are students' ideas and opinions worth something in this class? Do students help decide how to solve problems and how to get their work done? Do they get at the real reasons why certain things happen?)

   Below Average   Average   Good   Very Good   The Very Best

10. THE GENERAL (ALL-ROUND) TEACHING ABILITY OF THIS TEACH-ER? (All factors considered, how close does this teacher come to your ideal?)

    Below Average   Average   Good   Very Good   The Very Best

11. *PLEASE NAME ONE OR TWO THINGS THAT YOU ESPECIALLY LIKE ABOUT THIS TEACHER.

12. PLEASE GIVE ONE OR TWO SUGGESTIONS FOR THE IMPROVEMENT OF THIS TEACHER.

13. PLEASE NAME ONE OR TWO THINGS THAT YOU ESPECIALLY LIKE ABOUT THIS COURSE.

14. PLEASE GIVE ONE OR TWO SUGGESTIONS FOR THE IMPROVEMENT OF THIS COURSE.

*These four open-ended items normally appear on the reverse side of the questionnaire making it possible for the total instrument to occupy a single page.

Figure 8.6 (continued)

who are part of the intended test population but will not be part of the sample, attempts to determine whether questionnaire items possess the desired qualities of measurement and discriminability.

If a series of items are intended to measure the *same* variable (as would be true of the ten SOQ items in Figure 8.6), it is desirable to determine whether these items are measuring something in common. To determine this, the scale would be administered to a pilot sample, and, based on responses, correlations would be run between the scores obtained by each person on each item and the scores obtained by each person across the whole scale (see the discussion on item analysis in the previous chapter). The larger the correlation between an item score and the total score, the greater the relationship between what the item is measuring and what the total scale is measuring. Following the completion of this item analysis, the researcher can select those items having the highest correlations with the total score and use them to make up his final scale. Consider ten items to measure a person's attitude toward some object and the following correlations between each item score and the mean score across all ten items.

Item Number	Correlation
1	.89
2	.75
3	.27
4	.81
5	.19
6	.53
7	.48
8	.72
9	.33
10	.60

Based on these data, the decision would be to eliminate items 3, 5, 7, and 9 and use the other six items as the final scale, confident that the remaining items were measuring something in common.

Item analysis of items intended to measure the same variable in the same way is one important use of the data collected from a pilot test. However, item analyses are not as critical for the refinement of questionnaires as they are for the refinement of tests. Questionnaire items are usually reviewed for clarity and distribution of responses without necessarily running an item analysis.

A pilot test can uncover a variety of failings. For example, if all respondents reply identically to any one item, that item probably lacks discriminability. If you receive a preponderance of inappropriate responses to an item, examine it to see if it is ambiguous or poorly worded. Poor instructions and other administration problems become apparent on a pilot test. In addition, areas of extreme sensitivity often become apparent. If respondents refuse to answer certain items, try to desensitize such items by rewording them. Thus, a pilot run enables the researcher to "debug" his questionnaire by diagnosing and correcting the above kinds of failings.

8.5 SAMPLING PROCEDURES

Random Sampling

A researcher administers a questionnaire or interview to gain information about a particular group of persons, such as high-school graduates, school administrators in New England, or home economics teachers in New Jersey. This target group is termed the *population* of the study, and the first step in sampling is to define the population. Once this has been done, you must then select a *sample* or representative group from this population to serve as respondents. One way to insure that this sample will be representative of the larger population is to draw a *random* sample because random selection limits the probability that you choose a biased sample.* For example, you are interested in obtaining information about presidents of two-year colleges. The population is 2,800 presidents from which you want a sample of 300. Which three hundred should you choose? To draw a random sample, you might write the names of all the two-year colleges in alphabetical order† giving each a number in the sequence. Three hundred numbers would then be randomly selected using a table of random numbers (see Appendix B). The resulting list of 300 colleges, each yielding one president, is a random sample of the population from which it was drawn. No systematic biases in selection or selectees need be expected *as a result* of this procedure.‡ When certain sample variables are of special interest to the researcher (e.g., age) strati-

*Random assignment of subjects to groups was described in Section 5.5. The description here concerns the random selection of subjects from a population. While random assignment is a strategy for controlling threats to internal validity, random selection is a strategy for controlling threats to external validity. It is possible to use both procedures in a single study where experimental and control groups are to be employed. Where groups are to be obtained only by sampling and not assignment, random sampling or some variant would be used alone.

†Actually, you can write them in any order. Alphabetizing is merely a convenience. Indeed, in this particular instance, there is a directory available listing the colleges in alphabetical order which may be used as the selection source.

‡It is possible to determine statistically the extent to which the sample characteristics are equal to the population characteristics and thus that the sample is representative of the population from which it was drawn (as would be expected of a random sample). For a discussion of these statistics, see Ferguson, 1966.

fied sampling is employed with the variables of interest termed sampling parameters (see page 202).

Defining the Population

The population (or target group) used in a questionnaire or interview study is that group about which the researcher is interested in gaining information and drawing conclusions. If the researcher were interested in the educational aspirations of teachers, for example, the population of the study would be teachers. The term *defining the population* refers to the establishment of boundary conditions which specify who shall be included in or excluded from the population. In the above example, the population could be defined as elementary school teachers, or public school teachers, or all teachers, or some other choice.

Specifying the group that is to constitute the population is an early step in the sampling process that affects the nature of the conclusions that may be drawn from a study. If the population is broadly defined (like "all teachers" in the above example), external validity or generalizability will be maximized, although such a broad definition may make obtaining a representative sample difficult and require a large sample size. On the other hand, defining the population narrowly (e.g. as "female, elementary school teachers") may facilitate the selection of a suitable sample but will restrict conclusions and generalizations to the specific population used which may be inconsistent with the intent of the study.

The definition of the target population in a study is most reasonably based on the independent, moderator, and control variables in the study design along with practical considerations such as availability of subjects or respondents. When a control variable in a study deals with a population characteristic, the researcher must systematically include or exclude this characteristic in defining the population. (See also page 84.) For example, if a researcher were interested in a comparison between academic high-school graduates and vocational high-school graduates with the limitation that a student had attended one or the other school for three consecutive years, then the population would be defined to exclude all graduates who had switched from one school to the other. In studying school superintendents in urban and rural settings, to return to an earlier example, a researcher might define the population to exclude all superintendents not yet completing their second year in the district, thus somewhat controlling for longevity, a potentially important control variable. (Longevity might also be controlled through stratified sampling which will be discussed below.)

In addition to design considerations, practical considerations affect the definition of the population as well. In Sample Study I, Appendix A, for example, the availability of vocational school teachers was an influencing factor in leading the researchers to define the population for that study as teachers in vocational schools. However, because of the variables of interest, both teachers of vocational subjects and academic subjects in the vocational schools were included in the definition of the population making it possible for subject taught to serve as an independent variable. In general, independent and moderator variables require inclusion in defining a population while control variables require exclusion.

Thus, an early step in sampling is to define the population from which the sample is to be drawn. By referring to the variables of interest and taking into account practical considerations, the researcher is guided in choosing characteristics to be included in and excluded from the target population. A concrete sampling plan illustrating the process of exclusion in defining the population appears in Table 8.3.

Establishing Specifications for Stratified Random Sampling

The use of *stratified* random sampling will permit you to include parameters of special interest and to control for internal validity in terms of selection factors through the use of moderator or control variables. In addition, stratification represents a good operational strategy for screening members of the population into and out of the study and for reducing the variability of the sample.

The first step in stratified sampling is to identify the stratification parameters or variables. Each stratification parameter represents a control variable, that is, a potential source of error or extraneous influence which may provide an alternative explanation for the outcome of a study. Assume that you want to contrast the teaching techniques of male and female elementary school teachers. The study would restrict the population to elementary school teachers, since that is a specified control variable, and would sample across male and female teachers, since that is the independent variable of the study. You are concerned, however, that the number of years of teaching experience may be an extraneous influence. To offset this potential source of error, first determine the distribution of years of experience for male and for female elementary school teachers and then select the sample in proportion to these distributions. (The selection of specific subjects within each stratum or proportion would be on a random basis.) The other control variables would be treated similarly.

Consider samplings for national political polls. Results are usually reported separately for different age groups and for different sections of the country. Thus, age and geography are treated as moderator variables and are sampled

Table 8.3 *A sampling plan for sampling two-year colleges.*

Population: All two-year colleges in the U.S.A.

Variables controlled by exclusion:
  (1) College must have graduated a minimum of one class
  (2) President must have held position for a minimum of one year

Variables controlled by stratification:
  (1) Private-Public

25% private	75% public

  (2) Urban-Rural

15% urban	10% rural	60% urban	15% rural

  (3) Size of Student Body*

5% large	1% large	48% large	3% large
10% small	9% small	12% small	12% small

If the sample size were to be 300, it would be broken down as follows:

		Sample	Population
private, urban, large	5%	15	140
private, urban, small	10%	30	280
private, rural, large	1%	3	28
private, rural, small	9%	27	252
public, urban, large	48%	144	1344
public, urban, small	12%	36	336
public, rural, large	3%	9	84
public, rural, small	12%	36	336
	100%	300	2800

*Large - more than 2,000 students
Small = fewer than 2,000 students

separately. However, within each age and geographical group, sex, race, religion, socioeconomic status, and specific geographical location may be controlled for by proportional stratification. If half of the Northeastern youth are male, then half of the sample of Northeastern youth should be male. If 65% of the Southeastern middle-aged group is poor, then 65% of the sample of this group should be poor. (Of course, terms like middle-aged and poor must be operationally defined.) The pollsters then take these subpopulation differences into account in evaluating the outcomes of the study.

Consider the example given earlier (see page 200) on sampling 300 presidents of two-year colleges. One possible source of bias in this random selection would be overrepresentation of the private colleges. To control for this factor, use it as a variable or parameter for stratified sampling. Suppose one quarter or 700 of the two-year colleges are private and three quarters or 2100 are public. In proportional stratified sampling, you would want this percentage embodied in your sample. In a sample of 300 college presidents you would want 75 from private two-year colleges and 225 from public ones (the specific ones in each stratum being randomly chosen), making the sample systematically representative of the population. To accomplish this stratified sampling, it would be necessary to make two separate alphabetical lists, one of private colleges, the other of public. You would then use your table of random numbers to select 75 private and 225 public colleges from the two lists, respectively. Of course, you could go further and control also for factors such as urban versus rural setting or large versus small colleges. However, in considering stratification remember that each additional control variable complicates the sampling procedure and reduces the population per category from which each part of the sample is drawn. The sampling plan for this study is shown in Table 8.3.

While randomness is the key to overcoming selection bias in sampling, stratification adds precision in insuring that the sample contains the same proportional distribution of respondents on selected parameters as the population. If a non-random sample were to be drawn, its representativeness of the target population would *not* be insured. Stratification, in addition to random selection, increases the likelihood that the sample will be representative of the population. Where stratified sampling is used, it is important that *within each stratum, sample respondents are chosen randomly* from the population to increase the likelihood that selection sources of invalidity other than those controlled through stratification will be eliminated. Since stratification controls for selection invalidity based on pre-selected variables in a systematic way, it is recommended for use with those variables identified as representing the greatest potential source of selection bias.

Determining Sample Size

In designing a questionnaire study, a researcher will invariably ask: How large a sample should I employ? He will reasonably seek to use as small a sample as he can for reasons of time and cost, while keeping it large enough to insure its representativeness. Very often researchers select a sample size based on their own experience or choose a size utilized in a similar study. However, it is possible to obtain some guidance in choosing a sample size on a more systematic basis than those above.

The primary issue in choosing a sample size is that it be sufficient to assure the researcher that the sample will be representative of the population from which it is drawn. While he can never be certain of this representativeness unless he tests the entire population, he can establish that the sample is representative of the population on critical parameters *at an acceptable level of probability*. This probability level, called a *confidence level*, is usually set at 95% (the so-called .05 level) meaning that there is a 95% chance that the sample is distributed in the same way as the population. (Occasionally the confidence level is set more stringently at 99% (the .01 level) or less stringently at 90% (the .10 level).

A further issue in sampling is called *sampling error*, the extent to which the sample means of repeatedly drawn random samples deviate from one another and presumably from the population mean. It is desirable to minimize sampling error in order to maximize sample representativeness.

In stratified sampling, a researcher attempts to maintain the same proportionality on stratification parameters in the sample as occur in the population. If sex, for example, were a stratification parameter, and the population contained 50% males and 50% females, the researcher would want to maintain these same proportions in his sample. Thus the representativeness of the sample in terms of the population may be specified in terms of sampling error, acceptable confidence level, and distribution of a stratification parameter.

In studies where a single dichotomous stratification parameter is employed (e.g., private–public, urban–rural, large–small) and with random sampling within each category, the formula given below may be used for determining a sample size suitable for obtaining a sample representative on this parameter for a given confidence level and a given sampling error.

$$N = (z/e)^2 (p)(1 - p)$$

N is the sample size, z is the standard score corresponding to a given confidence level, e is the proportion of sampling error in a given situation, and p is the estimated proportion or incidence of cases in the population. Confidence level, again, refers to the *probability* that the sample proportion will reflect the population proportion on a given outcome with a specific degree of accuracy (this degree of accuracy being designated as e). For a 90% confidence level, $z = 1.65$; for a 95% confidence level, $z = 1.96$; for a 99% confidence level, $z = 2.58$. (See the sources recommended at the end of this chapter for further details.)

Consider the example in Table 8.3. Private two-year colleges account for 25% of all two-year colleges. The proportion of cases of private colleges in the population of two-year colleges is .25 ($p = .25$). If you wanted a confidence level of 95% ($z = 1.96$) with a tolerable amount of error no greater than plus or minus 0.10 you would calculate the necessary sample size as shown below.

$$N = (1.96/0.10)^2 \quad (0.25) \quad (0.75)$$
$$N = (19.6)^2 \quad (0.1875)$$
$$N = 72$$

Thus, a sample size of 72 private two-year colleges would create no more than a plus or minus 0.10 sampling error with a confidence limit of 95% for a population with the incidence of 25% private and 75% public two-year colleges. Note that in the example in Table 8.3, a sample of 75 private two-year colleges was designated. The above calculations indicate that the sample size will be adequate for maintaining sampling error within tolerable limits for a sample sub-divided into two categories—in this case private and public colleges.

When there is some question about sample size, you should select as large a sample as is practical since with a large sample the sampling error is likely to be small. In addition, large samples add to the stability of the findings obtained.

8.6 PROCEDURES FOR ADMINISTERING A QUESTIONNAIRE

This section will focus on procedures for mailing out a questionnaire, following it up, and subsequent sampling from among those in the sample who do not respond (hereafter called nonrespondents).

Initial Mailing

The initial mailing of a questionnaire to a sample of respondents typically includes a cover letter, the questionnaire itself, and a stamped, return-addressed envelope.

The cover letter is a critical part of the initial mailing because it must establish the legitimacy of the study and the respectability of the researcher. The cover letter should be brief but should focus on the following points.

(1) *The purpose of the study.* A respondent will be anxious to know what the data are to be used for to satisfy his intellectual curiosity and to allay any doubts that participation in the study will threaten his privacy or reputation. Therefore, the cover letter should indicate the purposes and intentions of the study. It is impossible, however, often to give the respondent complete details about the purposes of the study because such knowledge might bias his responses.

(2) *The protection afforded the respondent.* The respondent is entitled to know how his privacy and confidentiality will be treated; thus the letter should indicate whether the respondent is to identify himself and, if so, how his identity and his responses will be protected. If questionnaires will be destroyed after rostering, and if rostering will be done by number rather than name (both practices being recommended) be sure to include this information.

(3) *Endorsements of the study.* Because respondents will be more secure if they know that recognized institutions are behind the study, university or agency letterhead should be used. If respondents are being studied as a part of a professional group, then the cooperation and endorsement of this group should be obtained and mentioned in the letter. If the study is being undertaken as a doctoral dissertation, mention the dissertation advisor by name and/or ask the dean of the school to sign or countersign the letter. If any agency or organization is providing financial support for the study, then it should be acknowledged.

(4) *Legitimacy of the researcher.* Say who and what you are. Identify yourself both by name and by position.

(5) *Opportunities for debriefing.* If the respondent can obtain the results of the study or additional explanations of its purpose at some later date, tell him so.

(6) *Request for cooperation.* The letter constitutes an appeal from you for the respondent's help. If there are special reasons why he should help (e.g., the importance of the study for his profession) be sure to mention them.

(7) *Special instructions.* The questionnaire should be self-administering and self-contained, although general instructions may be contained in the cover letter. Be sure to set a deadline for return and to caution against omissions.

The above seven points are important in any research administration, whether it is done by mail or in person. Thus, a personal interview should, in effect, begin with an *oral* cover letter.

The initial mailing, however, may include more than one cover letter. For example, a letter of endorsement from a funding agency or from an organization to which the respondent belongs may help gain the cooperation of the person being interviewed. It is also wise *not* to put the respondent's name on the questionnaire to avoid alarming him on the privacy-confidentiality issue. Use of a code number is a much better method of identification. Because filling out a questionnaire is, at the very least, an imposition on the respondent's time, both it and the cover letter should be as brief as possible.

Figures 8.7 and 8.8 (pages 209 and 210, respectively) are two examples of a cover letter. The first letter accompanied the 1970 U.S. Census which for the first time was partly done by mail rather than by interview.

Follow-Ups

After a period of about two weeks to a month has elapsed, it is a good idea to correspond with those that have not yet returned their questionnaires (i.e., the nonrespondents). This second mailing can simply be another letter soliciting cooperation and should include another questionnaire and another stamped, return-addressed envelope in case the respondent cannot find the original ones.

Ordinarily from about one third to two thirds of the questionnaires sent out will be returned during the month after the initial mailing. Beyond this, about 10–25% can be stimulated to respond by additional urging. If the second mailing (first follow-up letter) fails to stimulate a response some researchers use a third mailing (second follow-up). It typically takes the form of a post card and follows the second mailing by about two to three weeks. Most researchers are unwilling to accept a return of less than 75% to 90% (and rightly so). Additional mailings, telephone calls, and a large sampling of nonrespondents (see below), are employed to elevate the return. Telegrams or telephone calls may be helpful in getting responses. If a study is worth doing, it is worth striving for the greatest return possible.

Sampling Nonrespondents

If from among those persons receiving the questionnaire, fewer than about 80% complete and return it, than an attempt must be made to reach and obtain

BUREAU OF THE CENSUS
U.S. Department of Commerce
Washington, D.C. 20233

Dear Resident:

This is your 1970 Census.

Our progress as a nation depends today, as it has in the past, on meeting our national challenges with knowledge and reason. To do so, we must constantly take stock of ourselves. The census is an essential tool for this purpose. It is provided for in Article I of the Constitution, and a census has been taken every ten years since 1790.

Every question asked in the 1970 Census has a national purpose. The Federal Government, our States, cities, schools, businesses, and citizen groups all use census figures to plan their work and to measure our country's problems and progress. It is most important, therefore, that you answer all questions which apply to you and your household to the best of your knowledge and ability.

Your answers to the census questions are confidential. They can be used only for statistical purposes. They can be seen only by census employees who are prohibited by law from disclosing them to anyone in or out of the Government.

The census is deeply rooted in America's heritage. I hope you will take pride, as you complete your questionnaire, in exercising the opportunity it gives us once again to strengthen our nation's development.

Sincerely,

Maurice H. Stans

Secretary of Commerce

Figure 8.7 *Sample cover letter I.* (*Reprinted by permission of the Bureau of Census, U.S. Department of Commerce.*)

RUTGERS UNIVERSITY   *The State University of New Jersey*

GRADUATE SCHOOL OF EDUCATION
Department of Vocational-Technical Education
New Brunswick, New Jersey 08903
Tel. 201-247-7636, 247-1766 Ext. 6937

ENDORSING AGENCIES
The Institute for the Certification of Engineering Technicians
American Society of Agricultural Engineers
American Society of Tool and Manufacturing Engineers
Instrument Society of America
National Aeronautics and Space Administration
Rutgers University - The State University of New Jersey
State of New Jersey Department of Education
State of New Jersey Department of Labor and Industry

Dear Certified Technician:

Your help is urgently needed.

The Institute for the Certification of Engineering Technicians has assisted me
in choosing you as a representative of a national stratified sample of
Certified Engineering Technicians to take part in a Rutgers University research
project of major importance.

This project is aimed at assessing the natural mobility of Certified Engineering
Technicians. The purpose of this study will be two fold: (1) the degree of
geographic and employer mobility which you have experienced will provide those
responsible for designing technical training with an indication of the degree to
which technicians sell their skills and knowledge on a local market, as opposed
to a national market, and (2) your mobility history will provide associations and
employers such as those endorsing this study, with an indication of the degree to
which you can be expected, given the proper incentive, to change geographic area.

All that you need do to render this very worthwhile contribution to education and
your association is complete the following questionnaire. Won't you please take
fifteen minutes now and provide the information needed and return the form in
today's mail?

Thank you for this very important contribution. You may be assured that after
the data are transferred to computer cards, this questionnaire will be destroyed
and your anonymity will be guaranteed.

Sincerely,

Charles H. Buzzell
Principal Investigator

Figure 8.8 *Sample cover letter II. (From C. H. Buzzell, Incidents of geographic
and occupational mobility among certified electronic technicians in the middle-
Atlantic states, New Brunswick, N.J., Rutgers University, unpublished doctoral
dissertation, 1970, pp. 158–159. Reprinted by permission of the author.)*

some data from a portion of those who failed to return the questionnaire (the so-called nonrespondents). Additional returns of all or critical portions of the questionnaire by 5 or 10% of the original nonrespondents is required for this purpose.

This additional procedure is necessary to establish that those who have not responded are not systematically different from those who have. If you do not check on the potential bias based on nonresponse, you may have both external and internal invalidity based on experimental mortality (selective, nonrandom loss of subjects from a random sample) as well as a potential increase in sampling error.

Obtaining data from nonrespondents is not easy when they have already ignored two or three attempts on your part to include them in the study. The first step is to select at random 5 to 10% of them from your list of nonrespondents, using the table of random numbers (Appendix B). Using their code numbers, go through the table of random numbers and pick those whose numbers appear first. Next prepare either a special cover letter, write, or call them. About 75 to 80% return from the nonrespondent's sample may be all that can be reasonably expected, but every effort should be made to achieve this.

8.7 CONDUCTING AN INTERVIEW STUDY

Procedures for conducting an interview may differ from those involved in obtaining data by questionnaire, but the aim is the same: to obtain the desired data with maximum efficiency and minimum bias.

Selecting and Training Interviewers

It is obviously preferable to select interviewers who are trained and experienced, but this if often difficult to do. Consequently, many researchers use students (both graduates and undergraduates) or housewives. The level of skill will depend on the nature of information you are trying to elicit; more personal, sensitive material will require more skilled interviewers.

The task of an interviewer is a responsible one, both in terms of his manner in conducting an interview and in his willingness to follow instructions. In training, he should observe interviews being carried out in the prescribed manner and should then have the opportunity to conduct practice interviews during which time he is observed. During such practice interviews, respondents should in some cases be "live" in the sense that they are potential subjects from the sample to be used in the study. In other cases, the researcher should arrange for respondents to present certain typical situations that the interviewer will have to cope with—"rigged" interviews to give the researcher the opportunity to present the trainee with a range of possible situations.

Training should also include familiarizing the interviewer with the forms that will be used in recording responses and keeping a record of his interviewing. In order to exercise some control over the sampling, he must learn how to determine whom he is to interview. It is also necessary to know how to set up an interview appointment, how to introduce himself and begin an interview in a manner that will put the interviewee at ease, how to use response-keyed questions and other nonlinear approaches, how to record the responses, and (if this is to be part of his job) how to code them.

All interviewers should be given similar training experiences where possible, for differences in interviewer style and approach represent a source of internal invalidity based on *instrumentation*. Interviewers are instruments for collecting data, and, as instruments, their own characteristics should affect the data as little as possible. Interviewers should reflect their respondents and not themselves. Of course, it is impossible to make them perfect "mirrors," but if they are chosen from the same population and receive the same training and instructions, they should tend to become standardized against one another as a function of their training. It is also useful not to divulge any more about the study to the interviewers than is absolutely necessary lest you subtly make confederates of those who may unconsciously attempt to bias the outcomes in the directions you desire.

Conducting an Interview

The first task of an interviewer may be to select his respondents, although in some studies, interviewers are given a list of people to contact. Unless the interviewer is both highly trained and experienced, it is much better to give him the names and addresses (and phone numbers) of the persons he is to interview along with a deadline for completion. He may be allowed then to choose his own interviewing order or an order may be recommended.

Typically, the interviewer proceeds by telephoning a potential respondent and essentially presents a verbal "cover letter." However, in a phone conversation, the interviewer has the advantage of being able to alter or expand upon the contents of that "letter" as a reaction to specific concerns raised by the potential respondent. During this first conversation, an interview appointment should also be made.

At the meeting, the interviewer again should brief the respondent as to the nature or purpose of the interview (being as candid as possible without biasing responses) and attempt to make the respondent feel at ease. He should explain the manner in which he will be recording responses, and if he plans to tape record, he should get the respondent's assent. At all times an interviewer must remember that he is a data collection instrument and try not to let his own biases, opinions, or curiosity affect his behavior. It is important that the interviewer not deviate from his format and interview schedule although many schedules will permit some flexibility in choice of questions. The respondent should be kept from rambling away from the essence of a question, but not at the sacrifice of courtesy.

8.8 CODING AND SCORING

Objectively-Scored Items

Data obtained from interviews and questionnaires (often called *protocols*) are not necessarily usable in the exact form in which they are collected but often have to be converted to a different form for analysis. This initial processing of information is called scoring or coding. Many questions, such as rating scales or checklists, are precoded; that is, each response can be immediately and directly converted into a score in an objective fashion. The researcher simply has to assign a score to each point on the list or scale.

Consider item 14 from the Organizational Climate Descriptive Questionnaire which appears in Figure 8.2 (page 182).

14. Teachers seek special favors from the principal.   RO   SO   OO   VFO

You might assign *rarely occurs* (RO) a score of 1, *sometimes occurs* (SO) a score of 2, *often occurs* (OO) a score of 3, and *very frequently occurs* (VFO) a score of 4. You could then add the scores on all the items to obtain a total score on the scale.

Sometimes items are written in both positive and negative directions to avoid response bias. Consider the following two items on a questionnaire measuring attitudes toward school.

- I enjoy myself most of the time in school.

| strongly agree | agree | disagree | strongly disagree |

- When I am in school I usually feel unhappy.

| strongly agree | agree | disagree | strongly disagree |

If you were to score the *strongly agree* for the first item as 4, then you would have to score the *strongly agree* response for the second item as 1 because strong agreement with the first item indicates liking school while strong agreement with the second item indicates disliking school. To be able to add the scores on these two items to get a measure of how much a student likes school, you have to score them in opposite directions.

Often a questionnaire or overall scale will contain a number of subscales each of which measures a different aspect of what the total scale measures. In analyzing subscale scores, a scoring key is most helpful. Typically such a scoring key is a cardboard sheet or overlay with holes punched so that when it is placed over an answer sheet it reveals only the responses to the items on a single subscale. One scoring key would be required for each subscale.

Thus, in scoring objective items, such as rating scales and checklists, the first step is identification of the direction of items—separating reversed and nonreversed ones. The second step is assigning a numerical score to each point on the scale or list. Finally, subscale items should be grouped and scored.

By their very nature ranking items have a score associated with them, i.e., the rank given each item in the list. For any particular item in the list, you can sum the ranks across respondents and divide by the number of respondents to get the average rank for that item. All ranking items can be dealt with in this way. This set of averages can then be compared to that obtained from another group of respondents using the Spearman rank correlation procedure (described in the next chapter).

Some scales, such as those using a true–false or yes–no format, lend themselves primarily to counting as a scoring procedure. Simply count the number of "true" or "yes" responses. However, you must still pay attention to reversed items. A "false" answer on a reversed item must be counted with a "true" response on a nonreversed item. On a positive item, for example, a "yes" would get a score of 1, a "no" a score of 0. In contrast, on a negative item, a "yes" would get a score of 0, a "no" a score of 1.

Another scoring procedure is to count people who fit into a particular category. For instance, in the case where respondents are asked to identify their sex, scoring can consist of counting the number who indicate "male" and the number who indicate "female."

Generally speaking there are then, four scoring procedures for objective items. These are summarized below.

(1) *Scale Scoring*. Where the item represents a scale, each point on the scale is assigned a score. After taking item reversal into account, you can add a respondent's scores on the items on a total scale or subscale to get his overall score.

(2) *Rank scoring*. Each item in a list is assigned a rank by the respondent. If some of the items have been keyed as a subscale, then their ranks can be averaged to obtain a subscale score. Here, typically, average ranks across all respondents are calculated for each item in the list.

(3) *Response counting*. Where categorical or nominal responses are obtained on a scale (such as true–false), you simply count the number of agreeing *responses* by a respondent and this total represents the total score on the scale for that respondent. A total score would be calculated in this way for each respondent. Response counting is used when a scale is made up of more than one item, all presumably measuring the same thing.

(4) *Respondent counting*. Where categorical or nominal responses are obtained on single items, you can count the number of respondents who give a particular response to that item. By properly setting up your answer sheet in advance, respondent counting can be done mechanically. Respondent counting enables one to generate a *contingency* table (a four-cell table that displays the number of respondents responding in each of the two possible ways on two items simultaneously) and to employ chi-square analysis (see the next chapter). A contingency table is illustrated in Figure 8.9.

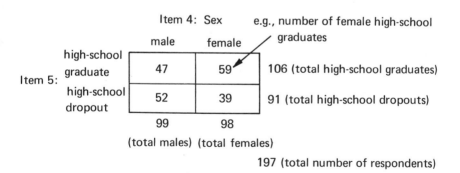

Figure 8.9 *An example of a contingency table.*

Fill-In and Free-Response Items

Although any one of the four techniques described above can be used to score fill-in and free-response items, the most common is respondent counting. However, before respondents can be counted, their responses must be coded. Coding is a procedure for reducing data to a form where response similarities and differences can be tabulated.

Suppose, for example, that an interviewer asks: Why did you leave school? Suppose, also, that the following potential responses to this question have been identified by the researcher:

_____ Couldn't stand it (or some indication of strong dislike)

_____ Wasn't doing well

_____ Waste of time

_____ Better opportunities elsewhere

_____ Other: _____

For purposes of efficiency, researchers often establish such precoded response categories for fill-in and free-response items. Although the respondent never sees these responses (if he did, the item would be a checklist) the interviewer has them on the answer form and, while the respondent is talking, judges which fits best. Thus, these precoded response categories become a nominal checklist enabling the interviewer to code immediately the unstructured response into checklist form. Or the interviewer might indicate which of the above reasons were given and their apparent importance to the respondent by ranking them. Coding, therefore, represents the superimposition of a response format onto a free or unstructured response.

Often coding is done before the data are collected, if the interviewer uses a precoded interview schedule. Thus, while he is asking an open-ended question and the respondent is giving a free response, the interviewer is attempting to catalog the response into one or more coding category sets. Here are a few examples to illustrate this point:

- Question: When you have a problem in school who do you go to?

  Answer: Mainly I go to my friends, especially my best buddy. Sometimes I talk to my rabbi.

  Coding: _____ Parents   X Friends
            _____ Teacher(s)   X Others: clergyman
            _____ Counselor

- Question: What is it about school that you like least?

  Answer: I would say the work. I don't find my subjects interesting. They don't have anything to do with what I'm interested in.

  Coding: ____ Teachers
  ____ Organization
  _X_ Schoolwork
        _X_ boring
        ____ irrelevant
        ____ too easy
        ____ too hard
  ____ Other:_____

Of course, the coding scheme you employ in converting a response into analyzable data will be a function of the problem and the hypotheses with which you are working. If you have hypothesized, for example, that youngsters in the upper third portion of the high school I.Q. distribution will be more likely to find their school work irrelevant than youngsters in the middle or lower thirds, then you must find out how youngsters view their school work and code it in terms of perceived relevance. The second example above represents an attempt to get such information.

The extent to which precoding is possible is an indication of the extent to which the question is likely to yield relevant information. Precoding has the additional advantage of eliminating coding as a separate step in data reduction and providing the interviewer with an easy format for data collection.

In designing response-scoring codes the basic consideration is what it is that you want to find out from the question. If you are testing to see whether tenured teachers are more or less interested in teaching effectiveness than non-tenured teachers, you might ask: How interested are you in the objective determination of your teaching effectiveness? The interviewer could be provided with a precoded rating scale such as the following:

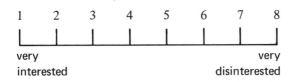

After listening to the teacher's free response to this question, the interviewer could summarize his opinion by placing a check on the above rating scale. This is an example of the use of *scale scoring* for coding and scoring an open-ended response. An examination of the ratings given the responses made by the two groups of teachers to this question would provide data to determine whether tenured or nontenured teachers were more interested in teaching effectiveness. Alternatively, the response could be precoded as simply:_____ seems interested, _____ seems disinterested. This represents the use of the respondent counting coding and scoring approach. There you would simply count the number of teachers in each group who were seen as interested and those seen as disinterested and place the findings into the contingency table shown below.

	interested in teaching effectiveness	disinterested in teaching effectiveness
tenured teachers		
nontenured teachers		

Thus far, the discussion of coding has focused on the use of precoded categories. The same kinds of coding precedures used for precoding can be used for coding after the data are collected. Precoding has the advantage of being more efficient than postcoding. For the latter, free responses must be recorded verbatim (usually by tape recorder) or summarized. These recordings are then transcribed by a typist and finally coded. Coding after data collection has as its principal advantage greater care in establishing coder reliability.

The issue of the reliability of coding judgments must be raised just as the previous chapter considered the reliability of rating and coding techniques used to describe behavior. If the interviewer codes every response, there is no way to do a reliability check on the coding decision of the interviewer since no record of the response exists. Where interviewers do all the coding live and free responses are not recorded, you should be concerned about coding unreliability as a threat to instrumentation validity. It is recommended that at least 20% of the responses be recorded verbatim and then coded by at least two judges or interviewers, thus providing a sample of responses to assess inter-coder reliability.

In the case of post-interview coding, the already existing response transcripts make it possible for a second coder to code a sufficient number of protocols to establish reliability with the first coder or for two coders to code all protocols to increase the reliability of the data.* Both first and second coders should be trained in the use of the coding system and have practice trials under the scrutiny of the researcher. In such instances reliabilities in the .70 to .90 range would be expected to guarantee sufficiency in dealing with instrumentation invalidity in coding.

*   *   *

Now that instruments have been designed and data collected, data analysis can begin. This is the subject of the next two chapters.

RECOMMENDED READINGS

Cochran, W. G. *Sampling techniques* (2nd ed.). New York: Wiley, 1963.

Fishbein, M. (Ed.) *Readings in attitude theory and measurement.* New York: Wiley, 1967.

Kahn, R. and Cannell, C. F. *The dynamics of interviewing.* New York: Wiley, 1957.

Kish, L. *Survey sampling.* New York: Wiley, 1967.

Miller, D. C. *Handbook of research design and social measurement.* New York: David McKay, 1964.

Snedecor, G. W. *Statistical Methods.* Ames, Iowa: The Iowa State University Press, 1962.

Where two coders code all protocols, their judgments can be averaged to obtain final coding scores. In such cases, the obtained reliabilities can be corrected by the Spearman-Brown formula (see page 138) since the average scores are more reliable than either individual set.

COMPETENCY TEST EXERCISES

1. Which of the following is *not* a purpose for which interviews and question-naires are used?
   a. finding out what a person thinks and believes
   b. finding out what a person likes and dislikes
   c. finding out how a person behaves
   d. finding out what experiences a person has had

2. Which of the following is not a shortcoming of a questionnaire or interview?
   a. The respondent may not know anything about the interviewer.
   b. The respondent may not know the information requested.
   c. The respondent may try to show himself in a good light.
   c. The respondent may try to help by telling you what you want to hear.

3. Match up the following correctly.
   a. indirect question
   b. specific question
   c. question of opinion
   d. statement
   e. response-keyed question

   1. declarative sentence form
   2. requests reaction to a single object
   3. next question depends on response to this one
   4. requests information for inferences
   5. how do you feel about X?

4. Match up the following correctly.
   a. scaled response
   b. fill-in response
   c. ranking response
   d. tabular response
   e. checklist response
   f. unstructured response
   g. categorical response

   1. My favorite subject is (check one):
      English _____
      Chemistry _____
      Calculus _____
   2. My favorite subject is calculus. (yes, no).
   3. How do you feel about chemistry?
   4. English is a subject I (like a lot, like a little, dislike a little, dislike a lot).
   5. My favorite subject is _____.
   6.

	English	Chem	Calc
Like			
Dislike			

   7. My order of preference of subjects is:
      English _____ (1, 2, 3)
      Chemistry _____ (1, 2, 3)
      Calculus _____ (1, 2, 3)

5. Below is a list of considerations. Write an I next to those that support use of an interview and a Q next to those that support use of a questionnaire.
   a. I want to collect data from at least 90% of my sample. ____
   b. I want to keep my problems of data reduction to a minimum ____
   c. I do not have very much money to conduct this project. ____
   d. I want good reliability of my data in this study. ____
   e. I'm not sure what questions are likely to get answered. ____
   f. I have to ask some intensive questions which may lead into sensitive areas. ____

6. Below are listed some considerations. Write an F next to those that support or describe the use of the fill-in response mode, an S for those that support scaled response, R for ranking, and C for checklist or categorical.
   a. I do not have to anticipate the respondent's response. ____
   b. I want to get ordinal data. ____
   c. This does not provide for degrees of responding and thus has too few options. ____
   d. I'll have a big scoring job (prescoring will be difficult). ____
   e. I may get response bias away from the extremes. ____

7. You are interested in finding out about the attitudes of teachers toward the administration, particularly with regard to procedures to be followed for ordering classroom supplies. Construct three sequential interview questions.

8. You are interested in finding out about the attitudes of administrators toward teachers, particularly as regards their use of procedures to be followed for ordering classroom supplies. Construct three questionnaire items (using three different structured response modes other than fill-in) to accomplish this).

9. You are planning to draw a stratified random sample of 200 from a high-school population that contains 60% males and 40% females. Among the males, 40% are college prep majors, 10% business majors, 20% vocational majors, and 30% general majors. Among the females, 50% are college prep majors, 25% are business majors, 5% are vocational majors, and 20% are general majors. How many respondents would you need in each of the eight categories?

10. You are going to interview 60 teachers in a school system of 200 teachers. In this system there are 100 elementary school teachers—20 men and 80 women; 50 junior high-school teachers—20 men and 30 women; and 50 high-school teachers—30 men and 20 women. How many teachers in each of the six categories would you include in your sample of 50?

11. Which of the following is *not* ordinarily covered in a cover letter?
    a. protection afforded the respondent
    b. anticipated outcome of the study
    c. legitimacy of the researcher
    d. purpose of the study

12. You are planning to do a study of the relationship between a teacher's amount of teaching experience and his (her) attitudes toward discipline of students. You are sending out a questionnaire including an attitude scale and a biographical information sheet. Construct a sample covering letter to accompany this mailing.

13. Which of the following is *not* ordinarily done in training an interviewer?
    a. familiarizing him with response-recording forms
    b. teaching him to code responses
    c. having him conduct mock interviews
    d. teaching him to conduct data analyses

14. Differences in interviewer style and approach represent a source of internal invalidity based on which of the following?
    a. testing
    b. multiple interactive effects
    c. history
    d. instrumentation
    e. maturation

15. Look at the Student Opinion Questionnaire (SOQ) shown in Figure 8.6. (pages 197-198). A teacher received the following ratings on the ten items:

    1. average
    2. good
    3. average
    4. very good
    5. good
    6. the very best
    7. very good
    8. below average
    9. very good
    10. good

    If a rating of "below average" is given a score of 1 and "the very best" a score of 5, what would be the teacher's score on the SOQ?

16. Look at the Student Opinion Questionnaire (SOQ) shown in Figure 8.6 (pages 197-198). Construct a response code (with five response categories) that might be used for coding the free responses to item 13.

9

Carrying Out
Statistical Analyses

OBJECTIVES

Choose a statistical test appropriate for different combinations of variables and different levels of measurement. / Calculate a mean, median, and standard deviation. / Analyze data and report statistical findings using (1) a *t*-test, (2) a Pearson product-moment correlational analysis, (3) an analysis of variance, (4) a Mann-Whitney *U*-Test, (5) a Spearman rank-order correlation, and (6) a Chi-square test.

9.1 SIGNIFICANCE TESTING

Statistical tests are a major aid for data interpretation. By statistical testing a researcher can compare groups of data to determine the probability that differences between them are based on chance, thereby providing evidence for judging the validity of a hypothesis or inference.*

Consider for example that you are comparing an experimental group to a control group on an achievement measure and have collected data from 50 students in each group. Now you want to ask the question: Are the two groups equal in achievement or is one group superior to the other? If you calculate the mean or average achievement score (i.e., the sum of the scores divided by the number of scores) for each group, upon inspection the scores may look different.

Such statistical tests are called inferential statistics. *Statistics used to describe a group of data (e.g., mean) are called* descriptive statistics. *This chapter deals with both, but primarily with the former.*

But, are they really? That is, how do you know that the differences are not merely due to the fluctuations of chance but are really due to the treatments being compared?

A statistical test can compare the means in the above example relative to the degree of variation among scores in each group to determine the *probability* that the differences obtained between the means are real differences and not chance occurrences. By considering the degree of variation within groups, statistical tests yield an estimate of the probability or *stability* of particular findings. Thus when a researcher reports that the difference between two means is significant at the .05 level (usually reported as $p < .05$ and read p less than .05), this means that the probability is less than 5 out of 100 that the difference is due to chance. (That is, the likelihood that the distribution of scores obtained in the study would occur simply as a function of chance is less than 5%.) On this basis, it is possible to conclude that the differences obtained were the result of the treatment.

When statistics are employed by behavioral scientists, the 5% level (i.e., $p < .05$) often is considered an acceptable level of confidence to reject the null hypothesis of equal means between the control and experimental groups. There is nothing magic about the .05 level. It is simply an arbitrary level that many researchers have chosen as a decision point in accepting a finding as reliable or rejecting it as sufficiently improbable to have confidence in its recurrence. Occasionally, mean differences in an experiment will be significant at the .01 confidence level. Differences at this level indicate that the probability is only 1 out of 100 that the differences would be accounted for by chance alone.*

9.2 MEASURES OF CENTRAL TENDENCY AND VARIABILITY

The two main measures of central tendency are the *mean* and the *median*. The principal statistical measure of variability is the *standard deviation*. Each is described below.

Mean

The mean or average is computed by adding a list of scores and then dividing by the number of scores. The algebraic formula used to determine the mean is:

$$\overline{X} = \frac{\Sigma X}{N}$$

While confidence levels are usually set at the 5% or 1% levels, findings which attain a degree of confidence between the 10 and 5 levels are often interpreted as trends.

$\overline{X}$ is a symbol for the mean while ΣX is a symbol for the sum of the X's or individual scores. N represents the number of scores.

Consider the following example. Fifteen students who took a mathematics exam had the following scores:

98	90	80
97	89	73
95	84	70
93	82	60
90	82	45

To determine the mean score on the math test, add the fifteen scores, that is, $\Sigma X = 1230$. Then divide this number by N, 15, to give $\overline{X} = 82.0$.

Median

The median is the score in the middle; 50% of the scores fall above it, and 50% of the scores fall below it. In the above list of fifteen scores the median score is 84. Seven scores are higher and seven scores are lower. In a list containing an even number of scores, the middle two scores would be averaged to get the median.

The median is not as sensitive to extreme scores as is the mean. Note that the mean of the fifteen scores is lower than the median because of the two or three extremely low scores.

Standard Deviation

The standard deviation (s) is a measure of the spread or dispersion of a distribution of scores. It can be calculated by using the following formula:

$$s = \sqrt{\frac{\Sigma(X - \overline{X})^2}{N - 1}}$$

Note that the deviation of each score from the mean $(X - \overline{X})$ is squared; these squared deviations are then summed, the result divided by $N - 1$, and the square root taken. This formula is offered because of its value in helping you see the basis for the standard deviation. For easier calculation, however, the following formula may be used.

$$s = \sqrt{\frac{N\Sigma X^2 - (\Sigma X)^2}{N(N-1)}}$$

The term ΣX^2 indicates that you square each score and then add the sum of the squares; first you square, then you sum. The term $(\Sigma X)^2$ indicates that you add the scores together and then square the total; first you sum, then you square. The calculations on the scores given in the preceding example are as follows:

$$s = \sqrt{\frac{(15)(103,546) - (1230)^2}{15(15-1)}}$$

$$s = \sqrt{\frac{1,553,190 - 1,512,900}{15(14)}}$$

$$s = \sqrt{\frac{40,290}{210}} = \sqrt{191.9}$$

$$s = 13.8$$

Thus, the scores have a spread or standard deviation of 13.8. This score is related to the range or difference between the highest and lowest score. That is, typically, the greater this range the greater the standard deviation.

The square of the standard deviation is referred to as the *variance* (s^2) of a group of scores. In the above example, the variance equals 191.9.

9.3 PARAMETRIC AND NONPARAMETRIC STATISTICAL TESTS

One group of statistical tests, called *parametric* tests, was conceived as tests based on interval measurement of the dependent variable. The use of these tests requires that the following assumptions be satisfied:

(1) *Normal distribution.* Parametric tests are more valid when they are performed on data that have a normal distribution. A normal distribution [see Figure 9.1 (a)] is a distribution which is perfectly *symmetrical* about its mean; it has a bell shape. When the distributions of scores on the dependent variable for the different groups compared in a study (or on both variables in the case of a correlation) are *nonsymmetrical* or *skewed* [see Figure 9.1 (b)], then conclusions based upon a parametric statistical test are less valid. The greater the skewness of the distributions, the greater the invalidity of a parametric test done on them.

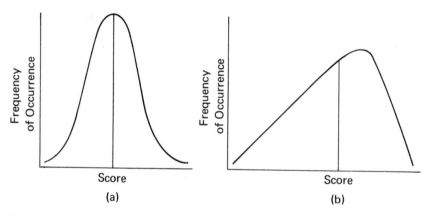

Figure 9.1 *Graphic examples of distribution curves: (a) normal and (b) skewed.*

(2) *Homogeneity of variance.* Scores are easiest to compare parametrically when the variance or spread within the two groups is equal (homogeneous). If two groups are given an achievement test with the distributions shown in Figure 9.2 resulting, a parametric test would be more difficult to interpret because of the differences in the spread or variance within the two groups.

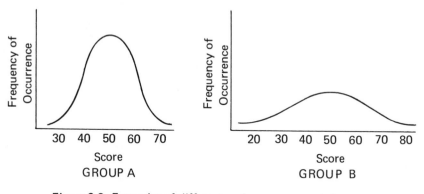

Figure 9.2 *Examples of different variances or spreads in scores.*

(3) *Continuous equal interval measures.* Parametric tests, as conceived, can only be done on scores (dependent measures) that represent an interval scale, that is, are continuous and of equal interval throughout. (This point will be discussed more thoroughly in the next section.)

Nonparametric tests make fewer assumptions about distributions; they do not require a normal distribution nor equal group variances. They are based on ordinal or nominal measurement and are highly useful for quick calculations. They are also useful for large samples where the parametric assumptions are not met and for studies involving hypotheses using ordinal measuring devices.

9.4 CHOOSING THE APPROPRIATE STATISTICAL TEST

As you recall, the purpose of a statistical test is to determine whether the data collected from two or more samples are equivalent, and, further, to determine the possibility that any difference between the samples can be accounted for by chance fluctuations.

To choose the appropriate statistic, first determine the number of independent and dependent variables in your study. (For statistical purposes, consider moderator variables as independent variables.) Next determine which variables are nominal, ordinal, or interval. (These terms are explained in Section 7.3.) Next refer to Figure 9.3 for more specific information.

You will notice in Figure 9.3 that if *both* independent and dependent variables are interval measures, correlation techniques (parametric correlations) may be employed. Tests such as *t-test* and *analysis of variance** are used when independent variables are nominal or ordinal and the dependent variable is interval. Ordinal measurement generally calls for the use of nonparametric techniques, with a chi-square analysis recommended for a combination of nominal independent and nominal dependent variables. Notice that it is difficult to analyze more than one dependent variable simultaneously without the use of a highly complex statistical procedure. Other procedures for handling more than one dependent variable at a time such as factor analysis and discriminant function analysis are also quite complex.

Consider an example. Suppose you are studying the effect of programmed science materials on learning with the I.Q. of the student as a moderator variable. One of the independent variables is a nominal variable—programmed learning versus traditional teaching—while the second is an interval variable—I.Q. The dependent variables, you decide, are subsequent performance on an achievement test (interval) and attitudes as measured by an attitude scale (interval). How to proceed? The first step is to convert the second independent variable (I.Q.) from an interval variable to a nominal variable. (Recall from Section 7.3 that *you can*

**These tests will be described in more detail in the subsequent pages.*

Type and Number of Independent Variables

Type and Number of Dependent Variables		Interval		Ordinal		Nominal	
		1	**More than 1**	**1**	**More than 1**	**1**	**More than 1**
Interval (Row 1)	0		Factor analysis	Transform ordinal variable into nominal and use C-1, or transform the interval variable into ordinal and use B-2, or transform both variables into nominal and use C-3			Analysis of variance
	1	Correlation	Multiple correlation			Analysis of variance (or t-test)	
	More than 1	Multiple correlation					
Ordinal (Row 2)	0	Transform ordinal variable into nominal and use C-1, or transform the interval variable into ordinal and use B-2, or transform the interval variable into nominal and use C-2			Coefficient of concordance (W)		
	1			Spearman correlation, Kendall's tau (τ)		Sign test, median test, U-Test, Kruskal-Wallis	
	More than 1						Friedman's two-way analysis of variance
Nominal (Row 3)	0						
	1	Analysis of variance (see C-1)		Sign test, median test, U-test. Kruskal-Wallis (see C-2)		Phi Coeff. (ϕ), Fisher exact test, chi-square	Chi-square
	More than 1	Analysis of variance (see C-1)		Friedman's two-way analysis of variance (see C-2)			
		Column A		**Column B**		**Column C**	

Figure 9.3 *Basis for selecting a statistical test.*

always convert from a higher order of measurement to a lower—from interval to ordinal or nominal or from ordinal to nominal—but that *converting from a lower to a higher order of measurement is not advised.*)

To convert an interval variable to a nominal variable, the students should be separated into groups based on their scores on the interval measure. By placing the scores on a variable (say, I.Q.) in numerical order (that is, essentially, recasting the interval data in ordinal form) and then locating the median score, you can label everyone above the median as high I.Q. and everyone below the median as low I.Q., thus assigning Ss to a high category or a low category. Or, the students can be broken into three groups: high, medium, and low by dividing the group into equal thirds or *tertiles*. Categorical assignment to groups represents nominal measurement.

Next, draw a diagram of the design and enter the data into it as shown in Figure 9.4. Since the dependent variables will be analyzed separately, draw one diagram for each variable.

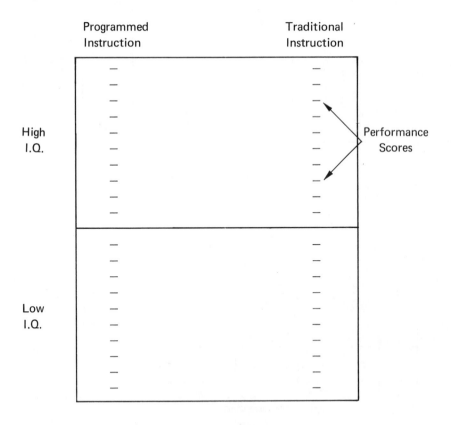

Figure 9.4

Now that you have two nominal independent variables and an interval dependent variable, the technique that can be used is analysis of variance.* Be sure to keep in mind the three conditions discussed in the previous section which must be met to justify the use of the different parametric statistical techniques.

There are basically six commonly used statistical tests. If you are dealing with *two interval variables,* use a parametric correlation (called a Pearson product-moment correlation). When dealing with *two ordinal variables,* most researchers use a Spearman rank-order correlation and with two nominal variables, the Chi-square statistic. When there are a nominal *independent variable* and an *interval dependent* variable, use a *t*-test if there are only two conditions or levels, or analysis of variance if there are two or more conditions or more than one independent variable. Finally, a *nominal independent variable* and *ordinal dependent variable* require a Mann-Whitney *U*-test (a nonparametric *t*-test).

Researchers often transform variables so they are able to use their data to perform a specific statistical test (which may be different from the one originally anticipated). For instance, if interval performance data is available in a two-condition study, but the conditions for a *t*-test (normal distribution, equal sample variance) are not met, you could transform the interval dependent variable into an ordinal measure and use a Mann-Whitney *U*-test.

There are a great many nonparametric statistical tests. Siegel's (1956) book *Nonparametric Statistics* is a helpful source and is within the grasp of most researchers. Within parametric statistics, there are many varieties of analysis of variance. A good source is *Statistical Principles in Experimental Design* by Winer (1962), although this is an advanced level book containing relatively difficult techniques.

9.5 CARRYING OUT PARAMETRIC STATISTICAL TESTS

The *t*-Test

A *t*-test is a statistical test that allows you to compare *two* means to determine the probability that the difference between the means is a real difference rather than a chance difference. A worksheet for a *t*-test is shown in Table 9.1.[†]

Note that you begin on the worksheet by calculating the sum of scores (ΣX),

---

*It would have been appropriate also to have used analysis of covariance prior to converting I.Q. scores to nominal form.

†Note that this worksheet is for a t-test for independent samples. Where matching with random assignment is used to compose groups or Ss are used as their own controls, a t-test for correlated samples is usually employed. Information on this latter test can be found in most statistics textbooks. (See the recommended readings at the end of this chapter.)

sum of squared scores (ΣX^2), and mean ($\overline{X}$) for each of the two groups. Next, formulas are given to calculate the variances for each of the two groups. These formulas are the same as $s^2 = \dfrac{\Sigma(X - \overline{X})^2}{N - 1}$ but have been altered so that the $\overline{X}$ term does not appear (it has been replaced by $\dfrac{\Sigma X}{N}$). The formulas on the worksheet are easier to use on a desk calculator.

Table 9.1 *t-test worksheet.*

GROUP	1	2
$N =$		
$\Sigma X =$		
$X^2 =$		
$\overline{X} =$		

1 Calculation of group variances.

$$s_1^2 = \frac{N_1 \, \Sigma X_1^2 - (\Sigma X_1)^2}{N_1 \, (N_1 - 1)} = \underline{\hspace{3cm}} \qquad s_1^2 = \underline{\hspace{2cm}}$$

$$s_2^2 = \frac{N_2 \, \Sigma X_2^2 - (\Sigma X_2)^2}{N_2 \, (N_2 - 1)} = \underline{\hspace{3cm}} \qquad s_2^2 = \underline{\hspace{2cm}}$$

2 Calculation of *t*-value.

Steps

1. $\dfrac{(N_1 - 1)s_1{}^2 + (N_2 - 1)s_2{}^2}{N_1 + N_2 - 2} = \underline{\hspace{3cm}}$

2. $\dfrac{N_1 + N_2}{N_1 N_2} = \underline{\hspace{3cm}}$

3. (Step 1 X Step 2) = $\underline{\hspace{3cm}}$

4. $\sqrt{\text{Step 3}} = \underline{\hspace{3cm}}$

5. $\overline{X}_1 - \overline{X}_2 = \underline{\hspace{3cm}}$

6. $t = \dfrac{\text{Step 5}}{\text{Step 4}} = \underline{\hspace{3cm}}$ $df = N_1 + N_2 - 2 = \underline{\hspace{3cm}}$

7. Look up *t* value in Table II, Appendix B.* $p = \underline{\hspace{3cm}}$

If t-value in Step 6 exceeds the table value at a specific p level, then the null hypothesis (i.e., that the means are equal) can be rejected at that p level.

In step 1 of the t-test, the variances are combined or pooled (specifically, averaged); in step 2, a term is calculated which is multiplied by the pooled variances in step 3. In step 4, a square root is taken of the value in step 3 to provide a standard deviation estimate. This, when divided into the difference between the two means, yields at t-value which is then compared with the t-value from a t table (see Table II, Appendix B) to determine if the calculated t-value is significant. If the obtained t-value exceeds the table t-value (for those degrees of freedom) at a specific p level, then the null hypothesis (which states that the means being compared are equal) can be rejected at that p level.

Parametric Correlation (Pearson Product-Moment Correlation)

The parametric correlation is used to deal with two interval variables, each of which is normally distributed. A correlation is an indication of the predictability of one variable given the other. It is an indication of covariation.

The relationship between two variables can be examined by plotting the paired measurements on graph paper. Such a plot in which each pair of observations is represented by a point is called a *scatter diagram*. Some appear in Figure 9.5. These plots enable you to assess visually the degree of relation between the two variables.

The basic formula for a correlation coefficient (indicated as r) is:

$$r = \frac{\Sigma(X - \bar{X})(Y - \bar{Y})}{Ns_x s_y}$$

Thus, it is the summation of the products of the deviations of each score from its mean divided by N times the product of the two standard deviations ($s_x s_y$). For calculation on a machine, this formula is altered to the formula shown on the worksheet (Table 9.2).

It is possible, when working on a desk calculator, to calculate all the basic terms of the formula simultaneously. By putting both X and Y values into the calculator at the same time, and both squaring and multiplying, you can calculate ΣX, ΣX^2, ΣY, ΣY^2, and ΣXY* simultaneously. (This procedure is described in detail in the next chapter.)[†] The remaining calculations proceed as shown on the worksheet (see Table 9.2 on page 235).

*The calculation on some machines provides $2\Sigma XY$ which is then halved to yield ΣXY.
†The procedure for computing correlations by computer is also described in the next chapter and is, in fact, recommended when a number of correlations must be computed.

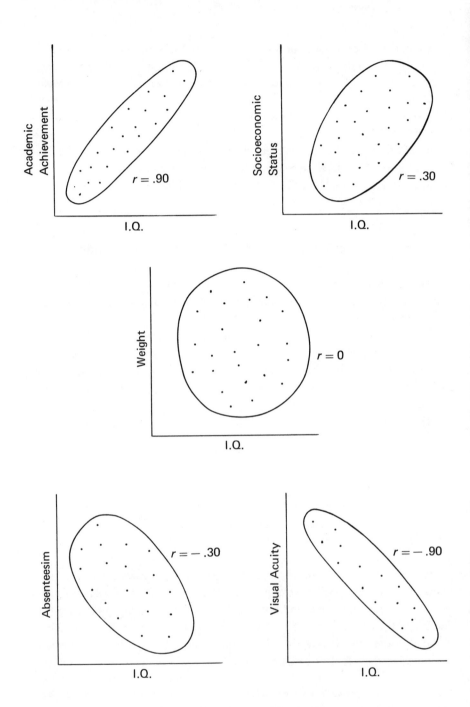

Figure 9.5 *Correlation scatter diagrams.*

Table 9.2 *Correlation worksheet.*

$$r = \frac{N \, \Sigma XY - (\Sigma X)\,(\Sigma Y)}{\sqrt{(N\Sigma X^2 - (\Sigma X)^2)\,(N\Sigma Y^2 - (\Sigma Y)^2)}}$$

Formula Steps	Calculations $X =$ $Y =$
1. N (Number of pairs)	
2. ΣX	
3. ΣX^2	
4. ΣY	
5. ΣY^2	
6. ΣXY	
7. $N\Sigma X^2 - (\Sigma X)^2$	
8. $N\Sigma Y^2 - (\Sigma Y)^2$	
9. Step 7 X Step 8	
10. $\sqrt{\text{Step 9}}$	
11. $N\Sigma XY - (\Sigma X)(\Sigma Y)$	
12. Step 11 ÷ Step 10 = r	
13. $df = N - 2$	
14. p (from Table III, Appendix B) *	

*If r obtained in Step 12 exceeds the r given in Table III, Appendix B, for df (Step 13) at a specific p level, then the null hypothesis that the variables are unrelated may be rejected at that p level.

A reminder about the algebraic terms ΣX^2 and $(\Sigma X)^2$: *The term ΣX^2 means that first you square each score and then you add the squares. The term $(\Sigma X)^2$ includes parentheses which tell you first to add all the X's together and then square the sum.* In algebra, the operation described within parentheses (in this case, adding) always precedes the operation described outside of the parentheses (in this case, squaring).

The significance level of a correlation can be obtained by looking in Table III, Appendix B (for $N - 2$ degrees of freedom).

If the obtained correlation exceeds the table value at a specific p level, then the null hypothesis that the variables are not related can be rejected at that p level. A correlation can be somewhat evaluated by squaring it to obtain an estimate of the amount of common variance, or overlap, between the two measures. For example, a correlation of .50 between two measures indicates an overlap of 25% while a correlation of .25 between two measures indicates an overlap of about 6%.

Analysis of Variance

All of the statistical techniques described thus far in this chapter can be used with only two variables at a time. On the other hand, analysis of variance can be used for almost any number of independent variables but is typically used for two, three, or four. When using a *factorial design* that includes an independent variable, moderator variable, and dependent variable the size of the analysis of variance is equal to the number of independent and moderator variables, called *factors.* * If one independent variable and one moderator variable exist (the case to be described), then a *two-factor* analysis of variance would be used. Only one dependent variable can be analyzed at a time using the kind of analysis of variance to be illustrated.

Suppose the independent variable is traditional teaching versus team teaching versus self-teaching. The independent variable is then one factor with three *levels* (or variations). Suppose the moderator variable is I.Q. and the interval I.Q. measure has been split at the median to give two levels: high and low. It would now be possible to use a 3 X 2 analysis of variance. The two digits indicate two factors, one having three levels and one having two levels. Since the independent (and moderator) variables must be nominal before an analysis of variance can be used, the *median-split* technique or other equal *n-split* techniques are useful as a prerequisite to analysis of variance. Often, the moderator variable is interval and can be transformed by median or other equal *n* splits. The dependent variable should be interval for the parametric analysis of variance to be employed.

Let us call *A* the independent variable and *B* the moderator variable. Analysis of variance will indicate the effect of the independent variable (the *A* effect), the effect of the moderator variable (the *B* effect), and the effect of both variables in *interaction* (the *AB* interaction). The concept of interaction will be explored more fully later.

Table 9.3 is a worksheet for performing a two-way or two-factor analysis of variance. In this design the number of levels of the independent variable is called *p* (equal to the number of columns in the design), and the number of levels of

---

The terms variable and factor are used synonymously here. Variables or factors are further subdivided into levels, treatments, or conditions—these three words being used interchangeably. For statistical usage, variables will be called factors, the subdivisions of which will be called levels.

Table 9.3 *Analysis of variance* (p × q *factorial*) *worksheet* (*with unequal n's*).

	p_1	p_2	p_i	
q_1	$n =$ $\dfrac{1}{n} =$ $\Sigma X =$ $(\Sigma X)^2 =$ $\Sigma X^2 =$ $\overline{X} =$ $SS^* =$			$B_1 =$
q_j				$B_i =$
	$A_1 = \rule{2cm}{0.4pt}$	$A_2 = \rule{2cm}{0.4pt}$	$A_i = \rule{2cm}{0.4pt}$	

$*SS = \Sigma X^2 - \dfrac{(\Sigma X)^2}{n}$ (All of these terms should be calculated for each cell.)

$A_{1,\,2,\,i} =$ sum of means in columns 1, 2, i, respectively.

$B_{1,\,j} \quad =$ sum of means in rows 1, j, respectively.

$G \qquad =$ sum of A's $=$ sum of B's $= \rule{3cm}{0.4pt}$

$p \qquad =$ number of columns $= \rule{3cm}{0.4pt}$

$q \qquad =$ number of rows $= \rule{3cm}{0.4pt}$

Steps

1. Add together all the *SS.* $\rule{4cm}{0.4pt}$ $= SS_w$
2. Add together all the $\dfrac{1}{n}$. $\rule{4cm}{0.4pt}$
3. pq/Step 2 $= \rule{4cm}{0.4pt}$ $= \tilde{n}$
4. $G^2/pq = \rule{4cm}{0.4pt}$
5. Square each A_i and add the squares together $= \rule{3cm}{0.4pt}$ $= \Sigma A^2$
6. Step 6/q $\rule{3cm}{0.4pt}$

Table 9.3 (continued)

7.   Square each B_j and add the squares together = _____

            $= \Sigma B^2$

8.   Step 7/p _____

9.   Square every $\overline{X}$ and add the squares together = _____

            $= \Sigma \overline{X}^2$

SS_A = Step 3 [Step 6 − Step 4]

SS_B = Step 3 [Step 8 − Step 4]

SS_{AB} = Step 3 [Step 9 − Step 6 − Step 8 + Step 4]

$$MS_A \;\; = \frac{SS_A}{p-1} = \text{_____}$$

$$MS_B \;\; = \frac{SS_B}{q-1} = \text{_____}$$

$$MS_{AB} \;\; = \frac{SS_{AB}}{(p-1)\,(q-1)} = \text{_____}$$

$$MS_w \;\; = \frac{\text{Step 1}}{(\text{Total of } n\text{'s} - pq)} = \text{_____}$$

$$F_A \;\; = \frac{MS_A}{MS_w} = \text{_____}$$

$$F_B \;\; = \frac{MS_B}{MS_w} = \text{_____}$$

$$F_{AB} \;\; = \frac{MS_{AB}}{MS_w} = \text{_____}$$

From Table IV, Appendix B

df_A $= p - 1 =$ _____

df_w $=$ total of n's $- pq =$ _____ $p =$ _____*

df_B $= q - 1 =$ _____

df_w $=$ _____ $p =$ _____

df_{AB} $= (p - 1)\,(q - 1) =$ _____

df_w $=$ _____ $p =$ _____

*If an obtained F value exceeds the value given in Table IV, Appendix B (for the appropriate df's) at a specific p level, then the null hypothesis that the variables are not related can be rejected at that p level.

the moderator variable is called q (equal to the number of rows in the design). The analysis of variance worksheet, Table 9.3, is for a $p \times q$ factorial where p runs from p_1 to p_i and q from q_1 to q_j to indicate that each variable may have more levels than shown in the worksheet. It is not necessary that $p_i = q_j$. Also, the analysis of variance shown in the worksheet is for unequal numbers of cell entries (called unequal n's). The unequal n problem is handled by the un-weighted means solution and should be used only when you have planned to have about the same number of students in each condition or have suffered random losses. (Also, this analysis is restricted to cases where each subject is used only once. It does not cover repeated measurements. See Winer, 1962.)

Once the analysis of variance calculations are completed, the results are displayed in an analysis of variance *source table* as shown.

Analysis of Variance of Dependent Variable by Independent Variable (A) and Moderator Variable (B)

Source	df	MS	F
A	$p - 1$	MS_A	F_A*
B	$q - 1$	MS_B	F_B†
AB	$(p - 1)(q - 1)$	MS_{AB}	F_{AB}*
error	(total of n's $- pq$)	MS_w	

*$p < .05$ †$p < .01$

The degrees of freedom (df) of the numerator will be $(p - 1)$ for F_A, $(q - 1)$ for F_B, and $(p - 1)(q - 1)$ for F_{AB}. For all three, the degrees of freedom for the denominator will be the total of the n's $- pq$. Indicate the significant F's in the source table with asterisks. If an obtained F value exceeds the value given in the table (for the appropriate df's) at a specific p level, then the null hypothesis that the variables are not related can be rejected at that p level.

One of the most valuable features of an analysis of variance is that it statistically identifies interactions. Return to the original example: a study in which the independent variable is team teaching versus traditional teaching versus self-teaching for high and low I.Q. students (moderator variable). The dependent variable is performance on an achievement test. Some sample graphs appear in Figure 9.6.

Notice in graph 1 that team teaching produces higher achievement than traditional teaching which in turn produces higher achievement than self-teaching for

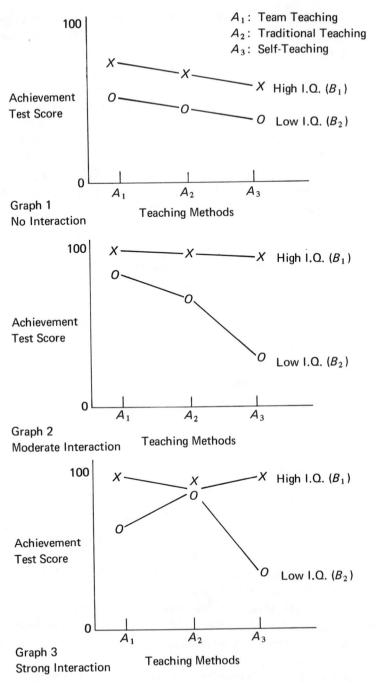

Figure 9.6 *Sample graphs illustrating statistical interactions or their absence.*

both I.Q. groups. Considering teaching technique as the A variable, the overall superiority of the team teaching approach (or inferiority of the self-teaching approach) would show up in the analysis of variance as a significant A effect. A significant B effect would also be obtained since the high I.Q. group out-performs the low group. In fact, it is likely that the data in all three graphs would produce significant B effects (as well as significant A effects although these seem less dramatic than the B effects). Notice in graph 1 that the I.Q. curves are parallel. The three teaching effects do not affect the two I.Q. groups differentially. The superiority of the high over the low I.Q. group is constant from one teaching technique to the other. Thus, in graph 1, there is *no interaction*.

In graph 2, however, the superiority of the high over the low I.Q. group increases from one teaching technique to the next. If students had not been separated by I.Q. level, it would not be known that team teaching produces very similar achievement among high and low I.Q. students, while low I.Q. students fare very poorly from self-teaching when compared to their high I.Q. counterparts. Thus, in graph 2, there is an *interaction*.

In graph 3, high and low I.Q. students fare equally well from traditional teaching; however, high I.Q. students achieve more after team teaching with this difference becoming even greater after self-teaching. Thus, the effects of the teaching techniques are strongly based on an *interaction with I.Q.* in graph 3. Had the effects of the three teaching techniques not been examined in terms of the two I.Q. levels, only a slight tendency for the self-teaching to be inferior (a small possible A effect) would be apparent. However, when the moderator variable (I.Q.) is introduced an interaction effect appears, revealing that the effect of the treatments is different for different I.Q. groups.

When group means are graphed and the lines between points for the different moderator variables depart from parallel, you can usually expect to find an interaction—at least be clued in to look for it. The greater the tendency toward non-parallelism, the more likely an interaction. This point is illustrated in Figure 9.6.

9.6 CARRYING OUT NONPARAMETRIC STATISTICAL TESTS

Mann-Whitney U-Test

The Mann-Whitney U-test is a nonparametric test which compares two samples for possible significant differences. The U-test is not bound by the same restrictions as the t-test (its parametric counterpart). Like all other nonparametric tests, it does not require that data be normally distributed or sample variances equal.

The U-test calls for a nominal independent variable (such as a treatment and a control) and an ordinal dependent variable. If the dependent variable is an interval measure, this is easily transformed to an ordinal measure by casting the scores into *ranks* and then analyzing the ranks.*

A worksheet for the U-test appears in Table 9.4. This worksheet has been set up for experiments where there are less than 20 and more than 8 observations in the larger of two samples. For larger sample sizes, use techniques described in Siegel (1956).

As you can see from the worksheet (Table 9.4), data from the two samples are combined and cast into ranks. Tied scores are given the same rank, that being the average of the ranks. For instance, if two scores, covering ranks 4 and 5 are tied, each is given the rank of 4.5. The next score would then have the rank of 6. If the three highest scores were tied, each would have the rank of 2, the fourth highest score would receive rank 4. The ranking technique transforms interval data into ordinal data.

Next, experimental group data and control group data are regrouped, and the ranks are summed for each group. Use the formulas at the bottom of the worksheet to calculate U twice, once for each group. The *smaller* of these two U values is then checked against the U value given in Table V, Appendix B, for the appropriate n's. If the value in the table is larger, then the groups are significantly different.

Example: a teacher of electronics wanted to know if a mnemonic device would aid students in memorizing the color code for electrical resistors. He gave this device to half of his class of 18 students and the other half practiced simply by trying to commit the list to memory. Two weeks later, on a follow-up test, he obtained the results shown in Figure 9.7. These data (representing the number of errors) were transformed to ranks and subjected to a Mann-Whitney U-test (rather than retained in interval form and compared by a t-test) because of the skewness of the distribution (i.e., the tendency of the distribution of the data to be nonnormal).

To interpret the U values calculated in Figure 9.7 look in Table V, Appendix B, under $n_1 = 9$, $n_2 = 9$; at the .05 significance level $U = 17$. Since the smaller U obtained in this experiment was 9, it was possible to conclude that the mnemonic device resulted in a significant improvement in learning.

Note, however, that the information value of data is reduced when they are transformed to a lower order of measurement.

Table 9.4 *Worksheet for Mann-Whitney U-test.*

Rank all data (both groups combined)

Observation (in decreasing order)	Rank	Group*	Observation	Rank	Group	Observation	Rank	Group
1.			13.			25.		
2.			14.			26.		
3.			15.			27.		
4.			16.			28.		
5.			17.			29.		
6.			18.			30.		
7.			19.			31.		
8.			20.			32.		
9.			21.			33.		
10.			22.			34.		
11.			23.			35.		
12.			24.			36.		

*E = experimental group C = control group

If two or more scores are tied, assign each the same rank—that being the average of the ranks for the tied scores.

E score	Rank (R_1)	C score	Rank (R_2)
	$\Sigma R_1 = \underline{\hphantom{xxx}}$		$\Sigma R_2 = \underline{\hphantom{xxx}}$
	$n_1 = \underline{\hphantom{xxx}}$		$n_2 = \underline{\hphantom{xxx}}$

$$U = n_1 n_2 + \frac{n_1 (n_1 + 1)}{2} - R_1 = \underline{\hphantom{xxxxxxxx}}$$

$$U = n_1 n_2 + \frac{n_2 (n_2 + 1)}{2} - R_2 = \underline{\hphantom{xxxxxxxx}}$$

$p = \underline{\hphantom{xxxxxxxx}}$†

†**Rule:** Use as U whichever of the two computed U values is smaller. *Look up this value in the table of critical values of* U *(Table V, Appendix B), to determine significance. If the smaller obtained* U *value is smaller than the table value at a given* p *level, then the difference is significant at that* p *level.*

	Score	Experimental	Control
1.	0	1.5	
2.	0	1.5*	
3.	1	4	
4.	1	4	
5.	1	4	
6.	2	7	
7.	2		7
8.	2		7
9.	3	9.5	
10.	3	9.5	
11.	4		11
12.	5		12
13.	6	13	
14.	7		14
15.	9		15.5
16.	9		15.5
17.	10		17
18.	10		18
		$\Sigma R_1 = 54.0$	$\Sigma R_2 = 117.0$

$$U = n_1 n_2 + \frac{n_1 (n_1 + 1)}{2} - R_1 = 126 - 54 = 72$$

$$U = n_1 n_2 + \frac{n_2 (n_2 + 1)}{2} - R_2 = 126 - 117 = 9$$

*There is a procedure for correcting for tied ranks (see Siegel, 1956). Since the ties in this example only cut across conditions in one case, the correction would add little in the way of accuracy and so has not been used.

Figure 9.7 *Sample data analyzed by Mann-Whitney U-test.*

Spearman Rank-Order Correlation

The Spearman rank-order correlation (r_s) is used to compare two sets of ranks to determine their degree of equivalence. (Remember that data set forth in ranks represent ordinal data; therefore, the rank-order correlation is the relation between two sets of ordinal data.) Where data have been collected in interval form, they can be converted to ordinal form to be analyzed by means of a Spearman correlation (rather than a Pearson product-moment correlation as would be used to compare sets of interval data).*

*An instance where this conversion might prove helpful is one in which judges using the same scale have different response tendencies—one to use the ends of the scale and the other the middle.

The most common use of the Spearman rank-order correlation is to compare judgments by a group of judges of two objects or the scores of a group of subjects on two measures (see Siegel, 1956, for an example of this use). A second valuable, but less frequent use of the test is to compare judgments by two judges of a group of objects or items (see Hays, 1963, for an example of this use). The second, use is essentially a technique for assessing inter-judge equivalence of judgments over a set of items or objects. In the case of multiple judges' rankings on two measures, N is equal to the number of judges or subjects. In the case of two judges ranking multiple objects, N is equal to the number of objects. In the case

Table 9.5 *Worksheet for rank-order correlation* (r_s).

$$r_s = 1 - \frac{6 \Sigma d^2}{N^3 - N}$$

Subject or Object	Rank for Test 1 or Judge 1	Rank for Test 2 or Judge 2	Difference between Ranks (d)	d^2
(1)				
(2)				
(3)				
(4)				
(5)				
(6)				
(7)				
(8)				
(9)				
(10)				
(11)				
(12)*				

1. $\Sigma d^2 = $ _____
2. $6 \times$ Step 1 = _____
4. $N = $ number of subjects or objects = _____
5. Step 2 $\div$ Step 4 = _____
6. $r_s = 1 -$ Step 5 = _____
7. p (from Table VI, Appendix B) = _____ †

This technique can be used for any number of subjects or objects. For this illustration, N = 12.

†*If r_s exceeds the table value at a given p level, then r_s is significant at that p level.*

EXAMPLE: A class of 10 students were given a test of science aptitude and a science achievement test. Their scores appear below.

Subject	Test 1: Science Aptitude Scores	Rank	Test 2: Science Achievement Scores	Rank	d	d²
1) Mary	98	2	85	6	4	16
2) Bill	53	10	65	10	0	0
3) Jean	85	5.5	90	4	1.5	2.25
4) Donna	72	8	75	9	1	1
5) Joe	65	9	80	8	1	1
6) Craig	75	7	85	6	1	1
7) Blair	98	2	100	1	1	1
8) Tommy	85	5.5	95	2.5	3	9
9) Bret	90	4	85	6	2	4
10) Jennie	98	2	95	2.5	0.5	0.25

1. $\Sigma d^2 = 35.5$
2. $6 \Sigma d^2 = 213$
3. $N = 10$
4. $N^3 - N = 1000 - 10 = 990$
5. Step 2 ÷ Step 4 = 213 ÷ 990 = .22
6. $r_s = 1 - $ Step 5 = 1 − .22 = $\boxed{.78}$
7. From Table VI, Appendix B: $p < .01$*

*From Table VI, Appendix B, an r_s of .564 would yield p = .05 for N = 10; an r_s of .746 would yield p = .01 for N = 10.

Figure 9.8 *An example illustrating the use of the Spearman rank-order correlation.*

of multiple subjects, the Spearman rank-order correlation answers the question, "Do the measures tend to agree—that is, are they measuring the same or a related thing?" Such would be applicable, for example, in assessing concurrent test validity or test-retest reliability. In the case of multiple objects, the Spearman rank-order correlation answers the question, "Do the judges tend to agree?" This would be applicable, for example, in assessing inter-rater reliability.*

*In the case of multiple judges and multiple objects, a Friedman two-way analysis of variance by ranks or a Kendall Coefficient of Concordance would be used (see Siegel, 1956).

The worksheet for the Spearman rank-order correlation (r_s) appears in Table 9.5. This worksheet can be used where multiple subjects are providing rankings on two measures as well as where two judges are providing rankings of multiple objects. An example of the first instance is given in Figure 9.8 (page 246) where a group of students are ranked on two measures.

As can be seen from Figure 9.8, there is a .78 rank-order correlation between the students' science aptitude and their science achievement. An examination of Table VI, Appendix B, shows that the probability of obtaining a .78 rank-order correlation for 10 students by chance is less than .01. Thus, the relationship determined in the example between the two measures is significant.

Chi-Square (X^2) Test

The X^2 test can be used for one, two, or more nominal variables but is commonly used for two.* Data in the two-variable case are cast into a *contingency table* such as the following.†

	College	Non-College	
First-Borns	75	30	105
Later-Borns	23	80	103
	98	110	208

The numbers in the contingency table represent the *frequency* of cases jointly satisfying a particular set of conditions specified by the variables (or the distributions of the two samples—first-borns and later-borns—across two categories—went to college and did not go to college). For instance, given the contingency of being a first born child going on to college, 75 students out of a graduating class of 208 are to be found.

The values obtained by summing the frequencies across rows and columns are called the *marginals* (e.g., 98, 105) so named because they appear in the margins of the table.

For information on the use of the chi-square test for one variable (called the one-sample case) or for two variables, with more than two levels per variable (called the K independent samples case, see Siegel (1956). The version described here is for two independent samples (in the illustration, first-borns and later-borns). However, in all three cases, the computations are highly similar.

†*Contingency tables were previously described in Section 8.8.*

The χ^2 test tells you whether the two independent samples (first-borns and later-borns) have significantly different distributions across the two categories (college and non-college) and may thereby be considered to have been drawn from different populations. That is, it tells you whether the frequencies obtained in the cells of the table are different from the frequencies you might expect based on chance variation alone. Thus, the χ^2 test compares *obtained* frequencies to *expected* frequencies and indicates the probability that they are different.

The basic formula for computing χ^2 is as follows

$$\chi^2 = \Sigma\Sigma \frac{(o - e)^2}{e}$$

where o is the obtained frequency in a cell and e is the expected frequency. The double summation sign indicates that summing is done across both the rows and columns of the contingency table. In calculating the expected frequency for each cell, if all the marginal values for a contingency table were the same, you would simply divide the total frequency by the number of cells. However, since the marginals are rarely the same, you calculate the expected frequencies for a cell by dividing the product of its marginals by the total frequency. In the example, the cell having an *obtained* frequency of 75 would have an *expected* frequency of (98 × 105) ÷ 208 or 49.4.

A worksheet for a 2 × 2 χ^2 test appears in Table 9.6. This worksheet employs a different formula which is easier to apply than the one above and is therefore recommended for computation purposes.* Note, however, that the worksheet formula can be used only in the case of a 2 × 2 contingency table. In other than the 2 × 2 case (i.e., more than 2 independent samples or more than 2 categories), the first formula should be used.†

The original example, illustrated again below, will now be re-examined and a χ^2 test performed on it using the worksheet. This analysis is shown in Figure 9.9.

	College	Non-College	
First-Borns	75	30	105
Later-Borns	23	80	103
	98	110	208

The worksheet formula has the additional advantage of incorporating a correction for continuity *which improves the approximation of the obtained distribution by the chi-square distribution.*

†*A point about the use of the chi-square test itself: it requires that the expected frequencies in each cell not be too small. If the smallest expected frequency is less than 5, the Fisher Exact Test should be used (see Siegel, 1956). Moreover, in all instances where sample sizes (N's) of less than 20 are employed, the Fisher Exact Test should also be employed.*

Table 9.6 *Worksheet for a chi-square* (X^2) *test for two independent samples* *(2 × 2 contingency table).*

A = _____	B = _____	A + B = _____
C = _____	D = _____	C + D = _____

A + C = _____   B + D = _____   N = _____

$$X^2 = \frac{N[(A \times D) - (B \times C) - \frac{N}{2}]^2}{(A + B)(C + D)(A + C)(B + D)}$$

Steps

1. $(A + B)(C + D)(A + C)(B + D) =$ _____
2. $A \times D =$ _____
3. $B \times C =$ _____
4. Step 2 − Step 3 = _____
5. Step 4 $- \dfrac{N}{2} =$ _____
6. $(\text{Step 5})^2 =$ _____
7. $N \times$ Step 6 = _____
8. Step 7 ÷ Step 1 $= X^2 =$ _____

   $df = (number\ of\ rows - 1)(number\ of\ columns - 1) = (2 - 1)(2 - 1) = 1$

   p (from Table VII, Appendix B) = _____ *

If the obtained X^2 value exceeds the value given in Table VII, Appendix B, at a given p level, then the obtained X^2 value can be considered significant at that p level.

The worksheet formula for a 2 × 2 contingency table when applied to the sample data yields a X^2 value of 48.4, which, for 1 degree of freedom, is significant well beyond the .001 level. This X^2 value and its corresponding p leads to the conclusion that first-borns and later-borns are distributed significantly differently

	College	Non-College	
First-Borns	$A =$ 75	$B =$ 30	$A + B =$ 105
Later-Borns	$C =$ 23	$D =$ 80	$C + D =$ 103
	$A + C =$ 98	$B + D =$ 110	$N =$ 208

$$\chi^2 = \frac{N[(A \times D) - (B \times C) - \frac{N}{2}]^2}{(A + B)\,(C + D)\,(A + C)\,(B.+ D)}$$

Steps

1. $(A + B)\,(C + D)\,(A + C)\,(B + D) = (105)\,(103)\,(98)\,(110) = 116{,}585{,}700$
2. $A \times D = 75 \times 80 = 6{,}000$
3. $B \times C = 30 \times 23 = 690$
4. Step 2 $-$ Step 3 $= 6{,}000 - 690 = 5{,}310$
5. Step 4 $- \frac{N}{2} = 5{,}310 - 104 = 5{,}206$
6. $(\text{Step 5})^2 = (5{,}206)^2 = 27{,}102{,}436$
7. $N \times$ Step 6 $= 208 \times 27{,}102{,}436 = 5{,}637{,}306{,}688$
8. Step 7 $\div$ Step 1 $= \dfrac{5{,}637{,}306{,}688}{116{,}585{,}700} = \chi^2 = \boxed{48.4}$

   $df = 1$

   p (from Table VII, Appendix B) $< .001^*$

---

*Note from Table VII, Appendix B, that a χ^2 of 10.83 is needed to attain significance at the .001 level for df = 1.

Figure 9.9 *An example illustrating the use of chi-square analysis for a 2 × 2 contingency table.*

across the two categories: college and non-college, justifying the inference that students who are first-born tend to go to college significantly more often than those who are later-born.

Occasionally, it is necessary to transform a variable from interval measurement to nominal measurement in order that both variables be nominal—making the use of the χ^2 possible.* This is usually best accomplished by *splitting* the interval measure at the *median* to obtain a high half and a low half. Considering students as high or low on a measure, rather than working with their actual scores, makes the use of a χ^2 test possible. However, it is preferable to retain the variable in interval form and employ a parametric test. In so doing, information will not be lost.

*   *   *

The high speed digital computer has made it possible to analyze data statistically by automation alone and, in fact, high speed data analysis is the subject of the next chapter. However, for fuller understanding of the statistical tests it is useful for a researcher to be able to perform them by hand before he tries to accomplish them by computer. Moreover, there are still occasions when the researcher will lack the resources or the necessary program to use a computer or, by virtue of the small amount of data collected, will still find it economical to do his analyses on a desk calculator. Thus, the reader is encouraged to master the procedures in this chapter before turning to the next.

RECOMMENDED READINGS

Edwards, A. L. *Statistical analysis* (3rd edition). New York: Holt, Rinehart, and Winston, 1969.

Ferguson, G. A. *Statistical analysis in psychology and education* (2nd edition). New York: McGraw Hill, 1966.

Hays, W. L. *Statistics for psychologists.* New York: Holt, Rinehart, and Winston, 1963.

Siegel, S. *Nonparametric statistics.* New York: McGraw Hill, 1956.

Tatsuoka, M. M. and Tiedeman, D. V. Statistics as an aspect of scientific method in research on teaching. In N. L. Gage (Ed.) *Handbook of research on teaching.* Chicago: Rand-McNally, 1963, pp. 142–170.

Winer, B. J. *Statistical principles in experimental design.* New York: McGraw-Hill, 1962.

*An alternative strategy may be to use a t-test or a point biserial correlation.

COMPETENCY TEST EXERCISES

1. You have a study with an independent variable: experimental treatment versus control; a moderator variable: I.Q.; and a dependent variable: performance on a criterion test. The statistical test you would be likely to employ would be
   a. a t-test
   b. correlation
   c. analysis of variance
   d. chi-square

2. You are analyzing the results of an experiment comparing the performance of Ss assigned to experimental and control groups. Your dependent measure is a score that, for purposes of analysis, has been converted to a rank assignment relative to the scores of other Ss. To statistically compare such experimental and control group scores, you would be likely to use
   a. Mann-Whitney U-test
   b. Spearman rank-order correlation
   c. chi-square
   d. t-test

3. Consider the following scores of two groups ($N = 20$ in each) of Ss on a performance measure:

Group 1				Group 2			
a. 75	k. 81			a. 72	k. 79		
b. 88	l. 89			b. 81	l. 83		
c. 80	m. 77			c. 70	m. 73		
d. 85	n. 84			d. 80	n. 85		
e. 78	o. 88			e. 70	o. 82		
f. 90	p. 93			f. 85	p. 90		
g. 82	q. 91			g. 73	q. 80		
h. 88	r. 81			h. 82	r. 78		
i. 76	s. 85			i. 72	s. 81		
j. 82	t. 87			j. 78	t. 74		

Calculate the mean, median, and standard deviation of the scores in Group 1.

4. Calculate the mean, median, and standard deviation of the scores in Group 2.

5. Compare the means for Groups 1 and 2 using a t-test. Report the t value and its level of significance (if any).

6. Compare the scores for Groups 1 and 2 (above) using a Mann-Whitney U-test. Report the smaller U value and its level of significance (if any).

7. Compare the scores for Groups 1 and 2 (above) using a Chi-Square test. (Split the scores into two categories.) Report the X^2 value and its level of significance (if any).

8. Consider the data from exercise 3 that you have been using in the above exercises. Assume that Group 1 is the experimental group and Group 2 is the control group and that together they constitute *variable A* (the independent variable). In addition, assume you have a moderator variable, *variable B* (high versus low I.Q., for example). Alternating members of each group (a), (c), (e), (g), . . . (s) are low on variable B; the remaining members (b), (d), (f), (h), . . . (t) are high on variable B. Run a two-way analysis of variance and report mean squares and F ratios for each source of variance (A, B, AB, error). Also report levels of significance (if any). (*Note*: you can use the forms for unequal n's even though this analysis has equal n's.)

9. Now use the data given in exercise 3 in a slightly different way. Instead of thinking of Groups 1 and 2 as they are labeled, think of them as Tests 1 and 2, administered to a single group of Ss. The letter appearing alongside each piece of data is now the subject identification code. Compute a Spearman rank-order correlation between the scores for the 20 Ss on Test 1 (Group 1) and the scores for these same Ss on Test 2 (Group 2). Report the r_s and the level of significance (if any).

10. Again, consider Groups 1 and 2 to be Tests 1 and 2, respectively, as was done above. But this time only consider the first 10 Ss. (Again use the letters alongside the data as Ss identification codes.) Compute a Pearson product-moment correlation between the Test 1 and Test 2 scores for the first 10 Ss. Report the r and the level of significance (if any).

10

Using Procedures
for Data Processing

OBJECTIVES

Demonstrate procedures for data coding and rostering. / Describe a punch card (and other input sources) and procedures for preparing data for punching and analysis. / Idenfity "canned" programs for data analysis and describe their characteristics. / Construct job control cards and program control cards required for program use. / Describe and interpret computer output (printouts). / Demonstrate procedures for correlational analysis using a standard desk calculator (rotary type).

10.1 DATA CODING

Ordinarily a researcher does not analyze data in name or word form. For instance, the fact that a subject was male or female cannot be conveniently conveyed to a data processing device through the use of the words male and female. The solution is to use a numerical *code*: each male subject could be coded as a 1 and each female subject as a 2. The numerical code is just another *name* for a piece of datum but one which is shorter than its word name and therefore easier to record, store, process, and retrieve.

Such codes are used regularly in data processing. It is possible to code the subject's name, sex, socioeconomic status, years of education completed, etc. Consider the sample data codes shown in Figure 10.1. Note that the data are collected in nominal categories designated by word name (e.g., single, married, divorced) and that the word name of each category is then replaced by a number.

The choice of which number represents which word is arbitrary. Typically, however, consecutive numbers are chosen; when appropriate, one number (usually the last in the series) is reserved for other or miscellaneous.

Example 1

Sex

1 = male
2 = female

Example 2

Marital Status

1 = single
2 = married
3 = divorced
4 = widowed

Example 3

Hair Color

1 = brown
2 = black
3 = blonde
4 = red
5 = other

Example 4

Years of
Education

1 = some high school
2 = high-school graduate
3 = some college
4 = college graduate
5 = professional or
    graduate training

Example 5

Occupational
*Categories**

1 = professional, techni-
    cal, and managerial
2 = clerical and sales
3 = service
4 = farming, fishery,
    forestry, and
    others related
5 = processing
6 = machine trades
7 = bench work
8 = structural work
9 = miscellaneous

Example 6

Subject
Matter

1 = English
2 = Social Studies
3 = Mathematics
4 = Science

*From the *Dictionary of Occupational Titles*

Figure 10.1 *Sample data codes.*

Numerical data codes are quite essential with nominal data which are typically collected in word form and must therefore be coded to obtain numerical categories. They can also be used for interval data (or ordinal data) if, for reasons of data storage or analysis, you desire to replace a long series of numbers with a shorter one, or if you choose to convert these data to nominal form. (Coding produces nominal data since it groups scores into categories.) For instance, if you have collected data on subjects' ages which run from a low of 16 to a high of 60, you can replace an interval scale of 45 possible scores with a compressed scale of five categories (which would then be considered nominal categories for computational purposes) by designating ages between 11 and 20 with the code 1; 21 to 30, 2; 31 to 40, 3; 41 to 50, 4; and 51 to 60, 5. Thus, the researcher has the following options with interval data. He can retain it in interval form and use the two-digit number for age as collected. Or, he can treat the data as classes or categories by coding it into nominal form, as described above. (If he chose to utilize a statistic requiring nominal data, such as a chi-square analysis, he would have to adopt the second option.)

It is also possible to code in categories in terms of the ordinal position of a score within a series of scores. Thus, 1 might represent those scores in the high 20% of a series of scores, 2 those in the second highest 20%, and so on, down to 5 for those in the lowest 20%. Consider the following example of scores from a class of 25 students.

	98	84	79	70	60
	96	84	78	69	58
	94	84	77	68	53
	92	80	77	68	42
	87	80	71	65	30
Code	1	2	3	4	5

This coding system insures that an equal number of scores will fall into each coding category; it is the system to use if an experiment requires that the number of scores in a category must be the same. (It can also be used to compare the distributions of two independent samples using chi-square analysis.)

Some examples of more complex coding systems for converting interval scores to ordinal categories appear in Figure 10.2. Computationally, such categories are still likely to be treated as nominal. Note that the code of 0 has been avoided. It is recommended that a coding category begin with 1 or 01 and that 0 be restricted in its use to designate *no data*. Note also that in each case the number of digits in the code must be the same as the number of digits in the last category of the code. Since the number 10 in Example 2 has two digits, a two-digit code must be used from the beginning. If there were 350 categories, then a three-digit code would be required, since the number 350 has three digits.

It is important to emphasize that all data should not be automatically coded. Actual data values may be rostered and analyzed. Data codes are used (1) when interval or ordinal data have been collected but discrete data categories (nominal data) are desired for analysis purposes, or (2) when the data themselves come in nominal form (that is, as words).

10.2 DATA ROSTERING

The step between data collection and data analysis is data rostering. It is the procedure by which data are *recorded* for use in a calculator or computer analysis.

Example 1	Example 2
Weight in Pounds	*Number of Correct Responses*
1 = under 121	01 = 0-5
2 = 121-140	02 = 6-10
3 = 141-160	03 = 11-15
4 = 161-180	04 = 16-20
5 = 181-200	05 = 21-25
6 = 201-220	06 = 26-30
7 = over 220	07 = 31-35
	08 = 36-40
	09 = 41-45
	10 = 46-50

Example 3	Example 4
Grade	*Grade*
1 = 90 and above	1 = top 10% (percentile 91-100)
2 = 80-89	2 = next to top 20% (percentile 71-90)
3 = 70-79	3 = middle 40% (percentile 31-70)
4 = 60-69	4 = next to lowest 20% (percentile 11-30)
5 = 59 and below	5 = lowest 10% (percentile 1-10)

Figure 10.2 *Complex data codes.*

In fact, the following discussion of data rostering will be predicated on the expectation that the next step will be key punching of the data onto cards for computer analysis, although data rostered in this form are equally ready for analysis with a desk calculator.

For example, suppose thirty-two children employed in a study concerning reading methods were grouped as follows: (1) eight children who were given readiness and then sight reading, (2) eight children who received sight reading only, (3) eight children who were given readiness only, and (4) eight children who received training using the Initial Teaching Alphabet (ITA). Type of treatment represents the major independent variable. As a moderator variable, half of the children in each treatment were boys. As a second moderator variable, half of the boys in each treatment and half of the girls were above the group mean on the Stanford-Binet I.Q. Test. The father's income was used as a control variable. Codes necessary for rostering these data (called the "Reading Experiment") appear in Figure 10.3.

Once you have prepared the code, the next step is preparation of the data sheet. Large, multiple-column pads,* such as accounting pads, are best for this

*Pads that are ruled into 80 columns, thus making card punching easier, are available from IBM.

Subject Number	*Treatment*
01 = Johnny J.	1 = Readiness and sight reading
02 = George T.	2 = Sight reading only
03 = Nancy R.	3 = Readiness only
.	4 = ITA
.	
.	
32 = Blair Z.	

Sex	*I.Q.*	*Father's Income*
1 = male	1 = high	1 = under $6,000
2 = female	2 = low	2 = $6,000–$10,000
		3 = over $10,000

Figure 10.3 *Data codes for the "Reading Experiment."*

purpose. At the top of the columns enter the relevant indentification or name for each variable. (It will also be helpful for your own purposes to indicate on a separate piece of paper which are the independent, moderator, control, and dependent variables for each analysis. Such information will be used later in preparing control cards for computer analysis; this is discussed in Section 10.4.)

The dependent variables in this study include scores on the school's own reading test (which provides scores of rate, accuracy, and comprehension) and scores on the Picture Reading Test. In addition, the number of days absent from school were rostered, as well as the scores on a group I.Q. test administered at the end of the experiment. The sample roster sheet appears in Figure 10.4.

Note that the first five items on the roster have been designated by code while the remaining six are actual data. This roster, as will be seen later, has been optimally set up for key punching. Decimal points have been eliminated (a common practice) since they are in a constant position for each variable and therefore add nothing to the data (but do take up space). They can be reinstated in the terms obtained from the subsequent analysis.

One more example of data rostering may be useful. Twenty-four teachers, half vocational and half academic, were rated by their students on a 20-item scale. The average judgment by the class for each teacher on each item was rostered on an IBM sheet (Figure 10.5; the "Teaching Style Experiment"). This sheet, suitable for both data rostering and coding, was also used to roster the data from a number of other measures obtained on the teachers in this study— such as mean score across the 20-item scale, three observer measures, and five

Subject Number	Treatment	Sex	I.Q.	Father's Income	Days Absent	School Reading Test			Picture Reading Test	Group I.Q.
						Rate	Accuracy	Comprehension		
01	1	1	1	2	00	21	07	18	2.4	115
02	1	1	1	3	01	19	10	16	3.1	095
03	1	1	2	3	01	09	04	17	0.9	101
04	1	1	2	1	05	17	02	10	1.6	097
05	1	2	1	2	00	22	14	04	1.8	122
06	1	2	1	2	11	14	06	11	2.0	124
07	1	2	2	1	08	13	12	18	1.1	110
08	1	2	2	1	07	16	03	16	1.2	104
09	2	1	1	1	01	11	04	17	0.3	122
10	2	1	1	2	04	18	09	12	0.9	100
11	2	1	2	1	01	25	02	14	2.9	101
12	2	1	2	2	03	23	12	15	1.0	099
13	2	2	1	3	06	11	08	10	2.1	133
14	2	2	1	3	09	17	11	14	2.1	130
15	2	2	2	2	06	29	14	11	1.0	129
16	2	2	2	1	00	13	08	16	2.0	103
17	3	1	1	3	02	15	10	12	3.0	092
18	3	1	1	1	06	17	10	09	2.8	104
19	3	1	2	2	08	27	06	23	2.0	101
20	3	1	2	2	10	25	14	17	1.7	093
21	3	2	1	1	01	13	12	16	2.2	109
22	3	2	1	1	02	24	09	21	2.7	131
23	3	2	2	2	06	31	10	14	2.5	105
24	3	2	2	3	03	15	15	18	2.9	108
25	4	1	1	2	05	19	10	17	1.8	111
26	4	1	1	1	11	13	12	18	0.6	130
27	4	1	2	2	01	25	08	12	1.5	090
28	4	1	2	1	10	30	09	13	1.9	100
29	4	2	1	3	07	19	19	24	2.6	119
30	4	2	1	1	03	11	15	23	2.0	124
31	4	2	2	2	03	18	10	20	3.5	101
32	4	2	2	3	09	24	15	15	2.1	095

Figure 10.4 *Data roster for the "Reading Experiment."*

IBM FORTRAN Coding Form

X28-7327-6 U/M 025
Printed in U.S.A.

Statement Number		1	2	3	4	5	6	7	8	9	10	11	12	13	14	15	16	17	18	19	20	$\bar{X}$	CON	DT	TSC	I	II	III	IV	S
01	1	58	64	55	65	45	60	59	63	62	43	52	45	58	52	63	47	58	50	66	46	55	50	49	71	13	02	09	12	1
02	1	64	62	62	56	69	62	64	64	45	42	48	54	60	61	66	54	49	58	47	38	56	71	67	99	06	05	11	14	1
03	1	48	58	54	58	58	55	58	63	55	27	52	50	52	54	52	53	48	50	35	38	52	47	53	60	08	04	12	12	1
04	1	55	73	38	45	75	56	69	82	60	73	51	60	48	68	55	53	45	49	44	55	55	38	49	58	04	09	11	12	1
05	1	56	70	46	53	68	49	65	60	59	58	48	54	53	55	47	42	69	48	54	33	51	60	56	60	07	07	10	12	1
06	1	56	65	51	55	63	56	63	65	56	49	50	53	54	58	57	50	54	51	49	42	54	53	55	70	08	08	09	11	1
07	1	50	56	55	58	62	73	63	60	56	41	50	50	56	50	47	41	57	51	45	48	52	38	42	30	10	06	10	10	2
08	1	51	60	79	57	84	50	67	79	69	23	50	50	61	76	64	51	60	66	44	39	56	42	51	40	07	11	08	10	2
09	1	58	62	61	64	72	57	63	60	63	32	58	50	63	49	52	48	53	61	32	38	52	38	40	50	09	08	09	10	2
10	1	60	65	62	64	62	61	64	59	61	46	58	51	67	54	64	62	48	62	42	46	54	30	49	27	06	07	13	10	2
11	1	90	70	49	60	82	41	53	74	58	63	65	61	63	83	69	81	73	63	78	61	63	65	69	36	10	05	11	10	2
12	1	62	63	61	61	72	56	62	66	61	41	56	52	62	62	59	57	58	61	48	46	55	43	50	37	10	10	08	08	2
13	2	43	57	41	55	60	59	68	57	57	40	49	41	58	43	44	51	54	55	40	32	49	41	41	44	11	05	07	13	1
14	2	62	32	25	21	32	26	50	55	27	23	28	51	33	54	24	55	37	26	25	27	37	31	35	38	08	07	08	13	1
15	2	38	47	32	36	43	48	47	64	49	30	38	53	60	45	31	43	44	41	45	39	45	47	46	65	05	07	11	13	1
16	2	49	55	29	46	55	36	61	59	51	28	37	39	49	53	44	48	46	43	43	42	48	44	44	45	12	02	10	12	1
17	2	41	45	42	52	74	56	43	71	28	10	44	30	48	85	29	37	40	41	46	38	42	62	64	67	07	06	11	12	1
18	2	48	56	42	56	75	59	56	65	60	45	61	51	46	41	44	57	46	58	41	34	46	21	24	24	07	04	14	11	1
19	2	48	61	43	61	54	45	49	54	56	39	61	53	51	51	34	46	56	53	46	30	49	43	45	50	09	05	12	10	2
20	2	61	57	30	63	61	26	42	60	45	37	40	42	45	68	41	50	50	38	50	35	46	21	24	08	10	09	09	08	2
21	2	57	53	42	54	63	52	58	59	54	42	51	45	50	56	45	45	51	50	40	42	47	29	31	01	10	08	08	10	2
22	2	48	54	39	33	60	53	71	56	52	18	40	49	53	54	19	25	41	35	38	42	43	37	40	15	10	08	09	09	2
23	2	41	46	49	57	53	54	57	52	51	58	46	40	56	62	26	43	49	45	36	21	45	68	48	80	12	08	07	09	2
24	2	44	58	56	53	61	43	41	57	55	45	43	51	53	66	47	45	50	51	29	47	48	55	45	50	12	07	08	09	2

*A standard card form, IBM electro 888157, is available for punching statements from this form.

Figure 10.5 *Data roster for the "Teaching Style Experiment."*

personality measures. The information identifying the data in each column or columns, as shown below in Figure 10.6, should help to explain the data layout in Figure 10.5.

Column Number		Column Number	
1–2	teacher code number	35–36	item 15
4	teaching area:	37–38	item 16
	1 = vocational	39–40	item 17
	2 = nonvocational	41–42	item 18
7–8	item 1	43–44	item 19
9–10	item 2	45–46	item 20
11–12	item 3	48–49	total scale mean score
13–14	item 4	51–52	consensus of judges'
15–16	item 5		judgments
17–18	item 6	54–55	best judgment of judges
19–20	item 7	57–58	judgments on checklist
21–22	item 8	61–62	personality I score
23–24	item 9	64–65	personality II score
25–26	item 10	67–68	personality III score
27–28	item 11	70–71	personality IV score
29–30	item 12	73	high–low on IV
31–32	item 13		1 = high
33–34	item 14		2 = low

Figure 10.6 *Column designations for the data roster (Figure 10.5) in the "Teaching Style Experiment."*

The data rostering format shown in Figure 10.5 is ideal for key punching and subsequent computer analysis. It is orderly and easy to read. In using it, work directly from the raw data rather than rostering the data and then transposing it.

Note that each subject is given a row while each measure accounts for a column. In some cases columns have been left empty to make it easier to read the data, although every column may be utilized if necessary.

The data shown in Figure 10.5 (the "Teaching Style Experiment") will be used for illustrative purposes in the next three sections of this chapter.

10.3 THE PUNCH CARD AND DATA ROSTERING

A major source of input to a high-speed digital computer is a punch card. Data is punched on cards by a key punch machine; these punched cards can then be "read" by a computer. An example of a blank punch card appears in Figure 10.7. Note that the card has 80 columns numbered 1 to 80, and 10 rows, with

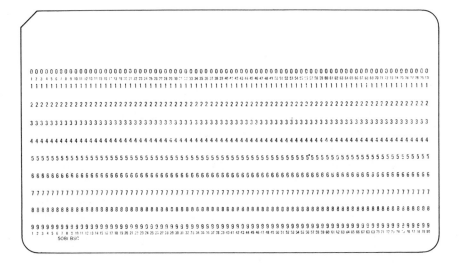

Figure 10.7 *Sample blank punch card.*

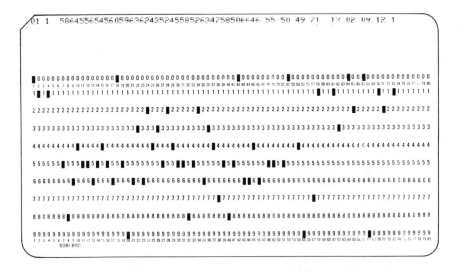

Figure 10.8 *Sample punch card with data punched from subject 1 on the data roster in Figure 10.5.*

the numbers 0 to 9. If you wanted to punch the number 103 onto a punch card, you would punch the number 1 in the first column, 0 in the second column, and 3 in the third column. Ordinarily data for a single subject goes on a single card, but if more than 80 columns are required per subject for the data, additional cards may be used. When this is the case, avoid confusion by punching a card sequence in column 80 and by punching a subject identification number in the initial columns of each card.

The card layout conforms to the roster format shown in Figure 10.5 insofar as each contains 80 columns and each column conforms to a single digit. Since each row on the data roster is for a single subject, and each punch card is for a single subject, then each row on the data roster is punched on a separate card. The card in Figure 10.8 contains data from subject number 01 in the data roster shown in Figure 10.5. The data are often printed out at the top of a card as well as being punched. Note that the punches conform to the numbers at the top.

Each measure or code recorded on the roster is referred to as a *data field*. If the measure or code employs only a single digit, it is referred to as a one-digit field. The code in column 4 of the roster (Figure 10.5) would be an example of a one-digit field. If the measure or code employs two digits, it is referred to as a two-digit field (as would be true of the code in columns 1 and 2), and so on. Each digit in a data field requires a column, and all recordings of the same measure must have the same size data field because inconsistent blanks in a punch card create confusion and errors. Thus, a single digit entry in an otherwise two-digit field is best prefixed by a zero to make it conform to a two-digit field; this system avoids the error that would result from placing the digit in the first rather than the second column causing the computer to read 90 rather than 9.

The data in Figure 10.5 require 24 cards, one for each subject, punched as illustrated for the first card in Figure 10.8. Each card contains 31 data fields, (because there are 31 measures), all but two of which are two-digit fields. The remaining two are one-digit fields. Thus, the data in Figure 10.5 require at least 60 columns per card to accommodate the 29 two-digit fields and 2 one-digit fields. Since 13 blank columns have been employed for spacing,* a total of 73 columns is utilized on each card out of a total of 80 possible columns. If more than 80 columns were required, two cards would be used per subject.

Ordinarily, blanks are read as zeroes, which do not affect the score following them on the card, and therefore may be used for spacing. Such blanks or zeroes are also typically inserted to fill in for (and thus designate) missing data. The variable format card, described in the next section, enables the researcher to communicate to the computer the columns in which data are to be found.

Inputs to large computers may also be made with magnetic tape and discs. Large amounts of data and frequently used programs are often stored this way for easy access and rapid processing.

It is vital that punch cards fed into a computer be consistent in their layout and size of data fields. The likelihood of achieving consistency is increased through the use of proper data rostering.

10.4 THE USE OF COMPUTER PROGRAMS FOR DATA ANALYSIS

Program Selection

The set of instructions which a computer employs to analyze data is called a *program*. A large number of such programs are currently available for common statistical analyses ranging from the calculation of means and variances to multiple regression analysis. Programs in general are referred to as *software* (to distinguish them from machine parts or *hardware*), and general-use programs already in existence are referred to as *canned* programs. Whenever possible, it is a good idea to use canned programs rather than undertaking the effort of writing an original program.

Canned programs appear in various series. One popular series is the UCLA Biomedical Series (BIMED) developed at UCLA initially for application in the biological and medical field. A list of BIMED programs for statistical analyses appears in Figure 10.9. The BIMED users' manual (Dixon, 1968) specifies the restrictions and characteristics of each BIMED program. In selecting a suitable program decide on the data analysis to be done and then scan the manual to find a possible program and the description of its characteristics (i.e., a general description including limitations, order of cards in deck, card preparation, computational procedure, and references).

As a concrete illustration, consider again the "Teaching Style Experiment" whose data deals with twenty-four teachers, each of whom is described by his students on a 20-item scale (Figure 10.5, page 260). The first task in data analysis is to perform an *item analysis* to determine the relation between each test item and the total test score (see Section 7.7). This analysis, which forms the basis for deciding which items are internally consistent and should be retained in the test, may be accomplished by correlating the scores on each item

Six Character Name	Descriptive Title	Six Character Name	Descriptive Title
BMD01D	Simple Data Description	BMD05R	Polynominal Regression
BMD02D	Correlation with Trans-generation	BMD06R	Asymptotic Regression
BMD03D	Correlation with Item Deletion	BMD01S	Life Table and Survival Rate
BMD04D	Alphanumeric Frequency Count	BMD02S	Contingency Table Analysis
BMD05D	General Plot Including Histograms	BMD03S	Biological Assay: Probit Analysis
BMD06D	Description of Strata	BMD04S	Guttman Scale Preprocessor
BMD07D	Description of Strata with Histograms	BMD05S	Guttman Scale no. 1
BMD08D	Cross-Tabulations with Variable Stacking	BMD06S	Guttman Scale no. 2, Part 1
BMD09D	Cross-Tabulation, Incomplete Data	BMD07S	Guttman Scale no. 2, Part 2
BMD10D	Data Patterns for Dichotomies	BMD09S	Transgeneration
BMD11D	Data Patterns for Polychotomies	BMD10S	Transposition of Large Matrices
BMD01M	Principal Component Analysis	BMD01T	Amplitude and Phase Analysis
BMD02M	Regression on Principal Components	BMD02T	Autocovariance and Power Spectral Analysis
BMD03M	Factor Analysis	BMD01V	Analysis of Variance for One-Way Design
BMD04M	Discriminant Analysis for Two Groups	BMD02V	Analysis of Variance for Factorial Design
BMD05M	Discriminant Analysis for Several Groups	BMD03V	Analysis of Covariance for Factorial Design
BMD06M	Canonical Analysis	BMD04V	Analysis of Covariance with Multiple Covariates
BMD07M	Stepwise Discriminant Analysis	BMD05V	General Linear Hypothesis
BMD01R	Simple Linear Regression	BMD06V	General Linear Hypothesis with Contrasts
BMD02R	Stepwise Regression		
BMD03R	Multiple Regression with Case Combinations	BMD07V	Multiple Range Tests
BMD04R	Periodic Regression and Harmonic Analysis	BMD08V	Analysis of Variance

Figure 10.9 *Library of BIMED (UCLA) programs for statistics.*

with their total or mean score for the total scale. To accomplish this on the computer, use a BIMED program labelled BMD02D, which is *correlation with transgeneration*. Part of the general description of this program appears in Figure 10.10. As can be seen from the description this program computes a matrix of simple correlation coefficients. That is, for the 20 items and scale mean score (a total of 21 variables), this program will provide a correlation of each variable with every other variable, although all this is really needed is the

BMD02D

Correlation with Transgeneration (Boolean Selection of Cases)

1. General Description
   a. This program computes simple correlation coefficients, averages, and measures of dispersion on entering variables and/or transgenerated variables from selected cases whose values for specified variables have a precise logical relationship in agreement with a specified Boolean expression.
   b. Output from this program includes:
      (1) Sums
      (2) Means
      (3) Cross-product deviations
      (4) Standard deviations
      (5) Variance—covariance matrix
      (6) Correlation matrix

   Optional output includes:
      (7) One-page cross-tabulation plots of any two variables, automatically scaled to 50 (vertical) by 100 (horizontal) character spaces or units.
   c. Limitations per problem:
      (1) p, number of original variables ($2 \leqslant p \leqslant 135$)
      (2) n, number of original cases ($2 \leqslant n \leqslant 99, 999$)
      (3) j, number of Plot Selection Cards ($0 \leqslant j \leqslant 99$)
      (4) q, number of variables added to the original set after transgeneration ($-133 \leqslant q \leqslant 133$)
      (5) b, number of Case Selection Cards ($0 \leqslant b \leqslant 9$)
      (6) m, number of Transgeneration Cards ($0 \leqslant m \leqslant 150$)
      (7) k, number of Variable Format Cards ($1 \leqslant k \leqslant 10$)

Revised 6-1-67

Figure 10.10 *Class D—description and tabulation. (From: W. J. Dixon (Ed.) Biomedical computer programs, Berkeley and Los Angeles, University of California Press, 1968. Reprinted by permission of the author and the Regents of the University of California.)*

correlations of each item with the scale mean score. (As is often the case, the computer gives you more than you need, but it is easier to disregard what you do not need than to alter the program.)

As you will note from the program description in Figure 10.10, there are seven limitations in using this program of which only the first (1), second (2), and seventh (7) are relevant for the purposes of this discussion. (The problem of analysis will not entail transgeneration—limitations 4 and 6, nor plot or case selection—limitations 3 and 5.) The problem of analysis includes 21 variables and 24 cases (or subjects) and is thus well within the first and second limitations. Moreover, all of the data for each subject will be contained on a single card and since the program will accommodate as many as 10 cards per subject (that is, 10 variable format cards), limitation number 7 can be met. (You will note later that when all the data for a subject are contained in a single card, only one variable format card is needed.)

Preparing Control Cards: An Example

After having selected a program and determined its suitability, the next step is to provide instructions for the computer so that it uses the appropriate program and reads in the data. Such instructions are presented by a series of program *control cards* which are specified in the users' manual. The manual also specifies the order in which these cards are to be read into the computer. Control cards for the correlational analysis described above (the "Teaching Style Experiment") were prepared, punched, and then the control cards and the data were printed out. The print-out for the control cards and data appears in Figure 10.11.

The first three control cards (shown on the first three lines of the printout) are called *system cards* and are often unique to the system employed by the particular computer center being used. These cards—as all the control cards in this illustration—are written in job control language, rather than in a language such as FORTRAN IV. (The BIMED programs themselves, however, are written in FORTRAN IV.)

The first card, usually referred to as the *job card*, identifies the analysis,* the user's code number, and the user's name. The second card instructs the computer to use the BMD02D program which has been stored on a disc. The third system card tells the computer to begin the operation; the fourth card is called a *problem card*. Columns 7 through 12 of the problem card are reserved for

---

*CØRREL *is an arbitrary name chosen to indicate that a correlational analysis is being used. Note that the letter O is made with a slash through it (Ø) to distinguish it from a zero.*

```
//CORREL    JOB  31750,'TUCKMAN, DR B. W.    ',CLASS=J
// EXEC BMDGO,PROG=BMD02D
//GO.SYSIN DD *
PROBLM    1 21    24        NONO
(6X,20F2.0,1X,F2.0)
                                                                                          1
01 1 5864556456059636243524558526347585060646 55 50 49 71 13 02 09 12 1
02 1 6462566962644645424854600166544958473 8  56 71 67 99 06 05 11 14 1
03 1 4858545855586355277525052545348503538    52 47 53 60 08 04 12 12 1
04 1 5573384575566982607351604868555354 94455 55 38 49 58 04 09 11 12 1
05 1 5670465368496560595848545354742694 85433 51 60 56 60 07 07 10 12 1
06 1 5665515563663490503545857505451494 2     54 53 55 70 08 08 09 11 1
07 1 5055555862736360564150650474157514548    52 38 42 30 10 08 09 10 2
08 1 5160795784506779692350506177664516066 4439 56 42 51 40 07 06 10 10 1
09 1 5862616472576360633258506349524853613238 52 38 40 50 09 11 09 10 2
10 1 6065626462616459614658516754646248624246 54 30 49 27 06 08 13 10 2
11 1 9070496082415374586365616383698173637861 63 65 69 36 10 07 11 10 2
12 1 6263616172566266614156262629575861 4846  55 43 50 37 10 05 08 08 2
13 2 4357415560596857574049415843445154554032 49 41 41 44 11 10 07 13 1
14 2 6232252132265055272328513354245537262527 37 31 35 38 08 10 08 13 1
15 2 3847323643484764493038536045313444145 39  45 47 46 65 05 07 11 13 1
16 2 4955294655366159512837399534448464 34342  48 44 44 45 12 05 11 13 1
17 2 4145452527456437128104430088529374041 4638 42 62 64 67 07 02 10 12 1
18 2 4856425675599660456151464144574665 84134  46 21 24 24 07 06 11 11 1
19 2 4861436154454549456396153151344665346 30  49 43 45 50 09 04 14 11 2
20 2 6157300636126426045374042456841505038 5035 46 21 24 08 10 05 12 10 2
21 2 5753425463525859544251455056454551 504042 47 29 31 01 10 09 09 08 2
22 2 4854393360537115652184049535419254 13842  43 37 40 15 10 08 08 10 2
23 2 4146495753545752515846405662264394 45362 1 45 68 48 80 10 08 09 09 2
24 2 4458565361434157554543515366474550 512947 48 55 45 50 12 07 08 09 2
FINISH
//
```

Figure 10.11 *Print-out of the control cards and data for a correlational analysis for the "Teaching Style Experiment."*

an alphanumeric* code that tells the researcher what analysis it is (the "1" is a code for his first analysis; the blanks are read as zeroes—see footnote, p. 263). The problem card then lists the number of variables (21) in columns 13-15, the number of cases (24) in columns 16-20, and the number of variable format cards (1) in column 72.[†] The next control card is called a *variable format card* and informs the computer where to find the data on the card. The 6X means skip the first six columns, since, as you can note on the data print-out, the first six columns are taken up by identification codes and blank columns (columns 1-2 contain a subject code; column 4 contains a treatment or condition code); 20 means read the next 20 data fields; and 2.0 means each of these data fields contains two digits. The IX means skip the next column (47) which is blank, and F2.0 means read the next two-column data field in which the scale mean score is punched.[‡]

Next in sequence come the data cards and, finally, the last two control cards are a *finish card* and a double-slash (//) card to terminate the analysis and operation.

The deck is now prepared and the analysis is ready to be run. To reach this point, the researcher has had to:

1. roster the data in a form suitable for key punching (including setting up data codes where necessary);
2. punch the data on key punch cards;
3. select a suitable program and check its limitations;
4. prepare control cards as instructed in the users' manual;
5. place the control cards (including system cards) and data in the proper sequence as specified in the users' manual;
6. drop the cards off at the local computer center (assuming you have an account there);
7. go back to the center as often as necessary to correct any errors, typically in the preparation of the program control cards or sequence of the cards, that may crop up and cause the program not to run as desired, and resubmit the deck for another run (or several) until the run is successfully completed.

Alphanumeric is a term used to refer to codes in which both letters and numbers are permitted. Alphabetic refers to letters only and numeric to numbers only.

†*The "NO" "NO" in columns 29-30 and 31-32 indicate that neither a matrix of cross products nor a covariance matrix is desired in the print-out.*

‡*Instructions about the preparation of control cards appears at the beginning of the BIMED Manual (Dixon, 1968). These instructions are reasonably simple and can be followed by the beginner; the use of BIMED programs does not require training in programming.*

In addition, of course, he has to interpret the print-out of the results, which will be covered in Section 10.5.

Another Example—"Teaching Style Experiment: Part Two"

It may be useful to provide a second example of steps leading up to the point where an analysis is ready to be run. For this illustration, parts of the same data from the "Teaching Style Experiment" (shown originally in Figure 10.5 and printed out in Figure 10.11) will be employed. Here analysis of variance will be used to determine if the teachers' subject area and personality affected his over-all ratings by students. Referring to Figure 10.5 (and the column designations and codes shown in Figure 10.6, pages 260 and 261, respectively), you will see that teachers are subdivided into vocational and nonvocational teachers, this information being presented in column 4 with vocational teachers coded as 1 and nonvocational teachers as 2. Personality scores for teachers are coded in column 73 with high IV teachers coded with a 1 and low IV teachers with a 2. Personality and the subject taught are the independent variables for the two-way analysis of variance. The dependent variable is mean score on the total test* (shown in columns 48 and 49). Each independent variable is a one-digit data field while the dependent variable is a two-digit data field. None of the other data on the roster will be used in this analysis. However, since the data to be used have already been punched on the cards in the last illustration (see the print-out of the data in Figure 10.11), the deck from that illustration will be used again, although a new program and new control cards will be needed; new control cards are necessary since the program, number of variables, and location of these variables on the cards are different from the previous analysis. In general, if you conduct both analyses in the same run, you need to construct two data decks. This can be accomplished while punching the first deck by using the duplicate key on the key punch and punching another card from the original or using a reproducer.†

Since the data have already been coded, rostered, and a second deck punched the next step is to select a program. The users' manual of BIMED programs is again consulted for this purpose. An examination of Figure 10.9, representing the complete contents of the BIMED users' manual, indicates that program BMD 02V is the likely program for the factorial analysis of variance. The first page of

*This test is a version of the SPOTS (shown on pages 163–164), a measure of a teachers nondirectiveness.

†It is also possible to store the data on discs or tape and use it repeatedly without the need of multiple data decks.

BMD02V
Analysis of Variance for Factorial Design

1. General Description
   a. This program computes an analysis of variance for a factorial design.
   b. Output for this program includes:
      (1) Analysis-of-variance table and the grand mean.
      (2) A breakdown of the sums of squares into orthogonal polynomial components for as many as four main effects and all of their first order interactions.
      (3) Main effects and first order interactions for the variables specified in (2).
      (4) Cell and marginal means.
   c. Limitations per problem:
      (1) W, number of variables or ways ($W \leqslant 8$)
      (2) R, number of replicates ($R \leqslant 999$)
      (3) L_i, number of categories or levels of any one variable ($L_1 \leqslant 999$) and ($L_1 \times L_2 \times L_3 \times \ldots \times L_w \leqslant 18,000$)
      (4) k, number of Variable Format Cards ($1 \leqslant k \leqslant 5$)
   d. Estimation of running time and output pages per problem:
      Number of seconds $= (W \cdot R + 90)$ (for IBM 7094)
      Number of pages $= 5$
                      $+ \Sigma L_i/60$ if marginal means requested
                      $+ \Pi L_i/60$ if cell means requested
   e. The program can perform transgenerations of input data, if desired, according to the codes specified on one Special Trangeneration Card. Codes 01 through 10 of the transgeneration list may be used.

Figure 10.12 *Class V—variance analysis. (From W. J. Dixon (Ed.), Biomedical* computer programs, *Berkeley and Los Angeles, University of California Press, 1968. Reprinted by permission of the author and The Regents of the University of California.)*

the description of this program has been reproduced as Figure 10.12. Since the desired analysis of variance includes two factors ($W = 2$; see Figure 10.12) with two levels each ($L_1 = 2, L_2 = 2$), and six replicates ($R = 6$ or six entries per cell), it is well within the limitations of the BMD02V program. (Also, all the data for a subject is on a single card so R, the number of variable format cards, equals 1—falling within the fourth limitation.)

The control card format and order are set forth in the users' manual. As in the previous analysis, three system cards, a problem card, a variable format card, a finish card, and a double-slash card are employed. These cards along with the data have been printed out in Figure 10.13. Note that the first system card is

```
//ANOVA     JOB 31750,'TUCKMAN, DR B. W.    ',CLASS=J
// EXEC BMDGO,PROG=BMD02V
//GO.SYSIN DD *
PROBLM020062 201       002002
(47X,F2.0)
03 1 485854558555863552752505254534850353 8 52 47 53 60 08 04 12 12 1
07 1 505655586273636056415050565047415751455 48 52 38 42 30 10 06 10 10 1
13 2 435741556059685757404941584344515545540 32 49 41 41 44 11 05 07 13 2
19 2 486143615445495456396153515134465565346 30 49 43 45 50 09 05 12 12 2
01 1 586455654560596362435245585263475850664 6 55 50 49 71 13 02 09 10 1
08 1 516079578450067796923505061766451606644 39 56 42 51 40 07 11 08 10 1
14 2 623225213226505272323285133554455372625 27 37 31 35 38 08 07 08 13 2
20 2 615730636122642604537404245684150503850 35 46 21 24 08 10 09 09 08 2
02 1 646226566996264645424854600616654495847 38 56 71 67 99 06 05 11 14 1
09 1 586261647257636063325850063495248536133 238 52 38 40 50 09 08 09 10 1
15 2 384732364348476449303853600453134344145 39 45 47 46 65 05 07 11 13 2
21 2 575342546352589544251455056453455150404 2 47 29 31 01 10 08 08 10 2
04 1 557338457556698260735160486855553454945 5 55 38 49 58 04 09 11 12 1
10 1 606562646261645961465851675464624862422 46 54 30 49 27 06 07 13 10 1
16 2 495529465536615952184073949534441925413 42 48 44 44 45 12 02 10 12 2
22 2 485439336053715652184049535474269484534 3 43 37 44 15 10 08 09 09 2
05 1 567046536849650595484545355474726941637 861 51 60 56 60 10 07 10 12 1
11 1 907049608241537458636616383693817363786 1 63 65 69 36 07 07 11 10 1
17 2 414542527456437128104430488529374041463 8 42 62 64 67 10 05 11 12 2
23 2 414649575354575251584640566226434945362 1 45 68 48 80 07 06 07 09 2
06 1 566551556356636556495053545857505451494 2 54 53 55 70 12 08 09 11 1
12 1 626361617256626661415652625957586148846 55 43 50 37 08 08 08 08 1
18 2 485642567755956560456151464144574654841 34 46 21 24 24 10 10 08 11 2
24 2 445856536143415755454351536647455051294 7 48 55 45 50 07 04 14 09 2
FINISH
//
```

Figure 10.13 Print-out of the control cards and data for a two-factor analysis of variance on the data from the "Teaching Style Experiment."

identical to that used in the correlation except that ANØVA (a name chosen for analysis of variance) has replaced CØRREL (for correlation). The second system card differs from the one in the correlational analysis only in program specification (BMD02V instead of BMD02D). The third system card is the same in both analyses.

The problem card specifies the code number of the run (02) in columns 7–8, the number of replicates or cases per cell (006) in columns 9–11, the number of variables (2) in column 12, a code to instruct the computer to print out cell and marginal means (2) in column 14, the number of input data fields per card (1)— since only one dependent variable is being used; see the variable format card—in columns 15–16, the number of levels of each independent variable or factor (002 in each case) in columns 22–24 and 25–27, and finally the number of variable format cards (1) in column 72. (The format for this card is laid out in the manual.)

The variable format card indicates where the data are to be found. The instruction (47X, F2.0) specifies that after skipping 47 columns, the appropriate single two-digit data field will be found. (For a single data field, no number need be put in front of the F.) You will notice in the roster (Figure 10.5) that the dependent variable appears in columns 48 and 49 and is labeled $\overline{X}$. No instruction about where to find the independent variables is necessary since they are handled in terms of the order of the data cards. If you examine columns 4 and 73 on the data print-out (Figure 10.13)—these are the independent variables— you will see that the cards are laid out in order with the six cards from cell 1–1 appearing in the first, fifth, ninth, thirteenth, seventeenth, and twenty-first positions; the six from cell 1–2 in the second, sixth, etc. positions; the six from cell 2–1 third, seventh, etc.; and finally 2–2 fourth, eighth, etc. The input format as required for this program in terms of cells, therefore, is 1–1, 1–2, 2–1, 2–2, 1–1, 1–2, 2–1, etc.

The steps to this point have included

1. coding and rostering the data (see Figure 10.5);
2. selecting a program suitable for the analysis desired;
3. preparing program control cards for the analysis, using the BIMED users' manual (which explains control card preparation in detail in the first chapter);
4. punching the data (in duplicate decks since it is also being used for the correlational analysis) and ordering the data cards by cells (see Figure 10.13).

The next step is to run the analysis and interpret the print-out.

10.5 COMPUTER OUTPUT: THE PRINT-OUT

Illustration 1. The "Teaching Style Experiment"—
Correlational Analysis

The results of an analysis performed by a computer are obtained in the form of a *print-out*. Figure 10.14 shows the print-out results from the correlational analysis performed in the first of the two illustrations of the "Teaching Style Experiment" (see Figure 10.11 for the print-out of the control cards and data). The print-out, as you can see, reports the program designation, the problem code (1 because it is the first of two analyses), the number of variables, the number of cases, the variable format card, and the sample size. Computationally, it reports the sums of the individual item scores, the sum of the total scale mean scores across subjects, the mean and standard deviation for each item and for the total scale mean score, and a matrix of correlations—each item and the total scale mean score with each other. As you will recall, the analysis involved 21 variables: 20 item scores and a total scale mean score. The objective of the analysis was to correlate each item score with the total scale mean score in order to obtain measures of item-whole consistency. This was accomplished by computing a matrix of correlations, 21 X 21, thus providing more information than the objective requires. Column 1 and row 1 in the print-out designate item 1; column 20 and row 20, item 20; and column 21 and row 21, the total scale mean score. The objective of the item analysis concerns only the correlations reported under column 21 since these are the correlations between each item and the total scale mean score. If you examine these 20 correlations (excluding the 21st which is the correlation of the total scale mean score with itself), you will note that all but three (items 6, 7, and 14) exceed 0.5000. Thus, the scale would seem to be high in internal consistency except for these three items.

It is wise to check a print-out to make sure that you have not erred on your control cards (that is, system cards, problem cards, etc.) or data cards, thus creating the possibility of an error in the analysis. (Note: Do not blame the computer for errors; computer errors occur but are rare compared to human errors in writing control cards.) Check, for example, the sum and mean reported for column 21, since they represent the sum and mean of the total scale mean score and are central in the analysis (and relatively easy to check by hand). Examine the array of sums; they are arranged by column designations as follows:

1	2	3	4	5	6	7	8
9	10	11	12	13	14	15	16
17	18	19	20	21			

BMD02D CORRELATION WITH TRANSGENERATION - REVISED JANUARY 29, 1970
HEALTH SCIENCES COMPUTING FACILITY,UCLA

```
PROBLEM CODE    1
NUMBER OF VARIABLES   21
NUMBER OF CASES   24

VARIABLE FORMAT CARD(S)
(6X,20F2.0,1X,F2.0)

REMAINING SAMPLE SIZE=   24
```

SUMS

1288.0000	1389.0000	1143.0000	1283.0000	1503.0000	1233.0000	1393.0000	1504.0000
1290.0000	953.0000	1176.0000	1175.0000	1299.0000	1400.0000	1123.0000	1184.0000
1236.0000	1206.0000	1063.0000	959.0000	1200.0000			

MEANS

53.6667	57.8750	47.6250	53.4583	62.6250	51.3750	58.0417	62.6667
53.7500	39.7083	49.0000	48.5583	54.1250	58.3333	46.7917	49.3333
51.5000	50.2500	44.2917	39.9583	50.0000			

STANDARD DEVIATIONS

10.7649	9.0569	12.7409	10.6198	12.1827	10.9656	8.7451	7.4872
9.8168	14.5944	8.6577	6.8492	7.4327	11.4119	14.1513	10.1582
8.4545	9.6920	11.0157	8.6601	5.6875			

CORRELATION MATRIX

ROW	COL. 1	COL. 2	COL. 3	COL. 4	COL. 5	COL. 6	COL. 7	COL. 8
1	1.0000	0.4294	0.1525	0.2125	-0.2990	-0.2099	0.0930	0.2850
2	0.4294	1.0000	0.4536	0.5914	0.5887	0.3218	0.4403	0.4321
3	0.1525	0.4536	1.0000	0.6061	0.5119	0.5334	0.3537	0.2808
4	0.2125	0.5914	0.6061	1.0000	0.4678	0.3901	0.0400	0.0955
5	-0.2990	0.5887	0.5119	0.4678	1.0000	0.3122	0.2826	0.6616
6	-0.2099	0.3218	0.5334	0.3901	0.3122	1.0000	0.5403	0.1488
7	0.0930	0.4403	0.3537	0.0400	0.2826	0.5403	1.0000	0.1722
8	0.2850	0.4321	0.2808	0.0955	0.6616	0.1488	0.1722	1.0000
9	0.1205	0.7420	0.5877	0.5575	0.4325	0.4145	0.5375	0.2337
10	0.3777	0.6197	0.0836	0.3190	0.2348	0.1569	0.2059	0.1797
11	0.3667	0.6743	0.5372	0.7419	0.5928	0.4900	0.2331	0.2824
12	0.5063	0.5312	0.2215	-0.0529	0.1962	0.0459	0.2519	0.3100
13	0.1793	0.5273	0.7108	0.5589	0.3751	0.5371	0.3718	0.1664
14	0.3545	0.1287	0.2099	0.1232	0.5113	-0.2359	-0.2637	0.5774

Figure 10.14 *The print-out of the correlational analysis results of the "Teaching Style Experiment."*

Correlation matrix (Figure 10.14, continued). Values are listed below each column heading in row order.

Rows 15–21 (upper fragment):

ROW	COL. 10	COL. 11	COL. 12	COL. 13	COL. 14	COL. 15	COL. 16
15	0.7549	0.6678	0.6175	0.5198	0.3152	0.3349	0.5229
16	0.3554	0.1871	0.3064	0.2934	-0.1511	-0.1378	0.3691
17	0.6589	0.1873	0.5823	0.4295	0.1151	0.1938	0.2061
18	0.6690	0.7888	0.7305	0.6806	0.5019	0.3487	0.3805
19	0.5551	0.1899	0.4005	0.1695	0.0599	0.3265	0.4235
20	0.5847	0.2292	0.1695	0.4293	0.1934	0.1579	0.5791
21	0.8525	0.6504	0.6227	0.5704	0.3674	0.4091	0.5330

Rows 1–21, COL. 9 – COL. 16:

ROW	COL. 9	COL. 10	COL. 11	COL. 12	COL. 13	COL. 14	COL. 15	COL. 16
1	0.1205	0.3777	0.3667	0.5063	0.1793	0.3545	0.5858	0.7311
2	0.7420	0.6197	0.6743	0.5312	0.5273	0.1287	0.7549	0.3554
3	0.5877	0.0836	0.5372	0.2215	0.7108	0.2099	0.6673	0.1871
4	0.5575	0.3190	0.7419	-0.0529	0.5589	0.1232	0.6175	0.3064
5	0.4325	0.2348	0.5928	0.1962	0.3751	0.5113	0.5198	0.2934
6	0.4145	0.1569	0.4900	0.0459	0.3718	-0.2359	0.3152	-0.1511
7	0.5375	0.2059	0.2331	0.3100	0.1664	-0.2637	0.3349	-0.0378
8	0.2337	0.1797	0.2824	0.5323	0.6261	0.5774	0.5229	0.3691
9	1.0000	0.4516	0.6676	0.4542	0.4331	-0.2018	0.6002	0.2180
10	0.4516	1.0000	0.4542	0.5323	0.2048	0.0437	0.4298	0.4456
11	0.6676	0.4542	1.0000	0.3813	0.5480	-0.0251	0.5958	0.4944
12	0.4542	0.5323	0.3813	1.0000	0.2239	-0.0621	0.4427	0.4664
13	0.4331	0.2048	0.5480	0.2239	1.0000	0.0338	0.5823	0.2286
14	-0.2018	0.0437	-0.0251	-0.0621	0.0338	1.0000	0.2158	0.2274
15	0.6002	0.4298	0.5958	0.4664	0.5823	0.2158	1.0000	0.6541
16	0.2180	0.4456	0.5886	0.5958	0.2286	0.2274	0.6541	1.0000
17	0.6035	0.4914	0.8384	0.5137	0.5137	0.1920	0.5958	0.4065
18	0.7497	0.3537	0.4386	0.7407	0.7407	-0.0869	0.7932	0.5238
19	0.2596	0.3846	0.3468	0.3643	0.3643	0.3506	0.5044	0.4113
20	0.3584	0.3123	0.4405	0.3675	0.3675	0.3561	0.5970	0.3738
21	0.6868	0.5280	0.6931	0.5357	0.6922	0.2606	0.9173	0.5870

Rows 1–21, COL. 17 – COL. 21:

ROW	COL. 17	COL. 18	COL. 19	COL. 20	COL. 21
1	0.5145	0.3096	0.5783	0.4998	0.5809
2	0.6589	0.6690	0.5551	0.5847	0.8525
3	0.4583	0.7888	0.1099	0.2292	0.6504
4	0.5823	0.7305	0.4069	0.1695	0.6227
5	0.4295	0.6806	0.3135	0.4293	0.5704
6	0.1151	0.5019	0.0599	0.1934	0.3674
7	0.1938	0.3805	0.0265	0.1579	0.4091
8	0.2061	0.3805	0.4235	0.5791	0.5330
9	0.6035	0.3537	0.2596	0.3584	0.6868
10	0.4914	0.7497	0.3846	0.3123	0.5280
11	0.5886	0.3537	0.4386	0.3468	0.6931
12	0.5137	0.3538	0.2197	0.4405	0.5357
13	0.1920	0.3643	0.3506	0.3675	0.6922
14	0.0869	0.7932	0.3561	0.5970	0.2606
15	0.5958	0.5238	0.5044	0.5870	0.9173
16	0.4065	0.6086	0.4113	0.3738	0.5870
17	1.0000	1.0000	0.3173	0.3186	0.7315
18	0.6086	1.0000	0.5056	0.3653	0.8014
19	0.6865	0.3173	1.0000	0.5056	0.6343
20	0.3186	0.3653	0.5056	1.0000	0.6462
21	0.7315	0.8014	0.6343	0.6462	1.0000

Figure 10.14 (continued)

The last one, for column 21, or the sum of the total scale mean scores, is 1200.0000 with a corresponding mean of 50.0000. To check this, add the numbers in columns 48–49 on the roster (Figure 10.5) corresponding to column 21 on the print-out. These numbers add to exactly 1200.0000, providing a check on the analysis.

Often the computer gives more information than is needed (in this case 20 X 20 extra correlations). However, this analysis requires only 0.02 minutes of computer time (less than two seconds), which indicates that the time-consuming part of data analysis is preparation rather than actual operation time. Thus, it takes the computer much less time to calculate a 21 X 21 matrix of correlations (441 correlations plus 21 sums, means, and standard deviations) than it would take to run the 20 desired correlations by hand.*

Illustration 2. The "Teaching Style Experiment: Part Two"—Analysis of Variance

Now consider the second illustration, the analysis of variance of mean scores on the total scale as a function of teachers' subject taught and personality (see Figure 10.13 for the input print-out of the control cards and data). Figure 10.15 gives the print-out of the results of this analysis. This print-out reports the program BMD02V, the problem number, the number of variables, levels per variable, replicates, variable format card, and grand mean (or mean across all conditions), along with a source table (the principal interest), and tables of cell and marginal means. To help understand the listing of cell and marginal means the following table can be used.

		Variable 1		
		Category 1 Vocational teachers	Category 2 Nonvocational teachers	
Variable 2	Category 1 High system IV	cell 1 (1–1)	cell 3 (2–1)	Marginal 2–1
	Category 2 Low system IV	cell 2 (1–2)	cell 4 (2–2)	Marginal 2–2
		Marginal 1–1	Marginal 1–2	*Grand mean*

**However, it is worth noting that it took the researcher three tries to get this program to run because of mistakes in the problem card (sloppily punching a number in the wrong column), and the variable format card (making a careless oversight). Thus, the total time required to get data analyzed by computer always exceeds computer time. However, the computer still is a great time-saver as well as an accurate data analyzer.*

PROBLEM NO. 02

NUMBER OF VARIABLES   2
NUMBER OF REPLICATES   6

VARIABLE   NO. OF LEVELS
    1   2
    2   2
VARIABLE FORMAT CARD(S)
(47X,F2.0)

GRAND MEAN   50.00000

SOURCE OF VARIATION	DEGREES OF FREEDOM	SUMS OF SQUARES	MEAN SQUARES
1	1	504.16635	504.16626
2	1	16.66661	16.66661
12	1	0.16724	0.16724
WITHIN REPLICATES	20	222.99986	11.14999
TOTAL	23	744.00000	

PROBLEM NO. 02

C E L L N U M B E R S	M E A N S
1 1	53.83333
1 2	55.33333
2 1	44.50000
2 2	46.33333

M A R G I N A L M E A N S		
VARIABLES	CATEGORIES	M E A N S
1	1	54.58333
	2	45.41666
2	1	49.16666
	2	50.83333

Figure 10.15 *Print-out of the analysis of variance results for the "Teaching Style Experiment."*

Consulting Figure 10.15, you can see from the listing of marginal means that vocational teachers (marginal 1-1 = 54.58333) greatly exceed nonvocational teachers (marginal 1-2 = 45.41666). This accounts for the large mean square for variable 1 as shown in the source table ($MS = 504.16626$). Two things need to be done with this print-out. The first is to check it by computing the means for each cell by hand and comparing them to the print-out. If the cell means check out, the analysis is probably correct. Secondly, the F-ratios should be computed by dividing each mean square by the within replicates mean square. This results in the following:

Source	F-Ratio
1	45.22*
2	1.49
12	0.01

p <.01

The results show that vocational teachers are significantly more nondirective than nonvocational teachers ($F = 45.22$, $p < .01$, means of 54.6 and 45.4, respectively), while high systems IV teachers and low systems IV teachers do not differ in directiveness ($F = 1.49$, $p > .10$, means of 49.2 and 50.8 respectively). Moreover, there is no interaction between these variables.

The total time to run this analysis was 0.02 minutes (about one second). However, it was in fact run three times. In the first run, a designation on the problem card was carelessly put in the wrong column, and in the second run the cards were in the wrong order because the researcher misunderstood the users' manual instruction on this point.*

Errors on the problem card cause the program not to run at all (at least in this case) while other errors cause inaccurate runs which must be diagnosed from the print-out. It is essential that problem cards, variable format cards, and data cards be perfect but often because of the researcher's haste or misunderstanding they are not. Sometimes the print-out will provide a number code which informs you about the error that was made. Other times you will have to diagnose it. In these latter cases, the computer cannot tell that an error has occurred.

10.6 CORRELATIONAL ANALYSIS ON A DESK CALCULATOR

Because there are many types and brands of desk calculators on which many different analyses can be done, it is impossible to discuss all of them. One analysis has been chosen for coverage because it provides a useful illustration of the use of the desk calculator in an instance where there is a shortcut for performing that particular statistical analysis on a desk calculator. The analysis is the calculation of a parametric correlation.

He put all the cards from a cell in order instead of alternating one card from each cell and then repeating this alternating order.

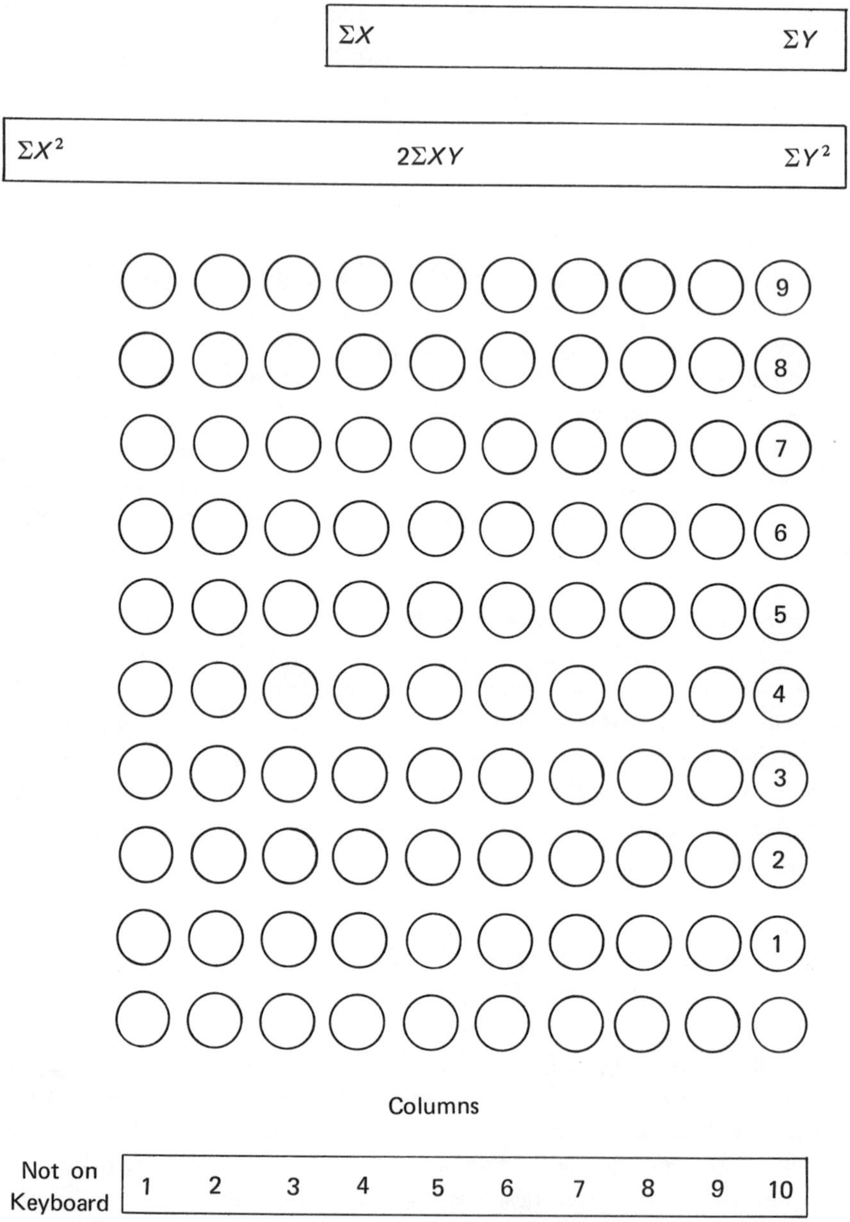

Figure 10.16 *Use of a Monroe rotary desk calculator for parametric correlational analysis* (X *is a score on one variable,* Y *is a score on the other variable*).

If you examine the statistics worksheet for parametric correlational analysis in Chapter 9, (page 235), you will notice that there are five basic computational terms that must be calculated: ΣX, ΣY, ΣX^2, and ΣXY. Each of the five would seem to require a separate operation on a desk calculator. However, each can be calculated simultaneously by using the following procedure (keyed to Figure 10.16):

1. Punch the first value of X in column 2 (or columns 2 and 3 if it is a two-digit figure or if any value of X in the analysis has two digits) and punch the corresponding first value of Y (that is, the value of Y for the same S who obtained that X) in column 10 (or columns 9 and 10 if two-digit values will appear).
2. Depress the ENTER MULTIPLIER key and hold it down (holding it down keeps the same keys depressed so that squaring may be done without re-entering the multipliers).
3. Depress the ACC MULT (accumulative multiplier) key which combines multiplying and summing.
4. Repeat the above three steps for each pair of X and Y values, being careful always to use the same columns on the keyboard.

What will result is shown in Figure 10.16. The calculator has two result rows at the top. At the left end of the shorter row, ΣX will appear while ΣY will appear at the right end. At the left end of the longer row, ΣX^2 will appear while ΣY^2 appears at the right end, and $2\Sigma XY$ in the middle. All you need do is divide $2\Sigma XY$ by 2 and you will have completed the first five steps on the worksheet for parametric correlation.

The user is cautioned to know where his decimal points are and/or where one computational term ends and the next begins. Location of the decimal points (and number of digits in each computational result) is often determined by hand calculating the approximate order of magnitude of each term.

RECOMMENDED READINGS

Borko, H. (Ed.) *Computer applications in the behavioral sciences.* Englewood Cliffs, N. J.: Prentice-Hall, 1962.
Bushnell, D. D. and Allen, D. W. (Eds.) *The computer in American education.* New York: Wiley, 1967.

Coman, H. L. and Smallwood, Clarice. *Computer language: an auto-instructional introduction to FORTRAN.* New York: McGraw-Hill, 1962.

Dixon, W. J. (Ed.) *Biomedical computer programs.* Berkeley: University of California Press, 1968.

Veldman, D. J. *FORTRAN programming for the behavioral sciences.* New York: Holt, Rinehart, & Winston, 1967.

COMPETENCY TEST EXERCISES

1. The following data have been collected:

36	92	74	85	39
98	41	40	90	45
47	73	58	70	22
49	62	67	71	52
54	68	81	78	50

   Develop a coding scheme using 5 coding categories and assign each score to a category.

2. Prepare 20 sets of data, each including the following: subject identification number, sex code (1 or 2), age, experimental condition code (1 or 2), and scores on each of 10 dependent variables (each score having two digits). Roster these data on a roster sheet.

3. Data are being prepared to be punched. In a set of three-digit I.Q. scores, the score 89 appears. For key punch purposes, it would be wise to
   a. add a zero after the 9
   b. add a zero before the 8
   c. both of the above.

4. In punching the data from a roster onto punch cards, researchers ordinarily put
   a. one subject per column and one digit of data per card
   b. two subjects per column and two digits of data per card
   c. one digit of data per column and one subject per card
   d. two digits of data per column and two subjects per card.

5. You have one independent variable and one dependent variable and are interested in doing an analysis of variance. From Figure 10.9, what is the six character name of the program you would be likely to use?

6. You are planning to run a matrix of correlations using the BMD02D program (see Figure 10.10). You are planning to correlate the scores of 500 subjects on 57 measures.
   a. This program _____ (will, will not) accommodate data from 500 subjects. Its maximum is _____ .
   b. This program _____ (will, will not) accommodate data on 57 measures. Its maximum is _____ .

7. Prepare a *problem card* for the analysis described in exercise (6). (All the data for a subject appear on a single card.)

8. Prepare a *variable format card* for the analysis described in exercise (6). (The first 3 columns on each card contain the subject identification code; column 4 is blank; 40 measures, each a one-digit data field, appear in the

next 40 columns; the next 2 columns are blank; 17 measures, each a two-digit data field, appear in the last 34 columns.)

9. From Figure 10.14, pages 275–276, what is the correlation between item 12 and item 20?

10. From Figure 10.15, page 278, what is the mean SPOTS (i.e., dependent variable) score for vocational teachers *low* on System IV?

11. In doing a correlation on a desk calculator as described in this chapter, which of the following statements is true:
    a. ΣX and ΣX^2 appear in the same row.
    b. ΣXY appears doubled and must be divided by 2.
    c. ΣY and ΣY^2 appear in the same row.
    d. ΣXY appears halved and must be multiplied by 2.

12. Consider the following data for 10 *Ss* on measures X and Y:

S	X	Y
1	12	10
2	4	6
3	6	6
4	8	7
5	3	3
6	10	8
7	8	10
8	7	7
9	4	4
10	5	6

Use a desk calculator and the procedures described in this chapter to determine the correlation between X and Y.

11

Writing a
Research Report

OBJECTIVES

Write a research proposal including an introductory section and a method section. / Write a final research report including the following sections: introduction, method, results, discussion, references and abstract. / Prepare tables to illustrate experimental designs and results of data analysis. / Prepare graphs to illustrate the results of data analysis.

11.1 THE RESEARCH PROPOSAL

A research proposal consists of two parts—an *introduction* and a *method* section. These two sections correspond to the first two sections of the final research report, the only difference being that the proposal is typically written in the present or future tense and the report is always written in the past tense. Since the introduction and method sections appear in both the proposal and final report in virtually identical form, there would be little purpose in describing each separately. Consequently, the remainder of this chapter will be devoted to final research report preparation.

The reader is reminded that proposal preparation is significant in the development and pursuit of a research project. In fact, whether a planned research undertaking is accepted by a dissertation committee or funding agency often depends on the quality of the proposal. The next two sections, "The Introduction Section" and "The Method Section", are pertinent to the preparation of a proposal.

11.2 THE INTRODUCTION SECTION

This and the next five sections deal with the preparation of the parts of a research report acceptable for the preparation of both dissertations and journal article manuscripts in educational research.*

The preparation of the introductory section, is described below. Depending upon the length of the section, subsection headings may or may not be used (for example, context of the problem, statement of the problem, review of the literature, statement of the hypotheses, rationale for the hypotheses, and so on).

Context of the Problem

The first paragraph or two of the introduction should acquaint the reader with the problem to be dealt with. This orientation is best accomplished by providing its background. One accepted way to establish a frame of reference for the problem is to quote authoritative sources. Consider the following opening paragraphs of the introductions drawn from each of two articles appearing in the *American Educational Research Journal*.

- *Context of the Problem[†]*
  School instruction is, by precept and by practice, primarily dependent upon communication in the form of language. At this date, the structure of children's language (e.g., Griffin, 1968) and of some instructional materials (e.g., Strickland, 1962) are receiving limited attention. Inevitably the perceptions and concepts learned in school pass through the several different linguistic screens of teachers, classmates, and materials. Within this construct, the relationship of teachers' language structure to children's language structure is a variable of major consequence. Yet the nature of the language of teachers rests in an area only tangentially studied (Davis and Kean, 1965; Bellack, et al., 1966; Blake and Amato, 1967) by either psycholinguistic or educational researchers. [Kean, 1968, p. 599]

*The three research reports in Appendix A may be used as models for preparing reports. Two of them have been taken from journal sources while the third was prepared by a student in a graduate educational research course.

†Because the use of headings is optional, the original material cited as examples often lacks these headings. When missing from the original, the appropriate heading has been added for clarity.

- *Context of the Problem*

  Although a number of studies have approached the leadership problem from an organizational context, little attention has been given to the orientation of organizational members. Basically, researchers have tended to focus upon the leader and his behavior, often to the virtual exclusion of organizational members, their behavior, and their orientation relative to the leader. In this paper, some of the pertinent research relative to conceptual structures of leadership behavior is examined, and a number of general hypotheses which relate need orientations of teachers to leadership style preferences are tested. [Sergiovanni, et al., 1969, p. 62]

Note that each introduction identifies the area in which the problem is to be found; additionally as the basis for undertaking the project, the introduction points out that the problem has not been fully studied. These particular illustrations are short since each was drawn from a journal where brevity of exposition is emphasized. In other forms of research reports (and in some journal articles as well), context statements may run somewhat longer. However, three paragraphs is recommended as a maximum.

Statement of the Problem

The next item in the introduction is the statement of the problem. Although some writers prefer to state the problem late in the introduction, the advantages of stating it early is that it provides the reader with an immediate basis from which to interpret subsequent statements (especially the review of the literature). Placing the statement of the problem near the beginning of the introduction makes it possible to quickly determine the purpose of the study; the reader will not have to search through the introduction to discover the problem being examined.

The statement of the problem should identify, if possible, all independent, moderator, and dependent variables, and should ask, in question form, about their relationships. Since at this point in the exposition the variables have not as yet been operationalized, the problem statement should identify the variables in their conceptual form rather than in operational form. The variables should be named; no description of how they were measured is necessary at this point.

One or two sentences will normally suffice to state the problem. Often the statement begins as follows: "The purpose of this study was to examine the relationship between ... ."* Here are the two studies referred to earlier:

*In a research proposal "is" or "will be" would be substituted for "was" since the proposal is written in the present or future tense rather than in the past tense as is the final report.

- *Problem*

    The purpose of this study was the cataloguing of teacher-spoken language. Specifically, the objectives of this study were to (1) describe the linguistic structure of elementary school teachers' classroom language, and (2) compare the linguistic structure of the classroom language of teachers working at 2nd and 5th grade level. [Kean, 1968, p. 599–600]

- *Problem*

    The...[study] examines the relationship between perceived "ideal" leadership style and need orientations of teachers. [Sergiovanni, et al., 1969, p. 62]

Consider some further problem statements taken from students' research projects.

- *Problem*

    The purpose of this study was threefold. An attempt was made to test the differential effects of the verbal praise of an adult (the type of reinforcement most often utilized by classroom teachers) (1) on a "culturally disadvantaged" as opposed to a white middle class sample, (2) as a function of the sex of the agent, and (3) as a function of the race of agent and recipient of this reinforcement.

- *Problem*

    The purpose of this study was to determine whether girls who plan to pursue careers in science are more aggressive, more domineering, less conforming, more independent, and have a greater need for achievement than girls who do not plan such careers.

- *Problem*

    It was the purpose of this study to determine what differences, if any, existed in the way principals of large and small schools and principals (collectively) and presidents of teacher organizations viewed the level of involvement of the principal in a variety of administrative tasks.

Review of the Literature

The purpose of the literature review is to expand upon the context and background of the study, to help further define the problem, and to provide an empirical basis for the subsequent development of hypotheses. The length of the review will depend upon the number of relevant articles available and the purpose for which the research report is being written. Dissertations are usually expected to provide a more exhaustive literature review than journal articles. Although some dissertation style manuals recommend devoting an entire chapter (typically the second) to a review of the literature, building the review into the introductory chapter has the advantage of forcing the writer to keep it relevant to the problem statement and hypotheses which surround it.

Strategy of Literature Searching. In order to search literature, you must have a key concept (or concepts). These key concepts, extracted from the problem statement, represent the major variables and their interrelationships. Consider, for example, a study concerned with the effect of group dynamics training on administrative decision-making. The key concepts for literature searching would be: (a) group dynamics and related training procedures and their outcomes or effectiveness; (b) administrative decision-making and factors that affect it; (c) specific relation between group-type training procedures and administrative decision-making.

The searching strategy gives the reviewer or searcher some further insight into the nature of his variables and their possible interrelation. While a reviewer must have some idea of what variables he is hoping to relate in order to identify his search concepts, the studies located in the search often help him to identify other variables of potential importance and to see how the variables relate. The literature search, therefore, should provide some empirical basis for formulating hypotheses.

Consider Sample Study I, Appendix A. In conducting a limited literature search for this sample study, studies were sought that examined the effectiveness of feedback as a change agent without regard to the source or target of the feedback, and others that examined the effectiveness of different feedback sources on the behavior of teachers. In addition, literature relevant to the methodology or mechanics of providing feedback was examined. Thus, the variables and their potential interrelationship were organizers and keys for the literature search, and the search, in turn, provided support for the expectation that these variables would be meaningfully related.

Consider a third example, a study of the relationship between five personality variables and teachers' innovativeness. The review should examine each of the personality variables, but, to keep it within manageable proportions, each personality variable should only be explored as it relates to innovativeness or conceptually similar outcomes. Innovativeness literature would then be reviewed both to give the reader an understanding of the variable and to identify its potential relationship to teacher personality. Considerations of each variable would be kept within the field of education.

Sources of Literature. Literature sources include the following: (a) books and monographs, (b) journal and periodical articles, (c) dissertations, (d) government reports, and (e) unpublished manuscripts. Relevant books and monographs can be located through the card catalog in the library, particularly as referenced by subject. Journal and periodical articles can be found through *index sources* such as the *Education Index* (N.Y.: H. W. Wilson Co., 1929–) and the *Readers' Guide to Periodical Literature* (N.Y.: H. W. Wilson Co., 1901–), each of which indexes by subject.

A further source of journal references is provided by *abstracting journals*, i.e., journals that list and abstract articles in a particular field by subject matter. These include *Child Development Abstracts* (Washington, D.C.: National Research Council of the Society for Research in Child Development, 1927–), *Psychological Abstracts* (Washington, D.C.: American Psychological Association, 1927–), and *Sociological Abstracts* (N.Y.: Sociological Abstracts, Inc., 1954–).

A third source of journal articles are *reviewing journals* that offer literature reviews for selected topics. These include *Review of Educational Research* (Washington, D.C.: American Educational Research Association, 1931–), *Psychological Bulletin* (Washington, D.C.: American Psychological Association, 1904–), and *Annual Review of Psychology* (Palo Alto, Calif.: Annual Reviews, Inc.).*

Still one more source of information on journal articles is the *Current Index to Journals in Education* (N.Y.: CCM Information Corporation, 1969–). It includes a listing of content area headings and articles appearing in journals. This publication is a highly useful index and is part of the Education Resources Information Center (ERIC) program and thus includes information on how each article can be obtained through ERIC Center sources.

Dissertations may be obtained primarily through two sources. The first of these is an abstracting journal called *Dissertation Abstracts* (Ann Arbor, Mich.: University Microfilms,† 1938–). A second source is DATRIX, a subsidiary of the Xerox company, in Ann Arbor, Michigan. DATRIX is an information retrieval system connected to the *Dissertation Abstracts* file. For a fee, a researcher gets a listing of dissertation titles selected according to key words that he provides—in effect, a selected bibliography.

Government document reference lists are most readily obtained through the network of ERIC centers across the country. An index to the holdings of these centers is provided by *Research in Education*—RIE (Washington, D.C.: Government Printing Office, 1966–). The ERIC Document Reproduction Service will provide microfilm or xerographic copies of the *Research in Education* articles

The American Educational Research Association is also planning an annual review publication to be published by F. E. Peacock, Inc. in 1973.

†*A subsidiary of the Xerox Company.*

290

which are cited by subject and referenced by the subject or a key word. Another abstracting journal, *Technical Abstract Bulletin* (Alexandria, Va.: Defense Documentation Center), provides abstracts of articles which have been produced through military sources. Subject 28 in this bulletin covers psychology and human engineering.

Unpublished manuscripts are not systematically referenced by any source, although some find their way into the ERIC centers and are thus covered in *RIE*.

Organization. A good guideline for selecting the literature in the review section is to cite references dealing with each of the variables in the study, paying special attention to those articles dealing with more than one of the variables. Literature concerning conceptually similar or conceptually related variables should likewise be cited.

Subheadings should reflect the major variables (key words) of the literature review. The more relevant the article to your study, the more detailed your description of it may be. Remember that the purpose of the literature review is to provide a basis for the formulation of hypotheses. In other words, articles are not reviewed for their own sake but as a basis for generalizing from them to your own study.

Consider the following organization of subheadings for the literature review section in a study of the relationship between teacher attitudes and teaching style

Teacher Attitudes
    Overview and Definitions
    Open-minded versus Closed-minded—General Studies
    Open-minded versus Closed-minded—Relation to Teaching
    Humanistic versus Custodial—General Studies
    Humanistic versus Custodial—Relation to Teaching

Teaching Style
    Overview and Definitions
    Directive versus Nondirective—General Studies
    Directive versus Nondirective—Relation to Teacher Attitudes

Organizing the literature review section by subheadings makes it easier for the reader to follow. To be most meaningful, these subheadings should reflect the variables and the problem (i.e., their relationship). The subheadings should also be your guide to the searching process as well as the reviewing process. The organization of the literature review section in terms of the problem, enables you to work toward establishing hypotheses, thus providing a logic for both the reader and yourself.

Statement of the Hypotheses

It has been recommended throughout this book (particularly in Chapter 2) that hypotheses be developed to describe the anticipated relationships between variables. Hypotheses help to focus a study and to give it direction and often make a study easier to follow. They need not be stated operationally but should be stated clearly and concisely in conceptual terms for greatest generality. They may also be underlined or italicized for emphasis and ease of locating.

Although examples of hypotheses have been given in Chapter 2, here are two examples.

- *Hypotheses*
  The following hypotheses were formulated:

  (a) *Ss* learn concepts more effectively in mediated than in nonmediated concept learning;

  (b) *Ss* of high intelligence learn concepts more readily than *Ss* of lower intelligence;

  (c) *Ss* of high intelligence demonstrate the greatest superiority over other *Ss* on a conceptual task which explicitly requires the use of mediation and other cognitive processes;

  (d) the effects of intelligence are most pronounced in the period prior to the first correct response, the period of response generation. [Jacobson et al., 1969, p. 110]

- *Hypotheses*
  It was expected that learners scoring high on anxiety, compulsivity, and convergent-minus-divergent thinking and those scoring low in exhibitionism would do relatively better in the programmed learning task situation. [Ripple, et al., 1969, p. 115]

Rationale for the Hypotheses

Hypotheses may be justified on two grounds—logical or empirical. Logical justification requires the development of arguments based on concepts or theories related to the hypotheses while empirical justification requires reference to other research. It is necessary to provide justification for each hypothesis to insure the reader of its reasonableness and soundness. (Justification is especially critical in the proposal.) To provide logical arguments in support of hypotheses, describe or allude to appropriate premises, concepts, or theories. For empirical justification, you may refer to literature cited in the review section although not necessarily in as much detail as in its first description.

The inexperienced researcher often neglects to provide a clear rationale for his hypotheses. All too often he assumes that the reasoning behind a hypothesis is obvious, an assumption that leads to confusion on the part of the reader who may react by saying (to himself), "What ever led you to expect that," or "I don't believe it," or after reading the results, "You must have made this one up after you collected the data!" A strong rationale with logical and empirical support, contiguous to the statement of the hypothesis, minimizes the likelihood of such reactions.

Construct your hypotheses and establish their logical and empirical support *prior* to data collection and analysis, not after, for hypotheses are tools for helping a researcher see the relationship between his theory and the work to be done. Writing hypotheses after seeing the data makes hypothesizing a sterile activity (although, hypotheses for future study may be identified).

Consider the following example.

- *Hypothesis*

  Directive teachers produce more satisfaction in and are more preferred by (and generate better performance in) students who are highly directive-oriented, viz., concrete-dependent Ss, and nondirective teachers produce more satisfaction in and are more preferred by (and generate better performance in) nondirective-oriented students, viz., abstract-independent Ss.

  Rationale

  As has been described above, concrete-dependent individuals are quite dependent upon other persons, particularly authorities, for guidance, structure, and ambiguity reduction. Their cognitive simplicity leads them to prefer situations that are structured for them, and in such situations they function best. Tuckman (1967a) has shown that concrete-dependent Ss perform better in structured situations, and that they prefer such situations to unstructured ones. Sieber and Lanzetta (1964) have shown that concrete-dependent Ss have a preference for certainty over uncertainty. Directive teaching represents a structured situation where the expected behavior of the student is prescribed by the teacher. Consequently, there is little ambiguity or uncertainty. In such a situation, concrete-dependent Ss should perform better and be more satisfied. They are expected to prefer the directive approach. Abstract-independent Ss, on the other hand, are independent and cognitively complex. They perform better in unstructured situations, and prefer them (Tuckman, 1967a). They have a preference for uncertainty (Sieber and Lanzetta, 1964). Since the nondirective teacher creates a somewhat unstructured and uncertain situation in which the students must provide some of their own guidance, abstract-independent *Ss* should perform better, be more satisifed and manifest a preference for the teachers involved. [Tuckman, 1968, p. 11-12]

Operational Definitions of the Variables

It is useful, in the introduction, to provide brief operational definitions of the independent, moderator, and dependent variables. Although the method section which follows will provide a detailed operational statement of how the variables are to be manipulated or measured, it is helpful for the reader to have an early idea of what the variables mean.

Many examples of operational definitions are offered in Chapter 4. Two additional examples appear below.

- In this situation the authors distinguished two basic types of strategies or problem-solving methods used by the children: (a) hypothesis scanning, (b) constraint seeking. In hypothesis scanning the child asked a series of unrelated specific questions, for example, "Is it the cow?" or "Is it the sailboat?"... In constraint seeking the child asked a question comprehensive enough to include at least two objects, for example, "Is it red?" or "Is it larger than a dog? ... . [Laughlin, et al., 1969, p. 188]

- 1. *Professional values*—held by teachers who identify themselves with the values and the goals of professionalism, knowledge and education, and their field of education.
  2. *Organizational values*—held by teachers who identify themselves with the values and goals of bureaucracy, conformity to system policy and rules, and promotion into supervisory positions.
  3. *Social values*—held by teachers who identify themselves with the values and goals of membership in their school work groups, home and family, and religion and convention. [Coughlan, 1969, p. 169]

Operational Restatement of the Hypotheses

While not absolutely essential, it is often helpful to restate your hypotheses in operational form to provide the reader with a more concrete picture of the aims of the study.* Since the hypotheses have already been stated conceptually and operational definitions of all the variables have been provided, it is now a simple matter to restate the hypotheses in operational terms. Such operationalized hypotheses are often referred to as *predictions*. Consider these examples.

- It was therefore hypothesized that teachers labelled as innovative by virtue of their applying for funds to develop an innovative classroom program would perceive their working environment to be more open as characterized by greater participation by teachers and students in the decision process, greater control by teachers over their own classroom behavior, and greater tolerance for dissent.

- Teachers who were given six weeks of training in a program aimed at increasing their ability to write behavioral objectives were expected to write behavioral objectives that more adequately met the three criteria for behavioral objectives than teachers given six weeks of training in an unrelated area.

- Specifically, teachers displaying more liberal political attitudes as measured by the Opinionation Scale and the Dogmatism Scale (both developed by Rokeach) were expected to show more liberal tendencies toward the treatment of students as evidenced by a greater emphasis on autonomy for students and allowing students to set their own rules and regulations and enforce them.

Significance of the Study

Readers of a research proposal or report are usually concerned with the relevance of the problem both to practice and to theory. Much value is placed on doing research which has primary or secondary value for the solution of practically-oriented educational problems. There is also a need in education for the establishment and verification of theories or models. To these ends, it is useful for the writer to indicate the value or potential significance of the problem area and hypothesized findings to educational practice, educational theory, or both.

Restatement is more appropriate in dissertations than in journal articles since space is at a premium in the latter.

Again, some examples are offered.

- Finally, the relevance of the problem to educational settings lies in the fact that the educator is anxious to foster learning by discovery (i.e., induction) in the classroom since, as the findings of Gagne and Brown (1961) and Katona (1940) show, such learning provides for greater transfer of the concepts and principles to new but related problems. Transfer and transferability are clearly goals of the educational process. [Tuckman, et al., 1968, pp. 60-61]

- *Significance of the Study*

  A central problem for educators is that of heightening children's interest in the learning activities to which they are exposed. Once interest in a given learning activity has developed, however, the question arises, "How long will it persist?" Clearly, the learner must continue or persist in his efforts until the educational goal is attained if the learning activity is to be considered effective.

  Current research in the areas of curiosity and exploratory behavior suggests that external stimulation may contribute to persistent attending on the part of the learner. It has been suggested, in fact, that external stimulation may be varied during the instructional sequence in a manner to suit the student's individual need for stimulation so that optimal interest in learning will be maintained.

  Stimulus novelty has been found to be one aspect of external stimulation which is related to attention and manipulation. Since these behaviors are invariably required of learners, it would appear most relevant to question how the variable of stimulus novelty may be exploited within instructional environments. To clarify the principles underlying persistence in response to novelty, however, it first is necessary that stimulus conditions and task complexity be differentiated and controlled in a school-related activity. Through such refinement, the feasibility of exploiting the novelty variable for pedagogical purposes may be demonstrated. [Perticone, 1969, pp. 1-2]

- *Significance of the Study*

  It is hoped that this study will begin to answer some of the questions that educators have concerning the relationships between race and sex of pupils and teachers and the effect that these variables have on the pupil's acquisition of academic skills. Also looked for are some further insights into teaching practices, especially in terms of the type of reinforcement employed in the learning situation as found in school. It is also hoped that the study will stimulate researchers to further investigation into the problem of helping minority group children toward more meaningful experiences within the educational system. [Student research paper]

It must be emphasized that the topical areas listed in this section and the order in which they are listed represent guidelines for a research proposal or report rather than absolute requirements. Specific types of studies and different writing styles may yield somewhat different topical areas and somewhat different orders.

11.3 THE METHOD SECTION

Following is a recommended set of categories for describing the methods and procedures of a study for purposes of either a proposal or final research report. In the actual report each category may serve as a subheading. Such a high degree of structure for the method section is recommended since this section contains detailed statements of the actual steps undertaken in the experiment.

Subjects

The purpose of the section entitled "Subjects" is to indicate *who* participated in the study and *how many* there were. Where relevant, this section should also indicate whether or not the subjects were volunteers (i.e., how their participation was arranged), how they were selected, and what their characteristics were. Characteristics typically reported include sex, age, grade, I.Q. (median and/or range). Providing such information makes it possible for another researcher to select a virtually identical sample if he chooses to replicate the study. In fact, the entire method section should be written in such a way as to provide another researcher with the possibility of replication of your methodology.
Consider the following examples.

- *Subjects*
  Ss were thirty-six students at a large West Coast high school; at the time of the investigation, all were currently enrolled in "regular" or "x" (accelerated) third- and fourth-year English classes. The student population of the school was primarily drawn from upper middle-class families, and a large proportion of the school's graduates go on to college. All Ss were volunteers for this investigation. [Weiss, et al., 1970, p. 84]

297

- *Subjects*

    The sample consisted of thirteen blind and thirteen partially-sighted white youngsters enrolled in public schools throughout the state of New Jersey. Children ranged from grades two through eight. Blind and partially-sighted youngsters were paired according to age, sex, and grade. It was assumed that I.Q. would be reasonably accounted for (i.e., both very high and very low ends eliminated) if the children were in the approximate grade for their chronological age. Other factors such as albinism, hearing loss, cerebral palsy, etc., were eliminated by not including those children in the study. None of the children went to special sight-saving classes. All had been in their homeroom class since September. [Sample Study III, Appendix A]

    For further examples, consult articles in research journals such as the *Journal of Educational Psychology* and the *American Educational Research Journal*.

Tasks

In some studies (but definitely not all), there are certain activities in which all subjects in the study participate. These tasks represent neither dependent nor independent variables; rather than being treatments themselves, they are a vehicle for introducing treatments. If, for instance, multiple-choice and completion-type response modes are being compared for a self-instructional learning program, the content of the learning program would constitute the task since *Ss* in both groups would experience this content. Apart from the content which is constant across conditions, one group would experience multiple-choice questions in its program, the second would experience completion-type questions. Program question format is thus the independent variable and would be described in the next section, "Independent Variables." *Program content* is the *task* and would be described in this section. Activities experienced by all groups are described in this section; activities experienced by one or some but not all of the groups are described in the next.

Some examples appear below.

- *The Task*

    The pictorial display was the same as used by Bruner, et al. (1966) consisting of forty-two drawings of common objects in a 6 × 7 matrix. The verbal display consisted of the lettered names of the same objects in the same arrangement. A smaller sample pictorial verbal array consisting of sixteen objects in a 4 × 4 matrix was used to demonstrate the problem during the initial instructions. [Laughlin, et al., 1969, p. 189]

In the study referenced above, all Ss received the same pictorial displays; the only difference consisted in the nature of the instructions they were given. However, in the following study, all Ss received the same tasks. What varied was the way these tasks were combined.

- *The Task*

The task was a 4 × 6 matrix of two-digit numbers as follows that were to be added:

18	18	18	18	18	18
10	10	10	10	10	10
24	24	24	24	24	24
79	79	79	79	79	79

Those problems identified as *search problems* could be solved by methods other than adding all twenty-four numbers. The example given above represents a search problem that could be solved (i.e., the sum could be found) by adding the numbers in the first column and multiplying by six since all the columns are identical. Other search problems featured two columns of numbers repeated three times each; others featured a row repeated four times although the order of the numbers was different from row to row. The common feature of search problems was that a shortcut method could be used to obtain a sum rather than adding all twenty-four numbers.

A *nonsearch problem* was a matrix of twenty-four numbers that only could be summed by adding all the numbers; no pattern existed so that no shortcut solution could be used. Search and nonsearch problems were equated in pairs in terms of the amount of time required to solve each by summing all twenty-four numbers. However, solving search problems via the shortcut required considerably less time once the shortcut was discovered. [Tuckman, et al., 1968, p. 61]

There are, however, frequent cases where there is no common activity, or task, and, in such cases, this section would be entirely eliminated.

Independent Variables

In this section, the independent (and moderator*) variables should be described, each under a separate heading. There are generally two types of independent variable. The first of these may be called a *treatment* variable. In the case of a treatment variable (i.e., something which has been manipulated), describe the manipulation or materials which constituted the treatment (such as, what you did or what you gave). Be specific enough so that someone else can replicate your treatment. Identify each level of the treatment, itemizing each for emphasis.

Following is an example of the description of a treatment, independent variable.

- *Independent Variable*
  1. Emotional appeal. This treatment consisted of a ten-minute taped speech containing statements which had severely threatening consequences for those who indulge in cigarette smoking, statements to the effect that "continued smoking will cause death through either lung cancer or heart attack." The speech also contained personalized threat references explicitly directed to the audience, statements to the effect that "this could happen to you." *E* established the credibility of the communicator through an acknowledgement of his status as an expert.
  2. Cognitive appeal. This treatment consisted of a ten-minute taped speech containing actual facts with a minimum of threat references. Impersonal language was used to describe the harmful consequences of smoking. Fewer references to the harmful consequences of smoking were made in this appeal than in the emotional one. Again, *E* established the communicator's credibility. [Student research paper]

The second form of independent variable may be called a *measured* variable. Such measured variables may have been used in addition to or instead of a treatment variable. In describing the measured independent variable (such as intelligence, personality, aptitude), indicate what instrument was used to measure it. If a standardized test was used, provide a published reference source for it, such as the test manual, and indicate the test's reliability and validity. If the instrument used was homemade, indicate whatever psychometric properties were determined and place a copy of the homemade test instrument in the appendix.

Recall from Chapter 3 that a moderator variable is a secondary type of independent variable, one that is included in a study to determine whether it affects or moderates the relationship between the primary independent variable(s) and the dependent variable. A moderator variable is, therefore, a special type of independent variable and is written up as an independent variable but labeled, for purposes of clarity, as a moderator variable.

Consider the following description of a measured independent variable, in this case a moderator variable.

- *Moderator Variable*

  1. High versus low authoritarian. *Ss* were classified as high authoritarian or low authoritarian based on their responses to the California Short Form of the *F*-Scale (twenty-eight items) developed by Adorno, et al., (1950). *Ss* scoring above the median were classified as high *F* and those below as low *F*. The *F*-scale is a measure of an individual's reliance on regimentation, structure, and authority in dealing with the world. High scorers are threatened by ambiguity and lack of standards. Nine subdimensions are reported by the authors. Satisfactory reliabilities and validities are reported. A copy of the *F*-scale has been appended. [Tuckman, 1968, p. 40]

In the above example, clearly more detail about the measure might have been given. The amount of detail reported will vary as a function of the familiarity of the instrument, the requirements of the readers, and the space allocation.

Dependent Variables

Each dependent variable should also be described. Since a dependent variable is typically a measured variable, it is necessary to describe the behavior measured, the instrument for measuring it, and the scoring procedure. Following are two examples.

- *Dependent Variable*

  ... The achievement criteria were scores on six subtests of the Metropolitan Achievement Test Series (MAT) administered in the ninth grade under the auspices of the Florida Ninth-Grade Statewide Testing Program. The MAT is a coordinated series of measures of achievement in the important skill and content areas of junior high school curriculum. The particular tests included in the battery are: reading (RD), language (LG), arithmetic computation (AC), and Science (SC). The language score is a composite of four subtests which measure usage, punctuation, capitalization, kinds of sentences, and parts of speech and grammar. [Khan, 1969, p. 217]

- *Dependent Variable*

  The dependent variable, level of learning attained as a result of completing the instructional program on Livestock Nutrition, was measured by means of a paper-and-pencil achievement test. This test was made by combining the two at the end of each unit of the original instructional booklet. The test was four pages long, three of which dealt with nutrition and one with vitamins. Thirty-six multiple-choice items in all were used to test *Ss'* knowledge of terminology and application of basic ideas as covered in the learning material. Forty-two responses were required on each item, providing a score range from 0 to 42. The group score was obtained by averaging the individual scores. Fifteen minutes in all were required to complete this measure. [Student research paper]

Procedures

The procedures section should describe any operational details which have not yet been described and which another researcher would need to know to replicate the method. Such details usually include (1) the specific order in which steps were undertaken, (2) the timing of the study, (e.g., time for different procedures and time between different procedures), (3) instructions given to *Ss*, and (4) briefings, debriefings, and safeguards.

Consider the following illustrations.

- *Procedures*

  Ss were recruited on a volunteer basis and completed the questionnaire on their own. They were all urged not to discuss the materials among one another until they were completed. The test booklet contained the occupational information questionnaire (with the satisfaction scale on the last page) followed by the ITI. In the initial briefing, *Ss* were told that the purpose of the study was to discover what kinds of people do best in what kinds of jobs in order to facilitate the guidance process. *Ss* were guaranteed complete privacy of response from both program sponsors and employers. [Tuckman, 1968, p. 547]

- *Procedures*

  The study was conducted in two consecutive days at each school. Each day's testing required about 1-1½ hours for each class. In every class, the first day was devoted solely to administering ability tests. The Inference Test was given first followed by the subjects from the PMA.

  The first task given on the second day was the learning materials. The four sets of materials were distributed serially throughout the class. The number of students who received each set of materials follows: VD, 108; VI, 100; FD, 107; and FI, 111.

Before the learning materials were distributed, *E* wrote each of the five basic concept words on the board and pronounced them. He explained that these words were the concepts to be learned. After being given the materials, students were instructed to study them carefully because they would be tested on their contents after finishing. As soon as each student completed the materials he was given the criterion test. [King, et al., 1969, pp. 245-246]

Data Analysis

The data analysis section describes the statistical design that was used and the statistical analyses that were undertaken. It is usually not necessary to describe these procedures step-by-step. If the statistical tests used were common ones (such as, analysis of variance, *t*-tests, chi-square analysis, correlation), then the test may simply be named and its source referenced. More unusual approaches require more detail.

These points are illustrated in the following examples.

- *Data Analysis*

  The following three-factor analyses of variance with repeated measures on two factors and unequal *n*'s (unweighted-means solution)—described by Winer (1962, p. 374)—were done on the data:

  1. A 4 X 2 X 2 analysis for: systems, I-IV; targets, best friend and casual acquaintance; and intimacy levels, nonintimate and intimate, on data from the Self-Disclosure Scale ($N = 112$).

  2. A 4 X 2 X 2 analysis containing the same factors and levels as above on data from the Probing Scale ($N = 112$).

  3. A 2 X 2 X 2 analysis for: exchange processes, probing and revealing, targets, best friend and casual acquaintance; and intimacy levels, nonintimate and intimate ($N = 224$).

  The three analyses were performed separately rather than as a single four-factor analysis because of heterogeneity of variance considerations. The third analysis was performed in order to compare the processes of revealing and probing directly. [Tuckman, 1966, p. 659]

- *Data Analysis*

  The hypotheses presented in an earlier section of this paper were tested statistically by use of sixteen 2 X 4 analyses of variance following the BMDO2V program for the IBM 7040 computer. Where significant effects occurred, the Scheffé method (Ferguson, 1966, pp. 296–297) was used to determine which differences in mean values were significantly different... . [McCall, 1969, p. 47–48]

In preparing a proposal or final research report (such as a dissertation), it may be very necessary and quite acceptable to provide more detail in each category of the method section than is evident in the examples given in this section. (The examples chosen for this text were selected in part for their brevity. Moreover, many of the examples were drawn from journal sources which place a premium on space, thus resulting in a very terse style.) In order to obtain some idea of length and level of detail, read research reports of the same form that you are about to prepare (i.e., dissertations, masters theses, journal articles), paying particular attention to form. Occasions will undoubtedly arise when a particular study will require fewer catagories or a different order than have been used in this section.*

11.4 THE RESULTS SECTION

Tables and graphs are usually essential to a results section, with the text describing in words what is shown in the tables and graphs. (Section 11.8 will deal with tables and Section 11.9 with graphs.)

The best way to structure the results section is in terms of the hypotheses which the study has set out to test. Hypothesis One would be the first heading, Hypothesis Two, the second, and so on. (Such subdivisions would not be necessary of course, in a study with only a single hypothesis.) Each heading would then be followed by a brief restatement of the hypothesis, a reference to an appropriate table or graph, and a descriptive statement of the outcome in testing the hypothesis, i.e., F ratios, t values, correlations, means, or whatever statistic was used. The description of statistical outcomes would parallel the table in which these data are found. You would conclude by indicating whether the data justified acceptance or rejection of the hypothesis.

A general rule is to prepare the text in sufficient detail so that the reader can comprehend the results by reading the text without consulting the tables or figures. Similarly, tables and figures should be prepared so that they can stand alone in describing the outcomes of the study.

*For information on the preparation of proposals and research reports according to U.S. Office of Education Standards (for grant purposes), see the manuals: Office of Education Support for Research and Related Activities and Preparing Reports Based on Research Supported by the Office of Education Bureau of Research.

The following six examples of text were drawn from the results sections of journal, dissertation, and research project sources. Each example represents only a portion of each particular section, typically pertaining to a single finding or cluster of related findings. In each case a table or figure or both are referred to and each illustration proceeds to identify the relevant statistical findings as set forth in the table or figure with little explanation or embellishment.

- **Results**

  Blind children were found to be less often rejected by their sighted peers than were partially-sighted children, as hypothesized, at the .001 level of significance (Mann-Whitney $U = 20.5, n = 13, n = 13$). Figure 1 shows the frequency with which the names of the two groups of visually-handicapped students appeared on their sighted classmates' questionnaires. In all instances but one, the names of partially-sighted children appeared more frequently. In most cases the partially-sighted student's name appeared at least twice as often as a blind student of the same age, sex, and at the same grade level. In two cases the name of the partially-sighted child appeared 17 and 44 times as often as the blind student with whom he was paired. [Sample Study III, Appendix A]

- **Results**

  Means and standard deviations for each of the eight cells of the experiment appear in Figure 1. The results of an analysis of variance of solution times for Ss in the first four cells of the experiment indicates that Ss having appropriate prior experience (Cells 1 and 2) took significantly less time to complete the criterion problem than Ss having inappropriate experience (Cells 3 and 4) $- F = 15.8, df = 1/133, p < .01$. A significant main effect of criterion problem was also obtained with the search criterion problem requiring less time to completion than the nonsearch criterion problem— $F = 30.6, df = 1/133, p < .001$.

  Cell means were further compared using the Duncan multiple-range test (Winer, 1962) and all mean differences *except* that between Cells 2 and 3 were significant at the .01 level. [Tuckman, et al., 1968, p. 63]

- **Results**

  Table 2 presents the 2 X 2 X 3 X 2 repeated-measures analysis of variance of mean time-to-criterion training and transfer scores for (a) level of GMA, (b) degree of initial acquisition, (c) group size, and (d) learning condition. As indicated, the interaction of the three main effects was significant ($p < .01$). Figure 1 presents the second order (ABC) interaction to be discussed later. Additionally, in the repeated measures, the Group Size X Learning Condition interaction was also significant. The interaction indicates that while transfer concepts are most efficiently attained by *Ss* trained as individuals, the performance of the group is more efficient on the training concepts. [Lemke, et al., 1969, pp. 76-77]

- *Hypotheses One and Two*

  Table 1 on page 67 shows the results for the total sample on the Social Desirability (SD) measure. A trend toward a significant interaction between the two perceptual factors is disclosed ($F = 2.96$; $df = 1, 84$; $p < .10$). The Multiple Range Test reveals no significant differences between subgroup means.

  For boys, the results presented in Table 2 on page 69 disclose a significant main effect for field articulation on the SD tendency ($F = 5.52$; $df = 1, 40$; $p < .05$). Analytic Perceivers display greater social desirability tendencies than Global Perceivers. A comparison of means, using the Multiple Range Test, demonstrates a trend toward a significant difference ($p < .10$) between the mean obtained by Global Perceivers who are Slow Closers and the means obtained by Analytic Perceivers who are Rapid Closers and Analytic Perceivers who are Slow Closers respectively. In each case, the Analytic Perceivers attained higher mean scores on the Social Desirability measure. [Cummings, 1967, pp. 66-68]

- *Hypothesis One*

  The results of the analysis of variance of the data indicate that pupils' I.Q. scores improved significantly when they were given the experience of taking three different intelligence tests. The mean gain in I.Q. scores between the first and second testing sessions was 2.7 points, and between the second and third session was 1.0 point. The former gain was statistically significant; the latter was not (Tables 5-6). [Kreit, 1968, pp. 616-617]

- *The First Results*

  Using a 7 X 7 correlation matrix the general hypotheses relating teacher perceptions of leader behavior to teacher-need orientations were tested. The results of this test with sex, age, experience, and teaching level held constant (variables 1, 2, 3, and 4 partialled out) are given in Table 3. The individual's CMS score was not found to be significantly correlated with either his score on the revised LBDQ subscore I (System) or subscore II (Person). Apparently, an individual's need-orientation as measured by the CMS was not related to his perception of the leader behavior of an ideal principal as measured by the LBDQ XII scores on the two global factors. The .517 correlation, however, suggests a positive relationship between preferences for systems and persons orientations. [Sergiovanni, et al., 1969, p. 71–73]

11.5 THE DISCUSSION SECTION

The discussion section considers the nuances and shades of the experiment; in it, the perceptiveness and creativity of the researcher and writer are finally given their chance. Perhaps the most critical part of the research report, this section is often the most difficult to write because it is the least structured. In the introductory, method, and results sections the details of the research dictate the content, but not in the discussion section.

The discussion section, however, does have a frame of reference—the introductory section. The points raised in the introduction must be responded to in the discussion. But within this frame of reference, the writer is free to use whatever art and imagination he can to show the range and depth of significance of his study. The discussion section ties the results of the study to both theory and application by pulling together the theoretical background, literature reviews, potential significance for application, and results of the study.

Because a discussion section is such a personalized expression of a particular study by a particular researcher, it would be unwise to recommend definite categories for this section as was done for previous sections. It may be helpful, however, to identify and describe the various functions of the discussion section.

To Conclude or Summarize

One very straightforward function of the discussion section is to summarize the findings of the study in the form of conclusions. If the study has been set up to test specific hypotheses, then the discussion section must report the outcome on each hypothesis, along with ancillary findings. It is useful to begin the discussion section with a summary of the main findings (numbered as the original hypotheses were numbered in the case of multiple, numbered hypotheses) under the heading of "Conclusions." As a starting-off point, this enables the reader to get the total picture of the findings in encapsulated form, and also helps to orient him to the discussion which follows. Some examples of conclusion summaries appear on the next page.

● *Conclusions*

The findings in this experiment led to the follow conclusions:

1. In an absolute sense, teachers of vocational subjects were *more nondirective* than teachers of nonvocational subjects.

2. Students were more satisfied with and preferred nondirective teachers, both in the vocational and nonvocational areas. However, students' preference for nondirective teachers was more marked among vocational teachers than among nonvocational teachers.

3. Students earned higher grades from nondirective, nonvocational teachers than they did from directive, nonvocational teachers. (Grades earned from the two groups of vocational teachers, however, were comparable.)

4. Abstract students showed a marked preference for nondirective, vocational teachers over directive ones while concrete students showed approximately equal preference for the two groups.

5. Nonauthoritarian students showed more marked course satisfaction and higher grades under nondirective, nonvocational teachers as compared to directive teachers than did authoritarian students. That is, nonauthoritarian students showed greater discrimination and a more differentiated outcome in favor of nondirective teachers than did their more authoritarian counterparts. [Tuckman, 1968, p. 66]

● *Conclusions*

All measures reported in the experiment showed consistant trends supporting the hypothesis that test performance and satisfaction would range from high to low for the Placebo, Experiment, and Time-Filler treatments, respectively. The same trends held for *Ss'* reports of number of agenda questions discussed as well as for their estimates of the completeness of the discussion. [Johnson and Foley, 1969, pp. 9–10]

To Interpret

What do the findings mean? What might have been happening within the methodology to account for the findings? Why did the results not turn out as hypothesized or expected? What circumstances accounted for the unexpected outcome? What were some of the shortcomings of the study? What were some of the limitations? The discussion section must address itself to these kinds of questions. There must be reasoned speculation. There may even be additional analyses of the data, referred to as *ad hoc* analyses, because they are done after the main findings are seen. Such analyses are introduced into the discussion section to help the interpretation and to account further for findings that on the surface appear inconsistent or negative.

For example, a doctoral study was done (Anderson, 1970) where one of the predictions was that students would spend less time on a difficult achievement test written at the 7th-grade level than at the 5th-grade level, an indication of a personality trait known as acquiescence. Results showed that students spent more time on the 7th-grade test than the 5th-grade test, contrary to the prediction. Anderson was still not convinced that students were attending more to the 7th-grade test so in his discussion section he introduced *ad hoc* analysis. He counted up the number of words in each test and divided it by the time taken to complete the test to get a measure of *reading rate*. Comparison of the two tests showed that the reading rate was faster for the more difficult test, thus providing partial support for the original expectation about acquiescence.

Further examples appear below.

- This study indicated that boys and girls achieved equally well for the two units whether their teachers used pupil-centered or teacher-centered techniques. This may imply that we should look more carefully at the considerable volume of material which implies that pupil-centered instruction produces greater achievement than teacher-dominated methods. The null hypothesis which stated that there would be no statistically significant differences in achievement between sex, level of group, and treatment was sustained.

   The implication is that teachers in the study were equally successful in the teacher-centered and pupil-centered instructional roles when pupil achievement and interest are considered. This, of course, presupposes that the teachers did in fact carry out the role expectations of the two treatments. How well they did this is supported by the data given under the topic of control of treatments reported under the procedures of the study. [Herman, et al., 1969, p. 237]

- An alternative interpretation is that the gains made by pupils in the experimental group over the three test sessions were related to the test-taking experiences which they received. Interestingly, a statistically significant change occurred between the first and second test sessions, but not between the second and third test administrations. This may mean that a limited amount of practice is related to the acquisition of test-taking skills and that further practice beyond the first test session yields little if any improvement. [Kreit, 1968, p. 623]

- The finding of no statistically significant interaction between initial I.Q. levels and test gains between sessions appear to contradict the hypothesis that the ability to learn is positively correlated with a pupil's I.Q. score. However, when one considers that the greatest gain was made by the high I.Q. group and the lowest was made by the low I.Q. group, it may be that the regression toward the mean phenomenon diminished the interaction which might otherwise have been significant. Another possibility is that the overlap in I.Q. scores of the high, medium, and low group prevented a statistically significant interaction. [Kreit, 1968, p. 624]

- The findings in the study appear to open several avenues of approach for application. However, because of the limitations of the research, caution must be exercised. The group was homogeneous and the size of the sample was small. It must be pointed out, also, that instruments such as projective techniques have no rigid structure for scoring and are prone to differential judgment. Even questionnaires and rating forms have traps that may pick up biases. With these shortcomings in mind, some issues may be raised. [Morrison, 1969, p. 172]

To Integrate

Not only must the discussion section unravel findings and inconsistencies as it does under interpretation, but it must also attempt to put the pieces together to achieve meaningful conclusions and generalizations. Often the results of a study are disparate and do not seem to "hang together." In the discussion section an attempt should be made to bring the findings—expected and unexpected, major and ancillary—together to extract meaning and principles. Some brief examples are given below.

- From the findings of the three experiments, it was possible to make an inference that was both important and unexpected, namely that *the strategy of search could be made more readily to transfer than the skill of search, as the result of limited prior experience.* [Tuckman, et al., pp. 66-67]

- This paper has viewed the reading of an organized passage as involving several factors, including goals or objectives, *Ss* skill repertoire, and the nature of the verbal material. These elements interact in a complex manner to produce various response outcomes, such as the use of appropriate strategies which *Ss* seem to be able to verbalize, retention of different words, and written response production. [Frase, 1969, p. 55]

To Theorize

When a study includes a number of related findings, it occasionally becomes possible not only to integrate these findings into some superordinate point or principle but to integrate them into an already existing theory or to use them to formulate an original theory. The goal is to make your findings part of a comprehensive body of theory either by working within an existing theory or by generating original theory. In the former case, you must state in the introductory section the existing theory that is to serve as the frame of reference.

Some brief examples follow.

- This research lends support to the contention that some children from homes in which a nonstandard dialect is spoken learn early in life to learn the standard dialect of the area. But, on the other hand, this research does not lead to the conclusion that the child who speaks a nonstandard dialect does not suffer adversely in a school setting as a result of language differences. The degree of social isolation, the attitude of the teacher, and the particular nonstandard dialect being studied are all variables which should be considered in evaluating the effects of subcultural language differences in the classroom setting. [Weener, 1969, p. 199]

- Although the sample was small, the study gives much support to the conception of underachievement among preadolescent boys as a form of passive aggression possibly stemming from strained adult-child interpersonal relations. [Morrison, 1969, p. 172]

To Recommend or Apply

Since education is essentially an applied field, research in education should yield some recommendations for alterations in educational practices.* In the discussion section, typically toward the end, you should examine your findings in the light of suggested applications.

Some examples of applications are illustrated below.

- One implication of this finding is that limited educational exposure to elegant thinking and problem-solving approaches may induce students

---

Dissertation writers often choose to follow the "Discussion" section with a separate "Conclusions and Recommendations" section, highlighting the conclusions and recommendations based on the results of the study.

to adopt the strategy to search when confronted by transfer situations but leave them lacking the skill to successfully apply this strategy. The result would be performance inferior to the inelegant technique, and perhaps frustration. Based on this implication, one must take care to provide a level of skill commensurate with a student's commitment to a strategy in order that he can use this strategy effectively, if at all. More extensive experience sequences than those provided in this experiment would be needed. [Tuckman, et al., p. 68]

- As has been shown, the natural response of curiosity is, at least in part, a function of the degree of novelty of the stimuli to which children are exposed. If such a proposition is valid, it behooves the teacher to provide an environment which not only is stimulating but which is exploration-inducing as well. Such an environment would be characterized by the strategic presence of varied and novel stimuli, changes in the intensity of sensory stimulation, and provision for the introduction of mild surprise. [Perticone, 1969, pp. 64–65]

- The brevity of the actual experimental portion of this study showed that teachers can experience perception and behavior changes in a relatively short time period when dissonance is aroused. This is more important for those working with in-service teachers than with practice teachers. Practice teachers are working full-time to perfect their skills whereas in-service teachers have a minimum amount of extra time available for such work. [McCall, 1969, p. 75]

To Suggest Extensions

Often the discussion section concludes with suggestions for further research, replications, or refinements, thus indicating directions that future research in the area might take. Such suggested extensions can be offered in general or more specific form.

- The results of this study suggest a need for comprehensive and systematic research on affective variables in academic achievement. Such research may have potential significance in educational decision making, guidance and placement of students, and identification of high and low achievers, for whom new educational environments ought to be devised so that their probable achievement can be heightened. [Khan, 1969, p. 220]

- A related issue which requires further research clarification concerned the possible existence of learning styles not observed in this study. Here many questions remain: How many different kinds of learning styles are there? How can they best be measured? Are new test instruments required? etc. And the same questions can be asked about instructional methods and subject-matter variables, since learning styles are best defined in these terms.

Answers to these questions will not be easy to find. The questions themselves seem to open up entirely new fields for investigation. It is apparent, however, that systems must be developed for classifying instructional-method variables and subject-matter variables in more meaningful ways than are currently available. [Tallmadge and Shearer, 1969, pp. 229-230]

11.6 THE REFERENCES

There are a variety of different formats for preparing references, two of which will be covered briefly here. The one used in this book is the style used in the psychological journals, such as the *Journal of Educational Psychology*. This format is described in detail in the *Publication Manual of the American Psychological Association* (1967 revision, pp. 39-48). In this format, footnotes are not used to cite references. Rather, references are cited in the text by author's surname and year of publication. A section headed "References," appearing at the end of the report, includes the full reference for each citation in alphabetical order according to the senior author's surname. A journal reference would appear as follows:

Samuels, S. J. and Wittrock, M. C. Word-association strength and learning to read. *Journal of Educational Psychology*, 1969, *60*, 248-252.

A book would be referenced as follows:

Pearl, A. and Riessman, F. *New careers for the poor*. New York: The Free Press, 1965.

Every item in the reference list must be specifically cited in the text and vice versa. To see how other types of reference (e.g., dissertations, government reports) are dealt with in this format, obtain a copy of the *Publication Manual of the APA* or examine references for articles appearing in the *Journal of Educational Psychology*.

Other reference formats are described in *Form and Style in Thesis Writing* (3rd edition; W. G. Campbell, 1969). Among these is one used in many educational research journals such as the *American Educational Research Journal* (*AERJ*). In this system, the reference in the text appears as the author's surname and year of publication exactly as it does in the psychological system. (In neither case are footnotes used for referencing.) However, a journal article listed in the references at the end of an article in the *AERJ* would appear as follows:

SAMUELS, S. JAY AND WITTROCK, MERLIN C. "Word-Association Strength and Learning to Read." *Journal of Educational Psychology* 60: 248–52; June, 1969.

A book reference in this format would appear as follows:

PEARL, ARTHUR and RIESSMAN, FRANK. *New Careers for the Poor.* New York: The Free Press, 1965. 265 pp.

Additional details on this second format can be obtained in W. G. Campbell (1969) or by examining reference lists in *AERJ*. You will notice that the two reference formats differ only slightly on matters such as capitalization, punctuation, and order of items, but the latter system includes the month when referencing an article and the number of pages when referencing a book. Both formats use the same technique for referencing in the text and both list citations alphabetically by senior author's surname at the end of the report in the reference section.

11.7 THE ABSTRACT

Journal articles and other research reports typically require an abstract written according to well-delineated standards. The number of words of the abstract is usually limited. Dissertations typically require a summary or what may be called a long abstract—often between 600 and 1,000 words. The rules for writing such a long abstract are essentially the same as that for writing a short one and may be obtained from W. G. Campbell (1969).

A short abstract for a journal article or research paper should run between 100 and 150 words. It should be written in block form (i.e., without indentations) and in complete sentences. The abstract should contain statements of the (a) problem, (b) method, (c) results, and (d) conclusions. Results are of major importance and, therefore, every abstract should contain at least the trend of the results. It is also recommended to state the number and kind of *Ss*, the type of research design, and the significance levels of the results. Results and conclusions may be itemized for brevity. Standard abbreviations and acronyms should be used where possible.* An example appears below.

- *Abstract*

  This study is aimed at determining whether learning might be enhanced by employing instructional methods which differ in design and use as a function of learner characteristics. Two separate subject-matter areas which represent two distinctly different learning situations were selected for investigation. Two separate courses were developed for each subject-matter area. One reflects an inductive instructional approach and the other a deductive method. Each of the four courses was administered to 55–60 Navy enlisted men. Twenty-eight measures of aptitude, interest, and personality were obtained on each *S*. The primary finding of the study is the significant ($p < .001$) interaction among instructional methods, learner characteristics, and subject matters. This finding strongly supports the existence of learning styles. [Tallmadge and Shearer, 1969, p. 222]

Other than the use of the present rather than the past tense (and in the use of some numerals in written rather than Arabic form—with regard specifically to APA format), the example above illustrates all the points about writing an abstract.

11.8 PREPARING TABLES

Tables are extremely useful for the presentation of results, both the results of statistical tests and means and standard deviations. Analyses of variance and correlations (when done in sufficient number) are statistical tests whose results are typically reported in tabular form.

Table 11.1, an analysis of variance table, indicates the source of variance, degrees of freedom (*df*) associated with each source, mean square of the variance (*MS*) for effects and error terms, and *F* ratios for main effects and interactions. The study involved two-rule conditions (variable *A*) which were applied to nine concept-solving problems (variable *B*). The same authors also prepared a table of means, Table 11.2. Table 11.3 is another example of a table of means.

In the APA format, all numerals should be in Arabic form, not spelled out, even at the beginning of a sentence—for purposes of saving space.

Table 11.1 *Analysis of variance of number of correct responses in nine concept problems for two-rule conditions. (From J. L. Dunham and C. V. Bunderson, Effect of decision-rule instruction upon the relationship of cognitive abilities in multiple-category problems,* Journal of Educational Psychology, *1969, 60, 123. Reprinted by permission of the authors and publisher.)*

Source	df	MS	F
Between Ss	135	82.54	1.85
Rule condition (A)	1	44.64	
Error between	134		
Within Ss	1088	392.75	64.24*
Problems (B)	8	8.33	1.36
A X B	8	6.11	
Error within	1072		

*$p < .001$

Table 11.2 *Mean number of correct responses on nine concept problems for two-rule conditions. (From J. L. Dunham and C. V. Bunderson, Effect of decision-rule instruction upon the relationship of cognitive abilities in multiple-category problems,* Journal of Educational Psychology, *1969, 60, 122. Reprinted by permission of the authors and publisher.)*

Groups	Problems								
	1	2	3	4	5	6	7	8	9
No-rule instruction	9.21	6.66	6.96	11.82	10.03	9.37	10.88	8.07	10.71
Decision-rule instruction	9.71	7.58	7.03	12.06	10.26	10.78	11.07	9.14	10.75

Table 11.3 *Pre/post means for Unit I achievement test. (From W. L. Herman, Jr. et al, The relationship of teacher-centered activities and pupil-centered activities to pupil achievement and interest in 18 fifth-grade social studies classes,* American Educational Research Journal, *1969, 6, 227–240. Reprinted by permission of the authors and publisher.)*

	Teacher-Centered Treatment		Pupil-Centered Treatment	
	Pretest	Posttest	Pretest	Posttest
Above-average group	20.42	31.92	18.53	26.45
Average group	21.02	25.90	17.71	24.40
Below-average group	16.75	25.63	16.69	22.64

Tables 11.4 and 11.5 are two examples of tables used to display correlations.

A final example of a tabular presentation (although this does not necessarily mean that all possible tables have been illustrated) is that called the *contingency table*, used in conjunction with a chi-square analysis—see Table 11.6 on page 318.

For further information on the preparation of tables, read Campbell's (1969) *Form and Style in Thesis Writing* and the American Psychological Association's (1969) *Publication Manual*. These sources are also instructive on the preparation of figures. Also examine tables and figures as they appear in journal articles.

Tables often play a useful role in the method section by depicting a complex arrangement among conditions, an experimental design, or a sequence of

Table 11.4 *Internal consistency coefficients of the five TPA factor scores (N = 192). (From R. J. Coughlan, The factorial structure of teacher work values, American Educational Research Journal, 1969, 6, 169-190. Reprinted by permission of the author and publisher.)*

Factor	Internal Consistency Coefficient
I. Administrative Focus	.74
II. Work Emphasis	.60
III. Source of Authority	.51
IV. Educational Concern	.67
V. Source of Support	.54

Table 11.5 *Relationships between student ratings, observer ratings, and personality structure. (Reprinted from Tuckman, 1968, p. 49.)*

	ORS_1	ORS_2	TSC_1	TSC_2	SIV
SPOTS $\bar{X}$	.12	.53**	.31	.15	.01
ORS_1		.76**	.88**	.84**	.50*
ORS_2			.75**	.63**	.40
TSC_1				.95**	.32
TSC_2					.59**

ORS_1, Mean, Observer Rating Scale
ORS_2, Best Judgment, Observer Rating Scale
TSC_1, Mean, Teacher Style Checklist
TSC_2, Consensus, Teacher Style Checklist
SIV, System IV, Interpersonal Topical Inventory

$*p < .05$ $**p < .01$

procedures. Table 11.7 illustrates the design and conditions of an experiment.*
To save space, means and standard deviations were also placed in this table (even
though those are results).

Table 11.6 *Comparison of school superintendents' perceived morality press and
innovativeness. (Reprinted from I. M. Peterson, 1968, p. 86, with permission
of the author.)*

Morality Press

		High	Low	
Innovativeness	High	12	8	20
	Low	5	25	30
		17	33	50

$\chi^2 = 8.20; p = .005$

Table 11.7 *Design of experiment II and mean times to completion in seconds
(and standard deviations) for each cell. (From B. Tuckman, et al., Induction and
transfer of search sets, Journal of Educational Psychology, 1968, 59–68. Reprinted by permission of the author and publisher.)*

	Appropriate Prior Experience	Inappropriate Prior Experience
Search Transfer Criterion Problem	Cell 1a 3 search problems search transfer criterion problem $N = 50$ $M = 107$ $SD = 6.9$	Cell 3a 3 nonsearch problems search transfer criterion problem $N = 52$ $M = 97$ $SD = 5.2$
Nonsearch Criterion Problem	Cell 2a 3 nonsearch problems nonsearch criterion problem $N = 51$ $M = 99$ $SD = 5.4$	Cell 4a 3 search problems nonsearch criterion problem $N = 47$ $M = 122$ $SD = 4.9$

*In some cases (such as this) it is somewhat arbitrary as to whether a diagram is referred to
as a table or a figure.

Table 11.8 illustrates the use of a table for displaying a sequence of procedures used in the methodology of an experiment. The table helps clarify the timing and time sequence of the study as well as the differences and similarities between treatments.

Table **11.8** *Feedback sequence. (Reprinted from K. M. McCall, 1969, p. 43, with permission of the author.)*

	Interaction Analysis Group	*Verbal Feedback*	*Tape Feedback*	*Control*
Week 1	Learned the Flanders I.A. system	Sheet number 1 was read to this group	Listened to 45 minutes of their own taped lessons	No treat- ment
Week 2	Observed 3 I.A. Group teachers in class	Sheet number 2 was read to this group	Listened to 45 minutes of their own taped lessons	No treat- ment
Week 3	Observed other 2 I.A. teachers in class	Sheet number 3 was read to this group	Listened to 45 minutes of their own taped lessons	No treat- ment

11.9 PREPARING FIGURES AND GRAPHS

Often figures are useful in the presentation of results. Data collected over time are often amenable to graphic presentation as are data displaying statistical interactions, means, and so on, as illustrated in Figures 11.1, 11.2, and 11.3

Figure 11.1 is illustrative of the use of a figure to display means in order to highlight an interaction. This figure would be more meaningful if the axes were more clearly labeled. The horizontal axis, labelled "Levels," refers to students' levels of intelligence. The unlabeled vertical axis represents scores on a measure of student interest in the colonization unit. This interest measure took the form of pairing social studies with all other school subjects and asking students to indicate their preference within each pair. The vertical might have been labeled: "Mean Number of Social Studies Choices," or "Mean Interest Inventory Score," and the horizontal axis, "Levels of Intelligence."

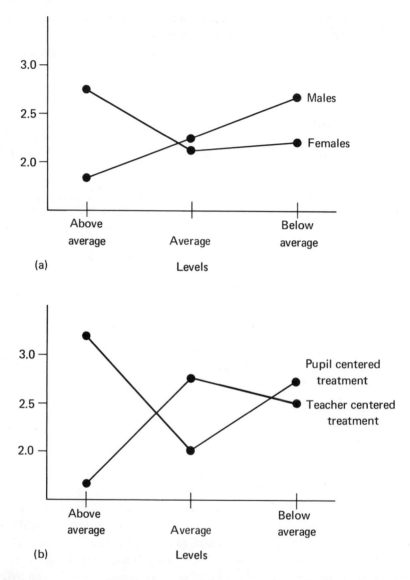

Figure 11.1 *(a) Interaction between sex and levels for interest inventory—colonization unit; (b) interaction between treatment and levels for interest inventory—colonization unit. (From W. L. Herman, Jr., et al. The relationship of teacher-centered activities to pupil achievement and interest in 18 fifth-grade social studies classes,* American Educational Research Journal, *1969, 6, 227–240. Reprinted by permission of the authors and publisher.)*

*These are separately labeled figures in the original source.

Figure 11.2 plots changes in a relationship (in this case, correlations) over time.

One final illustration represents a combined tabular and graphic display. Figure 11.3 (page 322) includes an analysis of variance source table, a table of means (of which there are four), indication of the mean comparisons, and a graph displaying the four means plotted together. This type of graph is purely an expositional device. Four points (particularly nominal ones) are typically not graphed.

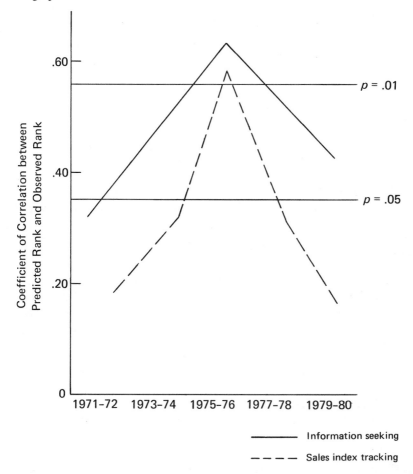

Figure 11.2 *Correlations between hypothesized and observed order of the groups on two task-related behavior dimensions over time.* (*From B. W. Tuckman, Personality structure, group composition, and group functioning, Sociometry, 1964, 27, 469–487. Reprinted by permission of the author and publisher.*)

Source	df	MS	F
A	1	4.92	1.0
B	1	9.65	1.0
A X B	1	78.80	5.50*
Error	84	14.32	

*$p < .05$

Analytic	Global	
24.9	27.6	52.5
26.4	25.1	51.5
51.3	52.7	

*GIRd > GISl $p < .05$
*GIRd > AnRd $p < .05$

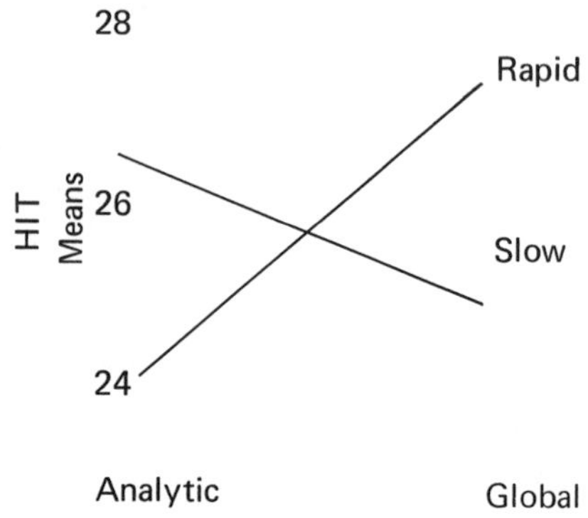

Figure 11.3 *Analysis of variance of feeling-value congruency (HIT) ratings from two levels of Gestalt perception (A) and field articulation (B), along with cell means, row and column mean totals, and significant mean contrasts—total sample, N = 88. (Reprinted from R. D. Cummings, 1964, p. 76, with permission of the author.)*

However, the use of the graph clearly illustrates the interaction between the two variables in question (i.e., analytic versus global perceivers, and slow versus rapid closers) on the independent measure (HIT score). Certainly it would be much more difficult to say in words what this graph depicts with relative ease.

RECOMMENDED READINGS

American Psychological Association. *Publication manual*. Washington, D.C.: American Psychological Association, 1967.

Ballou, D. V. *A model for theses and research papers*. Boston: Houghton-Mifflin, 1970.

Campbell, W. G. *Form and style in thesis writing*, 3rd ed. Boston: Houghton-Mifflin, 1969.

Gillooly, W. B. *The literature search*. Somerset, N.J.: Mariner Press, 1969.

Perrin, P. G. *Writer's guide and index to English* (4th ed.) Glenview, Ill.: Scott, Foresman and Company, 1968.

Wiersma, W. *Research methods in education*. Philadelphia: Lippincott, 1969.

COMPETENCY TEST EXERCISES

(In order to demonstrate competency in "Writing a Research Report," the reader should prepare a proposal and final report according to the specifications set forth in this chapter. However, for purposes of this test, an attempt will be made to help the reader assess his competency via short answer questions.)

1. In preparing the *introductory* section of a report, some of the sections listed below are usually included. Place a number before each section usually included to indicate its order in the sequence.
   - a. operational restatement of hypothesis ____
   - b. tasks ____
   - c. review of literature ____
   - d. problem context ____
   - e. conclusions ____
   - f. significance of study ____
   - g. problem statement ____
   - h. rationale for hypothesis ____
   - i. operational definitions of variables ____
   - j. statement of policy ____
   - k. statement of hypothesis ____

2. Given a study to relate teaching style to the degree to which children learn self-control and internal motivation, write a brief paragraph illustrating the significance of the study.

3. In preparing the *methods* section of a report, some of the sections listed below are usually included. Place a number before each section usually included to indicate its order in the sequence.
   - a. independent variables ____
   - b. procedures ____
   - c. data analysis (design) ____
   - d. outcomes ____
   - e. dependent variables ____
   - f. statement of hypothesis ____
   - g. tasks ____
   - h. subjects ____

4. Sample Study II in Appendix A does not have a subsection of its methods section entitled "independent variables." This information is contained under "method" but not in a separate section. Write a brief subsection entitled "independent variables" for Sample Study II.

5. A good way to structure the *results* section is to subdivide it into subsections for each _____.
   a. task
   b. independent variable
   c. operational definition
   d. hypothesis

6. Look at exercise 12 on the Competency Test Exercises for Chapter 10 (page 284). X represents ratings of a youngster's aggressiveness by the school psychologist while Y represents the number of demerits which each youngster has accumulated in school. It was hypothesized that the two were positively related. Using your result obtained in exercise 12, write a brief paragraph describing the results of this "study."

7. The *discussion* section of the report usually serves some of the functions listed below. Place an X next to those served by the discussion section.
   a. to abridge   _____
   b. to integrate   _____
   c. to suggest extensions _____
   d. to revise   _____
   e. to conclude   _____
   f. to theorize   _____
   g. to predict   _____
   h. to interpret   _____
   i. to recommend   _____
   j. to investigate   _____

8. It has been shown that youngsters in higher ability groups have better school attendance records than youngsters in lower ability groups. Write a brief paragraph interpreting this finding.

9. Construct an analysis of variance source table to show the results of the analysis of variance appearing in Figure 10.15 (page 278). Make sure to give your table the proper title. (The dependent variable is the rating of the teacher on a version of a scale called the SPOTS; the independent variable is the subject taught and the moderator variable is the teacher's personality.)

10. Construct a table to display the cell and marginal means for the analysis in Figure 10.15 (and for which the analysis of variance source table was constructed in the preceding item.) Make sure to title your table properly. Indicate significant mean differences that you know from the analysis of variance.)

11. Draw a graph to illustrate the cell means listed in the table for exercise 10. (Be sure to title it and label the axes.)

12. Draw a graph of the scores given in exercise 3 of the Chapter 9 Competency Test Exercises, page 252. Do not distinguish between groups. Plot all the data together in bar graph form showing the frequency distribution of each score or groups of scores.

12

Conducting
Evaluation Studies

OBJECTIVES

Distinguish between formative and summative evaluation. / Design a study to evaluate a treatment or intervention utilizing concepts of identification and operational definitions of variables, research design, and observation and measurement. / Analyze and interpret the data from an evaluation study and draw appropriate conclusions.

12.1 FORMATIVE VERSUS SUMMATIVE EVALUATION

Scriven (1967) has coined the labels *formative* and *summative* to describe two types of evaluation. Formative evaluation refers to the internal evaluation of a program, usually undertaken as part of the development process, in which the performance of students in a program is compared to the objectives of the program. It is an attempt to debug learning materials (or some other form of program) by trying them out on a test group as they are being developed. Such tryouts enable the developers to tell whether the materials are workable and to suggest changes to make in them. Formative evaluation often leads a program developer "back to the drawing board."

Summative evaluation—demonstration*—is a systematic attempt to determine whether a fully-developed program is meeting its objectives more successfully than alternative programs (or no program). Summative evaluation uses the comparison process to evaluate a full-blown program, while formative evaluation is part of the development process and thus preceeds demonstration-evaluation.

When, in Chapter 1, the terms evaluation *and* demonstration *were linked, it was summative evaluation being referred to.*

The techniques for formative evaluation are varied and not quite as systematic as those for summative evaluation. Since the purpose of formative evaluation is to help the program developer judge the adequacy of his materials as they are being developed, he often asks the pilot subjects to fill out questionnaires or to take performance tests. The developer then evaluates the success or failure of the material and rewrites it accordingly. By comparison, summative evaluation should proceed in a more systematic fashion, should conform to a model, and should provide a comparison between programs or products.

There are a variety of summative evaluation models. The one that will be described in detail in this chapter conforms to the logical base and process of research described in this book, and yet it is general enough to be applied in a variety of situations.

12.2 A MODEL FOR SUMMATIVE EVALUATION

The model that will be used here for evaluating an intervention or program will be based on the model of experimental design which has been described in detail throughout the preceding chapters of this book.* This model includes the techniques of formulating a hypothesis, constructing operational definitions, identifying variables, building a design, developing measuring instruments, and conducting statistical analyses. The reason that the research design model is appropriate for purposes of evaluation is threefold: (1) it is a logical and consistent approach, (2) it allows a researcher to establish cause and effect relationships (or at least, to make inferences about cause and effect), and (3) it provides the conditions for making systematic comparisons.

The overall evaluation model in Figure 12.1 includes five steps, each of which has already been dealt with in detail in the preceding chapters. The first step provides for the *identification of the dependent variables* of the evaluation study, namely the aims of the intervention or experimental program. The second step *transforms these aims into operational definitions* by stating them in behavioral terms. Step 3 then *develops tests or measuring devices for the dependent variables* in a manner which assures content validity. The fourth step involves the *establishment of an independent variable* in a situation that has an experimental group (the group receiving the intervention) and a comparison or control group. An additional part of this step is insuring or demonstrating that the members of both groups are equivalent on selection factors. Finally in the

---

*This chapter is not an attempt to survey the literature on evaluation and describe all possible evaluation models. Rather, the intention of this chapter is to provide one model for evaluating programs. There are, of course, alternative models that the researcher may employ.

Step 1 Identification of the aims and objectives of the program (the dependent variable)

Step 2 Restatement of the aims and objectives in behavioral terms (an operational definition)

Step 3 Construction of a content valid test to measure the behaviorally-stated aims and objectives (measurement of the dependent variable)

Step 4 Identification and selection of a control, comparison, or criterion group against which to contrast the test group (establishing the independent variable)

Step 5 Data collection and analysis

Figure 12.1 *An evaluation model.*

fifth step, *data collection and statistical analyses are undertaken* as a prerequisite to drawing conclusions. Each of these steps will be described in some detail.

Note that this model with step 4 removed can serve as a formative evaluation model. Since formative evaluation attempts to determine whether a program is successfully meeting its own objectives, it may be carried out by specifying these objectives, operationalizing them, building a test to measure them, and then using this test with a group of subjects that are completing the program, Formative evaluation, then, differs from summative evaluation in the absence of step 4— the lack of a control or comparison group.

12.3 DEFINING THE GOALS OF A PROGRAM

Identifying the Aims of the Intervention: The Dependent Variable

When an intervention* is undertaken in a school system—whether it is a specific course of study, a facility, or the introduction of a special piece of equipment—there are usually aims or objectives that exist in the minds of the people introducing the intervention as to what outcomes can be hoped for and expected. These aims and objectives, which will be different for different specific interventions, represent the goals of success of the intervention. Some educational programs may list as their aim mastery of the content of a certain course of study, while others locate their aim very specifically in the future adult life

---

The terms program *and* intervention *are used interchangeably although a program is only one form of intervention.*

of the student. In vocational programs, for example, specific trade competencies and entry level and potential advancement level job skills are often identified as the aims or objectives to which the program is addressed.

The decision concerning aims and objectives should rest with the user of the intervention. It is up to those who decide to try the intervention to determine their expectations. They must ask themselves: What do we expect of students who have completed the experience that we do not expect of students who have never had the experience or who have had other experiences? They may look to the developer of the intervention to help them answer these questions.

Thus, the first step in the evaluation process is to approach the user of the intervention and ask: What are the aims and objectives of this intervention? What are your expectations regarding what the students can do after having had the experience of the program? In response to such questions, the user may make statements such as the following: (a) the program will help the students develop an appreciation of art, (b) it will help them better understand themselves, (c) it will provide them with the skills for entering the carpentry trade, (d) it will make them more likely to be constructive citizens, (e) they will know more American history than they did before they started, (f) they will have a greater interest in science, and so on.*

Each of the above statements is an example of the kinds of aims that program users identify and the way they are likely to be expressed. Thus, in step 1 the dependent variable of the evaluation is identified, but it is identified to a large degree in conceptual terms, or, in vague and ambiguous terms—all being equally difficult to measure.

Operationally Defining the Dependent Variable: Behavioral Objectification

In the first step described above, the evaluator has identified the dependent variable. He has also, in a large sense, formulated a hypothesis about the dependent variable which states that its occurrence may be more likely to happen after experiencing the intervention as compared to experiencing some other or no other intervention. The next step is to produce an operational definition of the dependent variable, which will move the evaluator one step closer to the concrete terms and dimensions with which he can work.

In completing this second step, the evaluator says to himself and to the user (and occasionally to the developer): How can we tell whether the aims and

---

Consideration, in the subsequent measurement stage, should also be given to unintended or unanticipated outcomes since these often occur and help in the evaluation process.

objectives of the intervention which have been outlined in the first step have been achieved? What observable and measurable behaviors will the students perform if these aims and objectives have been achieved that they will not perform if these aims and objectives have not been achieved? That is to say, the question is not how will they be different after the intervention, but what can we *see* about them that is different? Unfortunately, it is impossible to get "inside the head" of the student to determine whether he appreciates, understands, is interested in, or motivated by the treatment. We are limited in our judgments to his overt actions and self-reports—that is, we can only study his behavior. Any conclusions about thoughts, fears, and the like can only be made inferentially from the study of behavior. Thus, the aims and objectives of the intervention must be operationally defined in behavioral terms. The conceptual (and vague and ambiguous) terms of aims and objectives must be replaced by statements of behavior.

It is entirely likely that an intervention of any size will have many aims or objectives, rather than just one. Moreover, in transforming these objectives into behaviors which define them or imply their presence, it is often necessary to deal with a number of behaviors associated with each aim and objective rather than with one behavior per objective. For this reason, it is necessary to think in terms of a *series* of behavioral objectives that will represent the dependent variable.

The first characteristic of the operational definition of a program aim is that it is written in specific behavioral terms, that is, it includes the use of an *action verb*. Upon completion of the program the student will be able to (1) *identify*, or point to something that has the following properties; (2) *describe*, or tell about those properties; (3) *construct*, that is, make something having the following properties; or (4) *demonstrate*, or use a procedure of a particular nature. To identify, describe, construct, demonstrate, and so on, represent the kinds of action verbs that are indicative of behavior and thus required for behavioral objectives. To specify something in behavioral terms, use behavioral words that specify "doing" rather than "knowing." Words such as "knowing," "appreciating," "understanding," are not action verbs and therefore should not be used in an operational definition.

Figure 12.2 gives a list of suggested action verbs originally developed by the American Association for the Advancement of Science. (The specific illustrations of the use of each one have been added by the author.) By using one of these action verbs, a researcher can be sure that he is writing a behavioral objective. In addition, this standardization enables researchers to compare objectives with a degree of certainty that a specific word has the same meaning in various experimental situations.

The second element of a behavioral objective is its *content*. What is it that a student shall be able to identify? What is it that a student shall be able to

Identify

Given a list of eight statements, the student shall identify all that are instances of hypotheses.

Distinguishing

Given a list of eight statements, the student shall distinguish between those that are hypotheses and those that are inferences.

Describing

The student shall describe two characteristics that distinguish between a hypothesis and an inference.

Naming

The student shall name four statistical tests that can be done to compare two treatments when the n's are small and outcomes are not normally distributed.

Stating a Rule

The student shall state a rule limiting the transformation of interval, ordinal, and nominal measurement, one to the other.

Ordering

Given a list of ten statements, the student shall order them in terms of their sequence in the research process.

Demonstrating

Given a set of data, the student shall demonstrate the procedure for analysis of this data using analysis of variance procedures on a desk calculator.

Constructing

Given the following set of data which are to be analyzed by analysis of variance, the student shall construct program control cards suitable for the use of the BMD02V program.

Applying a Rule

Given the following set of interval data, the student shall convert this data to nominal (high, middle, low) using the rule of the tertile split.

Interpreting

Given the following set of analyzed data and the following hypothesis, the student shall interpret the outcome of the experiment in terms of the hypothesis.

Figure 12.2 *A list of action words for constructing behavioral objectives.*

describe; What is it that a student shall be able to construct? The specific content in which mastery or competence is to be shown through behavior represents the second element of the behavioral objective.

The third element of the objective is a specification of the *exact conditions* under which the behavior is to take place. "Given a list of twenty items, the student shall identify," or "using the following pieces of equipment, the student shall construct or demonstrate," are examples of the specification of conditions.

Finally, if possible, try to specify in a behavioral objective the *criterion* such as the amount of time the student will have and how many correct responses he is likely to be able to make in that amount of time, although at this stage of behavioral objectification, it is not completely necessary to include this level of detail. It will often suffice to include an action verb, a statement of content, and any specific conditions.

Evaluators should not discourage users from the inclusion of creative and imaginative goals because of the difficulty in writing these in behavioral terms. If, for instance, a program user hopes to heighten his students' awareness of form in art, the evaluator should have the user help him identify behaviors that would be indicative of attainment of this goal (such as: given a painting and asked to describe it, the student will include an identification of the form in his description). Since the user will look for subjective evidence of the attainment of his more creative or imaginative goals, the evaluator must work with the user or other experts to identify behaviors associated with these outcomes.

Thus, the second step in the suggested evaluation model is to convert the aims and objectives which represent the dependent variable into more concrete and observable statements of behavior—that is, to transform the dependent variable statement into operational definitions or behavioral objectives.

12.4 MEASURING THE GOALS OF A PROGRAM (THE DEPENDENT VARIABLE)

Now that the program's goals—the dependent variable—have been transformed into operational definitions taking the form of behavioral objectives, the next step is to devise an instrument to measure the extent to which those behaviors representing the objectives of the program have been achieved. Building a test from behavioral objectives is a relatively straightforward process.*

Figure 12.3 illustrates a few behavioral objectives and test items that have been written to measure them.

The critical quality that a test of the behavioral objectives of a program must possess is content validity (see Chapter 7, page 141). The test must reflect

---

*We ordinarily tend to think of tests as a basis for evaluating individuals and individual performance. However, when a group of individuals who have commonly experienced an intervention or training program are given a test, and their test data are pooled and examined on a group basis with proper comparisons (this will be discussed in the next section), it is possible to use such test data for evaluating the intervention or program.

1. Demonstrating a Procedure for Expressing Improper Fractions as Mixed Numbers.

   Express $1\frac{1}{16}$ as an improper fraction.

2. Describing the Function of Information Conveyed in a Purchase Order.
   Circle the letter next to the correct answer.

   A purchase order is used when:
   A. A retailer orders merchandise from a wholesaler
   B. A retailer orders services from a consumer
   C. A wholesaler orders merchandise from a retailer
   D. A foreman orders stock from an inventory.

3. Demonstrating an Interest in the Study of Science.
   List any books or articles you have read on your own that have to do with science.

   Do you have a chemistry set? A microscope?
   Did you get these before or after your new science program?

4. Demonstrating a Procedure for Preparing Permanent Microscope Slides.
   Below are a sequence of steps in making a permanent microscope slide of a tissue speciment. Arrange the steps in their proper order.
   A. Soak in baths of progressively lower alcohol content
   B. Fix and mount
   C. Section
   D. Stain
   E. Soak in baths of progressively higher alcohol content

5. Constructing a Magnetic Field Using Current.
   Identify what material you would need to construct a magnetic field using current and describe the procedure you would use.

Figure 12.3 *Sample behavioral objectives and appropriate test items for each.*

accurately upon the intervention or program, and must be representative of those skills, competencies, aims, and objectives which the program has set for itself. By systematically delineating each objective associated with the program and then mapping out measurement items for each of these objectives, it is possible to guarantee that such test items, when taken together, will be representative of the program, and thus have content validity. This concept is illustrated in Figure 12.4.

As can be seen from this figure, breaking down an intervention or program into its separate units, identifying the competencies and skills to be obtained from each unit, and then developing test items to measure each competency or skill make it possible to build a test that is representative of the content which is

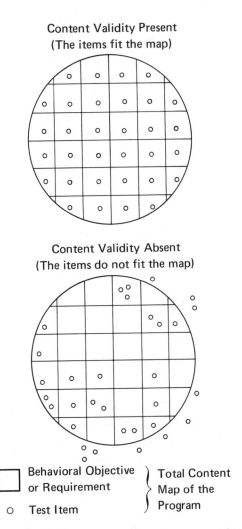

Content Validity Present
(The items fit the map)

Content Validity Absent
(The items do not fit the map)

☐ Behavioral Objective
 or Requirement

○ Test Item

} Total Content
 Map of the
 Program

Figure 12.4 *A schematic representation of content validity (achieved when the items testing the achievement of content fit or represent the objectives making up that content).*

presented in the program. The more representative the test, the higher its content validity. Without a content outline or breakdown, it is difficult to identify areas which must be covered in the test, or to determine that test items once developed are representative of the program's content or objectives. The content outline and its objectives is a guideline for writing items that will accurately reflect the effect of exposure to that content. A test so written will have content validity.

The objectives of a program will sometimes appear to require physical performances by the students to evaluate them. It is useful to try to think in terms of paper-and-pencil items that might as accurately capture the measurement of objectives which involve performance albeit less directly but more efficiently. However, one must be careful in attempting to replace performance items with paper-and-pencil items not to lose the essential characteristic which the item intends to measure. Items 4 and 5 in Figure 12.3 illustrate how performance judgments appropriate for objectives which call for demonstrations and constructions can be accomplished in the paper-and-pencil modes of identifications and descriptions.

12.5 ASSESSING ATTAINMENT OF A PROGRAM'S GOALS

Identifying a Comparison Group: The Independent Variable

Up to this point, we have really been dealing with a process that in and of itself could serve as formative evaluation. It is in this next step, the comparison process, that formative and summative evaluation are distinguished. The important difference is that summative evaluation is not simply an attempt to describe what behaviors a student has acquired as a result of specific experiences, but to judge further these acquired behaviors and their level of performance against some standard of success or effectiveness. Thus, summative evaluation, unlike formative evaluation, distinctly implies comparison of some sort.

There are three kinds of groups that may be used in contrast to the experimental group to assess the effect of the treatment or intervention. The first of these contrast groups may be called a *control* group. A control group is a group of subjects who have not experienced the treatment or any other similar or related treatment. The purpose of a control group is to answer the question: Would the behavioral objectives of the program have been met anyway, even if the program had not occurred? Or, Can these objectives be expected to occur spontaneously or be produced by some unspecified means other than the program? The fact that students who complete a program can now do more than they could before they completed the program might have been caused by history or maturation—sources of internal invalidity. In order to assure that neither history nor maturation is responsible for the change but that the intervention or program is responsible, an equivalent group of individuals who have not experienced the program can be compared to those who have, thus utilizing the basic experimental-control group contrast.

Very often, however, problems in evaluation take a somewhat different form, posing the question: Is the treatment or program producing the behaviors to a greater degree or perhaps more efficiently than alternative programs or interventions? When stated in this way, the problem becomes one not merely of control, but of *comparison*. Thus, the second group to which the intervention or program group could be compared would be a group of students who have presumably been trained to attain the same behavioral objectives in a different (and in many cases more traditional) way. A comparison of the performance of the two groups would answer the question: Is the new way better than the old way?

Occasionally, evaluation questions take even a third form. In this third form, the standard is developed in reference to some ideal state that is to be attained. Thus, the question might be: Has the vocational student developed a level of job skills which are sufficient for reasonable success in the occupation for which he was trained? Or, if the objective of a program is to give the student enough competence in calculus so that he can subsequently succeed in solving specific problems in physics and aerodynamics that require calculus to solve, we would say: How does his knowledge of calculus compare to the knowledge of calculus by those persons who are succeeding at solving physics and aerodynamics problems? Thus, we are asking for a contrast, not in terms of a control group which has had no experience, nor in terms of a comparison group, which has had an alternative experience, but in terms of a *criterion* group which is able to display the behavior in another context, namely that context in which the knowledge to be acquired in the treatment is applied.

Very often in vocational programs or professional programs where the aim is to prepare individuals to have on-the-job competence, the criterion group can be chosen from among those workers who are demonstrating such competence. Of course, the identification of these individuals as a criterion group must be accomplished using a measuring instrument other than the one which is being developed for purposes of evaluating the intervention. Typically this group is chosen on the basis of criteria such as supervisors' judgments, promotion rate, salary, or some indication of mastery other than direct measurement of competence and skill.

Further, one important consideration is the validity factor of selection. In selecting a control, comparison, or criterion group it is necessary that other potentially-relevant individual difference characteristics be controlled for in order to avoid selection bias. Often in an evaluation study it is not possible to use random assignment because individuals have come to participate in the procedure or its alternatives on a voluntary basis or on some basis other than assignment by the evaluator. The evaluator is brought in on an after-the-fact basis. That is, the evaluator is not often provided with a pool of subjects who can then be randomly assigned—half to the treatment, half to the control. More often, he begins with an intact group of subjects, possibly volunteers, who are already experiencing the treatment (or will so, imminently). Beginning with an intact group, the evaluation study thus calls for the nonequivalent control group design. However, if the evaluator does not arrive on the scene before the training starts and is thus unable to give the posttest instrument as a pretest (as is typically done in this design), it is necessary for him to select a control or comparison group that is as similar to the treatment group as possible.

When you begin with an experimental group that has already been composed, you should attempt either to select control subjects on a random basis from the same population as experimental Ss, or to select them on a systematic basis so that they are reasonably equivalent to the experimentals. Where you have reason to believe that experimental group assignment has been essentially unbiased, (although completed prior to your arrival as the evaluator), control group assignment should be random where possible. Where either, or both, treatment and comparison groups has been pre-assigned, you can compare the groups on selection factors on an after-the-fact basis to determine their equivalence. Age, for instance, is an important variable for comparison as are sex, I.Q. (or some other measure of ability or aptitude), socioeconomic status and achievement data. It is important that treatment and control groups, treatment and comparison groups, or treatment and criterion groups be as equivalent as possible on all potentially-relevant individual difference measures. In addition, where possible, all groups should be pretested on the dependent variable measure developed in the preceding step.

Ideally again, potential subjects should be assigned on a random basis by the evaluator to experimental and control (or comparison or criterion) groups; however, this is often beyond the realm of possibility. Thus, when a true experimental design cannot be used (or the dependent variable measured on a pretest basis), the evaluator must make every effort to show that experimental and control groups are equivalent on all potentially-relevant individual difference measures to minimize selection threats to internal validity. This is best accomplished by random selection of control Ss from the same population as experimental ones and after-the-fact comparing of the presumably equivalent groups.*

Data Collection and Analysis

The measure of the dependent variable developed in the third step is administered in this fifth step to all the students in the intervention (or a random

---

Where after-the-fact comparisons show the groups to be nonequivalent on relevant selection factors, differences can be somewhat adjusted for by analysis of covariance procedures.

sample drawn from among them if there are too many to test conveniently) and all the students in the control, comparison, or criterion group(s) (again, selecting a random sample from among these if there are too many to test conveniently). After both groups or samples from each have been tested, group means can be determined and t-tests run in order to determine if the difference between these means is significant.

Very often, the evaluation study will proceed most effectively if more than one group is used for contrast purposes. It may, for instance, be very useful to include both a control group and a criterion group to determine the level of achievement which the intervention produces as identified by or bounded by no-experience at one end (the control group) and operational competence at the other end (the criterion group). Thus, three groups would be tested. In this case, a one-way analysis of variance would be most appropriate in order to determine whether differential effects were being produced by these three conditions.*

12.6 ILLUSTRATIONS OF SUMMATIVE EVALUATION STUDIES

Evaluating a Job Training Program

Suppose that you had designed a one-semester secondary school level training program to prepare women to enter the occupation of key-punch operator upon high-school graduation. Furthermore, you had put this program into operation with a group of twenty female high-school seniors and were now interested in evaluating the outcome.

The first step would be to identify the aims and objectives of the training program. Broadly speaking, these would be to provide the subjects with entry-level job skills in key punching. More specifically, they would be to produce a worker who could operate a key punch at acceptable rates of speed. A second objective might be to increase the interest of potential dropouts in staying in school after the age of 16.

*Following the analysis of variance, it would be possible to do multiple range tests such as the Newman-Keuls Multiple Range test or the Scheffé test in order to compare the three means simultaeously using the error term from the analysis of variance. These techniques are aptly described in Winer (1962) and other statistics books. Where pretest data are available, analysis of covariance of the posttest scores with pretest scores as the covariate may be done.

The second step in implementing the evaluation model would be to construct an operational definition of the dependent variable—operating a key punch at acceptable rates of speed. For example;

Demonstrating a procedure for punching proper data into proper columns at the rate of X entries per hour after having planned and prepared a key punch for programmed control.

This particular behavioral objective could then be broken into four components.

1. Demonstrating a procedure for activating the proper functional control switches at the proper times.
2. Demonstrating a procedure for planning and punching a program card from punching and verifying instructions.
3. Demonstrating a procedure for mounting a program card on a program drum and removing it.
4. Demonstrating a procedure for punching a card from an original source document.

The second aim of the study might be stated operationally very simply as increasing attendance and decreasing the probability of dropping-out.

A third step would require a test to measure the dependent variables. In this instance the key-punching skills could be tested by placing a student at a key punch, telling her to punch data cards using a program card (see components (2) and (3) above), timing her, and measuring her accuracy. She could be scored for each of the four subtasks in terms of time or errors (or both) and then these scores could be summed for a total score. As for a secondary objective of the program, both drop-out rate and number of days absent could be used as measures.

One approach to the last step, the identification of comparison groups, would be to locate a commercial firm that ran its own training program for female key-punch operators. After collecting information about the age, I.Q. and socio-economic status (SES) of the students in the company program to determine equivalency, you could use them as a comparison group. Another possibility would be to establish a criterion group of women already successfully employed as key-punch operators. The difficulty with this suggestion is that key-punching skills improve with practice and employed key punchers are likely to have had considerably more practice than students. To eliminate the practice effect (i.e., to control it out as history bias), it would be necessary to compare two student groups, as in the first suggestion. However, successfully employed key punchers could be used as a basis for determining skill criterion levels. A key-punching performance test could be standardized against the employed criterion group and then used as a competency measure to assess the performance of the group in training.

A way to assess the retention value of the program would be to identify a control group in the same school as the key punch student test group—a sample of female students comparable to the test group on age, I.Q., and SES but not enrolled in the training program. Then draw a random sample of twenty control girls from this equated pool. It must be recognized that the control group and experimental group may be different in terms of initial motivation—if the training group represents volunteers and continuing motivation—for reasons of Hawthorne and expectancy effects. In the latter case, it might be useful to try to find a control group to control for Hawthorne and expectancy effects, such as, girls involved in a neighborhood social program or involved in a school social activity. For these procedures, see Chapter 6 on research design.

The last step in the evaluation would be the collection and analysis of the data. Administer the performance test developed in the third step to the test and comparison groups, score it, and analyze it and the attendance records using a t-test or Mann-Whitney U-test, or chi-square test.

Assuming that the test group outperformed the comparison group and out-attended the control group, you could then conclude that the high school key-punch training program was effective both in providing job skills and in increasing interest in school.

Evaluating a Reading Program

Another illustration of an evaluation is taken from the work of Lockmiller and Di Nello (1970) which was used illustratively in Chapter 5. (The problem and method sections of this study were reproduced in that chapter on pages 93–95.) The purpose of this study was to evaluate a reading program called *Words in Color,* designed to improve reading achievement and phonics skills among a group of second graders. The authors considered these purposes or objectives to be measureable by two standardized tests, the *California Reading Test* (Lower Primary) and the *McKee Inventory of Phonetic Skills.*

A comparison group was employed, namely: a group of second graders using a different reading program. To control for selection bias, Ss were randomly assigned to the two reading programs (the ideal arrangement). Moreover, selection factors (for example, I.Q., color vision) were compared after assignment to insure equivalent samples. Sex was used as a control variable to insure equal numbers of boys and girls in each group.

Both the California and McKee tests were administered on a pre-and posttest basis to both test and comparison groups. Alternate forms of the California Reading Test were employed to reduce instrumentation bias.

Because analysis of variance showed the two programs to have similar effects on reading and phonetic skills, it was concluded that the *Words in Color* program was not superior to the comparison program.

$$* \qquad * \qquad *$$

Summative evaluation as described in this chapter is an application of the research approach described and advocated in this book. The research model is consistent and systematic and often allows the researcher to attribute cause and effect or to make inferences. Since decision-makers must make decisions about cause and effect, this information is invaluable. Where necessary, quasi-experimental designs may be employed for evaluation purposes. Though alternative evaluation models (which do not include the many requirements of research design) are probably more efficient and easier to use, they are also further removed from cause and effect, and thus more judgmental or intuitive. The purpose of this chapter has not been to contrast these approaches, but to develop one that is a natural outgrowth of the rest of the book. In a sense, this chapter represents a strategy for summarizing and illustrating the research approach developed in the book.

RECOMMENDED READINGS

American Educational Research Association. Curriculum evaluation. *Review of Educational Research*, 1969, *39,* whole no. 3.

American Education Research Association. Educational evaluation. *Review of Educational Research*, 1970, *40,* whole no. 2.

National Society for the Study of Education. *Education evaluation: New roles, new means.* Sixty-eighth yearbook, Part II. Chicago: University of Chicago Press, 1969.

Smith, B. O. (Ed.) *AERA monograph series on curriculum evaluation.* Chicago: Rand McNally, 1967–1970.

Tuckman, B. W. and Edwards, K. J. A systems model for instructional design and management. *Educational Technology*, 1971, *XI* (no. 9), 21–26.

COMPETENCY TEST EXERCISES

1. You have run a training program and have collected data describing trainee performance at the end of the program. At the same time, another program has been in operation presumably to meet the same objectives as yours. You have also administered your performance test to the trainees in this other program at the end of training. This is called _____(formative, summative) evaluation.

2. You are designing training materials. After each unit is written, you try it out on a test group. The performance of this group on the end-of-unit test is then reported to the materials developers who use this information to evaluate and revise the unit. This is called _____(formative, summative) evaluation.

3. Listed below are a number of statements. Some of them represent steps in an evaluation study. Write a number next to those that are steps in an evaluation study, indicating their order in the sequence.
   a. selecting a comparison group
   b. developing feedback forms
   c. stating program objectives in behavioral terms
   d. collecting and analyzing data
   e. constructing a test to measure program objectives
   f. identifying the intervening variables
   g. identifying program objectives

4. Design an evaluation study to evaluate this book. Describe each step in the process, being as concrete as possible.

References Cited in the Text

American Psychological Association. *Publication manual* (revised). Washington, D. C.: American Psychological Association, 1967.

Anderson, H. L. Acquiescence response bias to difficult achievement-type true-false tests of male high-school students exhibiting rule breaking or rule obeying behavior. New Brunswick, N.J.: Rutgers University, unpublished doctoral dissertation, 1969.

Bales, R. F. *Interaction process analysis: a method for the study of small groups.* Reading, Mass.: Addison-Wesley, 1950.

Bales, R. F. *Personality and interpersonal behavior.* New York: Holt, Rinehart, and Winston, 1970.

Borkowski, F. T. The relationship of work quality in undergraduate music curricula to effectiveness of instrumental music teaching in the public schools. *Journal of Experimental Education,* 1970, *39,* 14–19.

Brower, E. The office employment expectations of white and nonwhite business education students. Philadelphia: Temple University, unpublished doctoral dissertation, 1970.

Brown, J. A. C. *The social psychology of industry.* Middlesex, England: Penguin Books, 1954.

Bryan, R. C. *Reactions to teachers by students, parents, and administrators.* Kalamazoo, Mich.: Western Michigan University (U.S. Office of Education Cooperative Research Project No. 668), 1963.

Buros, O. K. (Ed.) *The sixth mental measurement yearbook.* Highland Park, N.J.: The Gryphon Press, 1965.

Buzzell, C. H. Incidents of geographic and occupational mobility among certified electronic technicians in the middle-Atlantic states. New Brunswick, N.J.: Rutgers University, unpublished doctoral dissertation, 1970.

Campbell, D. T.   Reforms as experiments. *American Psychologist,* 1969, *4,* 409–429.

Campbell, D. T. and Stanley, J. C.   Experimental and quasi-experimental designs for research on teaching. In N. L. Gage (Ed), *Handbook of research on teaching.* Chicago: Rand-McNally, 1963, pp. 171–246.

Campbell, J. P. and Dunnette, M. D.   Effectiveness of T-group experiences in managerial training and development. *Psychological Bulletin,* 1968, *70,* 73–104.

Campbell, W. G.   *Form and style in thesis writing* (3rd ed.) Boston: Houghton-Mifflin, 1969.

Childers, P. R., and Haas, Virginia J.   Effect of detailed guidance on the writing efficiency of college freshmen. *Journal of Experimental Education,* 1970, *39,* 20–23.

Clark, C. A. and Walberg, H. J.   The influence of massive rewards on reading achievement in potential urban school dropouts. *American Educational Research Journal,* 1968, *5,* 305–310.

Coughlan, R. J.   The factorial structure of teacher work values. *American Educational Research Journal,* 1969, *6,* 169–190.

Cummings, R. D.   Defensiveness and academic achievement in sixth-grade children as a function of the interaction of the perceptual attitudes, field articulation and gestalt perception. New Brunswick, N.J.: Rutgers University, unpublished doctoral dissertation, 1967.

Dixon, W. J. (Ed.) *Biomedical computer programs.* Berkeley: University of California Press, 1968.

Dunham, J. L. and Bunderson, C. V.   Effect of decision-rule instruction upon the relationship of cognitive abilities to performance in multiple-category concept problems. *Journal of Educational Psychology,* 1969, *60,* 121–125.

Edwards, A. L.   *Techniques of attitude scale construction.* New York: Appleton-Century-Crofts, 1957.

Edwards, A. L.   *Manual: Edwards personal preference schedule* (revised). New York: The Psychological Corporation, 1959.

Eninger, M. U. (Project director) *The process and product of T and I high-school level vocational education in the United States: the product.* Pittsburgh: American Institutes for Research, 1965.

Feshbach, Norma D.   Student teacher preferences for elementary school pupils varying in personality characteristics. *Journal of Educational Psychology,* 1969, *60,* 126–132.

Flanders, N. A.   Teacher influence, pupil attitudes, and achievement. Washington, D. C.: U.S. Office of Education (Cooperative Research Monograph No. 12), 1965.

Frase, L. T. Cybernetic control of memory while reading connected discourse. *Journal of Educational Psychology*, 1969, *60*, 49–55.

Halpin, A. W. *Theory and research in administration*. New York: Macmillan, 1966.

Hays, W. L. *Statistics for psychologists*. New York: Holt, Rinehart, and Winston, 1963.

Herman, W. L. Jr., Potterfield, J. E., Dayton, C. M., and Amershek, K. G. The relationship of teacher-centered activities and pupil-centered activities to pupil achievement and interest in 18 fifth-grade social studies classes. *American Educational Research Journal*, 1969, *6*, 227–240.

Jacobson, L. I., Dickinson, T. C., Fleishman, Joyce M., and Haraguchi, Rosemary S. Relationship of intelligence and mediating processes to concept learning. *Journal of Educational Psychology*, 1969, *60*, 109–112.

Johnson, H. H. and Foley, Jeanne M. Some effects of placebo and experiment conditions in research on methods of teaching. *Journal of Educational Psychology*, 1969, *60*, 6–10.

Kaufman, J. J., Schaefer, C. J., et al. *The role of the secondary schools in the preparation of youth for employment*. University Park, Pa.: The Pennsylvania State University, Institute for Research on Human Resources, 1967.

Kean, J. M. Linguistic structures of second- and fifth-grade teachers' oral classroom language. *American Educational Research Journal*, 1968, *5*, 599–615.

Khan, S. B. Affective correlates of academic achievement. *Journal of Educational Psychology*, 1969, *60*, 216–221.

King, F. J., Roberts, D., and Kropp, R. P. Relationship between ability measures and achievement under four methods of teaching elementary set concepts. *Journal of Educational Psychology*, 1969, *60*, 244–247.

Kreit, L. H. The effects of test-taking practice on pupil test performance. *American Educational Research Journal*, 1968, *5*, 616–625.

Laughlin, P. R., Moss, Irene L., and Miller, Susan M. Information-processing in children as a function of adult model, stimulus display, school grade, and sex. *Journal of Educational Psychology*, 1969, *60*, 188–193.

Lemke, E. A., Randle, K., and Robertshaw, C. S. Effect of degree of initial acquisition, group size, and general mental ability on concept learning and transfer. *Journal of Educational Psychology*, 1969, *60*, 75–78.

Lewin, K., Lippitt, R., and White, R. K. Patterns of aggressive behavior in experimentally created "social climates." *Journal of Social Psychology*, 1939, *10*, 271–299.

Lippitt, R. and White, R. K. An experimental study of leadership and group life. In E. E. Maccoby, *Readings in social psychology* (3rd ed.). New York: Holt, Rinehart, and Winston, 1958, pp. 496–510.

Lockmiller, Pauline and DiNello, M. C. Words in color versus a basal reader program with retarded readers in grade 2. *Journal of Educational Research*, 1970, *63*, 330–334.

McCall, K. M. Modification of teacher behavior and self-perception: effects of dissonance and coded feedback. New Brunswick, N.J.: Rutgers University, unpublished doctoral dissertation, 1969.

Morrison, Evelyn. Underachievement among preadolescent boys considered in relationship to positive aggression. *Journal of Educational Psychology*, 1969, *60*, 168–173.

Osgood, C. E., Suci, G. J., and Tannenbaum, P. H. *The measurement of meaning*. Urbana, Ill.: University of Illinois Press, 1957.

Perticone, E. X. The effects of incidental stimulus variation on task persistence in children. New Brunswick, N.J.: Rutgers University, unpublished doctoral dissertation, 1969.

Peterson, I. M. School superintendents' perceptions of influential factors in the adoption of secondary-school curricular innovations. New Brunswick, N.J.: Rutgers University, unpublished doctoral dissertation, 1968.

Ripple, R. E., Millman, J., and Glock, M. D. Learner characteristics and instructional mode: a search for disordinal interactions. *Journal of Educational Psychology*, 1969, *60*, 113–120.

Rosenthal, R. *Experimenter effects in behavioral research*. New York: Appleton-Century-Crofts, 1966.

Rosenthal, R. and Jacobson, Lenore. *Pygmalion in the classroom*. New York: Holt, Rinehart, and Winston, 1968.

Schachter, S. *Obesity and eating*. Science, 1968, *161*, 751–755.

Scriven, M. The methodology of evaluation. In R. W. Tyler, R. M. Gagne, and M. Scriven (Eds.), *Perspectives of curriculum evaluation*. Chicago: Rand-McNally, 1967, pp. 39–83.

Sergiovanni, T. J., Metzcus, R., and Burden, L. Toward a particularistic approach to leadership style: some findings. *American Educational Research Journal*, 1969, *6*, 62–79.

Sieber, S. D. Survey research in education. The case of the misconstrued technique. *Phi Delta Kappan*, 1969, *50*, 273–276.

Siegel, S. *Nonparametric statistics for the behavioral sciences*. New York: McGraw-Hill, 1956.

Smith, M. P. Mud-pie research. Paper presented at meeting of Eastern Psychological Association, New York, 1966.

Spenciner, Loraine J. Differences between blind and partially-sighted children in rejection by sighted peers in the integrated classrooms, grades 2–8. New Brunswick, N.J.: Rutgers University, unpublished study, 1969.

345

Tallmadge, G. K., and Shearer, J. W. Relationships among learning styles, instructional methods, and the nature of learning experiences. *Journal of Educational Psychology*, 1969, *60*, 222–230.

Thorndike, E. L. *Human learning.* New York: The Century Company, 1931.

Thorndike, R. L. and Hagen, Elizabeth. *Measurement and evaluation in psychology and education* (2nd ed.) New York: John Wiley and Sons, 1961.

Townsend, J. C. *Introduction to experimental method.* New York: McGraw-Hill, 1953.

Trow, M. Education and survey research. In C. Clock (Ed.), *Survey research in the social sciences.* New York: Russell Sage, 1967.

Tuckman, B. W. Personality structure, group composition, and group functioning. *Sociometry*, 1964, *4*, 469–487.

Tuckman, B. W. Interpersonal probing and revealing and systems of integrative complexity. *Journal of Personality and Social Psychology*, 1966, *3*, 655–664.

Tuckman, B. W. *A study of the effectiveness of directive versus nondirective vocational teachers as a function of student characteristics and course format.* New Brunswick, N.J.: Rutgers University (U.S. Office of Education, Bureau of Research Project No. 6-2300) 1968.

Tuckman, B. W. A technique for the assessment of teacher directiveness. *Journal of Educational Research*, 1970, *63*, 395–400.

Tuckman, B. W., Henkelman, J., O'Shaughnessy, G. P., and Cole, Mildred B. Induction and transfer of search sets. *Journal of Educational Psychology*, 1968, *59*, 59–68.

Tuckman, B. W., and Oliver, W. F. Effectiveness of feedback to teachers as a function of source. *Journal of Educational Psychology*, 1968, *59*, 297–301.

Webb, E. J., Campbell, D. T., Schwartz, R. D., and Sechrest, L. *Unobtrusive measures; nonreactive research in the social sciences.* Chicago: Rand-McNally, 1966.

Weener, P. D. Social dialect differences and the recall of verbal messages. *Journal of Educational Psychology*, 1969, *60*, 194–199.

Weiss, R. L., Sales, S. M., and Bode, S. Student authoritarianism and teacher authoritarianism as factors in the determination of student performance and attitudes. *Journal of Experimental Education*, 1970, *38*, 83–87.

Welch, W. W., and Walberg, H. J. Pretest and sensitization effects in curriculum evaluation. *American Educational Research Journal*, 1970, *7*, 605–614.

Winer, B. J. *Statistical principles in experimental design.* New York: McGraw-Hill, 1962.

APPENDIX A: SAMPLE STUDIES

Sample Study I

EFFECTIVENESS OF FEEDBACK TO TEACHERS AS A FUNCTION OF SOURCE[1]

Bruce W. Tuckman and *Wilmot F. Oliver*
Rutgers, The State University

Two hundred eighty-six teachers were separated by years of teaching experience and subjected to 1 of 4 conditions: (a) feedback from students only, (b) from supervisors, i.e., vice-principals only, (c) from both students and supervisors, and (d) from neither (no feedback). It was found that student feedback led to a positive change among teachers (as measured by change in students' ratings across a twelve-week interval). Supervisor feedback added nothing to this effect when combined with student feedback, and when alone, produced change in a direction opposite to the feedback as compared to the no-feedback condition. Less experienced teachers showed greater receptivity to student feedback than their more experienced counterparts while the reverse held true for receptivity to supervisor feedback.

The problem of modifying the behavior of teachers is one that has been

SOURCE: Effectiveness of feedback to teachers as a function of source, from *Journal of Educational Psychology*, 1968, *59*, 297–301. Reprinted by permission of authors and publisher.

[1] This study was, in part, the doctoral dissertation of the junior author. It was supported, in part, by Grant No. 6–8327 from the United States Office of Education.

submitted to close scrutiny from a variety of vantage points. Techniques such as microteaching and the use of interaction process analysis have been employed, primarily with student teachers, as a means of altering their behavior. Underscoring the entire rationale for this approach, Daw and Gage (1967) recently said:

> It is highly plausible that feedback regarding how others feel about one's behavior will affect one's behavior. Whether this maxim will hold under a given set of practical circumstance must, however, be determined empirically (p. 181).

This study was an attempt to extend this "maxim" to conditions as yet untested.

Bryan (1963) has shown that teachers will alter their behavior as the outcome of receiving feedback from their students. The purpose of this study was to replicate Bryan's basic finding, using his instrument, and then to extend this finding by determining the relative effects of feedback from students and from supervisors (i.e., administrators responsible for instruction) on teachers' behavior. Moreover, Bryan's study did not include control over the variable of amount of teaching experience of teachers whose behavior was to be changed. His experimental and control groups showed an imbalance on this variable at the conclusion of his experiment with the preponderance of less experienced teachers appearing in the experimental group. An additional purpose of the present study was to systematically introduce years of teaching experience as an experimental variable so that its effects, if any, could be determined.

Finally, the present study was carried out with vocational teachers, in order to demonstrate additional generalizability for the basic finding obtained by Bryan using primarily teachers of academic subjects.

The fact that teachers change as the result of student feedback has also been demonstrated by Gage, Runkel, and Chatterjee (1960). Their study also showed that amount of change was related to the interval between pretest and posttest. Daw and Gage (1967) have shown, furthermore, that feedback from teachers can be used to alter the behavior of principals, but that the amount of change is not a function of the pretest-posttest interval.

In this study, as in previous studies in this area, the measurement of change in teacher behavior was inferential. Students were asked to rate their teacher twice, with a twelve-week interval separating these ratings (during which time the treatments could take effect). Behavior change by teachers was inferred from a difference between post-interval and pre-interval ratings. Remmers (1963) has shown that students, as a measuring instrument, are as reliable as the best mental and educational paper-and-pencil tests and can discriminate between aspects of teacher behavior (see also Tuckman, 1967). Thus, the dependent variable was identified as change in teachers' behavior with the recognition that this was inferential.

The expectation that years of teaching experience would be a significant variable was based on studies such as that of Ryans (1964) and Peterson (1964) who have shown that teachers' behavioral patterns change in a systematic fashion as a function of age. While age and years of teaching experience are not the same variable, they are assuredly related, with the latter being perhaps the more conceptually meaningful in an educational context.

PROBLEM

To determine the relative effects of students and supervisors as feedback sources for teachers, four conditions were run. In the first condition student feedback alone was employed; in the second, supervisor feedback was employed alone (the supervisor being an administrator, usually a principal or vice-principal responsible for the teaching activities of teachers); in the third, both feedback sources were employed concomitantly; and in the fourth, no feedback was given. Teachers were further classified as to teaching experience and systematically assigned to conditions on that basis.

It was hypothesized that: (a) teachers receiving feedback would change more than teachers not receiving feedback (essentially a replication of Bryan's results); (b) amount of change in teachers' behavior would vary as a function of feedback source; (c) years of teaching experience and amount of change would be inversely related.

METHOD

Sample

The sample consisted of 286 teachers of vocational subjects at the high school or technical institute level. Schools were selected from New Jersey and surrounding out-of-state counties and virtually all the vocational teachers in the schools used took part in the study. Participating teachers had a median class size of 15 students who were either in the tenth, eleventh, or thirteenth grade.

Measurement of Teacher Behavior

Teacher behavior was measured by the Student-Opinion Questionnaire (SOQ) developed by Bryan (1963). This instrument includes ten rating scales on which teacher is judged as to: his (a) knowledge of his subject, (b) ability to explain, (c) fairness, (d) ability to maintain discipline, (e) degree of sympathetic understanding, (f) ability to make you learn, (g) ability to be interesting, (h) ability to get things done efficiently, (i) ability to get students to think for themselves, and (j) general all-round teaching ability. Each scale has five points labeled: below average, average, good, very good, and the very best.

Bryan (1963) has reported reliability coefficients for the ten items on the SOQ of from .75 to .95 for chance-half averages for 50 classes. For whole classes of 28 students on the average, coefficients of from .86 to .92 were obtained.

On the reverse side of the SOQ are four open-ended questions dealing with the course and teacher, reflecting on things that are liked about each and suggestions for the improvement of each.

Feedback Conditions

Students only. Students completed the SOQ, and their ratings on the ten scales were averaged. The teacher was presented with a graph showing the average student judgment for each item. In addition, a summation of the students' responses on the open-ended questions were provided. Teachers were told that the feedback was from their students.

Supervisor only. The teacher's supervisor (either the principal, vice-principal, or assistant principal) completed the SOQ, and his ratings on each item were given to the teacher in graphical form along with a summary of his answers to the open-ended questions. The teacher was told that this rating was made by the supervisor. (In this condition, student ratings were also obtained although these were not made available to the teacher.)

Students and Supervisor. The teacher's supervisor and students completed the SOQ, and feedback from each was given separately, along with identification of source in the same manner as in the first two conditions.

No feedback. Students completed the SOQ but no feedback was provided to the teachers.
All initial testing was done in the late fall.

Years of Teaching Experience

Based on information from a personal information form, teachers were categorized as having 1–3 years of teaching experience, 4–10 years of teaching experience, or 11 or more years of teaching experience. Teachers from each group were then randomly assigned to each condition. The overall design of the study and assignment of teachers to conditions is shown in Table 1.

Measurement of Change in Teacher's Behavior

In the late spring, following a twelve-week interval after the initial testing, students of each of the teachers in the study completed the SOQ. The measure of change in each condition was the sum of the differences between the pre-interval judgments by the students on the ten items and their post-interval judgments. Ratings on each item were averaged across students and the pre-interval average on each item was then subtracted from the post-interval

Table 1 *Design of the experiment: assignment of teachers to treatment and experience groups.*

Condition	Years of Experience of Instructor					
	1–3 years (A_1)		4–10 years (A_2)		11 or more years (A_3)	
	B_1	B_2	B_1	B_2	B_1	B_2
Student Feedback (C_1)	14	18	19	18	18	13
No Student Feedback (C_2)	39	32	25	31	32	27

Note: Cell entries are number of observations per cell; $N = 286$; Abbreviations B_1 = supervisory feedback, B_2 = no supervisory feedback.

average to yield a change score on each of the ten items. These ten-item change scores were summed to obtain a total change score. Student judgments were used throughout as a measure of change to maintain a constant measuring instrument across conditions. This was seen as justifiable since pre-interval ratings by students did not differ significantly from those of supervisors in conditions where both were obtained and the latter were used as the feedback source.

All test administration was accomplished by the local vocational guidance counselor.

Analysis

For purposes of analysis, the four feedback conditions (conditions 1–4) were treated as two factors: supervisor feedback and student feedback with two levels on each: present and absent. The four conditions were thus labeled as follows: $(B_1 C_1)$ student and supervisor feedback, $(B_1 C_2)$ supervisor feedback only, $(B_2 C_1)$ student feedback only, and $(B_2 C_2)$ no feedback (see Table 1). Years of teaching experience was the first factor and had three levels. Subsequently, a $3 \times 2 \times 2$ analysis of variance using the unweighted means solution for unequal cell entries (Winer, 1962) was carried out on the total change score of each teacher. (Each teacher was used only once in the design.) In addition, direct mean comparisons were made using the Duncan multiple range test (Duncan 1955).[2]

---

[2] A fifth condition, called the posttest-only control group by Daw and Gage (1967), was also run with an additional 15 teachers. These teachers were rated by their students only at the end of the interval. The purpose of this condition was to determine whether the pretest or pre-interval measurement had a sensitizing effect on the raters or teachers (cf. Campbell and Stanley, 1963). A comparison of the mean for this posttest-only control group to the mean on the post-interval measurement for the no-feedback group showed them to be comparable. Thus, it was concluded that test sensitization was not a source of invalidity.

RESULTS

The results of the analysis of variance for the total change score showed that the presence of student feedback (factor C) had a significant effect on teachers' behavior as compared to its absence ($F = 5.941; df = 1/274; p < .025$) while the presence of supervisor feedback (factor B) produced no significant effect ($F = 1.064; df = 1/274$). The years-of-experience variable (factor A) also failed to produce a significant effect ($F = 0.701; df = 2/274$), and none of the interactions achieved significance at the .05 level ($F < 1$ in each case).

In an effort to delineate further the feedback effects, means for the four feedback conditions were compared, as shown in Table 2. From the table it can be seen that both conditions involving student feedback showed significantly greater change than both conditions not involving student feedback.[3] Feedback from students alone and from students and supervisors combined were statistically comparable, indicating a failure for feedback from supervisors to generate any change beyond that accounted for by student feedback alone. Finally, feedback from supervisors alone produced a significantly greater negative shift (i.e., a change in the opposite direction of that recommended by the feedback) than no feedback at all.

Thus, student feedback "improved" teacher behavior as compared to no feedback. Supervisor feedback produced no additional effect when combined with student feedback, and an adverse effect when used alone.

Table 2 *Mean total change scores by feedback condition and their comparison by Duncan multiple range test.*

Students Only	Students and Supervisors	Supervisors Only	No Feedback
−.054	−.385	−2.449*	−1.234*

*Significantly different from all other means, $p < .01$ (with exception of difference between second and fourth means, where $p < .05$)

[3]Throughout this description, results are referred to as changing "more" or "less". However, in the light of the fact that almost all of the means are negative, changing more means showing a lesser negative shift (i.e., a smaller negative change score) while changing less means showing a greater negative shift (i.e., a larger negative change score). This tendency for ratings to be less positive following the interval as compared to those preceding the interval were not attributable to a testing effect (see the preceding footnote). One must conclude that students as raters are more negatively inclined toward their teachers in the spring (after experiencing them for a year) than in the fall. Thus, the positive effect of feedback, when it occurred, was to reduce this tendency toward greater negativity of ratings (i.e., make the negative score smaller or positive).

DISCUSSION

The first hypothesis of this study predicted that feedback (source unspecified) would yield a greater positive change than no feedback, while the second hypothesis predicted different effects for the different feedback sources. The surprising finding of this study was that teachers receiving feedback from supervisors changed more in the opposite direction from the feedback than the spontaneous shift obtained in the no-feedback condition. Thus, the first hypothesis holds true for student feedback (a replication of Bryan's findings) which led to effects in excess of the no-feedback condition. Supervisory feedback added nothing to the student feedback effect when they were combined. (If anything it reduced it, but not significantly so.) Since supervisor feedback had the opposite effect than predicted, the second hypothesis was confirmed—that is, the feedback sources did have different effects. If in the first hypothesis, it was simply predicted that feedback would produce greater changes than no feedback, it would have been confirmed. Certainly this experiment suggests that teachers react to feedback, irrespective of source, with these reactions being positive only in the case of student feedback.

The question of why teachers reacted to feedback from supervisors as they did is immediately raised. It can only be surmised that teachers are defensive toward (or even hostile to) administrators who, in the absence of much basis for judgment, attempt to tell them how to teach. Of interest, though, is the fact that within the educational milieu, the only source of feedback to teachers, typically, are their supervisors. The data collected here indicate that such feedback is doing more harm than good, with the "best" source of feedback, students, overlooked.

The third hypothesis of the present study predicted an inverse relation between years of experience and receptivity to feedback. While the obtained relationship was not sufficiently strong to prove significant, the most experienced teacher group tended to show the least receptivity to feedback from their students, as the hypothesis predicted. However, the least experienced teacher group tended to show the least receptivity (i.e., the least relatively positive shift) to feedback from their supervisor – the reverse of the hypothesis.

Finally, a last question must be raised. Why do all the change scores tend to be negative with positive change being measured in terms of the "smallness" of the negative score? The use of a group of teachers whose students made only the post-interval ratings indicated that the test-retest phenomenon was not responsible for this shift from pre- to postratings. It appeared that students are more critical of their teachers at the end of the term than at the middle. At the time when the teacher is about to evaluate and grade the student, the student perhaps replies in kind. Thus, a positive change appeared as lessening in the "naturally" occurring negative shift. Researchers interested in using student judgments are cautioned to use the same starting and ending times for all groups to avoid the confusion of this end-of-term effect. September to January will not lead to the same effect as February to June.

REFERENCES

Bryan, R. C. Reactions to teachers by students, parents, and administrators. (United States Office of Education, Cooperative Research Project No. 668). Kalamazoo: Western Michigan University, 1963.

Campbell, D. T. and Stanley, J. C. Experimental and quasi-experimental designs for research on teaching. In N. L. Gage (Ed.), *Handbook of research on teaching*. Chicago: Rand-McNally, 1963.

Daw, R. W. and Gage, N. L. Effect of feedback from teachers to principals. *Journal of Educational Psychology*, 1967, *58*, 181–188.

Duncan, D. B. Multiple range and multiple *F* tests. *Biometrics*, 1955, *11*, 1–42.

Gage, N. L., Runkel, P. J., and Chatterjee, B. B. *Equilibrium theory and behavior change: an experiment in feedback from pupils to teachers*. (Report No. 6 in "Studies in the generality and behavioral correlates of social perception.") Urbana: Bureau of Educational Research, College of Education, University of Illinois, 1960.

Peterson, W. A. Age, teacher role, and the institutional setting. In B. J. Biddle and W. J. Ellena (Eds.), *Contemporary research on teacher effectiveness*. New York: Holt, Rinehart, and Winston, 1964.

Remmers, H. H. Rating methods in research on teaching. In N. L. Gage (Ed.), *Handbook of research on teaching*. Chicago: Rand-McNally, 1963.

Ryans, D. G. Characteristics of teachers. In B. J. Biddle and W. J. Ellena (Eds.), *Contemporary research on teacher effectiveness*. New York: Holt, Rinehart, and Winston, 1964.

Tuckman, B. W. *A study of the effectiveness of directive versus nondirective vocational teachers as a function of student characteristics and course format*. (United States Office of Education, Project No. 6–2300, Progress Report No. 1) New Brunswick, N. J.: Rutgers, The State University, 1967.

Winer, B. J. *Statistical principles in experimental design*. New York: McGraw-Hill, 1962.

Sample Study II

THE INFLUENCE OF MASSIVE REWARDS ON
READING ACHIEVEMENT IN POTENTIAL URBAN SCHOOL DROPOUTS

Carl A. Clark
Chicago State College

Herbert J. Walberg
Educational Testing Service[1]

Most theories of learning emphasize reinforcement as an important deter-
minant of behavior, and yet no randomized, controlled experiments have been
done in school classrooms (Parton and Ross, 1965). This study reports an investigation of this problem in an after-school reading program for children in the
Chicago Public Schools.[2] The experiment took place in the south side of the
innercity, an area populated by rural, Negro migrants from Alabama, Georgia,
and Mississippi and their first and second generations. The neighborhood is
characterized by low standards of living and high rates of social pathology:
unemployment, crime, and school attrition. Nationally-standardized achievement tests of children in this part of the city show that they are from one to
four years behind typical levels of children in the same age and grade. One
can imagine—and confirm by observation—that for these children, school work

SOURCE: From *American Educational Research Journal*, 1968, *5*, 305–310. Copyright by
American Educational Research Association. Reprinted by permission of authors and
publisher.

1. Now at Harvard University.
2. This research was supported by a Ford Foundation grant to the Chicago Public Schools
under the Great Cities School Improvement Program.

is frustrating and negatively reinforcing. The object of this study was to make the reinforcement positive with massive verbal rewards given by the teacher and tallied by each child, and to observe its effect on reading achievement.

There were three problems faced in conducting this experiment. The first had to do with the random assignment of pupils to experimental and control conditions necessary for statistical tests. If there is random assignment within classrooms, there is the problem of interaction between experimental and control subjects. If intact classes are assigned to experimental and control conditions, there is the problem of non-chance differences and there are usually not enough classes available for an adequate "groups within treatments" or "random replications" design (Lindquist, 1953). Fortunately, for our experiment, the administrators and teachers cooperated insofar as to enable random assignment of pupils to class as well as classes to experimental and control conditions.[3]

The second problem was the control and measurement of rewards. For the present study we used individual cards given daily to each pupil, each card containing numbered squares the pupil could circle when rewarded and told to do so by the teacher. The basic reason for the use of the cards was not to introduce a special reward system, but to have a means of quantifying the number of rewards received by each pupil. Other systems are possible, one being to have observers record the rewards; but this system involves an intrusion into the normal classroom situation, and could have its own effect, hard to assess. Another way is to have the teacher record the rewards given to each pupil, but this method takes a good deal of the teacher's time and attention from his work.

With the card system used, the cards could be collected at the end of the period and the number of rewards for each pupil tallied. Of course this system is not foolproof; a pupil could mark his card when he is not receiving rewards. In order to help control for this possibility, the pupils were given special blue pencils with blue-colored "leads" that they were to pick up and use only when, after being praised, they were told to circle a number. Numbers circled with their ordinary pencils would not count, and it would be fairly obvious if a pupil picked up and used the special blue pencil—obvious to the teacher and to the other pupils.

A special problem with the use of the blue pencil and card reward recording system was the possible "gadget effect." So far as this effect in itself contributed a reward there was not much of a problem since we were more concerned with the fact of reward than the type of reward. We did two things, however, to lessen and to control for a "gadget effect" and for the so-called "Hawthorne effect." One was to have both the experimental and control groups use the cards for tallying rewards, and the other was to have both groups go through a control period of several sessions, during which time the novelty effect could wear off.

Finally, there was the problem of measuring the effect of rewards on the dependent variable, which was reading achievement in this experiment. When pre and post test scores are used over a comparatively short time interval, several problems are introduced into the analysis: there are the effects of regression

[3]The writers wish to thank Louise Dougherty and Alfred Rudd for administrative support, the cooperating teachers for their participation, and Ina Turner for clerical assistance.

toward the mean, item memory practice, and others which obscure the results. It was decided, therefore, that the main analysis would be based on a single reading test given at the end of the experiment. Some control over initial individual differences would be attained by using IQ as a control variable in an analysis of covariance procedure.

METHOD

Subjects

The 110 children in the experiment were from 10 to 13 years of age and from one to four years behind in their school work. For these reasons they were considered potential dropouts and were assigned on a random basis to nine classes in an after-school remedial reading program with from 10 to 15 children in each class.

Procedure

At the beginning of the experiment all the teachers and children were asked to follow the same instructions. Each child received the especially prepared tally card which we have described, and the teachers were asked to distribute the praise rewards so that each child, even the very slow ones, would get at least several each day. After the teacher made a rewarding remark, she directed the rewarded child to make a tally mark on his card on a list of numbers, from 1 to 50. The child made the marks sequentially, beginning with number one. At the end of the class session he wrote down the total number of tally marks (therefore of rewards) he had received for the day. The teachers checked the card markings for accuracy, and sent the cards to the experimenters after each class.

After six sessions the reward rates per child and per teacher appeared to stabilize, and the five teachers (randomly determined) of the experimental groups were confidentially asked to double or triple the number of rewards while the four teachers of the control groups were asked to "keep up the good work." After these requests were made, large increments appeared in the number of tally marks on cards for the experimental group while the number for the control group remained at approximately the same levels.

At the end of the second three week period, the 62 children in the experimental groups and the 48 in the control groups took the Science Research Associates Reading Test, Intermediate Form. The total raw scores only were used in the analyses.

RESULTS

The mean for the experimental groups was 31.62, with a standard deviation of 7.43, and the mean for the control groups was 26.86, with a standard deviation of 8.60. The analysis of variance for the unadjusted raw scores produced an F-ratio of 9.52 (p less than 1 percent; see Table 1). In the covariance analysis with Kuhlman-Anderson IQs as the control variable, the F-ratio was 7.90 (p less than 1 percent). This F-ratio is smaller than the one for unadjusted scores, even though the error mean square is smaller, because the between treatments mean square for adjusted scores was only slightly lower. The mean IQ for the experimental group, 92.05, was slightly but not significantly higher than the control group mean, 90.73.

Table 1 *Analyses of variance and covariance for SRA reading and K-A intelligence test scores*

Scores	Sum of Squares	df	Mean Squares	F-Ratio
SRA Reading				
Between	616.82	1	616.82	9.52*
Within	6,994.45	108	64.76	
Total	7,611.27	109		
K-A Intelligence				
Between	176.55	1	176.55	1.84
Within	10,337.41	108	95.72	
Total	10,513.96	109		
Adjusted SRA**				
Between	488.40	1	488.40	7.90*
Within	6,614.43	107	61.82	
Total	7,102.83	108		

*Significant at the 1 percent level.
**The correlation between the SRA and the KA was .26.

DISCUSSION

The hypothesis was strongly supported: children who were massively rewarded scored significantly higher on a standardized reading test. Although the idea that reinforcement enhances learning has long been known in the field of psychology, it seemed revolutionary to the teachers and children in this experiment. It is not enough apparently, simply to instruct student teachers or regular teachers to use rewards to control behavior. The use of a reward tally card which focused the attention of the teacher and the child on the rewards seemed much more convincing. The request to distribute the rewards to insure that each child got at least a few each time also had a beneficial effect.

Some logical steps follow from this study. One would examine the effects of distinct reward schedules (ratio and interval); the ones used in this study were mixed. Another would determine the long term efficacy of massive rewards. One interesting hypothesis is that it is the increase differential across time that increases learning rather than continuous high rates which may lead to satiation. A third possible avenue of research would be to investigate the validity of these findings across children grouped by age, socioeconomic class, sex, school class and other relevant factors.

Parton and Ross (1965) in a review of research on social reinforcement of children's motor behavior have criticized the methods of previous studies in this area particularly with regard to the common omission of the control group. Methodologically, we have shown here that it is possible to randomly assign children to experimental and control groups in school classrooms, to randomly administer (with the class as the unit) an experimental treatment (massive verbal rewards) in measured amounts (tallied on cards by the pupils themselves), and to demonstrate significant differences between groups on a measure of achievement (a standardized reading test). Theoretically, we have confirmed the hypothesis from reinforcement theories of learning that verbal rewards have efficacy in the control of operant behavior in human subjects. And lastly, from a practical point of view, we have shown in an actual educational setting, that the teacher's increased use of verbal praise has a positive effect on the scholastic learning of children who are potential dropouts from inner-city schools.

REFERENCES

Lindquist, E. F. *Design and analysis of experiments in psychology and education.* Boston: Houghton-Mifflin, 1953.

Parton, David A. and Ross, Allan O. Social reinforcement of children's motor behavior: a review. *Psychological Bulletin*, 64:65–73, 1965.

Sample Study III

DIFFERENCES BETWEEN BLIND AND PARTIALLY-SIGHTED CHILDREN IN REJECTION BY SIGHTED PEERS IN INTEGRATED CLASSROOMS, GRADES 2-8*

Loraine J. Spenciner
Rutgers, The State University

Thirteen blind and 13 partially-sighted white children ranging in grades 2-8 were paired according to age, sex, and grade. Their sighted classmates were given questionnaires which contained the following questions: "List 5 boys or girls with whom you would *least* like to eat lunch. List 5 boys or girls whom you would *least* like to elect class leader. If you were having a party, who are the 5 boys or girls you would *least* like to invite?" It was found that blind children were significantly less rejected by their sighted peers than were partially-sighted children (at .05 level).

Educators of the visually handicapped have debated for many years the merits and disadvantages of placing blind and partially-seeing youngsters in integrated school programs with sighted youngsters as opposed to a residential program for the visually handicapped. However over the past years, one finds

---

*This study was completed by a graduate student in a course called Introduction to Educational Research and Methodology as part of the course requirement. It is intended to exemplify the kind of research undertaking from which students can learn in a course. This study is uncopyrighted. Reprinted by permission of the author.

more and more of a trend toward integrated programs with the handicapped child being served by an itinerant teacher or counselor.

Blind youngsters in such a program are fortunate in that the visiting counselor usually meets with them three to five times a week to work on Braille skills and other aids to help them keep up with their class. Problems which may have arisen with his classmates, teachers, or through other contacts are talked out. The partially-sighted youngsters are usually not seen as frequently: partly because they are usually able to keep up with their class by using a few visual aids. However it is often observed that these children have the more difficult time in making and keeping friends.

The purpose of this study was to examine the differences between blind and partially-sighted children and their rejection by sighted peers in integrated classrooms. Many authors feel that the attitudes present in the visually-handicapped child's milieu are significant in the kind of adaptation he makes with his handicap. Lukoff and Whiteman (1961) found in an attitude survey of blind and sighted respondents that social relations with sighted individuals were related to an independent-dependent component of attitudes toward blindness. However Greenberg, Herbert, and Jordan (1957) found one particular personality trait to be linked to degree of vision: the totally blind group was found to be less authoritarian than the partially-sighted group.

The present study hypothesized that blind children are less rejected by their sighted peers than are partially-sighted children in grades two through eight. The hypothesis is based in part on the work done by the following authors.

In a study observing sighted children's reactions to blind and partially-seeing children in nursery school and kindergarten (Wolman 1958), it was concluded that blindness does not prevent a child from being accepted by his sighted peers. Partially-sighted children were found to present more difficult problems.

Bateman and Wetherell (1967) obtained responses from teachers of the partially sighted. It was found that children with mild and severe visual defects revealed the former to be better socially adjusted. Both groups were better adjusted than the moderate defect group.

Using the Adolescent Emotional Factors Inventory, Baumen (1964) found that the partially seeing were more insecure than those who had less than travel vision.

Phelps (1955) explored the dynamics of partial sightedness. "As a child becomes aware that his perception is not quite the same as others about him, he tries to account for the difference he finds. Since he is physically unable to do this, his repeated attempts end in frustrating experiences and he learns to resort to round-about means." A partially-sighted child may react to his handicap in a number of ways. Sometimes he may be unable to handle the classroom situation and turns to gratification by other means or withdraws and refuses to participate with the others. He may become hyperactive, making a pest of himself in overdoing things, to draw the attention of others away from his visual defect. He may strike out at his tormentors; or he may capitalize on his visual defect to gain favor and attention (Phelps 1955).

In the present study, children with partial sight were defined as those with 20/70 or less vision in the better eye with correction but who were print readers (either large or regular print). Children defined as blind had light perception or less vision in the better eye and read only by Braille. Rejection was determined by sighted children's preferences on a questionnaire.

This study has direct significance in terms of the need for further counseling services in our integrated elementary schools. Often the child with enough usable vision for reading print is left to fend for himself in working out personal problems; whereas a blind child is given much time and counseling help. Itinerant teachers of the visually handicapped should carefully consider these findings in working with partially-sighted youngsters.

METHOD

Sample

The sample consisted of 13 blind and 13 partially-sighted white youngsters enrolled in public schools throughout the state of New Jersey. Children ranged in grades two through eighth. Blind and partially-sighted youngsters were paired according to sex, age, and grade. It was assumed that IQ would be reasonably accounted for (i.e. both very high and very low ends eliminated) if the children were in the approximate grade for their chronological age. Other factors such as albinism, hearing loss, cerebral palsy, etc., were eliminated by not including those children in the study. None of the children went to special sight-saving classes. All had been in their homeroom class since September.

Procedure

Homeroom teachers of both groups of visually-handicapped children were asked to administer the questionnaire to all the children in their class. They were given the following instructions:

> Please give one questionnaire to each child. If you run short, don't worry. Please do not tell the children these questionnaires were given to you by an educational counselor from the Commission for the Blind; and when returning them to the counselor, do not do so in front of the children. This is an untimed questionnaire. The following instructions should be read aloud to the class:
>> "Do *not* write your name on this paper. Please answer each question as carefully as possible by writing the names of five *classmates*. Use only those names of children in your home-room class. Use first names and last initials in your answers."
>
> Thank you for your cooperation.

The questionnaire contained the following three questions:

List 5 boys or girls with whom you would *least* like to eat lunch.

List 5 boys or girls whom you would *least* like to elect class leader.

If you were having a party, who are the 5 boys or girls you would *least* like to invite?

The questionnaire was scored by giving the blind or partially-sighted youngster one point for each time his name appeared on the questionnaires gathered from his class.

Analysis

Since the variances of the two groups were not homogeneous, the Mann-Whitney U statistic was employed; $\alpha = .05$ level of significance was used.

RESULTS

Blind children were found to be significantly less rejected by their sighted peers than were partially-sighted children at the .05 level of significance. The results were also significant at the .001 level.

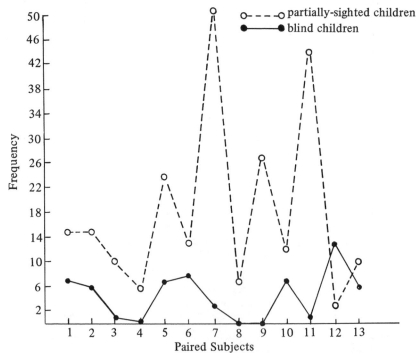

Figure 1 *Frequency with which the names of partially-sighted and blind children appeared on a rejection questionnaire submitted to their sighted classmates.*

Figure 1 shows the frequency with which the names of the two groups of visually-handicapped students appeared on their sighted classmates question-naires. In all instances but one, the names of partially-sighted children appeared more frequently. In most cases the partially-sighted student's name appeared at least twice as often as a blind student his same age, sex, and at the same grade level. In two cases the name of the partially-sighted child appeared 17 and 44 times as often as the blind student with whom he was paired.

Paired subjects are seen in ascending order of grade level in Figure 1, i.e., the children of pair 1 are in the second grade; pair 13 are in the eighth grade. It would not appear that grade level is a factor in determining the number of times the child's name is listed on the questionnaire. Names of blind or partially-sighted children appear neither more nor less frequently as grade level increases.

Table 1 *Frequency according to question with which
the names of partially-sighted and
blind children appeared on a
rejection questionnaire
submitted to sighted classmates.*

Question 1: List 5 boys or girls with whom you would *least* like to eat lunch.	Question 2: List 5 boys or girls whom you would *least* like to elect class leader.	Question 3: If you were having a party who are the 5 boys or girls you would *least* like to invite?
Blind Children 21	22	16
Partially-sighted Children 85	85	67

Table 1 shows the frequency with which the names of the visually-handicapped children appeared on each question of the questionnaires. Again, on each ques-tion the partially-sighted youngsters appeared more frequently than the blind student. Neither group appeared as frequently on question 3 as they did on questions 1 and 2.

Average class sizes of the blind children and the partially-sighted children were approximately the same. This was eliminated as a possible factor in influencing the results.

Examination on the data in terms of sex differences showed that boys and girls tended to be equally rejected (or accepted).

DISCUSSION

Results of this study strongly support the hypothesis that blind students are less rejected by their sighted peers than are partially-sighted students. The names of partially-sighted children appeared more frequently on all three rejection questions; however, neither group appeared as frequently on the party question as the other two questions. This may have been due to an ordering effect; however it would seem more likely that there are other reasons to account for this. Probably the idea of having a party and making a guest list is more remote than eating lunch with a classmate or choosing a class leader. These latter two events are immediate—either in the just-past or very-near-future. Thus the children have explicit ideas concerning their classmates. Or it may be that both the blind and partially-sighted youngsters are classmates with whom the sighted child must "put up with" in class and does not consider as a social prospect outside of school. Also, some of the younger children may be unfamiliar with giving a party.

In attempting further study in this area, design of the questionnaire should carefully be considered. Many schools as well as individual students refused to participate in this study because the questions were given a negative tone. In fact out of the 26 pairs that were to participate originally, half of the questionnaires were not allowed to be given. Some teachers only agreed to the study if their class could also answer the questions substituting "most" for "least." The present study has given several indications that the names of some blind students would appear in a most category if included in the design. In future study it would be valuable to include questions of this nature.

Itinerant teachers of the visually handicapped should keep these results in mind. Some of the time and help afforded our blind youngsters might be spent as well in helping partially-sighted children talk out their problems. The present study would indicate that many partially-sighted youngsters are not meeting with the social success every child needs. Somewhere we have forgotten about this youngster who may see well enough to read a book but who has difficulty in making and keeping friends.

REFERENCES

Bateman, B. Sighted children's perceptions of blind children's abilities. *Exceptional Children*, 1962, *29*, 42–46.

Bateman, B., and Wetherell, J. L. Some educational characteristics of partially-seeing children. *International Journal for the Education of the Blind*, 1967, *17* (2), 33–40.

Bauman, M. Group differences disclosed by inventory items. *International Journal for the Education of the Blind*, 1964, *13* (4), 101–106.

Greenberg, H., and Jordan, S. Total blindness and partial sight. *Exceptional Children*, 1957, *24*, 123–124.

Lukoff, I., and Whiteman, M. Attitudes toward blindness: some preliminary findings. *New Outlook for the Blind*, 1961, *55* (2), 39–44.

Phelps, C. Psychological implications of visual defects in children. *Education*, 1955, *76*, 91–96.

Wolman, M. Preschool and kindergarten children's attitudes toward the blind in an integrated program. *New Outlook for the Blind*, 1958, *52*, 128–133.

Zahran, H. A study of personality differences between blind and sighted children. *British Journal of Educational Psychology*, 1965, *35* (3), 329–338.

APPENDIX B: TABLES

Table I Random Numbers*

```
22 17 68 65 84   68 95 23 92 35   87 02 22 57 51   61 09 43 95 06   58 24 82 ⌐
19 36 27 59 46   13 79 93 37 55   39 77 32 77 09   85 52 05 30 62   47 83 51 6
16 77 23 02 77   09 61 87 25 21   28 06 24 25 93   16 71 13 59 78   23 05 47 4
78 43 76 71 61   20 44 90 32 64   97 67 63 99 61   46 38 03 93 22   69 81 21 9
03 28 28 26 08   73 37 32 04 05   69 30 16 09 05   88 69 58 28 99   35 07 44 7

93 22 53 64 39   07 10 63 76 35   87 03 04 79 88   08 13 13 85 51   55 34 57 7
78 76 58 54 74   92 38 70 96 92   52 06 79 79 45   82 63 18 27 44   69 66 92 1
23 68 35 26 00   99 53 93 61 28   52 70 05 48 34   56 65 05 61 86   90 92 10 7
15 39 25 70 99   93 86 52 77 65   15 33 59 05 28   22 87 26 07 47   86 96 98 2
58 71 96 30 24   18 46 23 34 27   85 13 99 24 44   49 18 09 79 49   74 16 32 2

57 35 27 33 72   24 53 63 94 09   41 10 76 47 91   44 04 95 49 66   39 60 04 5
48 50 86 54 48   22 06 34 72 52   82 21 15 65 20   33 29 94 71 11   15 91 29 1
61 96 48 95 03   07 16 39 33 66   98 56 10 56 79   77 21 30 27 12   90 49 22 2
36 93 89 41 26   29 70 83 63 51   99 74 20 52 36   87 09 41 15 09   98 60 16 0
18 87 00 42 31   57 90 12 02 07   23 47 37 17 31   54 08 01 88 63   39 41 88 9

88 56 53 27 59   33 35 72 67 47   77 34 55 45 70   08 18 27 38 90   16 95 86 7
09 72 95 84 29   49 41 31 06 70   42 38 06 45 18   64 84 73 31 65   52 53 37 9
12 96 88 17 31   65 19 69 02 83   60 75 86 90 68   24 64 19 35 51   56 61 87 3
85 94 57 24 16   92 09 84 38 76   22 00 27 69 85   29 81 94 78 70   21 94 47 9
38 64 43 59 98   98 77 87 68 07   91 51 67 62 44   40 98 05 93 78   23 32 65 4

53 44 09 42 72   00 41 86 79 79   68 47 22 00 20   35 55 31 51 51   00 83 63 2
40 76 66 26 84   57 99 99 90 37   36 63 32 08 58   37 40 13 68 97   87 64 81 0
02 17 79 18 05   12 59 52 57 02   22 07 90 47 03   28 14 11 30 79   20 69 22 4
95 17 82 06 53   31 51 10 96 46   92 06 88 07 77   56 11 50 81 69   40 23 72 5
35 76 22 42 92   96 11 83 44 80   34 68 35 48 77   33 42 40 90 60   73 96 53 9

26 29 13 56 41   85 47 04 66 08   34 72 57 59 13   82 43 80 46 15   38 26 61 7
77 80 20 75 82   72 82 32 99 90   63 95 73 76 63   89 73 44 99 05   48 67 26 4
46 40 66 44 52   91 36 74 43 53   30 82 13 54 00   78 45 63 98 35   55 03 36 6
37 56 08 18 09   77 53 84 46 47   31 91 18 95 58   24 16 74 11 53   44 10 13 8
61 65 61 68 66   37 27 47 39 19   84 83 70 07 48   53 21 40 06 71   95 06 79 88

93 43 69 64 07   34 18 04 52 35   56 27 09 24 86   61 85 53 83 45   19 90 70 99
21 96 60 12 99   11 20 99 45 18   48 13 93 55 34   18 37 79 49 90   65 97 38 20
95 20 47 97 97   27 37 83 28 71   00 06 41 41 74   45 89 09 39 84   51 67 11 52
97 86 21 78 73   10 65 81 92 59   58 76 17 14 97   04 76 62 16 17   17 95 70 45
69 92 06 34 13   59 71 74 17 32   27 55 10 24 19   23 71 82 13 74   63 52 52 01

04 31 17 21 56   33 73 99 19 87   26 72 39 27 67   53 77 57 68 93   60 61 97 22
61 06 98 03 91   87 14 77 43 96   43 00 65 98 50   45 60 33 01 07   98 99 46 50
85 93 85 86 88   72 87 08 62 40   16 06 10 89 20   23 21 34 74 97   76 38 03 29
21 74 32 47 45   73 96 07 94 52   09 65 90 77 47   25 76 16 19 33   53 05 70 53
15 69 53 82 80   79 96 23 53 10   65 39 07 16 29   45 33 02 43 70   02 87 40 41

02 89 08 04 49   20 21 14 68 86   87 63 93 95 17   11 29 01 95 80   35 14 97 35
87 18 15 89 79   85 43 01 72 73   08 61 74 51 69   89 74 39 82 15   94 51 33 41
98 83 71 94 22   59 97 50 99 52   08 52 85 08 40   87 80 61 65 31   91 51 80 32
10 08 58 21 66   72 68 49 29 31   89 85 84 46 06   59 73 19 85 23   65 09 29 75
47 90 56 10 08   88 02 84 27 83   42 29 72 23 19   66 56 45 65 79   20 71 53 20

22 85 61 68 90   49 64 92 85 44   16 40 12 89 88   50 14 49 81 06   01 82 77 45
67 80 43 79 33   12 83 11 41 16   25 58 19 68 70   77 02 54 00 52   53 43 37 15
27 62 50 96 72   79 44 61 40 15   14 53 40 65 39   27 31 58 50 28   11 39 03 34
33 78 80 87 15   38 30 06 38 21   14 47 47 07 26   54 96 87 53 32   40 36 40 96
13 13 92 66 99   47 24 49 57 74   32 25 43 62 17   10 97 11 69 84   99 63 22 32
```

*Table I is taken from Table XXXIII of Fisher, *Statistical Methods for Research Workers*, published by Oliver and Boyd, Ltd., Edinburgh, and by permission of the author and the publisher.

Table I (continued)

```
27 53 96 23    71 50 54 36 23    54 31 04 82 98    04 14 12 15 09    26 78 25 47 47
41 50 61 88    64 85 27 20 18    83 36 36 05 56    39 71 65 09 62    94 76 62 11 89
21 42 57 02    59 19 18 97 48    80 30 03 30 98    05 24 67 70 07    84 97 50 87 46
81 77 23 23    82 82 11 54 08    53 28 70 58 96    44 07 39 55 43    42 34 43 39 28
15 18 13 54    16 86 20 26 88    90 74 80 55 09    14 53 90 51 17    52 01 63 01 59

76 21 64 64    44 91 13 32 97    75 31 62 66 54    84 80 32 75 77    56 08 25 70 29
97 79 08 06    37 30 28 59 85    53 56 68 53 40    01 74 39 59 73    30 19 99 85 48
46 18 34 94    75 20 80 27 77    78 91 69 16 00    08 43 18 73 68    67 69 61 34 25
98 99 60 50    65 95 79 42 94    93 62 40 89 96    43 56 47 71 66    46 76 29 67 02
37 59 87 21    05 02 03 24 17    47 97 81 56 51    92 34 86 01 82    55 51 33 12 91

62 06 34 41    94 21 78 55 09    72 76 45 16 94    29 95 81 83 83    79 88 01 97 30
47 23 53 90    34 41 92 45 71    09 23 70 70 07    12 38 92 79 43    14 85 11 47 23
68 62 15 43    53 14 36 59 25    54 47 33 70 15    59 24 48 40 35    50 03 42 99 36
60 92 10 77    88 59 53 11 52    66 25 69 07 04    48 68 64 71 06    61 65 70 22 12
88 87 59 41    65 28 04 67 53    95 79 88 37 31    50 41 06 94 76    81 83 17 16 33

57 45 86 67    73 43 07 34 48    44 26 87 93 29    77 09 61 67 84    06 69 44 77 75
54 14 13 17    48 62 11 90 60    68 12 93 64 28    46 24 79 16 76    14 60 25 51 01
50 16 43 36    28 97 85 58 99    67 22 52 76 23    24 70 36 54 54    59 28 61 71 96
29 62 66 50    02 63 45 52 38    67 63 47 54 75    83 24 78 43 20    92 63 13 47 48
55 58 26 51    76 96 59 38 72    86 57 45 71 46    44 67 76 14 55    44 88 01 62 12

55 36 63 70    77 45 85 50 51    74 13 39 35 22    30 53 36 02 95    49 34 88 73 61
71 98 16 04    29 18 94 51 23    76 51 94 84 86    79 93 96 38 63    08 58 25 58 94
20 56 20 11    72 65 71 08 86    79 57 95 13 91    97 48 72 66 48    09 71 17 24 89
17 26 99 76    89 37 20 70 01    77 31 61 95 46    26 97 05 73 51    53 33 18 72 87
48 60 82 29    81 30 15 39 14    48 38 75 93 29    06 87 37 78 48    45 56 00 84 47

08 02 80 72    83 71 46 30 49    89 17 95 88 29    02 39 56 03 46    97 74 06 56 17
23 98 61 67    70 52 85 01 50    01 84 02 78 43    10 62 98 19 41    18 83 99 47 99
08 96 21 44    25 27 99 41 28    07 41 08 34 66    19 42 74 39 91    41 96 53 78 72
37 06 08 43    63 61 62 42 29    39 68 95 10 96    09 24 23 00 62    56 12 80 73 16
21 34 17 68    68 96 83 23 56    32 84 60 15 31    44 73 67 34 77    91 15 79 74 58

29 09 34 04    87 83 07 55 07    76 58 30 83 64    87 29 25 58 84    86 50 60 00 25
43 28 06 36    49 52 83 51 14    47 56 91 29 34    05 87 31 06 95    12 45 57 09 09
43 67 29 70    80 62 80 03 42    10 80 21 38 84    90 56 35 03 09    43 12 74 49 14
88 88 39 54    86 97 37 44 22    00 95 01 31 76    17 16 29 56 63    38 78 94 49 81
59 59 19 51    85 39 52 85 13    07 28 37 07 61    11 16 36 27 03    78 86 72 04 95

47 10 25 62    97 05 31 03 61    20 26 36 31 62    68 69 86 95 44    84 95 48 46 45
04 14 63 19    75 89 11 47 11    31 56 34 19 09    79 57 92 36 59    14 93 87 81 40
06 54 18 66    09 18 94 06 19    98 40 07 17 81    22 45 44 84 11    24 62 20 42 31
72 77 63 48    84 08 31 55 58    24 33 45 77 58    80 45 67 93 82    75 70 16 08 24
40 24 13 27    79 26 88 86 30    01 31 60 10 39    53 58 47 70 93    85 81 56 39 38

40 35 89 95    01 61 16 96 94    50 78 13 69 36    37 68 53 37 31    71 26 35 03 71
43 80 69 98    46 68 05 14 82    90 78 50 05 62    77 79 13 57 44    59 60 10 39 66
31 31 96 82    00 57 25 60 59    46 72 60 18 77    55 66 12 62 11    08 99 55 64 57
38 07 10 05    24 98 65 63 21    47 21 61 88 32    27 80 30 21 60    10 92 35 36 12
14 30 05 39    28 10 99 00 27    12 73 73 99 12    49 99 57 94 82    96 88 57 17 91

13 19 76 16    94 11 68 84 26    23 54 20 86 85    23 86 66 99 07    36 37 34 92 09
76 59 61 81    43 63 64 61 61    65 76 36 95 90    18 48 27 45 68    27 23 65 30 72
13 05 96 47    55 78 99 95 24    37 55 85 78 78    01 48 41 19 10    35 19 54 07 73
17 77 72 73    09 62 06 65 72    87 12 49 03 60    41 15 20 76 27    50 47 02 29 16
11 60 76 83    44 88 96 07 80    83 05 83 38 96    73 70 66 81 90    30 56 10 48 59
```

Table II Critical Values of *t**

df	Level of significance for one-tailed test					
	.10	.05	.025	.01	.005	.0005
	Level of significance for two-tailed test					
	.20	.10	.05	.02	.01	.001
1	3.078	6.314	12.706	31.821	63.657	636.619
2	1.886	2.920	4.303	6.965	9.925	31.598
3	1.638	2.353	3.182	4.541	5.841	12.941
4	1.533	2.132	2.776	3.747	4.604	8.610
5	1.476	2.015	2.571	3.365	4.032	6.859
6	1.440	1.943	2.447	3.143	3.707	5.959
7	1.415	1.895	2.365	2.998	3.499	5.405
8	1.397	1.860	2.306	2.896	3.355	5.041
9	1.383	1.833	2.262	2.821	3.250	4.781
10	1.372	1.812	2.228	2.764	3.169	4.587
11	1.363	1.796	2.201	2.718	3.106	4.437
12	1.356	1.782	2.179	2.681	3.055	4.318
13	1.350	1.771	2.160	2.650	3.012	4.221
14	1.345	1.761	2.145	2.624	2.977	4.140
15	1.341	1.753	2.131	2.602	2.947	4.073
16	1.337	1.746	2.120	2.583	2.921	4.015
17	1.333	1.740	2.110	2.567	2.898	3.965
18	1.330	1.734	2.101	2.552	2.878	3.922
19	1.328	1.729	2.093	2.539	2.861	3.883
20	1.325	1.725	2.086	2.528	2.845	3.850
21	1.323	1.721	2.080	2.518	2.831	3.819
22	1.321	1.717	2.074	2.508	2.819	3.792
23	1.319	1.714	2.069	2.500	2.807	3.767
24	1.318	1.711	2.064	2.492	2.797	3.745
25	1.316	1.708	2.060	2.485	2.787	3.725
26	1.315	1.706	2.056	2.479	2.779	3.707
27	1.314	1.703	2.052	2.473	2.771	3.690
28	1.313	1.701	2.048	2.467	2.763	3.674
29	1.311	1.699	2.045	2.462	2.756	3.659
30	1.310	1.697	2.042	2.457	2.750	3.646
40	1.303	1.684	2.021	2.423	2.704	3.551
60	1.296	1.671	2.000	2.390	2.660	3.460
120	1.289	1.658	1.980	2.358	2.617	3.373
∞	1.282	1.645	1.960	2.326	2.576	3.291

*Table II is abridged from Table III of Fisher, *Statistical Methods for Research Workers*, published by Oliver and Boyd, Ltd., Edinburgh, and by permission of the author and the publisher.

Table III Critical Values of the Pearson Product Moment Correlation Coefficient*

	Level of significance for one-tailed test				
	.05	.025	.01	.005	.0005
	Level of significance for two-tailed test				
$df = N-2$	.10	.05	.02	.01	.001
1	.9877	.9969	.9995	.9999	1.0000
2	.9000	.9500	.9800	.9900	.9990
3	.8054	.8783	.9343	.9587	.9912
4	.7293	.8114	.8822	.9172	.9741
5	.6694	.7545	.8329	.8745	.9507
6	.6215	.7067	.7887	.8343	.9249
7	.5822	.6664	.7498	.7977	.8982
8	.5494	.6319	.7155	.7646	.8721
9	.5214	.6021	.6851	.7348	.8471
10	.4973	.5760	.6581	.7079	.8233
11	.4762	.5529	.6339	.6835	.8010
12	.4575	.5324	.6120	.6614	.7800
13	.4409	.5139	.5923	.6411	.7603
14	.4259	.4973	.5742	.6226	.7420
15	.4124	.4821	.5577	.6055	.7246
16	.4000	.4683	.5425	.5897	.7084
17	.3887	.4555	.5285	.5751	.6932
18	.3783	.4438	.5155	.5614	.6787
19	.3687	.4329	.5034	.5487	.6652
20	.3598	.4227	.4921	.5368	.6524
25	.3233	.3809	.4451	.4869	.5974
30	.2960	.3494	.4093	.4487	.5541
35	.2746	.3246	.3810	.4182	.5189
40	.2573	.3044	.3578	.3932	.4896
45	.2428	.2875	.3384	.3721	.4648
50	.2306	.2732	.3218	.3541	.4433
60	.2108	.2500	.2948	.3248	.4078
70	.1954	.2319	.2737	.3017	.3799
80	.1829	.2172	.2565	.2830	.3568
90	.1726	.2050	.2422	.2673	.3375
100	.1638	.1946	.2301	.2540	.3211

*Table III is taken from Table VII of Fisher, *Statistical Methods for Research Workers*, published by Oliver and Boyd, Ltd., Edinburgh, and by permission of the author and the publisher.

Table IV Critical Values of F*

n_1 degrees of freedom (for greater mean square)

n_2	1	2	3	4	5	6	7	8	9	10	11	12	14	16	20	24	30	40	50	75	100	200	500	∞
1	161 / 4,052	200 / 4,999	216 / 5,403	225 / 5,625	230 / 5,764	234 / 5,859	237 / 5,928	239 / 5,981	241 / 6,022	242 / 6,056	243 / 6,082	244 / 6,106	245 / 6,142	246 / 6,169	248 / 6,208	249 / 6,234	250 / 6,258	251 / 6,286	252 / 6,302	253 / 6,323	253 / 6,334	254 / 6,352	254 / 6,361	254 / 6,366
2	18.51 / 98.49	19.00 / 99.00	19.16 / 99.17	19.25 / 99.25	19.30 / 99.30	19.33 / 99.33	19.36 / 99.34	19.37 / 99.36	19.38 / 99.38	19.39 / 99.40	19.40 / 99.41	19.41 / 99.42	19.42 / 99.43	19.43 / 99.44	19.44 / 99.45	19.45 / 99.46	19.46 / 99.47	19.47 / 99.48	19.47 / 99.48	19.48 / 99.49	19.49 / 99.49	19.49 / 99.49	19.50 / 99.50	19.50 / 99.50
3	10.13 / 34.12	9.55 / 30.82	9.28 / 29.46	9.12 / 28.71	9.01 / 28.24	8.94 / 27.91	8.88 / 27.67	8.84 / 27.49	8.81 / 27.34	8.78 / 27.23	8.76 / 27.13	8.74 / 27.05	8.71 / 26.92	8.69 / 26.83	8.66 / 26.69	8.64 / 26.60	8.62 / 26.50	8.60 / 26.41	8.58 / 26.35	8.57 / 26.27	8.56 / 26.23	8.54 / 26.18	8.54 / 26.14	8.53 / 26.12
4	7.71 / 21.20	6.94 / 18.00	6.59 / 16.69	6.39 / 15.98	6.26 / 15.52	6.16 / 15.21	6.09 / 14.98	6.04 / 14.80	6.00 / 14.66	5.96 / 14.54	5.93 / 14.45	5.91 / 14.37	5.87 / 14.24	5.84 / 14.15	5.80 / 14.02	5.77 / 13.93	5.74 / 13.83	5.71 / 13.74	5.70 / 13.69	5.68 / 13.61	5.66 / 13.57	5.65 / 13.52	5.64 / 13.48	5.63 / 13.46
5	6.61 / 16.26	5.79 / 13.27	5.41 / 12.06	5.19 / 11.39	5.05 / 10.97	4.95 / 10.67	4.88 / 10.45	4.82 / 10.27	4.78 / 10.15	4.74 / 10.05	4.70 / 9.96	4.68 / 9.89	4.64 / 9.77	4.60 / 9.68	4.56 / 9.55	4.53 / 9.47	4.50 / 9.38	4.46 / 9.29	4.44 / 9.24	4.42 / 9.17	4.40 / 9.13	4.38 / 9.07	4.37 / 9.04	4.36 / 9.02
6	5.99 / 13.74	5.14 / 10.92	4.76 / 9.78	4.53 / 9.15	4.39 / 8.75	4.28 / 8.47	4.21 / 8.26	4.15 / 8.10	4.10 / 7.98	4.06 / 7.87	4.03 / 7.79	4.00 / 7.72	3.96 / 7.60	3.92 / 7.52	3.87 / 7.39	3.84 / 7.31	3.81 / 7.23	3.77 / 7.14	3.75 / 7.09	3.72 / 7.02	3.71 / 6.99	3.69 / 6.94	3.68 / 6.90	3.67 / 6.88
7	5.59 / 12.25	4.74 / 9.55	4.35 / 8.45	4.12 / 7.85	3.97 / 7.46	3.87 / 7.19	3.79 / 7.00	3.73 / 6.84	3.68 / 6.71	3.63 / 6.62	3.60 / 6.54	3.57 / 6.47	3.52 / 6.35	3.49 / 6.27	3.44 / 6.15	3.41 / 6.07	3.38 / 5.98	3.34 / 5.90	3.32 / 5.85	3.29 / 5.78	3.28 / 5.75	3.25 / 5.70	3.24 / 5.67	3.23 / 5.65
8	5.32 / 11.26	4.46 / 8.65	4.07 / 7.59	3.84 / 7.01	3.69 / 6.63	3.58 / 6.37	3.50 / 6.19	3.44 / 6.03	3.39 / 5.91	3.34 / 5.82	3.31 / 5.74	3.28 / 5.67	3.23 / 5.56	3.20 / 5.48	3.15 / 5.36	3.12 / 5.28	3.08 / 5.20	3.05 / 5.11	3.03 / 5.06	3.00 / 5.00	2.98 / 4.96	2.96 / 4.91	2.94 / 4.88	2.93 / 4.86
9	5.12 / 10.56	4.26 / 8.02	3.86 / 6.99	3.63 / 6.42	3.48 / 6.06	3.37 / 5.80	3.29 / 5.62	3.23 / 5.47	3.18 / 5.35	3.13 / 5.26	3.10 / 5.18	3.07 / 5.11	3.02 / 5.00	2.98 / 4.92	2.93 / 4.80	2.90 / 4.73	2.86 / 4.64	2.82 / 4.56	2.80 / 4.51	2.77 / 4.45	2.76 / 4.41	2.73 / 4.36	2.72 / 4.33	2.71 / 4.31
10	4.96 / 10.04	4.10 / 7.56	3.71 / 6.55	3.48 / 5.99	3.33 / 5.64	3.22 / 5.39	3.14 / 5.21	3.07 / 5.06	3.02 / 4.95	2.97 / 4.85	2.94 / 4.78	2.91 / 4.71	2.86 / 4.60	2.82 / 4.52	2.77 / 4.41	2.74 / 4.33	2.70 / 4.25	2.67 / 4.17	2.64 / 4.12	2.61 / 4.05	2.59 / 4.01	2.56 / 3.96	2.55 / 3.93	2.54 / 3.91
11	4.84 / 9.65	3.98 / 7.20	3.59 / 6.22	3.36 / 5.67	3.20 / 5.32	3.09 / 5.07	3.01 / 4.88	2.95 / 4.74	2.90 / 4.63	2.86 / 4.54	2.82 / 4.46	2.79 / 4.40	2.74 / 4.29	2.70 / 4.21	2.65 / 4.10	2.61 / 4.02	2.57 / 3.94	2.53 / 3.86	2.50 / 3.80	2.47 / 3.74	2.45 / 3.70	2.42 / 3.66	2.41 / 3.62	2.40 / 3.60
12	4.75 / 9.33	3.88 / 6.93	3.49 / 5.95	3.26 / 5.41	3.11 / 5.06	3.00 / 4.82	2.92 / 4.65	2.85 / 4.50	2.80 / 4.39	2.76 / 4.30	2.72 / 4.22	2.69 / 4.16	2.64 / 4.05	2.60 / 3.98	2.54 / 3.86	2.50 / 3.78	2.46 / 3.70	2.42 / 3.61	2.40 / 3.56	2.36 / 3.49	2.35 / 3.46	2.32 / 3.41	2.31 / 3.38	2.30 / 3.36
13	4.67 / 9.07	3.80 / 6.70	3.41 / 5.74	3.18 / 5.20	3.02 / 4.86	2.92 / 4.62	2.84 / 4.44	2.77 / 4.30	2.72 / 4.19	2.67 / 4.10	2.63 / 4.02	2.60 / 3.96	2.55 / 3.85	2.51 / 3.78	2.46 / 3.67	2.42 / 3.59	2.38 / 3.51	2.34 / 3.42	2.32 / 3.37	2.28 / 3.30	2.26 / 3.27	2.24 / 3.21	2.22 / 3.18	2.21 / 3.16

*Reprinted by permission from *Statistical Methods*, 5th edition, by George W. Snedecor, ©1956 by the Iowa State University Press, Ames, Iowa.

Table IV (continued)

n_1 degrees of freedom (for greater mean square)

n_2	1	2	3	4	5	6	7	8	9	10	11	12	14	16	20	24	30	40	50	75	100	200	500	∞
14	4.60 / 8.86	3.74 / 6.51	3.34 / 5.56	3.11 / 5.03	2.96 / 4.69	2.85 / 4.46	2.77 / 4.28	2.70 / 4.14	2.65 / 4.03	2.60 / 3.94	2.56 / 3.86	2.53 / 3.80	2.48 / 3.70	2.44 / 3.62	2.39 / 3.51	2.35 / 3.43	2.31 / 3.34	2.27 / 3.26	2.24 / 3.21	2.21 / 3.14	2.19 / 3.11	2.16 / 3.06	2.14 / 3.02	2.13 / 3.00
15	4.54 / 8.68	3.68 / 6.36	3.29 / 5.42	3.06 / 4.89	2.90 / 4.56	2.79 / 4.32	2.70 / 4.14	2.64 / 4.00	2.59 / 3.89	2.55 / 3.80	2.51 / 3.73	2.48 / 3.67	2.43 / 3.56	2.39 / 3.48	2.33 / 3.36	2.29 / 3.29	2.25 / 3.20	2.21 / 3.12	2.18 / 3.07	2.15 / 3.00	2.12 / 2.97	2.10 / 2.92	2.08 / 2.89	2.07 / 2.87
16	4.49 / 8.53	3.63 / 6.23	3.24 / 5.29	3.01 / 4.77	2.85 / 4.44	2.74 / 4.20	2.66 / 4.03	2.59 / 3.89	2.54 / 3.78	2.49 / 3.69	2.45 / 3.61	2.42 / 3.55	2.37 / 3.45	2.33 / 3.37	2.28 / 3.25	2.24 / 3.18	2.20 / 3.10	2.16 / 3.01	2.13 / 2.96	2.09 / 2.89	2.07 / 2.86	2.04 / 2.80	2.02 / 2.77	2.01 / 2.75
17	4.45 / 8.40	3.59 / 6.11	3.20 / 5.18	2.96 / 4.67	2.81 / 4.34	2.70 / 4.10	2.62 / 3.93	2.55 / 3.79	2.50 / 3.68	2.45 / 3.59	2.41 / 3.52	2.38 / 3.45	2.33 / 3.35	2.29 / 3.27	2.23 / 3.16	2.19 / 3.08	2.15 / 3.00	2.11 / 2.92	2.08 / 2.86	2.04 / 2.79	2.02 / 2.76	1.99 / 2.70	1.97 / 2.67	1.96 / 2.65
18	4.41 / 8.28	3.55 / 6.01	3.16 / 5.09	2.93 / 4.58	2.77 / 4.25	2.66 / 4.01	2.58 / 3.85	2.51 / 3.71	2.46 / 3.60	2.41 / 3.51	2.37 / 3.44	2.34 / 3.37	2.29 / 3.27	2.25 / 3.19	2.19 / 3.07	2.15 / 3.00	2.11 / 2.91	2.07 / 2.83	2.04 / 2.78	2.00 / 2.71	1.98 / 2.68	1.95 / 2.62	1.93 / 2.59	1.92 / 2.57
19	4.38 / 8.18	3.52 / 5.93	3.13 / 5.01	2.90 / 4.50	2.74 / 4.17	2.63 / 3.94	2.55 / 3.77	2.48 / 3.63	2.43 / 3.52	2.38 / 3.43	2.34 / 3.36	2.31 / 3.30	2.26 / 3.19	2.21 / 3.12	2.15 / 3.00	2.11 / 2.92	2.07 / 2.84	2.02 / 2.76	2.00 / 2.70	1.96 / 2.63	1.94 / 2.60	1.91 / 2.54	1.90 / 2.51	1.88 / 2.49
20	4.35 / 8.10	3.49 / 5.85	3.10 / 4.94	2.87 / 4.43	2.71 / 4.10	2.60 / 3.87	2.52 / 3.71	2.45 / 3.56	2.40 / 3.45	2.35 / 3.37	2.31 / 3.30	2.28 / 3.23	2.23 / 3.13	2.18 / 3.05	2.12 / 2.94	2.08 / 2.86	2.04 / 2.77	1.99 / 2.69	1.96 / 2.63	1.92 / 2.56	1.90 / 2.53	1.87 / 2.47	1.85 / 2.44	1.84 / 2.42
21	4.32 / 8.02	3.47 / 5.78	3.07 / 4.87	2.84 / 4.37	2.68 / 4.04	2.57 / 3.81	2.49 / 3.65	2.42 / 3.51	2.37 / 3.40	2.32 / 3.31	2.28 / 3.24	2.25 / 3.17	2.20 / 3.07	2.15 / 2.99	2.09 / 2.88	2.05 / 2.80	2.00 / 2.72	1.96 / 2.63	1.93 / 2.58	1.89 / 2.51	1.87 / 2.47	1.84 / 2.42	1.82 / 2.38	1.81 / 2.36
22	4.30 / 7.94	3.44 / 5.72	3.05 / 4.82	2.82 / 4.31	2.66 / 3.99	2.55 / 3.76	2.47 / 3.59	2.40 / 3.45	2.35 / 3.35	2.30 / 3.26	2.26 / 3.18	2.23 / 3.12	2.18 / 3.02	2.13 / 2.94	2.07 / 2.83	2.03 / 2.75	1.98 / 2.67	1.93 / 2.58	1.91 / 2.53	1.87 / 2.46	1.84 / 2.42	1.81 / 2.37	1.80 / 2.33	1.78 / 2.31
23	4.28 / 7.88	3.42 / 5.66	3.03 / 4.76	2.80 / 4.26	2.64 / 3.94	2.53 / 3.71	2.45 / 3.54	2.38 / 3.41	2.32 / 3.30	2.28 / 3.21	2.24 / 3.14	2.20 / 3.07	2.14 / 2.97	2.10 / 2.89	2.04 / 2.78	2.00 / 2.70	1.96 / 2.62	1.91 / 2.53	1.88 / 2.48	1.84 / 2.41	1.82 / 2.37	1.79 / 2.32	1.77 / 2.28	1.76 / 2.26
24	4.26 / 7.82	3.40 / 5.61	3.01 / 4.72	2.78 / 4.22	2.62 / 3.90	2.51 / 3.67	2.43 / 3.50	2.36 / 3.36	2.30 / 3.25	2.26 / 3.17	2.22 / 3.09	2.18 / 3.03	2.13 / 2.93	2.09 / 2.85	2.02 / 2.74	1.98 / 2.66	1.94 / 2.58	1.89 / 2.49	1.86 / 2.44	1.82 / 2.36	1.80 / 2.33	1.76 / 2.27	1.74 / 2.23	1.73 / 2.21
25	4.24 / 7.77	3.38 / 5.57	2.99 / 4.68	2.76 / 4.18	2.60 / 3.86	2.49 / 3.63	2.41 / 3.46	2.34 / 3.32	2.28 / 3.21	2.24 / 3.13	2.20 / 3.05	2.16 / 2.99	2.11 / 2.89	2.06 / 2.81	2.00 / 2.70	1.96 / 2.62	1.92 / 2.54	1.87 / 2.45	1.84 / 2.40	1.80 / 2.32	1.77 / 2.29	1.74 / 2.23	1.72 / 2.19	1.71 / 2.17
26	4.22 / 7.72	3.37 / 5.53	2.98 / 4.64	2.74 / 4.14	2.59 / 3.82	2.47 / 3.59	2.39 / 3.42	2.32 / 3.29	2.27 / 3.17	2.22 / 3.09	2.18 / 3.02	2.15 / 2.96	2.10 / 2.86	2.05 / 2.77	1.99 / 2.66	1.95 / 2.58	1.90 / 2.50	1.85 / 2.41	1.82 / 2.36	1.78 / 2.28	1.76 / 2.25	1.72 / 2.19	1.70 / 2.15	1.69 / 2.13

Table IV (continued)

n_1 degrees of freedom (for greater mean square)

n_2	1	2	3	4	5	6	7	8	9	10	11	12	14	16	20	24	30	40	50	75	100	200	500	∞
27	4.21 / 7.68	3.35 / 5.49	2.96 / 4.60	2.73 / 4.11	2.57 / 3.79	2.46 / 3.56	2.37 / 3.39	2.30 / 3.26	2.25 / 3.14	2.20 / 3.06	2.16 / 2.98	2.13 / 2.93	2.08 / 2.83	2.03 / 2.74	1.97 / 2.63	1.93 / 2.55	1.88 / 2.47	1.84 / 2.38	1.80 / 2.33	1.76 / 2.25	1.74 / 2.21	1.71 / 2.16	1.68 / 2.12	1.67 / 2.10
28	4.20 / 7.64	3.34 / 5.45	2.95 / 4.57	2.71 / 4.07	2.56 / 3.76	2.44 / 3.53	2.36 / 3.36	2.29 / 3.23	2.24 / 3.11	2.19 / 3.03	2.15 / 2.95	2.12 / 2.90	2.06 / 2.80	2.02 / 2.71	1.96 / 2.60	1.91 / 2.52	1.87 / 2.44	1.81 / 2.35	1.78 / 2.30	1.75 / 2.22	1.72 / 2.18	1.69 / 2.13	1.67 / 2.09	1.65 / 2.06
29	4.18 / 7.60	3.33 / 5.42	2.93 / 4.54	2.70 / 4.04	2.54 / 3.73	2.43 / 3.50	2.35 / 3.33	2.28 / 3.20	2.22 / 3.08	2.18 / 3.00	2.14 / 2.92	2.10 / 2.87	2.05 / 2.77	2.00 / 2.68	1.94 / 2.57	1.90 / 2.49	1.85 / 2.41	1.80 / 2.32	1.77 / 2.27	1.73 / 2.19	1.71 / 2.15	1.68 / 2.10	1.65 / 2.06	1.64 / 2.03
30	4.17 / 7.56	3.32 / 5.39	2.92 / 4.51	2.69 / 4.02	2.53 / 3.70	2.42 / 3.47	2.34 / 3.30	2.27 / 3.17	2.21 / 3.06	2.16 / 2.98	2.12 / 2.90	2.09 / 2.84	2.04 / 2.74	1.99 / 2.66	1.93 / 2.55	1.89 / 2.47	1.84 / 2.38	1.79 / 2.29	1.76 / 2.24	1.72 / 2.16	1.69 / 2.13	1.66 / 2.07	1.64 / 2.03	1.62 / 2.01
32	4.15 / 7.50	3.30 / 5.34	2.90 / 4.46	2.67 / 3.97	2.51 / 3.66	2.40 / 3.42	2.32 / 3.25	2.25 / 3.12	2.19 / 3.01	2.14 / 2.94	2.10 / 2.86	2.07 / 2.80	2.02 / 2.70	1.97 / 2.62	1.91 / 2.51	1.86 / 2.42	1.82 / 2.34	1.76 / 2.25	1.74 / 2.20	1.69 / 2.12	1.67 / 2.08	1.64 / 2.02	1.61 / 1.98	1.59 / 1.96
34	4.13 / 7.44	3.28 / 5.29	2.88 / 4.42	2.65 / 3.93	2.49 / 3.61	2.38 / 3.38	2.30 / 3.21	2.23 / 3.08	2.17 / 2.97	2.12 / 2.89	2.08 / 2.82	2.05 / 2.76	2.00 / 2.66	1.95 / 2.58	1.89 / 2.47	1.84 / 2.38	1.80 / 2.30	1.74 / 2.21	1.71 / 2.15	1.67 / 2.08	1.64 / 2.04	1.61 / 1.98	1.59 / 1.94	1.57 / 1.91
36	4.11 / 7.39	3.26 / 5.25	2.86 / 4.38	2.63 / 3.89	2.48 / 3.58	2.36 / 3.35	2.28 / 3.18	2.21 / 3.04	2.15 / 2.94	2.10 / 2.86	2.06 / 2.78	2.03 / 2.72	1.98 / 2.62	1.93 / 2.54	1.87 / 2.43	1.82 / 2.35	1.78 / 2.26	1.72 / 2.17	1.69 / 2.12	1.65 / 2.04	1.62 / 2.00	1.59 / 1.94	1.56 / 1.90	1.55 / 1.87
38	4.10 / 7.35	3.25 / 5.21	2.85 / 4.34	2.62 / 3.86	2.46 / 3.54	2.35 / 3.32	2.26 / 3.15	2.19 / 3.02	2.14 / 2.91	2.09 / 2.82	2.05 / 2.75	2.02 / 2.69	1.96 / 2.59	1.92 / 2.51	1.85 / 2.40	1.80 / 2.32	1.76 / 2.22	1.71 / 2.14	1.67 / 2.08	1.63 / 2.00	1.60 / 1.97	1.57 / 1.90	1.54 / 1.86	1.53 / 1.84
40	4.08 / 7.31	3.23 / 5.18	2.84 / 4.31	2.61 / 3.83	2.45 / 3.51	2.34 / 3.29	2.25 / 3.12	2.18 / 2.99	2.12 / 2.88	2.07 / 2.80	2.04 / 2.73	2.00 / 2.66	1.95 / 2.56	1.90 / 2.49	1.84 / 2.37	1.79 / 2.29	1.74 / 2.20	1.69 / 2.11	1.66 / 2.05	1.61 / 1.97	1.59 / 1.94	1.55 / 1.88	1.53 / 1.84	1.51 / 1.81
42	4.07 / 7.27	3.22 / 5.15	2.83 / 4.29	2.59 / 3.80	2.44 / 3.49	2.32 / 3.26	2.24 / 3.10	2.17 / 2.96	2.11 / 2.86	2.06 / 2.77	2.02 / 2.70	1.99 / 2.64	1.94 / 2.54	1.89 / 2.46	1.82 / 2.35	1.78 / 2.26	1.73 / 2.17	1.68 / 2.08	1.64 / 2.02	1.60 / 1.94	1.57 / 1.91	1.54 / 1.85	1.51 / 1.80	1.49 / 1.78
44	4.06 / 7.24	3.21 / 5.12	2.82 / 4.26	2.58 / 3.78	2.43 / 3.46	2.31 / 3.24	2.23 / 3.07	2.16 / 2.94	2.10 / 2.84	2.05 / 2.75	2.01 / 2.68	1.98 / 2.62	1.92 / 2.52	1.88 / 2.44	1.81 / 2.32	1.76 / 2.24	1.72 / 2.15	1.66 / 2.06	1.63 / 2.00	1.58 / 1.92	1.56 / 1.88	1.52 / 1.82	1.50 / 1.78	1.48 / 1.75
46	4.05 / 7.21	3.20 / 5.10	2.81 / 4.24	2.57 / 3.76	2.42 / 3.44	2.30 / 3.22	2.22 / 3.05	2.14 / 2.92	2.09 / 2.82	2.04 / 2.73	2.00 / 2.66	1.97 / 2.60	1.91 / 2.50	1.87 / 2.42	1.80 / 2.30	1.75 / 2.22	1.71 / 2.13	1.65 / 2.04	1.62 / 1.98	1.57 / 1.90	1.54 / 1.86	1.51 / 1.80	1.48 / 1.76	1.46 / 1.72
48	4.04 / 7.19	3.19 / 5.08	2.80 / 4.22	2.56 / 3.74	2.41 / 3.42	2.30 / 3.20	2.21 / 3.04	2.14 / 2.90	2.08 / 2.80	2.03 / 2.71	1.99 / 2.64	1.96 / 2.58	1.90 / 2.48	1.86 / 2.40	1.79 / 2.28	1.74 / 2.20	1.70 / 2.11	1.64 / 2.02	1.61 / 1.96	1.56 / 1.88	1.53 / 1.84	1.50 / 1.78	1.47 / 1.73	1.45 / 1.70

Table IV (continued)

n_1 degrees of freedom (for greater mean square)

n_2	1	2	3	4	5	6	7	8	9	10	11	12	14	16	20	24	30	40	50	75	100	200	500	∞
50	4.03/7.17	3.18/5.06	2.79/4.20	2.56/3.72	2.40/3.41	2.29/3.18	2.20/3.02	2.13/2.88	2.07/2.78	2.02/2.70	1.98/2.62	1.95/2.56	1.90/2.46	1.85/2.39	1.78/2.26	1.74/2.18	1.69/2.10	1.63/2.00	1.60/1.94	1.55/1.86	1.52/1.82	1.48/1.76	1.46/1.71	1.44/1.68
55	4.02/7.12	3.17/5.01	2.78/4.16	2.54/3.68	2.38/3.37	2.27/3.15	2.18/2.98	2.11/2.85	2.05/2.75	2.00/2.66	1.97/2.59	1.93/2.53	1.88/2.43	1.83/2.35	1.76/2.23	1.72/2.15	1.67/2.06	1.61/1.96	1.58/1.90	1.52/1.82	1.50/1.78	1.46/1.71	1.43/1.66	1.41/1.64
60	4.00/7.08	3.15/4.98	2.76/4.13	2.52/3.65	2.37/3.34	2.25/3.12	2.17/2.95	2.10/2.82	2.04/2.72	1.99/2.63	1.95/2.56	1.92/2.50	1.86/2.40	1.81/2.32	1.75/2.20	1.70/2.12	1.65/2.03	1.59/1.93	1.56/1.87	1.50/1.79	1.48/1.74	1.44/1.68	1.41/1.63	1.39/1.60
65	3.99/7.04	3.14/4.95	2.75/4.10	2.51/3.62	2.36/3.31	2.24/3.09	2.15/2.93	2.08/2.79	2.02/2.70	1.98/2.61	1.94/2.54	1.90/2.47	1.85/2.37	1.80/2.30	1.73/2.18	1.68/2.09	1.63/2.00	1.57/1.90	1.54/1.84	1.49/1.76	1.46/1.71	1.42/1.64	1.39/1.60	1.37/1.56
70	3.98/7.01	3.13/4.92	2.74/4.08	2.50/3.60	2.35/3.29	2.23/3.07	2.14/2.91	2.07/2.77	2.01/2.67	1.97/2.59	1.93/2.51	1.89/2.45	1.84/2.35	1.79/2.28	1.72/2.15	1.67/2.07	1.62/1.98	1.56/1.88	1.53/1.82	1.47/1.74	1.45/1.69	1.40/1.62	1.37/1.56	1.35/1.53
80	3.96/6.96	3.11/4.88	2.72/4.04	2.48/3.56	2.33/3.25	2.21/3.04	2.12/2.87	2.05/2.74	1.99/2.64	1.95/2.55	1.91/2.48	1.88/2.41	1.82/2.32	1.77/2.24	1.70/2.11	1.65/2.03	1.60/1.94	1.54/1.84	1.51/1.78	1.45/1.70	1.42/1.65	1.38/1.57	1.35/1.52	1.32/1.49
100	3.94/6.90	3.09/4.82	2.70/3.98	2.46/3.51	2.30/3.20	2.19/2.99	2.10/2.82	2.03/2.69	1.97/2.59	1.92/2.51	1.88/2.43	1.85/2.36	1.79/2.26	1.75/2.19	1.68/2.06	1.63/1.98	1.57/1.89	1.51/1.79	1.48/1.73	1.42/1.64	1.39/1.59	1.34/1.51	1.30/1.46	1.28/1.43
125	3.92/6.84	3.07/4.78	2.68/3.94	2.44/3.47	2.29/3.17	2.17/2.95	2.08/2.79	2.01/2.65	1.95/2.56	1.90/2.47	1.86/2.40	1.83/2.33	1.77/2.23	1.72/2.15	1.65/2.03	1.60/1.94	1.55/1.85	1.49/1.75	1.45/1.68	1.39/1.59	1.36/1.54	1.31/1.46	1.27/1.40	1.25/1.37
150	3.91/6.81	3.06/4.75	2.67/3.91	2.43/3.44	2.27/3.14	2.16/2.92	2.07/2.76	2.00/2.62	1.94/2.53	1.89/2.44	1.85/2.37	1.82/2.30	1.76/2.20	1.71/2.12	1.64/2.00	1.59/1.91	1.54/1.83	1.47/1.72	1.44/1.66	1.37/1.56	1.34/1.51	1.29/1.43	1.25/1.37	1.22/1.33
200	3.89/6.76	3.04/4.71	2.65/3.88	2.41/3.41	2.26/3.11	2.14/2.90	2.05/2.73	1.98/2.60	1.92/2.50	1.87/2.41	1.83/2.34	1.80/2.28	1.74/2.17	1.69/2.09	1.62/1.97	1.57/1.88	1.52/1.79	1.45/1.69	1.42/1.62	1.35/1.53	1.32/1.48	1.26/1.39	1.22/1.33	1.19/1.28
400	3.86/6.70	3.02/4.66	2.62/3.83	2.39/3.36	2.23/3.06	2.12/2.85	2.03/2.69	1.96/2.55	1.90/2.46	1.85/2.37	1.81/2.29	1.78/2.23	1.72/2.12	1.67/2.04	1.60/1.92	1.54/1.84	1.49/1.74	1.42/1.64	1.38/1.57	1.32/1.47	1.28/1.42	1.22/1.32	1.16/1.24	1.13/1.19
1000	3.85/6.66	3.00/4.62	2.61/3.80	2.38/3.34	2.22/3.04	2.10/2.82	2.02/2.66	1.95/2.53	1.89/2.43	1.84/2.34	1.80/2.26	1.76/2.20	1.70/2.09	1.65/2.01	1.58/1.89	1.53/1.81	1.47/1.71	1.41/1.61	1.36/1.54	1.30/1.44	1.26/1.38	1.19/1.28	1.13/1.19	1.08/1.11
∞	3.84/6.64	2.99/4.60	2.60/3.78	2.37/3.32	2.21/3.02	2.09/2.80	2.01/2.64	1.94/2.51	1.88/2.41	1.83/2.32	1.79/2.24	1.75/2.18	1.69/2.07	1.64/1.99	1.57/1.87	1.52/1.79	1.46/1.69	1.40/1.59	1.35/1.52	1.28/1.41	1.24/1.36	1.17/1.25	1.11/1.15	1.00/1.00

Table V Critical Values of U in the Mann-Whitney Test*

n_1 \ n_2	9	10	11	12	13	14	15	16	17	18	19	20
1												
2	0	0	0	1	1	1	1	1	2	2	2	2
3	2	3	3	4	4	5	5	6	6	7	7	8
4	4	5	6	7	8	9	10	11	11	12	13	13
5	7	8	9	11	12	13	14	15	17	18	19	20
6	10	11	13	14	16	17	19	21	22	24	25	27
7	12	14	16	18	20	22	24	26	28	30	32	34
8	15	17	19	22	24	26	29	31	34	36	38	41
9	17	20	23	26	28	31	34	37	39	42	45	48
10	20	23	26	29	33	36	39	42	45	48	52	55
11	23	26	30	33	37	40	44	47	51	55	58	62
12	26	29	33	37	41	45	49	53	57	61	65	69
13	28	33	37	41	45	50	54	59	63	67	72	76
14	31	36	40	45	50	55	59	64	67	74	78	83
15	34	39	44	49	54	59	64	70	75	80	85	90
16	37	42	47	53	59	64	70	75	81	86	92	98
17	39	45	51	57	63	67	75	81	87	93	99	105
18	42	48	55	61	67	74	80	86	93	99	106	112
19	45	52	58	65	72	78	85	92	99	106	113	119
20	48	55	62	69	76	83	90	98	105	112	119	127

*Adapted and abridged from Tables 1, 3, 5, and 7 of Auble, D. 1958. Extended tables for the Mann-Whitney statistic. *Bulletin of the Institute of Educational Research at Indiana University, 1*, No. 2, with permission of the author and the publisher.

For additional Mann-Whitney U-tables for other n's and other α (p) levels, see Siegel (1956).

Table VI Critical Values of r_s, the Spearman Rank Correlation Coefficient*

N	Significance level (one-tailed test)	
	.05	.01
4	1.000	
5	.900	1.000
6	.829	.943
7	.714	.893
8	.643	.833
9	.600	.783
10	.564	.746
12	.506	.712
14	.456	.645
16	.425	.601
18	.399	.564
20	.377	.534
22	359	.508
24	.343	.485
26	.329	.465
28	.317	.448
30	.306	.432

*Adapted from Olds, E. G., Distributions of sums of square of rank differences for small numbers of individuals, *Annals of Mathematical Statistics*, 1938, *9*, 133–148, and from Olds, E. G. The 5% significance levels for sums of squares of rank differences and correction, *Annals of Mathematical Statistics*, 1940, *20*, 117–118, by permission of the author and the publisher.

Table VII Critical Values of Chi Square*

	Level of significance for one-tailed test					
	.10	.05	.025	.01	.005	.0005
	Level of significance for two-tailed test					
df	.20	.10	.05	.02	.01	.001
1	1.64	2.71	3.84	5.41	6.64	10.83
2	3.22	4.60	5.99	7.82	9.21	13.82
3	4.64	6.25	7.82	9.84	11.34	16.27
4	5.99	7.78	9.49	11.67	13.28	18.46
5	7.29	9.24	11.07	13.39	15.09	20.52
6	8.56	10.64	12.59	15.03	16.81	22.46
7	9.80	12.02	14.07	16.62	18.48	24.32
8	11.03	13.36	15.51	18.17	20.09	26.12
9	12.24	14.68	16.92	19.68	21.67	27.88
10	13.44	15.99	18.31	21.16	23.21	29.59
11	14.63	17.28	19.68	22.62	24.72	31.26
12	15.81	18.55	21.03	24.05	26.22	32.91
13	16.98	19.81	22.36	25.47	27.69	34.53
14	18.15	21.06	23.68	26.87	29.14	36.12
15	19.31	22.31	25.00	28.26	30.58	37.70
16	20.46	23.54	26.30	29.63	32.00	39.29
17	21.62	24.77	27.59	31.00	33.41	40.75
18	22.76	25.99	28.87	32.35	34.80	42.31
19	23.90	27.20	30.14	33.69	36.19	43.82
20	25.04	28.41	31.41	35.02	37.57	45.32
21	26.17	29.62	32.67	36.34	38.93	46.80
22	27.30	30.81	33.92	37.66	40.29	48.27
23	28.43	32.01	35.17	38.97	41.64	49.73
24	29.55	33.20	36.42	40.27	42.98	51.18
25	30.68	34.38	37.65	41.57	44.31	52.62
26	31.80	35.56	38.88	42.86	45.64	54.05
27	32.91	36.74	40.11	44.14	46.96	55.48
28	34.03	37.92	41.34	45.42	48.28	56.89
29	35.14	39.09	42.69	46.69	49.59	58.30
30	36.25	40.26	43.77	47.96	50.89	59.70
32	38.47	42.59	46.19	50.49	53.49	62.49
34	40.68	44.90	48.60	53.00	56.06	65.25
36	42.88	47.21	51.00	55.49	58.62	67.99
38	45.08	49.51	53.38	57.97	61.16	70.70
40	47.27	51.81	55.76	60.44	63.69	73.40
44	51.64	56.37	60.48	65.34	68.71	78.75
48	55.99	60.91	65.17	70.20	73.68	84.04
52	60.33	65.42	69.83	75.02	78.62	89.27
56	64.66	69.92	74.47	79.82	83.51	94.46
60	68.97	74.40	79.08	84.58	88.38	99.61

*Adapted from Table IV of Fisher, *Statistical Methods for Research Workers*, published by Oliver and Boyd, Ltd., Edinburgh, and by permission of the author and the publisher.

Answers to Exercises

Chapter 1

1. (a) i, (b) e, (c) e, (d) i, (e) e

2. d

3. a

4. a

5. external

6. internal

7. See Section 1.3.

8. step 1, d; step 2, k; step 3, h; step 4, a; step 5, i; step 6, f; step 7, b; step 8, e

9. a, c, d, f

10. See Section 1.5.

Chapter 2

1. (a) specific hypothesis, (b) general hypothesis, (c) observation

2. (a) general hypothesis, (b) observation, (c) specific hypothesis

3. General hypothesis: speculates on relation between general classes (i.e., all possible instances).

Specific hypothesis: speculates on relation between specific instances.

Observation: identifies an event that has occurred (or been seen).

4. Blind children will be better liked than partially-sighted children by their sighted peers.

Blind children will be less well liked than partially-sighted children by their sighted peers.

Blind children and partially-sighted children will be equally well liked by their sighted peers.

5. Students who use this textbook will learn

        more   less   the same amount

about research methods than students who use the Brand X textbook.

6. (a), because a child will more likely prefer one of two teachers than one of one; and two teachers means that one can be male and one female.

7. i. deductive, ii. inductive

8. Environmental relevance, unrestrictedness, and motivation.

9. Environmental relevance and appropriateness might apply to the match or correspondence between the subject-matter and the learning location; unrestrictedness might apply to freedom of movement outdoors; motivation might apply to the pleasure associated with being outside of the school.

10. (a) Enjoyment of school by youngsters will be unrelated to their reading grade level.
   (b) Intelligence and ordinal position of birth are unrelated, i.e., first-borns and later-borns are equally intelligent.
   (c) A combination of reading readiness training and programmed reading instruction will not be more effective in teaching reading than normal classroom instruction in sight reading.

11. Check answer with chapter.

12. Check answer with chapter.

Chapter 3

1. Check these answers with the definitions in the chapter.

2. (a) 3, (b) 5, (c) 4, (d) 1, (e) 2

3. (a) blind versus partially-sighted children

(b) rejection by sighted peers

(c) none

(d) sex, age, grade level, integrated classrooms

(e) acceptability, compensation for handicap, security, adjustment

4. Examples: acceptability among sighted peers versus acceptability among other blind or partially-sighted children, sex, number of years in an integrated classroom

5. See Section 3.9.

6. (a) perceptual-motor training versus no perceptual-motor training

   (b) sex

   (c) I.Q.

   (d) coordination

   (e) performance on eye-hand coordination tasks

7. (a) microteaching experience versus no microteaching experience

   (b) experienced versus inexperienced teachers

   (c) sex (males only)

   (d) dissonance

   (e) change in attitudes toward teaching

Chapter 4

1. a, c, d

2. a (See Sample Study III, Appendix A.)

3. b, c

4. (a) A, (b) C, (c) B

5. (a) C, (b) A, (c) B

6. (a) Example: state induced by giving a person training in a course intended to increase his desire for success.

   (b) Example: telling members of a group that test data indicate that they should all get along well.

7. (a) Example: state evidenced by a person showing persistence, competitiveness, and aggressiveness in a difficult task situation.

   (b) Example: state evidenced by a lack of open fighting, hostility, or disagreement and a predominance of sociability and group maintenance activity.

8. (a) Example: state evidenced by a person relating fantasies of task accomplishments when confronted by an ambiguous stimulus.

(b) Example: state evidenced by group members showing many intragroup friendship choices on a sociometric measure.

9. b

10. State of being able to do whatever you want short of interfering with another person's individual or civil rights and without breaking civil or criminal laws.

11. Example: the higher the income level of a person's father, the higher will be his grade-point average in high school.

12. Example: the fewer the rules and sanctions imposed by a teacher in a classroom, the greater the likelihood that students will generate novel (i.e., uncommon) yet appropriate responses in a classroom task situation.

Chapter 5

1. b

2. c

3. 1(a) selection   2(a) instrumentation
    1(b)   2(b) mortality
    1(c) history   2(c)
    1(d) maturation   2(d) history

4. (a) 2, (b) 6, (c) 1, (d) 3

5. See Section 5.4.

6. See Section 5.5.

7. Matched pairs: sex, age, grade.

Limiting the population: to children in the approximate grade for their chronological age.

8. History: use a control group, i.e., persons given nonprogrammed math instruction.

Maturation: use control Ss of the same age as experimental Ss.

Testing: use different forms of the math achievement test for pretest and posttest.

Instrumentation: use a standardized math achievement test.

Selection: randomly assign Ss to experimental and control groups.

Regression: use Ss whose math achievement covers a wide range.

Mortality: same as Selection answer.

9. Reactive effect of testing: use a standardized math achievement test.

   Interaction effects of selection bias: use Ss with a wide range of math achievement levels.

   Reactive effect of experimental arrangements: use experimental and control material as part of regular classroom activity.

   Multiple treatment interference: isolate Ss from other experiments while this one is being conducted.

10. History: use a control group of Ss who do not see the film.

    Maturation: select experimental and control Ss of the same age.

    Selection: assign Ss randomly.

11. One check would be to develop type B operational definitions of directive and nondirective counselors. Have trained observers listen to tapes of counseling sessions and check to see how many directive and nondirective acts each counselor makes in the two roles. Other checks are possible.

12. One approach would be to use a rating scale on which each S would rate his level of anger after the manipulation. Ss in anger condition should show significantly higher ratings of anger than Ss in non-anger condition. Other approaches are possible.

Chapter 6

1. (a) 5, (b) 4, (c) 1, (d) 3, (e) 6, (f) 2

2. (a) 2, (b) 3, (c) 4, (d) 6, (e) 1, (f) 5

3. (1) c, (2) a, (3) b

4. (1) c, (2) d, (3) a, (4) b

5. Example: R X O_1
            R O_2

   X $\equiv$ urban school experience
   $O_1 O_2 \equiv$ choice of teaching assignment

6. Example:

R	O_1	X	Y_1	O_5
R	O_2	X	Y_2	O_6
R	O_3		Y_1	O_7
R	O_4		Y_2	O_8

$O_1, O_2, O_3, O_4 \equiv$ math achievement pretest
$X \qquad\qquad \equiv$ programmed math instruction
$Y_1 Y_2 \qquad\quad \equiv$ high and low math aptitude
$O_5, O_6, O_7, O_8 \equiv$ math achievement posttest

7. a, d

8. b, d

9. c

10. (a) The experimenter cannot assign Ss to conditions. They choose their own conditions, thus creating potential selection bias.

   (b) $O_1 \qquad X \qquad O_3$

   $O_2 \qquad\qquad O_4$

   $O_1, O_2 \equiv$ control variables to assess group equivalence
   $X \qquad \equiv$ urban school experience
   $O_3, O_4 \equiv$ subsequent choice of assignment

11. (a) All Ss must participate in the experiment. This leaves no perfect way to control for history.

   (b) $O_1 \quad O_2 \quad O_3 \quad X \quad O_4 \quad O_5 \quad O_6$ $\qquad O \equiv$ number of cavities
   $\qquad\qquad\qquad\qquad\qquad\qquad\qquad X \equiv$ dental hygiene program

12. (a) Because the study compares two criterion groups, blind and partially-sighted children, after the fact of their becoming blind or partially-sighted.

   (b) $O_1 \qquad C_1 \qquad O_2$ $\qquad O_1, O_3 \equiv$ control variables

   ----

   $O_3 \qquad C_2 \qquad O_4$ $\qquad C_1, C_2 \equiv$ blind and partially-sighted children
   $\qquad\qquad\qquad\qquad\qquad O_2, O_4 \equiv$ number of peers choosing child as "friend"

13. (a) Because the experimenter is not creating the broken home, he is selecting children from it after-the-fact.

   (b) $R \qquad C \qquad O_1$ $\qquad C \qquad\quad \equiv$ children from broken homes
   $\quad R \qquad\qquad O_2$ $\qquad O_1, O_2 \equiv$ number of demerits

14. (a) Because the extra experience and feelings of importance for being singled out might enhance development.

   (b) $R \quad X \quad O_1$ $\qquad X \qquad\qquad\quad \equiv$ dance program
   $\quad R \quad H \quad O_2$ $\qquad H \qquad\qquad\quad \equiv$ reading program (irrelevant treatment)
   $\quad R \qquad\quad O_3$ $\qquad O_1, O_2, O_3 \equiv$ measurements of physical and social skills

15. (a) Because the extra experience and feelings of importance growing out of being included in the program might contribute to an increase in verbal I.Q.

(b) Because teachers who expect the treatment to work might contribute to its working.

(c)

R	O_1	X	E_P	O_5
R	O_2	X	E_N	O_6
R	O_3	H	E_P	O_7
R	O_4	H	E_N	O_8

$O_1, O_2, O_3, O_4 \equiv$ pretest verbal I.Q.

$X \equiv$ special program

$H \equiv$ irrelevant program

$E_P \equiv$ positive teacher expectations

$E_N \equiv$ neutral teacher expectations

$O_5, O_6, O_7, O_8 \equiv$ posttest verbal I.Q.

Chapter 7

1. (a) 2, (b) 4, (c) 1, (d) 3

2. For test-retest reliability administer scale to same group of Ss on two occasions. Correlate Ss score at time 1 with those at time 2 (as compared to split-half which involves one administration and the correlating of scores on odd-numbered items with those on even-numbered items).

3. (a) 3, (b) 4, (c) 2, (d) 1

4. To establish the concurrent validity give test to a sample along with a standard, more accepted I.Q. test. Correlate scores on the two tests (as contrasted to relating the test score to school achievement or some other behavior that would be related to the construct of intelligence).

5. (a) 3, (b) 1, (c) 2

6. true

7. (a) 2, (b) 1, (c) 3

8. (a) 43, (b) 430, (c) 40

9. (a) 531, (b) 823, (c) Joseph L. French, (d) Houghton-Mifflin Company, (e) 45 minutes, (f) 3–8, (g) 7, (h) one form (plus short form), (i) $24.00, (j) 1964

10. I would use the Sex Knowledge Inventory, Experimental Edition as compared to the Sex Knowledge Test because the former has a manual and reports norms and reliability (.88) while the latter does not.

11. (a) 7, (b) 8, (c) 5, (d) 2, (e) 1, (f) 4

12. d

13.

	Number of high 1/3 who pass	Number of low 1/3 who pass	Index of difficulty	Index of discrimin-ability
Item 1	2	0	.50	1.00
Item 2	2	1	.75	.67
Item 3	1	1	.50	.50
Item 4	2	0	.50	1.00

Eliminate item 3.

14. 1st – c   2nd – f   3rd – e   4th – d   5th – a   6th – b

15. item scores and total scores

16. evaluation, potency, activity

17. correlating their ratings

18. sign, time

19. .92

Chapter 8

1. c

2. a

3. (a) 4, (b) 2, (c) 5, (d) 1, (e) 3

4. (a) 4, (b) 5, (c) 7, (d) 6, (e) 1, (f) 3, (g) 2

5. (a) I, (b) Q, (c) Q, (d) Q, (e) I, (f) I

6. (a) F, (b) R, (c) C, (d) F, (e) S

7. Examples: How do you feel about procedures for ordering classroom supplies?

   What is it about the procedure that leads you to feel the way you do?

   Who do you feel is responsible for the procedure?

8. Examples: The ability of teachers to correctly follow procedures for ordering supplies is   very good   good   poor   very poor.

   I am pleased about the way teachers follow instructions for ordering supplies. TRUE or FALSE

Which of the following groups is *least* satisfactory in following instructions for ordering supplies (check one):

administrators   _____

teachers   _____

clerical staff   _____

9. male, college prep: 48   female, college prep: 40
   male, business: 12   female, business: 20
   male, vocational: 24   female, vocational: 4
   male, general: 36   female, general: 16

10. male, elementary: 6   female, elementary: 24
    male, junior high: 6   female, junior high: 9
    male, high school: 9   female, high school: 6

11. b

12. Example:

    I am conducting a study to examine the attitudes of different teachers toward problems of disciplining students and would like to enlist your co-operation. If you would fill out the two forms enclosed and return them to me in the stamped, return-addressed envelope which has been enclosed, I would be most appreciative.

    You are *not* asked to write your name on the questionnaires. Moreover, after the data are rostered by number, these questionnaires will be destroyed. No individual data will be released under any circumstances.

    The Dean of my school and doctoral committee have endorsed this study. It is being funded under a small grant from the university. Successful completion of the study will enable me to earn my doctoral degree.

    Again, I ask for your cooperation. Studies like this enable us to learn more about the process of education.

    Thank you.

(Note that the specific problem to which the study addresses itself has not been revealed in order to avoid a bias.)

13. d

14. d

15. 31

16. Examples: good discussions
    easy (not too much work)
    interesting (stimulating, learn a lot)
    good demonstrations (good audio-visuals, etc.)
    other

Chapter 9

1. c

2. a

3. mean $= 84.0$, median $= 84.5$, sd $= 5.2$

4. mean $= 78.4$, median $= 79.5$, sd $= 5.6$

5. $t = 3.27, p < .01$ $(df = 38$, two-tailed test)

6. $U = 96.5, p < .05$ $(n_1 = 20, n_2 = 20)$

7.

	Group		
	1	2	
High	(9.5) 13	(9.5) 6	19
Low	(10.5) 7	(10.5) 14	21
	20	20	40

$\chi^2 = 3.61, p < .10$ $(df = 1)*$

8.

Source	df	MS	F	p
A	1	348.0	16.49	$< .01$
B	1	313.0	14.83	$< .01$
AB	1	30.0	1.42	
error	36	21.1		

9. $r_s = .83, p < .01$ $(N = 20)$

10. $r = .89, p < .01$ $(df = 9)$

Chapter 10

1.

Category	Scores
1	22, 36, 39, 40, 41
2	45, 47, 49, 50, 52
3	54, 58, 62, 67, 68
4	70, 71, 73, 74, 78
5	81, 85, 90, 92, 98

*When computed by the $\sum\sum \dfrac{(o-e)^2}{e}$ formula, $\chi^2 = 4.92, p < .05$. The difference between the two χ^2 values indicates the effect of the correction for continuity built into the worksheet formula only. Note also that the same two sets of interval data when compared in interval form (t-test) differ at the .01 level, when compared in ordinal form (U-test) differ at the .05 level, and when compared in nominal form (χ^2 test with a correction for continuity) differ at the .10 level.

2.

S's 10			Sex			Age		Treat.		Mod.	1		2		3		4		5		6		7		8		9		10				
1	2	3	4	5	6	7	8	9	10	11	12	13	14	15	16	17	18	19	20	21	22	23	24	25	26	27	28	29	30	31	32	33	34
	0	1	1	2	4			1		1	4	3	1	2	3	3	0	7	1	8	9	0	4	3	3	8	1	2	1	1			
	0	2	2	2	0			1		2	4	0	0	9	2	4	0	2	2	4	8	0	4	1	1	9	2	4	1	3			
	0	3	1	2	1			1		1	3	7	0	8	4	1	1	0	1	6	6	7	5	5	2	1	2	0	0	1			
	.		.			.		.		.	.		.		.		.		.		.		.		.		.		.				
	.		.			.		.		.	.		.		.		.		.		.		.		.		.		.				
	.		.			.		.		.	.		.		.		.		.		.		.		.		.		.				
	2	0	2	2	2			2		2	4	1	1	9	3	1	0	9	2	9	7	3	5	5	2	9	1	4	2	1			

3. b

4. c

5. BMD01V

6. (a) will, 99,999   (b) will, 135

7.
```
 1  2  3  4  5  6  7  8  9 10 11 12 13 14 15 16 17 18 19 20 21 22 23 24 25 26 27 28 29 30 31 32 ... 72
 P  R  O  B  L  M              1        5  7        5  0  0                          N  O  N  O     1
```

8.
```
 1  2  3  4  5  6  7  8  9 10 11 12 13 14 15 16 17 18 19 20 21
 (  4  X  ,  4  0  F  1  .  0  ,  2  X  ,  1  7  F  2  .  0  )
```

9. 0.4405

10. 55.33333

11. b

12. $r = .875$, $\Sigma X = 67$, $\Sigma X^2 = 523$, $\Sigma Y = 67$, $\Sigma Y^2 = 495$, $\Sigma XY = 500$

Chapter 11

1. (a) 7, (c) 3, (d) 1, (f) 8, (g) 2, (h) 5, (i) 6, (k) 4

2. Example: An important function of the educational process in general and classroom experiences in particular is to help children learn self-control and internal motivation. This might be called the socialization function of education. If it fails to occur, the child can expect to have difficulty in school and later life. It would be helpful to know about the kind of teaching behavior or style that is most likely to produce these socialized behaviors. Knowing this, we can train teachers in the use of such a style in order to maximize the socialization function of education.

3. (a) 3, (b) 5, (c) 6, (e) 4, (g) 2, (h) 1

4. Example: *Independent Variable*
The independent variable was frequency of positive verbal reinforcement

(i.e., praise) for schoolwork and classroom activities. Two conditions were created: (1) experimental-reward frequencies two or three times the "normal" rate; (2) control-reward frequencies at the "normal" rate. The normal rate was established over a six session period. Children marked down their own rewards using a special pencil and a tally card. At the end of each session, the tally cards were turned in to the teacher and checked. Teachers were asked to distribute the praise rewards so that each child, even the very slow ones, would get at least several each day. After this initial period, teachers in the experimental condition were found to give considerably more rewards, as instructed, than teachers in the control condition. The treatment ended at the end of the sixth week.

5. d

6. Example: It was hypothesized that the ratings given each S by the school psychologist and the number of demerits each S had accumulated would be positively related. A Pearson product-moment correlation was run for the 10 Ss resulting in $r = .875$ $(df = 9)$. This correlation is significant at beyond the .01 level, indicating that, as predicted, judgments of aggressiveness by a professional and actual acting out behavior were positively related. This provides considerable validity for the judgments of the school psychologist on the aggressiveness variable.

7. x: b, c, e, f, h, i

8. Example: It was not completely surprising to find that students assigned to higher ability groups had better attendance than those assigned to lower groups. Two interpretations can be offered. It may be that higher ability youngsters are more motivated, this motivation accounting for their superior performance. This same motivation would also yield better attendance. It may also be that schools are "designed" to satisfy those youngsters in high ability groups—better teachers, more influence and privileges, etc., thus making them more inclined to come to school than youngsters in low ability groups whose school experience lacks these desirable features. Low ability youngsters may also be led to believe that school will have less payoff for them.

9.
Analysis of Variance of Students' Judgments
of Teacher Directiveness as a Function
of Teachers' Subject Areas (A) and Teachers' Personality (B)

Source	df	MS	F
A	1	504.17	45.22*
B	1	16.67	1.49
AB	1	0.17	0.01
error	20	11.15	

*$p < .01$

10.   Means of Students' Judgments of Teacher Directiveness
          as a Function of Teachers' Subject Area and Personality

	Vocational Teachers	Nonvocational Teachers	Combined
High System IV	53.8	44.5	49.2
Low System IV	55.3	46.3	50.8
Combined	54.5*	45.4*	

*Significantly different, $p < .01$

11.   Means of Students' Judgments of Teacher Directiveness
          as a Function of Teachers' Subject Area and Personality

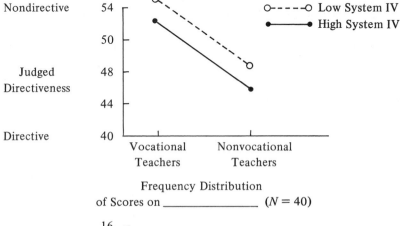

12.   Frequency Distribution
          of Scores on _____ ($N = 40$)

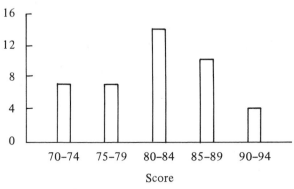

Chapter 12

1. summative

2. formative

3. (a) 4, (c) 2, (d) 5, (e) 3, (g) 1

4. The aims and objectives of this book are to enable students to design, conduct, and write research studies. A behavioral statement of these goals can take one of two forms. The first is the statement of objectives offered at the beginning of each chapter. The second is that the student actually conduct a study, report it, and evaluate it against the criteria set forth in the book. Measurement of the behavioral objectives set forth in the book is easily accomplished via the Competency Test Exercises at the end of each chapter. Measurement of the quality of an experiment could be accomplished by having a group of experts, working with the criteria in the book, evaluate each piece of research completed. A group of graduate students in education could be identified and half randomly assigned to the evaluation group, half to the control. Control *Ss* might use another book, take a course, or have no treatment, while experimental *Ss* would be given the book to read. Both groups would then take all of the Competency Test Exercises (or parallel forms of each) and both groups would design, carry out, and report in writing an experiment. Experts would judge each and judgments across groups would be compared.

Index of Names and Titles

(Page numbers in italics refer to figures and tables, *n* refers to footnotes.)

Index of Subjects

(Page numbers in italics refer to figures and tables, *n* refers to footnotes.)

examples, 24–25, 26, 27, 28, 29, 32,
35, 38–40, 43, 44, 45, 48–50, 66–67,
292, 293, 295
formulation, 12, 24–29
general, 25–26
null. *See* Null hypothesis
operational restatement, 294–295
rationale, 292–294
results of, 304
specific, 25–26
statement, 292
testing, 31

I

Independent variable:
definition, 36–37
in evaluation, 334–336
examples, 36, 38, 40, 43, 45, 46,
48–50, 300
in population definition, 201, 202
in problem statement, 287
relationship to dependent, 37–40, *39,
41, 42, 47*
use in data processing, 257, 270
use in statistics, 228–231, 236, 239,
242
writing up, 300
Index sources, 290
Induction, 26–29
Instrumentation bias, 76, 89, 90, 96, 137,
212, 340
controlling for, 89
Intact group, 104, 117–118, 126, 335,
336
Intact-group comparison, 105–106, 120,
123
Intelligence tests, 150–151
group, 150–151
individual, 151
specific, 151
Interaction analysis, *168*
Interaction, statistical, 112*n*, 236,
239–241, *240, 320*
Interest tests. *See* Vocations tests
Inter-judge agreement. *See* Inter-rater
reliability
Internal validity, 3–8, 74–79, 200*n*
designs to control for, 106–123
factors affecting, 74–79. *See also*
History bias; Instrumentation bias;
Maturation bias; Mortality bias;
Selection bias; Statistical regression;
Testing bias

Inter-rater reliability, 89, 165, 218–219,
245, 246
Interval scale, 143, 157, 181, 186,
189–190, 227, 228–231, 236, 244,
251, 254–256
Intervening variable, 36, 45–46, 79*n*, 84*n*
examples, 36, 45, 46, 48–50
Interviewers, 211–213
Interview schedules, 173–219
administering, 211–213
choice of, 187, *188*
coding, 215–219
construction of, 186–200
examples, *192*
question formats, 174–176, 187–188
response modes, 177–186, 188–191
Item analysis, 154–156, *155,* 159, 199,
264

K

Kendall:
coefficient of concordance, *229,* 246*n*
tau, *229*
Kruskal-Wallis test, *229*
Kuder-Richardson (test) reliability, 139,
156
formula, 20, 139

L

Level, 38
Likert scale, 157–159, *158. See also*
Rating scale; Scaled response mode
Literature review, 288–292
organization, 291–292
sources, 290–291
strategy, 289
Literature sources, 290–291
abstracting journals, 290
dissertations, 290
government documents, 290–291
reviewing journals, 290
Lockmiller-DiNello study, 92–95, 109,
339
Logical stages of research, 67

M

Manipulation, success of, 97–100, *99*
Mann-Whitney *U*-test, *229,* 231, 241–242,
243, 244, 339
Matched-group technique, 83
Matched-pair technique, 82–83, 108*n*
Maturation bias, 75, 90, 96, 105, 121

Treatment, 72, 103, 236n, *319*
True experimental designs:
  in evaluation, 336
  posttest-only control group design, 106–107
  pretest-posttest control group design, 107–109, 120
t-test, 228, *229*, 231–233, *232*, 242, 251n, 337, 339

U

Unstructured response mode, 177–178, 216–217
Unweighted means solution, 239
U-test. *See* Mann-Whitney *U*-test

V

Validity, 2–3. *See also* External validity; Internal validity; test validity
Variables:
  choice considerations, 50–52
  combined, *47*
  dispositional, 43
  identifying and labeling, 13, 36–52
  See also Control variable; Dependent variable; Independent variable; Intervening variable; Moderator variable
Variance, 226, *227*, 232, 235
  homogeneity of, 227–228
  analysis of. *See* Analysis of variance
Vocations tests, 153
Volunteers, 119, 335, 339